TRADITIONAL
FESTIVALS

a multicultural encyclopedia

TRADITIONAL
FESTIVALS

a multicultural encyclopedia

VOLUME II

CHRISTIAN ROY

A B C ⬤ C L I O

Santa Barbara, California • Denver, Colorado • Oxford, England

Library of Congress Cataloging-in-Publication Data

Roy, Christian, 1963-
Traditional festivals : a multicultural encyclopedia / Christian Roy.
p. cm.
Includes bibliographical references and index.
ISBN 1-57607-089-1 (hardback : alk. paper)—ISBN 1-85109-689-2
(ebook) 1. Festivals—Encyclopedias. I. Title.

GT3925.R69 2005
394.26'03—dc22
2005010444

07 06 05 / 10 9 8 7 6 5 4 3 2 1

This book is also available on the World Wide Web as an e-book.
Visit http://www.abc-clio.com for details.

ABC-CLIO, Inc.
130 Cremona Drive, P.O. Box 1911
Santa Barbara, California 93116–1911

This book is printed on acid-free paper.
Manufactured in the United States of America

To Lionel Rothkrug,
for first suggesting that I be entrusted with this project
that owes much to his groundbreaking work
on the history of religious mentalities

CONTENTS

Preface, xi

TRADITIONAL FESTIVALS
a multicultural encyclopedia

VOLUME I   A–L

VOLUME II M–Z

APPENDIXES

M

MADONNA DEL PONTE

See Conception and Birth of the
Virgin Mary

MAHALAYA AMAVASHYA, MAHANAVAMI

See Navaratra and Dusshera

MAHASHIVARATRI (HINDUISM)

Shivaratri is the Sanskrit word for the "**Night of Shiva**"—that of the fourteenth lunar day (*tithi*) of the waning or "dark half" (*krishna-paksha*) of every lunar month. Though both this time of day and this time of the month are the most inauspicious as the darkest, they are also the most sacred to Shiva in another sense. Especially auspicious is the last **Shivaratri** of the year—either in the month of Magha (January–February) or in that of Phalguna (February–March), depending on whether the months are counted from the new moon or the full moon in a particular region of the Indian subcontinent. For this is **Mahashivaratri**—the "Great **Night of Shiva**"—the year's major festival for every *shaiva* or devotee of Mahadeva—the "Great God" Shiva. Followers of other deities often mark it, too, especially the *Smarta* brahmins of South India and Gujarat State, who make a point of embracing all Hindu gods.

The Darkest Night When All Are Equal Before God

The night is the best time to worship Shiva because this is when he walks the earth and meditates at midnight in charnel grounds and crematoria—his favorite haunts—where ghosts, ghouls, and other fiends are his friends. The last night of the lunar cycle is particularly dark and has added meaning around **New Year**'s Eve and the end of winter, when the established order of the old year breaks down into chaos at its lowest point before being reinstated on a clean slate. Thus, "all persons of whatever birth or station may celebrate **Shivaratri** on the fourteenth tithi, even low caste people and women," as the *Ishanasamhita* points out. It goes on to say that "when, after observing a fast on that day, Shiva is worshipped with *bilva* leaves, and a vigil for the whole night is observed, Shiva saves man from hell and bestows enjoyment of happiness and liberation (*moksha*), and a man becomes like Shiva himself. Gifts, sacrifices, austerities, pilgrimages, and observances of vows are not equal to even one ten-millionth part of **Shivaratri**" (Kane 1930–1962, Vol. V, Part 1, p. 229). This ritual may therefore have been devised by Hindu leaders over a thousand years ago to give the populace easy access to heavenly rewards, as an incentive not to be swayed

Hindu devotees light candles during the Mahashivaratri festival at the Shiva temple in Trakeshawar, 75 kilometers (46 miles) west of Calcutta, February 18, 2004. (Jayanta Shaw/Reuters/Corbis)

by the competing egalitarian and atheistic teachings of Jainism and Buddhism.

Unwitting Devotion and Boundless Merit

This was done by circulating different versions of the story of a cruel huntsman of low caste with bad karma who got lost in a forest and found refuge in a tree overnight. Unbeknownst to him, the *bilva* (wood-apple) tree was sacred to Shiva, and it was the night of the fourteenth that he spent without food or sleep in it, shaking leaves and water onto the god's phallic idol or *linga* below, and involuntarily getting all the merit of these timely offerings—as did his wife just by being kept awake by worry all night. The next day, his heart had inexplicably softened, and they were soon both taken from this life to Shiva's realm and/or royal human births. The god's consort Parvati spread their story and the fame of the extraordinary redemptive efficacy of **Shivaratri** (as **Mahashivaratri** is commonly referred to), a ritual so powerful it could work even when people accidentally went through the motions. But in the words of the *Garuda Purana* (I:124), "if one worships the *linga* in this way, knowingly and willfully, then the merit accrued therefrom will be limitless and inexhaustible." This merit can translate into any of the following benefits, in order of importance: (i) worldly happiness and wish-fulfillment in terms of long life, power, family, fame, and fortune; (ii) safe passage across hell; (iii) liberation from the cycle of death and rebirth; (iv) becoming an attendant of Shiva; (v) becoming one of his companions in his heaven on Mount Kailash in the Himalayas; (vi) taking the same form as Shiva; or (vii) becoming completely one with him.

Communal Feast or Personal Vow?

If these blessings and rewards make **Shivaratri** desirable though optional (*kamya*), it is also obligatory (*nitya*) because its rites need to be performed every year if one is not to succumb to certain sins and their dire consequences. In this, despite the prominence of song, dance, drama, and popular fairs in places such as West Bengal, they represent less a cyclical community festival (*utsava*) than a voluntary personal vow (*vrata*)—one of well over a thousand known in Hinduism. The performance of this one happens to be expected of all faithful devotees of Shiva, to reaffirm the mutual interdependence of earthly and divine realms. For the divine realm is sustained by humans' physical and spiritual discipline, offerings of cooked food, and hymns of praise, while the earthly realm receives from it physical and spiritual well-being. It is in turn incumbent upon humans to redistribute to all creatures and gods the material goods and inner strength that allow them to perform such religious duties in the first place. Among the latter, the main three that constitute **Shivaratri** are fasting for the whole lunar day, holding a vigil, and worshipping the linga overnight with offerings of flowers, leaves, foods, precious objects, its anointing (*abhisheka*) with a variety of substances (ranging from sugar water to cow excrements) and the muttering (*japa*) of mantras. The pattern remains the same whether the rites are performed in a temple or at home, though it is reversed in some places where the fast (*upavasa*) and vigil (*jagara*) take place at night, and the worship (*puja*) in daytime. They can also last between a day and a day and a half, depending on the extent of the ritual used in a particular setting. In most cases today, people do not go through all the rites described in ancient texts but stick to the three basic elements (*svarupa*) and also listen to stories of Shiva's deeds, which brings great merit too. In parts of India, people still drink *bhang*, Shiva's favorite beverage: rosewater that has first been filtered through hemp leaves and is later mixed with opium and sprinkled with almonds and other ingredients.

Some Local Observances

Thousands of pilgrims come from India to the great Pashupatinath Temple near Kathmandu, the capital of Nepal—a Himalayan kingdom so wholly devoted to Shiva that many Buddhists too celebrate **Shivaratri**. All day, military gun salutes are heard crackling from Kathmandu's Tundikhel parade ground, and in the evening, the royal family comes with gifts to pay homage to Lord Pashupati—"Protector of Animals," as Shiva is known in this holy place. This is but one of the god's many names, which the fasting devotees who throng the surrounding slopes chant around campfires throughout the night, while many ritually bathe in the river below and return to temple grounds every three hours to shower countless lingas with flowers and holy water. Throughout Kathmandu Valley, at all crossroads and in each courtyard in town and country, relatives gather to praise Shiva around bonfires fed with wood collected by boys who have gone door to door chanting:

> *Two sticks of firewood we beg of you,*
> *For Mahadev is feeling cold.*

In the neighboring Indian state of Himachal Pradesh that day, groups of children go from door to door decorating each one with branches and often getting grain as a reward for singing:

> *The doors have been decked*
> *with thorny bush and wild cherry,*
> *Therefore, oh witch, run away to the peak.*

That night, the whole family sings and dances in honor of Shiva around a mandala checkerboard pattern traced on the floor with flour paste, in which a cowdung linga and a rice Parvati have been placed along with three breads and the many fried cakes prepared during the day. They are eaten when the fast is broken at four in the morning, as the idols are placed in the middle of a field. The priest gets one of the loaves, while remaining cakes are taken to absent relatives.

In Kerala State at the other end of India, people smear their bodies with ashes (an attribute of Shiva as a naked ascetic) after bathing near temples where the *puja* or service lasts all night and a strict vigil is kept until a final bath the next morning, marking the end of Shiva's meditation. Several thousand pilgrims from all castes and of all persuasions especially gather on the vast sandbank of Periyar River where the linga is erected near the Shiva temple of Aluva. Merchants sell their wares in row upon row of booths, while an array of performances attracts sightseers and helps the pilgrims keep awake all night. Most of them also make offerings to their ancestors the next morning. The rest of the day is celebrated with feasting and fairs, in commemoration of Shiva's rescue of the world from annihilation—either by mediating between the Creator, Brahma and the Sustainer, Vishnu, or by swallowing the poison released by the snake with which the gods churned the milk-ocean of early Creation so it would not contaminate the *amrita* elixir of immortality they were trying to recover from the bottom.

In the state of Andhra Pradesh, special foods are offered to the gods around one in the afternoon and are then eaten by the whole family, before portions are taken to relatives and friends to renew social ties as a conclusion to the festival. Over the previous night, when all temples remain open, nearly everyone would have visited several of them. Many begin the evening by going to watch devotional films—of which there are three showings on **Mahashivaratri**. For some, this is even a substitute for going to the temple, as crowds offer flowers and break hundreds of coconuts under the screen in the middle of a showing. This appears to be a development of the seasonal practice of temple storytelling by a "straight" narrator who keeps on being interrupted by a sidekick's gibes. Though the goal of his jokes and horseplay is to keep people awake during a long night vigil, they also ensure the festival's popularity among children.

Members of the South Indian Lingayat sect of iconoclastic "linga-wearers," also called Vira-Shaivas as "virile" spiritual heroes (though men and women of all castes wear these phallic symbols in place of the sacred thread of higher-caste Hindu men), give gifts to their guru or spiritual master on the day after the Great **Night of Shiva**.

See also Holi

References

P. V. Kane. *History of Dharmaśastra (Ancient and Medieval Religious and Civil Law)*. Poona, India: Bhandarkar Oriental Research Institute, 1930–1962, Vol. V, Part 1, pp. 225–236.

Bruce Long. "Mahaśivaratri: The Śaiva Festival of Repentance," in Guy R. Welbon and Glenn E. Yocum. *Religious Festivals in South India and Sri Lanka*. New Delhi: Manohar, 1982, pp. 189–217.

Swami Shivananda. *Hindu Fasts and Festivals and Their Philosophy*. Rishikesh, India: The Shivananda Publication League, 1947.

MAHAVIRA'S BIRTHDAY
See Paryushana and Dashalakshana

MAIKRAHV
See May Day

MAIMUNA
See Passover

MAMANDABARI-MALIARA
See Kunapipi

▶ MANKIND (DAY OF)

See Sekku

▶ MARDI GRAS

See Carnival

▶ MARTINMAS (CHRISTIANITY)

Martinmas is the November 11 feast of **Saint Martin**, who was buried on this day in 397. He has thus become the focus of rich and varied European folklore, because the date of his commemoration can serve both as a late **Thanksgiving** festival—bringing an end to the harvest season, or as an early winter solstice festival—anticipating the **Christmas** season in some of the same ways as the feast of **Saint Nicholas** on December 6. The feast of **Saint Eligius** on December 1 bridges those of **Saint Nicholas** and **Saint Martin**.

Martin, Eligius and Nicholas

At the height of his popularity in the Middle Ages, **Saint Martin** was often depicted as a young Roman officer on horseback who, upon encountering a beggar, cut his own cloak in two with his sword to give half of it to him, in literal obedience to the Gospel command. (He is thus known by this clothing attribute in German folklore as *Pelzmärtel*—"Pelt Marty," a kind of "wild" version of Saint Nicholas.) Since he pioneered the evangelization of Gaul's peasantry as bishop of Tours, Martin would become the first patron saint of France under the early medieval Merovingian kings. Still famous today from an old French children's song, **Saint Eligius** was an influential councillor to one of them—*le bon roi Dagobert*, the "Good King Dagobert" of its title. The December 1 feast of his passing in 659 complements in France (where it is known as *Saint-Éloi*) those of **Saint Nicholas** on December 6 and **Saint Martin** on November 11, with a seasonal blessing of horses, using a hammer—the animal and the tool being attributes of this former blacksmith (or goldsmith, depending on

the tradition, since both trades claim him as their patron saint). In Belgian Luxembourg, the *Fête de Saint-Éloi* is celebrated on the first Sunday of December in Bouillon with an early morning procession, carrying around town on stretchers loads of cakes to be given out after a special mass.

A traditional story from French Flanders links all three saints to account for the origin of the **Martinmas** lantern procession—formerly using hollowed out vegetables (such as beets), called "death's heads" on the northern coast of France, in Belgium, and in Holland. (Nowadays, however, paper lanterns made in school are used in the latter country as in Luxembourg and Germany, and as far away as in long German-dominated Estonia.) The story goes that **Saint Nicholas** once stopped to pray at a chapel dedicated to **Saint Eligius** in Dunkirk (though he never left Asia Minor and died there three centuries before the French saint!). Meanwhile, his donkey—or **Saint Martin**'s in some accounts—wandered off; hence the "donkey's droppings" (*volaeren*)—round raisin cakes left overnight on either December 5 or most often November 10, in remembrance of the local children who went and looked for the beast through the dunes and fields all night, carrying lanterns (although naughty children might get real droppings instead, or even get caned!). This was given as the reason why masked children go from door to door on **Martinmas**, singing and dancing in expectation of a reward. Money and candies have come to replace apples and nuts in this trick-or-treating quest of a kind to be found on various dates in different parts of Europe until the **Twelfth Night** of **Christmas**.

Between Halloween and Christmas

Like related **Christmas** customs, this continental equivalent of **Halloween** often involved the use as musical accompaniment of a *Rummelpott* (German for "rumble pot"), built like a drum with a swine's bladder through which a stick moves up and down, to produce a low, grating, vaguely obscene, and distinctly comical, noise. In Düsseldorf, the children's **Martinmas** trick-or-treating song seems to announce the still-distant lengthening of daylight with the winter solstice—the return of the sun as king: "I am a little king, don't give me too little/Don't leave me waiting too long for my journey's still long." Looking forward to **Christmas** rather than back to **Halloween**, as well as recalling the saint's famous charitable act (as in German parades led by a Roman soldier on horseback who mimes the saint's gift of his cloak), many local traditions of Northern Europe grant to **Saint Martin** the role of bringer of gifts to children, attributed elsewhere to Saint Nicholas. Likewise, just as there are **Saint Nicholas** cookies, there are also "**Saint Martin**'s horns": cakes baked in the shape of the saint with his arms arched to touch his hips like the ears of a pot—or the circle of the sun waxing and waning over the course of the year. In the West, the **Advent** season of fasting before **Christmas** was first known as "**Saint Martin**'s **Lent**," because it was instituted by Perpetuus, a late fifth-century successor of Martin as bishop of Tours who set it to begin on the local saint's November 11 feast, with fasting rules applicable only on Mondays, Wednesdays, and Fridays. **Saint Martin**'s **Lent** was adopted by other Frankish churches at the Council of Mâcon in 583, though it was later superseded by the standard Roman use for **Advent**.

A Harvest Festival

If **Martinmas** remained entrenched in rural custom, it was mostly due to its significance in the agricultural year, coming at its effective end with the onset of the cold—even though a belated return of fair weather was sometimes called "**Saint Martin**'s summer," and was explained as a favor granted to the saint by God so his donkey could graze. It was at this time that the contracts of apprentices and seasonal workers came to an end, and they were let off with the gift of a goose, before getting hired for a new contract until **Midsummer** or the next **Martinmas**. There is a story that **Saint Martin** was once annoyed by a goose and had it served for dinner, to account for the sacrifice of "Martin's goose" on his feast in France, the Netherlands, Germany, Switzerland, Austria, Denmark, and Sweden—though chicken as well as goose is eaten in Estonia. In Scotland, **Martinmas** is also a day when quarterly payments and yearly rents are due. Throughout Great Britain, **Martinmas** used to be the time for hiring servants, as well as for slaughtering the cattle to be salted for the winter, as was also the case on the Continent. There, the cattle might not be yoked on the feast of **Saint Martin** as the patron of plowmen, as he was known in some French provinces such as Touraine and Alsace on account of a story that he once used his cloak to cross a river with his cattle while he was plowing a field. The inflexibly regular fate of farm animals was the source of a quaint English expression of hope that people we have reason to dislike will eventually get their comeuppance: "His **Martinmas** will come as it does to every hog." For pigs were to be killed on this day in order to become the centerpiece of the **Christmas** meal they used to provide before turkeys came along, as they still do in many parts of Europe. In Estonia, old folk songs testify that sausages used to be made in order to be handed out to maskers going from door to door on **Martinmas** Eve.

Happy to have their pay in hand, farm employees could partake of the new wine that would be tried on this occasion of its cellaring, often at evening parties following the children's lantern procession and preceding the lighting of **Martinmas** bonfires. From Portugal to the Rhineland, these fires were kindled to clear the air; baskets of nuts and fruits were shaken over them in the Low Countries. **Saint Martin** was sometimes popularly known as the patron of drinkers—or even of drunkards, on account of excesses clerical authorities could hardly con-

Gothic painting of Saint Martin of Tours sharing his cloak with the poor. Anonymous, fifteenth century, Hungarian National Gallery, Budapest. (Archivo Iconografico, S.A./Corbis)

done on his feast, when, aside from wine, revellers might drink a potent seasonal liqueur made from its must, called *Martinsminne* in Germany; in the Netherlands, the Calvinist clergy long vainly tried to ban it along with Martin's goose. The custom of getting drunk that night prevailed from Western Germany to Northern France, where it has given rise to typical expressions such as "**Martinmas** sickness"—a hangover.

In Sigillo near Perugia, chestnuts are offered to the public along with the new wine on **Martinmas**. But elsewhere in Italy, harvest festivals equivalent to **Martinmas**, complete with blessings of farm produce and bonfires, are held on slightly different dates, like the Feast of **San Rocco** on November 16 in Roccanova near Potenza, and the **Fugarena** on November 19 in Terra del Sole near Forlì. Throughout much of Europe, many products of the year's harvest are also first consumed on **Martinmas**, as a kind of **thanksgiving** offering of their **first-fruits** to **Saint Martin**. Yet this festival is now somewhat overshadowed by **Armistice Day**—the civic day of the war dead its date has become (under this name in France, Belgium, and Britain, and that of **Remembrance Day** in Canada and Australia, while it was renamed **Veterans Day** by the U.S. Congress in 1954), in commemoration of the armistice that put an end to the slaughter of the First World War in 1918, coming into effect on the eleventh hour of the eleventh day of the eleventh month. In Rhineland towns down to southern Holland, this just happens to be the traditional moment when a council of eleven citizens begins preparations for the coming **Carnival**: at eleven past eleven on **Martinmas**, because eleven is the number symbolizing fools, who will then rule supreme for a few days.

> **See also** Carnival; Christmas; Days of the Dead (West); Epiphany; Lent; Midsummer; Saint Nicholas

References

Dien est Amour (Remes, France: Librarie Pierre Téqui), No. 15, "Saint Martin," October 1979.

H. Pomeroy Brewster. *Saints and Festivals of the Christian Church.* Detroit: Omnigraphics, 1990.

Jennifer M. Russ. *German Festivals and Customs.* London: O. Wolff, 1982.

Simon Schama. *The Embarrassment of Riches. An Interpretation of Dutch Culture in the Golden Age.* New York: Knopf, 1987.

▶ MARTYRDOM OF GURUS
See Gurpurb

▶ MARTYRDOM OF THE BAB
See Ridván

▶ MASQAL
See Elevation of the Cross

▶ MATRALIA (ROME)

It is on June 11 that Servius Tullius (578–534 B.C.E.), the sixth king of Rome, was said to have dedicated the temples of Fortuna and of Mater Matuta on the city's cattle market—the Forum Boarium. The latter goddess, "Mother Dawn," was henceforth honored at dawn every June 11 by the good mothers of Rome, provided they had been married only once. Mater Matuta forbade servants access to her temple; yet they were deliberately taken inside by their mistresses, so they could be slapped, beaten with sticks, and thrown out, as part of the rites of **Matralia**.

Why Dawn Frowns on Slaves and Shines on Nephews

Ovid accounted for the hostility of the Italic goddess Matuta toward slaves in terms of her identification with the Theban princess Ino of Greek mythology. For Ino's husband, King Athamas of Boeotia, slept with one of her servants and thus heard about a vital part of his wife's plot to get him to kill his children from a previous marriage.

Georges Dumézil (1898–1986) thought it more likely that the slaves stood in for the dark shadows that Dawn chases away every morning. The French historian went even further afield than the Roman poet to try to explain another enigmatic feature of her festival: the fact that, in Ovid's words, "no pious mother should pray to her for her child;/She seemed not the happiest of parents" (*Fasti* 6:559–560, p. 155).

According to Ovid, Ino had cast herself into the sea with her son Melicertes after her other son Learchus had been killed by Athamas. She did this in a fit of madness induced by Juno, who wanted to get back at Ino for saving her sister Semele's child by Jupiter. The Nereids (Greek sea deities who helped sailors in distress) then took Ino to the mouth of the River Tiber. "You will do better to give her another's child/She aided Bacchus more than her children" (*Fasti* 6:561–562, p. 155), when she took care of this orphan god. His father Jupiter's full glory as the god of thunder and lightning had consumed Semele when she had insisted on seeing her lover as he really was. Semele was following the deceptive advice of Jupiter's jealous wife Juno, who had come to her disguised as an old neighbor. For Ovid, Ino's care for her sister Semele's son Bacchus was the reason why, on **Matralia**, Roman matrons took their sisters' children, never their own, to commend them to Ino as Mater Matuta.

Taking seriously her ancient identification with Dawn—all the way to common Indo-European roots—Dumézil maintained that "at her festival the Roman ladies mime her mythic actions, in the hope of making her perform them when she makes her brief appearance every day of the year. These actions are the driving out of the shades and the attentive, affectionate welcoming of the sun, the child of night—according to Vedic mythology, her sister's child" (Dumézil 1996, Vol. 2, p. 388). In this interpretation, when mothers prayed to Mater Matuta for their nephews and nieces, they were assisting Dawn in cherishing the Sun as a newborn child of departed Night—her own sister.

How a Pair of Greek Suicides Became Roman Sea Deities

But this is a modern reconstruction of the hypothetical archaic origins of the rites of **Matralia**. By Ovid's time, Matuta was taken to be the name by which Ino was known to the Romans as a sea goddess; while to the Greeks she was Leucothea, the "White Goddess" worshipped in a wide range of initiatory festivals featuring social inversion and ritual trangressions of morality. (Hence perhaps her identification with Ino, who for a while raised Bacchus as a girl and also founded a contest for boys in Miletus.) For the Greeks, Melicertes had been deified as Palaemon, meaning the same as Portunus, as the Romans called him, since he had been given power over ports. This was believed to have happened once mother and son had found refuge on Italy's

shores after their miraculous rescue from drowning in the Tiber's waters. The temple of Portunus was therefore built only a stone's throw away from the Tiber on the Forum Boarium, like the temple of his mother Matuta.

The blessing of these new divine identities had been prophesied to Ino soon after their arrival by the goddess Carmentis, who had offered them the hospitality of her hearth. She even went so far as to hurriedly bake some cakes on it with her own hands for the hungry mother and child. Tradition held this to be the origin of the crunchy golden cakes that were specially baked by Rome's mothers in earthenware vessels to please Matuta on the festival of **Matralia**. For in her hour of direst need, "rustic kindness delights her more than art," as Ovid wrote in his *Fasti* (6:534, p. 154).

See also Carmentalia; Dionysia

References

Georges Dumézil. *Archaic Roman Religion, with an Appendix on the Religion of the Etruscans.* Tr. Philip Krapp. Baltimore, MD: Johns Hopkins University Press, 1996.

Robert Graves. *The Greek Myths.* London: Penguin Books, 1960.

Ovid. *Fasti.* Tr. A. J. Boyle and R. D. Woodard. London: Penguin Books, 2000.

▶ MATRONALIA (ROME)

As their name indicates, the **Matronalia** or *Matronales Feriae* constituted a private festival concerning only married women—the matrons of Rome. At home, they prayed for marital bliss and put on a feast for their female slaves, while their husbands would give them presents and pocket money at the calends of March. As on the new moon of every month, public sacrifices were also offered to Juno.

Sacred Groves for Deities of Childbirth

The difference was a question of emphasis and specialization. For March 1, aside from having long been the first day of the year until the religious reforms attributed to King Numa (715–673 B.C.E.), marked the anniversary of the dedication in 375 B.C.E. of the temple of Juno Lucina, protectress of childbirth, on her ancient sacred grove (*lucus*) on Esquiline Hill in an outlying area to the east of Rome. This cult and festival were said to have been established by Latin women under Titus Tatius, king of the Sabines and joint ruler of the city with its own founding king Romulus. The **Matronalia** therefore symbolized the peace that was sealed between the two founding peoples by their women's intercession after the crisis caused by the abduction and rape of the Sabine women by the first Romans, desperate for a boost to their demographics.

The prayer that Ovid attributes to the matrons who went in a procession to worship Juno as the goddess of childbirth at her temple on the Esquiline points to another possible etymology for her name Lucina in this capacity: "You have given us the light (*lucem*), oh Lucina," they would say as they brought her flowers, wearing them as garlands as well, because she loved blooming plants (*Fasti* 3:255, p. 61). They would also say: "Be present for the prayers of birth"(*Fasti* 3:256, p. 61). But an expectant mother had to make sure to let her hair loose before she prayed, so that Juno might in turn gently release the fruit of her womb by a simple application of sympathetic magic; any tie on the mother would be a hindrance to a smooth delivery of her child.

By the same principle, when Ovid proceeded to tell the story of another sacred grove: that of Nemi where Diana too was worshipped as patron goddess of pregnant women and young mothers (who left many *ex-votos* there to thank her), he did so as a poet to invoke the power of the muse Egeria. She was the goddess of the brook that came out of the grove, and she could draw the proper words and expressions out of him in the same way that she favored the delivery of the children expected by the women who came to offer her sacrifices. With a name that the ancients liked to relate to *egero*, "to cause to come out," the nymph Egeria of the brook of Nemi could confer her blessings on both the literal and the literary act of giving birth.

Man's Genius and Woman's Juno Meet at Nemi

The grove of Nemi in the Alban mountains is mostly famous as an archaic testing ground of manhood: for it had as a sacred king the man who succeeded in killing the previous one, until he himself was in time inevitably overcome by a stronger contender. The muse of the brook of Nemi may have inspired Ovid's odd insistence on a meaningful connection between the festival of Juno and the month of Mars, which was unconvincing except in this parallel: "Latin mothers rightly observe the fertile times;/ Childbirth embraces soldiery and prayer" (*Fasti* 3:243–244, p. 61). Labor could be seen as the female equivalent of combat, as it was in many ancient cultures from India to Mexico. The comparison went so far as to grant death in childbirth a heroic and supernatural postmortem status parallel to that of death on the battlefield. That was probably where a man's spirit would become most clearly manifest as something "larger than life"—a *genius* or personal deity of both familial generation and individual fortune hovering protectively about him. If such a genius was most evident in Caesar and his kin and was, as such, the object of a public cult on **Caristia**, every man in Rome possessed and privately honored his own genius. In the same way, Romans eventually came to feel that every woman too had the equivalent of a genius in her own personal Juno, which became manifest in a woman's ultimate experience: risking her life by giving birth.

It may then seem fitting after all that the Juno specific to childbirth was honored in Rome in temporal conjunction with the start of the month of the god of war Mars, as the other goddesses of childbirth—Diana and Egeria—were worshipped in spatial conjunction with the old religious center of the confederate Latin tribes at Nemi. For their foundational violence was long kept alive there, at a safe distance from civilization up in the hills, in a bloody contest between fugitive slaves under cover of the woods.

See also Caristia; Lupercalia; May Day; New Year (West)

References

Georges Dumézil. *Archaic Roman Religion, with an Appendix on the Religion of the Etruscans.* Tr. Philip Krapp. Baltimore, MD: Johns Hopkins University Press, 1996.

Sir James George Frazer. *The Golden Bough. A Study in Magic and Religion.* One-Volume Abridged Edition. New York: Macmillan, 1985.

Ovid. *Fasti.* Tr. Sir James George Frazer. Cambridge, MA: Harvard University Press, 1977.

▶ MATSURI (JAPAN)

A **matsuri** is a religious and/or civic festival, usually rooted in Japan's indigenous Shinto nature-worship. A number of **matsuri**s have been included in the national calendar of "**annual events**"—*nenchu gyoji,* going back over a thousand years to the Heian period, and incorporating Asian (and more recently Western) celebrations of relevance to the State, that then trickled down to Japanese society at large. But there are almost as many **matsuri**s as there are sacred spots in Japan, as these festivals are essentially shrine-based, local in character, and archaic in origin, although the larger ones attract visitors from outside the community. This often results in the prevalence of business and entertainment concerns, to the point where some new **matsuri**s have arisen solely in order to draw crowds for such secular festive purposes.

Marking Off the Sacred from the Profane

The sometimes boisterous celebration of human fellowship within a community of what-

ever scale has always been a vital part of the **matsuri**. But originally, it was never divorced from its ultimate purpose, defined by the pioneering folklorist Kunio Yanagita (1875–1962) as "man's attending to and living in the company of the gods" (Ito 1983, p. 253). This entailed above all offering them food; the verb *matsuru* for this also meant "to rule" in the eighth century, because such was the Emperor's chief priestly function. Today still, the term *matsuri-goto,* which literally means "affairs of religious festivals," also means "government" in everyday speech. This is because the supervision of the religious ceremonies of Shinto was long a key concern of the State, in a context where public as well as private life called for petitions and reports to the gods.

As a focus of extraordinary attention at a particular place, a god or *kami* is offered special foods on special occasions by people wearing particular clothing: all these things, places, and times have as a common denominator the out-of-the-ordinary, "sacred" character of *hare,* as opposed to *ke,* the mundane everyday or "profane" realm. The "turning point" (*oribe*) or "day marking change" (*sechibi*) from one to the other is in itself *hare,* whether it be a birthday or a wedding for a family, **New Year**'s Day, or some other **matsuri** for a local community or *ujiko.* The latter will itself be purified for the occasion, with a sacred area set apart for the main rituals by a sacred straw rope called a *shimenawa.* The signal used to alert the gods that a **matsuri** is ready to start in their honor is also *hare,* whether it be a white flag with their name or the shrine's name on it, or streamers on tall poles like the *sasatake* seen on the streets during the **Festival of the Weaver** on July 7, or the pine and bamboo *kadomatsu* decorations hanging in front of every home and business during the **New Year** festive season.

Members of an *ujiko* have their own *ujigami* shrine where a select few will assist the Shinto clergy in preparing and carrying out the **matsuri**. Ritual contact with the divine is usually the exclusive province of Shinto priests, who therefore remain in their own specially prepared quarters within shrine grounds for the duration of the festival—watching their diet and avoiding forbidden acts. However, the heads or *toya* of the exclusive *miyaza* lay brotherhoods of the Kyoto area must undergo the same austerities in order to represent the people in the ceremonies. Before modern times, certain purifying *monoimi* rites were a prerequisite for participation in a **matsuri**, but they have since been considerably relaxed. Depending on the place and the occasion, they formerly might have included washing oneself often or not washing one's hair or clothes at all, refraining from everyday tasks or from the use of sharp objects, or cooking food over a special fire. The priests of Sada Shrine in the Shimane Peninsula must light such a fire by rubbing a wooden stick against a board during the week of seclusion that precedes for them the end-of-September seat-changing rite of the local kami, or *Gozakae* **Matsuri**. *Imoni* **Matsuri** and *Amazake* **Matsuri** are named after the main offerings they call for—respectively, boiled taro roots and a sweet malted wine made from glutinous *mochi* rice, the *hare* food *par excellence* that is synonymous with festivals in Japan as it is in China. This is because rice was eaten only on special occasions in pre-modern times when millet was the staple crop. It was then that most **matsuri**s were developed in relation to the growing cycle of rice. Thus, the most important **matsuri**s are held in the spring, when the rice god goes from the houses or the hills to dwell in the paddies and is welcomed there to ensure plentiful crops, and in the fall, when he goes back to his home and is sent off with **thanksgiving** for a plentiful harvest. In between, during the month of June, comes another agricultural rite: the **Rice-Transplanting Festival**, called *Hana Taue.* A fine example of its traditions is now preserved by the government as a "folk-culture asset" in Chiyoda, where local residents of this valley town of the southern

mountains revived it in 1930 independently of the feudal system it reflected until the land reforms of 1900. Crews of female peasants can therefore still be seen singing traditional tunes to the beat of male drummers to summon the rice spirit to the paddies as they ceremonially put the seedlings in their new homes.

Summer **matsuri**s are often celebrated in the countryside in order to protect the crops from natural disasters. Yet they have grown in importance along with Japanese cities from the late medieval Muromachi Period, at first to ward off the urban hazards of plague and pestilence, and lately as colorful popular entertainment featuring parades of brightly decorated floats. This recent resurgence has generated new voluntary associations to put up festivities that had previously been the responsibility of the traditional *ujiko* "parishes" one was born into. While these local religious communities have been considerably undermined by increasing social mobility and secularization, liquor-store owners, rice dealers, and other merchants with a distinct economic interest in the continuation and development of street celebrations have taken over from them by banding together in syndicates to organize urban **matsuri**s.

Communicating with the Kami

Whatever the setting or the season, the better part of a **matsuri** is always taken by actual communication with the kami, once it has descended into its festive object of temporary residence—*shintai*. But first, the shrine's inner doors have been opened while a drum, bells or music were sounding and the priest made an eerie "*oo*" call. Next, the food offerings (*shinsen*) are presented, sometimes as well as other offerings called *heihaku,* which means "cloth," though nowadays the term also covers paper, jewels, weapons, money, and utensils. The head priest says prayers (*norito*) asking for prosperity in the form of local seasonal staples, or giving thanks for them. They can also take the form of feasting with the deity for its pleasure and the humans' nourishment, with *sake* rice-wine often playing a central role, whether it is formally sipped or unabashedly guzzled, depending on the **matsuri**. To entertain the deity, ceremonial music (*gagaku*) and dance (*bugaku*) is performed. Individual worshippers also present offerings of sacred *tamaguchi* branches.

For the community at large, a procession is the main opportunity for coming into contact with the deity. The Japanese word translates as an "august divine-going" through the *ujiko* or parish, taking the kami to or from its special shrine or favorite place and at the same time blessing the homes and people it passes on the way. For the procession, the kami is taken from the shrine's inner sanctum and transferred to an ornate and gilded palanquin serving as its portable shrine or *mikoshi*. Not that the object within which the kami resides is physically removed from its permanent seat; instead, it is symbolically transferred to a substitute object like a sacred mirror or *shinkyo*. Most often, as at the famous **Asakusa Shrine Festival** or *Sanja Matsuri* held in Tokyo in mid-May, the palanquin is carried by sturdy local youths in ritual white *hanten* (short kimonos) and *fundoshi* loincloths who zigzag down the crowded road with it. They shout: "*wassho, wassho!*"—supposedly to cheer the kami; but this is a fairly modern innovation, and some shrines have stuck to the original solemn style of procession. Others though, like Tokyo's Yushima Tenjin Shrine, have recently gone so far as to introduce female teams of mikoshi carriers. Ordinary parishioners often join in such processions with palanquins they have built to carry a symbolic token of the kami: a piece of paper with its name on it. There are even small palanquins for the children, and often floats (*dashi*) shaped like mountains, shrines, and the like are drawn or carried by men or by oxen. Also walking in this parade are priests in full ceremonial dress, delegations of parishioners, musicians, and dancers in traditional costumes.

In other cases, all these rites have come to lose much of their original significance and are held on to largely as a pretext for magnificent costume pageantry. For instance, the May 15 **Hollyhock Festival** (*Aoi Matsuri*) is a reenactment in Heian period costume of a courtiers' procession to offer leaves of this plant at Kyoto's Lower Kamo Shrine in order to secure good conditions for the rice harvest. It started out as a seasonal propitiatory ritual before the seventh century. Today, it is much closer to the **Period Festival** (*Jidai Matsuri*) held at Heian Shrine in Gion on October 22 since 1895 as a showcase of the history of national costumes. Yet **Aoi Matsuri** remains the best example of a type of procession to be found in many other Shinto festivals that annually retraces the steps of imperial messengers (*chokushi*) or feudal lords who came to a particular shrine on some historic occasion, or in a fondly remembered era.

A **matsuri**'s special events now often look like sports competitions; nonetheless, even in such forms, like the ancient **games** of Greece and Rome, they have sacred origins, either as entertainment for the gods or as a way for them to express their will by choosing the winner. This is as true of the teams of young men bearing on their shoulders the heavy mikoshi as it is of tug-of-war contests or *tsunahiki,* and of horse and boat races, which arose from medieval times onwards as a way to forecast disasters such as crop failures. As for sumo wrestling, though nowadays it is more often found in sports arenas than in shrine compounds, its Shinto roots are still in evidence in its rules. Thus, the referees, who are actually shrine priests, will stop the match at the slightest hint of a nosebleed, because blood is taboo around consecrated areas, and the sumo wrestling mat counts as one. Similarly, if the *kagura* ceremonial dances are now done just as a performance in honor of the gods, they used to be a way to induce an ecstatic trance in the dancer who, once possessed by one, would start uttering oracles as its temporary embodiment.

Communion and Send-Off

A more general communion with the gods is still possible, though, in many festivals, by partaking of the food offered to them in their shrine, in what is called the *naorai*. This term is sometimes used more loosely to include the eating of these offerings outside the **matsuri** site after the festival. The *monoimi* rites were meant to detach the participants from the daily realm of *ke* so as to usher them into a different one marked off as *hare*—a special realm delimited in space by sacred ropes or evergreen branches and delimited in time by elaborate rites. Conversely, a genuine *naorai* is intended as a formal transition from the sacred spatial and temporal confines of the **matsuri** back into the everyday world, at once linking and distinguishing the two sides of Japanese life.

The **matsuri** is formally closed when the offerings are withdrawn from the kami's presence in the shrine. Before going through procedures similar to the ones used to welcome it, like shutting the sanctuary's door, the kami is politely asked to go back to its customary otherworldly dwelling place among or beyond the natural elements. For it would be impossible to keep it at ease on the human plane for more than short festive periods—let alone permanently—due to the difficulty of maintaining ritual purity, as well as the impossibility of providing such an honored guest with non-stop entertainment.

See also Games (Greece); Games (Rome); Hollyhock Festival; New Year (Japan); Sekku

References

Mikiharo Ito. "Festivals," in *Kodansha Encyclopedia of Japan.* New York: Kodansha: International, 1983, Vol. 2.

Yoshida Mitsukuni and Sesoko Tsune, eds. *Naorai—Communion of the Table.* Tr. Lynne E. Riggs and Takechi Manabu. Hiroshima, Japan: Mazda Motor Corp., 1989.

Inoue Nobutaka, ed. *Matsuri: Festival and Rite in Japanese Life.* Tokyo: Institute for Japanese Culture and Classics, Kokugakuin University, 1988.

Kunio Yanagita. *About Our Ancestors: The Japanese Family System.* Tr. Fanny Hagin Mayer and Ishiwara Yasuyo. New York: Greenwood Press, 1988.

▶ MATZU'S BIRTHDAY (CHINA)

A *pai-pai* (pronounced "bye-bye") is a Chinese community festival celebrating the birthday of a deity, or some other important date. The rituals it involves differ little according to which one is being honored, whether it be the sages Confucius and Lao-Tzu, the female bodhisattva of compassion Kuan Yin, deified folk heroes like the third-century warrior Kuan Kung, or the tenth-century saintly maiden Matzu. The latter's birthday on the twenty-third day of the third lunar month being both typical and the most popular today—as the major festival of seafarers. It will serve as an example of a *pai-pai*, in the way it is observed in one of the many Taiwanese centers of her cult, native to southeastern China.

The Cult of Matzu, China's Stella Maris

Like that of other deified heroes (or of the saints of various religions), the cult of Matzu has its roots in wonders performed in her lifetime, but which also continued whenever people turned to her in times of crisis after her death. This proven and ongoing wonder-working efficacy is what turned her into a deity. She is called "Holy Mother up in Heaven" or "Queen of Heaven" (*Tienkou*) for the story goes that she went straight up to heaven after her death at the age of twenty-eight. It relates that she was born in 960 under the name of Lin Moliang (meaning "silent girl") near Meizhou Bay on the coast of the mainland province of Fujien, after her mother had a dream about being given medicine by the merciful Buddhist female deity Kuan Yin—who would later visit Matzu in person, and therefore remain associated with her cult. At sixteen, Matzu gained extraordinary powers upon miraculously coming out of a well into which she had fallen. At twenty, at the height of a terrible drought, she was thus asked by the people to perform a ritual for getting rain, which proved remarkably successful.

Another time, Matzu did not hesitate to put fire to the family home so that it would serve as a beacon to fishermen, upon sensing that they were caught in a sudden and violent storm. There is also a story that though she was asleep when her father and two brothers were caught in a typhoon while fishing, her spirit left her body to fly to them. She then took a brother in each hand and her father in her teeth but dropped the latter when, back home, her mother induced her to talk in her sleep. Thereafter, she would often appear out of the clouds to sailors in peril at sea to extend a helping hand and even still the storm—rather like her Western counterparts the Virgin Mary (another "Queen of Heaven" whose main festival is celebrated on the twenty-fifth day of the third month as the **Annunciation**) in her capacity as *Stella Maris* (Star of the Sea), or **Saint Nicholas** as patron of sailors. As in the latter's case, her cult was widely diffused by the twelfth century largely by virtue of becoming a patron of sailors (officially entering as such the Taoist liturgy due to a heavenly revelation after many petitions earned her various titles and dignities from the Emperor), whom all Chinese emigrants would eventually turn to for divine insurance against the perils of sea journeys. They thus took her cult to all the coasts of Southeast Asia, well beyond those of China, where the name of the former Portuguese colony of Macao is derived from that of a famous old temple of Matzu by the harbor, and it spread to the entire country—wherever it has survived decades of official State repression of popular religion. For when Matzu's pious parents tried to arrange a marriage for her, she refused, insisting that she had dedicated her life to the poor and suffering of the whole world. She thus saved many lives during a plague by going to the mountains to gather healing herbs. Matzu has proved able to dispel all manners of harmful spirits at the root of situations of distress ranging from shipwreck to disease. Her protection of a Chinese diplomatic mission to Korea earned Matzu the special plaque an imperial decree ordered to be put in the temple at her birthplace in Meizhou, where a local medium cult of her spirit was first centered around her embalmed body. Likewise, she was promoted "Queen of Heaven" in 1683 for having assisted the Chinese invasion fleet that conquered Taiwan. Since her cult was brought to the island by the mainland settlers who followed and felt indebted to her for a safe crossing, Matzu has been the most worshipped deity there, with some five hundred temples currently.

A Pai-Pai in Taiwan

In the port of Beigang on the west coast of Taiwan, a parade is held on **Matzu** birthday on the twenty-third of the third month (around April), with floats depicting scenes from Chinese history and literature, acted out by women in beautiful traditional dresses and men wielding ancient weapons, as well as children who thus make their parents proud. In its wake, men run with palanquins containing images of Matzu, brought from local shrines in order to be annually recharged with her blessings from contact with the one in her main temple. Firecrackers are thrown on their way so as to promote the transfer of auspicious energies to every home being passed and to all bystanders. Each village delegation of about forty people is admitted to the temple in turn to solemnly hand over to attendants their image of Matzu, wrapped in a bundle of pennants and flowers. It is taken over a series of altars all the way to the main one at the back of the temple courtyard. While it is placed in front of the temple's Matzu altar, bowing and chanting goes on around it for a few minutes. Then the bundle is handed back across the other altars to the people who brought it. They can now break their expectant silence with a shout of joy, holding the powerfully rededicated bundle aloft in triumph as they leave the temple, while another group of villagers comes in with its own image, to have it recharged following the same procedure. All these images are carried back through the streets on palanquins, again amid firecracker smoke so thick it has to be dispersed with bellows by assistants to the carriers—who are already wearing masks, since they may have trouble breathing.

Of all the processions from local temples to Beigang, the most famous is that from the hundred-year-old one of Tachia in Taichung county, a 280-kilometer journey known as *chin-hsiang* ("carrying the incense") through some thirty villages and towns and fifty-nine temples, lasting eight days and seven nights. However, due to a dispute between the two temples over the ranking of their respective deities, the destination was changed from Beigang to the nearby Worshipping Heaven Taoist Hall of Hsinkang near Chiayi in 1987, and the journey back and forth has become a blessing-imparting procession through a series of local towns. The precise date of the procession is decided each year three months before in Chenlan Taoist Hall at the **Lantern Festival** by casting lots. Scriptures for a peaceful journey are chanted before the Matzu image is taken from the inner hall and placed in her palanquin between two attendants—one named Chien-li Yen ("thousand-mile vision"), and the other, Hsun-feng Erh ("listening-on-the-winds hearing"). The flags of different temple organizations open the procession of the religious floats, palanquin, and incense burner. The ashes from the latter, like the tea offered to Tachia Matzu as "Rain Mother" or "Crossing-the-Waters Mother," have curative powers, so the procession is greeted everywhere by enthusiastic crowds lining up to get small red bags of incense ashes and other amulets, aside from

burning spirit money or prostrating under the passing palanquin. Taking part—on foot or on wheels—is the most reliable way to receive the blessings of the goddess—and transfer them to the home altar Matzu idol many take along, so that tens of thousands of people (many of them physically or mentally handicapped) join the *chin-hsiang* journey each year, plodding day and night in a line that stretches miles, with only five hours of sleep a night, as a matter of personal discipline and reverence for the surrounding nature. This does not prevent them from leaving an endless garbage trail in its wake, and it is far from being just a solemn affair; for it is accompanied by loud fireworks and acrobatic martial arts displays, with many entertainment floats on trucks for ongoing puppet-shows, karaoke, and dancing girls—often scantily clad or even stark naked.

On the Beigang temple grounds themselves, hundreds of people will mill about through the ceremonial of a ***pai-pai,*** going from one attraction to another. In their midst may be found individuals who have a special connection to the spirit world, be it a woman diviner in a trance as she writes messages from there in a tray of sand, or a man piercing his back with long brass skewers with weights attached, yet feeling no pain in his own trance-like state. Visitors hardly pay any attention to the Buddhist priest in yellow robes as he chants sutras (sacred scriptures) so as to bring another set of blessings to the occasion. But they do light joss sticks and bow before ancestral plaques and other images displayed in the Matzu temple's secondary shrines. Some go on making such offerings in other temples and at the home shrines of their ancestors as the evening winds down—though it long keeps buzzing with the wild festive spirit of the ***pai-pai.***

See also Annunciation; Chiao; Games (Greece); Lantern Festival; Saint Nicholas; Thaipusam

References

Richard C. Bush. *Religion in China.* Niles, IL: Argus Communications, 1977.

Muslims gather in a small square for celebrations on Mawlid-an-Nabi, the birthday of the Prophet Mohammed in I-n-Gall, Niger. (Tiziana and Gianni Baldizzone/Corbis)

Mary Flanangan. *Matzu Interactive World.* Peitou, Taiwan: National Institute of the Arts, 1999 (www.maryflanagan.com/Matsu).

Michael R. Saso. *Taiwan Feasts and Customs. A Handbook of the Principal Feasts and Customs of the Lunar Calendar on Taiwan.* Hsinchu, Taiwan: Chabanel Language Institute, 1966.

Kristofer Schipper. *The Taoist Body.* Tr. Karen Duval. Foreword by Norman Girardot. Berkeley: University of California Press, 1993.

▶ MAUNDY THURSDAY

See Holy Week

▶ MAWLID (ISLAM)

The Arabic word *mawlid* refers to the time, the place, and the festival associated with the memory of a holy person. For Muslims, **Mawlid** an-Nabi marks the **Nativity of the Prophet**—in the early hours of Monday, August 20, 570. Celebrated on 12 Rabi' I, a date held to also be that of Mohammed's death in 623, it is a late addition to the list of Islamic celebrations. Though it has an ambivalent status in terms of religious orthodoxy, it is firmly entrenched in mystical devotion and popular piety in most Muslim countries.

Evolution

Many Muslim saints even have their own **mawlid**s, often taking the form of annual pilgrimages, as to the seat of the Sufi contemplative order they may have founded. For instance, pilgrims come from far and wide each year for the largest such **mawlid** in East Africa, laying flowers and saying a brief prayer at the tomb of Lamu Sayyid Salih bin Abdallah-al-Aidrus and gathering to sing hymns by the illuminated mosque of Aidrus from ten at night to three in the morning—not so much on the anniversary of his death in 1935 as on the birthday of Mohammed, the Prophet's and the saint's **mawlid**s having merged.

As for the Prophet Mohammed, the term "**Mawlid** an-Nabi" was first applied to the house where he was born in Mecca. It was only recorded two centuries later, when the humble dwelling had been transformed into a house of prayer by the mother of Haroun al-Raschid, the fifth Abbasid Caliph of Baghdad, who appears in the *Arabian Nights*. The cult of the Prophet's person had just begun to develop, extending to his belongings and to his grave in Medina. It was thus only natural that pilgrims to Mecca would also make a point of visiting his birthplace, both to express their reverence and to take in its blessings. But it was only in the twelfth century that a special date was set aside for visits to the *mawlid* house, when it would be open all day to receive more visitors. The ceremonies they carried out did not initially differ from the ones surrounding the cult of any Muslim saint. It was only later that the cult of the Prophet evolved special forms that raised it above the cult of other holy persons, to give it the typical, universal features of the **mawlid**.

Under the Fatimid dynasty based in Egypt, it was still limited there to a discrete observance by temporal and religious court officials, consisting in solemn daytime processions and three sermons in front of the Caliph. It took place six times a year, commemorating alongside the Prophet, and with **mawlid**s of their own, members of his family like Ali and Fatima—eponymous ancestor of the ruling Caliph, whose birthday was therefore also observed in similar fashion. The last Shiite Fatimid Caliph was deposed in 1171 by the Sunni Sultan Saladin when he took over Egypt; he would also take Jerusalem from the Western Christian Crusaders in 1187. It was his brother-in-law, Prince Al-Malik Muzaffar al-Din Kokburi, who celebrated the first public **Mawlid an-Nabi** recognized by Sunnis at the beginning of the thirteenth century in Irbil, near Mosul in Iraq. Scholars and jurists, poets and mystics from far and wide started gathering two months in advance, followed within a month by all kinds of entertainers, who warmed up the venue for the actual anniversary. Two days prior to it, countless camels, sheep, and oxen were sacrificed, and on its eve, a torchlight procession across town was held. On the morning of the celebration, after the outdoor sermon for a mass audience and the military in full array, religious dignitaries received special robes as ceremonial gifts, and then all the people present were free to enjoy the party that the prince was throwing.

Future **mawlid**s would normally follow the same general outline (though not always on this lavish scale). It owed a lot to the celebration of the **Nativity of Christ** (the Arabic word for **Christmas** is *Milaad*—a form of *mawlid*), that many Muslims would have been familiar with and even regularly joined in, as well as to the mystical devotion of the Sufis. The broadly based international Sufi brotherhoods were actually responsible for popularizing this festival throughout the Islamic world, over the objections of many orthodox religious leaders. The latter were weary of any focus of devotion aside from the transcendent One God who had chosen Mohammed as His Messenger. This is still an issue for the rigorist Wahhabite brotherhood, which is dead set against the cult of saints in general and **Mawlid an-Nabi** in particular, and which has long been allied with the Saudi dynasty ruling over Mohammed's native Arabia since 1925.

Nevertheless, the celebration of Mohammed's birthday has been officially set on the twelfth day, a Monday, of the third month—Rabi' al-Awwal—since 1292; this took place more than seven centuries after the event itself, and independently of authentic tradition. It therefore has more of the character of a civic observance. Indeed, the Young Turks made the day into a national holiday in 1910, after they took control of the Ottoman Empire, and it was kept as such by the secular Turkish Republic that soon succeeded it.

Popular Piety

Regardless of its official status with civic and religious authorities, **Mawlid** remains above all a tremendous outpouring of popular piety, stretching over the entire "birth month" of the Prophet. On the eve of **Mawlid**, and often on the previous days of the month as well, the faithful gather in Koranic schools, shrines and mosques, as much as a display of Islamic solidarity as to hear lectures on the Prophet's life, and then prayerful poems in his praise—appropriately called **mawlid**s. This abundant literary genre is central to the festival as a flamboyant expression of devotion to Mohammed and is also popular over the year on other occasions. For instance, **mawlid**s may be recited to commemorate departed relatives. This is largely in imitation of one of the most famous, among the earliest Turkish poems that is still widely known, which Süleyman Çelebi—or Dede—concluded in 1409 with a moving account of the Prophet's encounter with the Angel of Death.

A festive meal follows the yearly recitation of such poems on **Mawlid** an-Nabi. Then the children go out in the streets, singing as they hold candles to evoke the souls of the dead, or dressed up in clown masks to make fun of *Bu Shikha*—"the Humpback," who is a kind of Arab bogeyman. Great bonfires are lit, as people dance and munch candies. The city of Cairo, founded by the Fatimids as their capital, and where **Mawlid** an-Nabi first caught on, is spectacularly illuminated on the eve of the festival, as if to give a sense of the dazzling light that is said to have filled the whole world on the night the Prophet was born.

In some parts of India, the night may be spent in large-scale feeding of the poor, and non-Muslims often listen alongside believers to speeches in praise of the Prophet at public gatherings where a town's faithful converge in several prayerful processions, like the ones seen in Islamic countries.

In Ghana's Upper West Region, people of all traditions and ethnic backgrounds join in the tribal **Damba** celebrations derived from **Mawlid**, but which have now taken on the character of a seasonal **New Yam festival** toward August. It is spread between **Somba Damba**, **Mawlid** proper, which is set on the first day of the month in the local lunar calendar, and **Naa Damba**, which commemorates the **Naming of the Prophet** on the seventeenth day. The latter, more than the first, centers on joyful displays of loyalty to tribal chiefs in song and dance, after general feasting upon a cow that has been led around by some attendants reading verses from the Koran. The finale is a procession out of town with the dance troupe after the next day's "horse display"—when everybody who owns one adorns it to visit friends and notables.

In Tunisia, **Mawlid** actually ranks first among religious observances—rather like its European counterpart **Christmas**. For it is a reminder of the enduring miracle of Creation, as well as of the birth of the Prophet as the channel of God's grace upon all creatures. To Muslims, this makes **Mawlid** an-Nabi the anniversary of the most important event of all time, because the Koran (21:107) describes the Seal of the Prophets as "Mercy for all creatures." (Abdullah Yusuf Ali translation, 1946). As Süleyman Dede wrote for the occasion, alluding to the angels who threw shooting stars at the demons (as they peered from the sublunar regions of the heavens to see what was going on among men down on earth) and to other phenomena (such as the sacred fires of Zoroastrian temples going out in Persia):

On this night the sun of the world was born . . .
On this night they sounded prophecy's drum,
on this night they cast
the Devil out of the heavens.
How many idol houses,
heathen temples, fetishes were torn down,
to the infidels' chagrin!

(Freely translated from the German version in Engelke 1926)

See also Christmas; New Yam Festival

References

Tarek Atia. *Mulid! Carnivals of Faith.* Photos by Sherif Sonbol. Cairo: American University in Cairo Press, 1999.

Irmgard Engelke. *Sülejman Tschelebi's Lobgedicht auf die Geburt des Propheten (Menlid-I-Serif).* (Dissertation for the University of Kiel.) Halle (Saale), Germany 1926.

N. J. G. Kaptein. *Muhammad's Birthday Festival: Early History in the Central Muslim Lands and Development in the Muslim West until the Tenth/Sixteenth Century.* Leiden, The Netherlands: E. J. Brill, 1993.

J. W. McPherson. *The Moulids of Egypt.* Cairo: 1941.

▶ MAY DAY (WEST)

Throughout Europe, the month of May, and its first day more specifically, is the focus of abundant and lively folklore symbolizing the struggle of the forces of the coming summer and the retreating winter, fighting the latter with fire and promoting growth with flowers, trees, and greenery, while celebrating young love over against its untimely marital fulfillment.

Beltane Fires

Though the sources of **May Day** folklore are too varied and archaic to be traced precisely in every case, a good portion of it could well be derived from an ancient Celtic festival known in the British Isles as **Beltane**. As the polar opposite of **Samhain,** it originally marked the end of the dark half of the year and the start of the bright half—since, as in many ancient cultures (such as those of Mesopotamia), the year was divided between two seasons or half-years. The name refers to "the fire of Bel"—a light principle identifiable with the Gauls' god Belenus and even the Greek Apollo. As at **Samhain** and many another such **New Fire Ceremony**, the druids would light this sacred fire by a special method using wood friction. Every fire in the land would then be rekindled from its embers after having been extinguished the night before this ceremony, in which the cattle was driven between two bonfires to protect it from disease over the coming year. These practices were carried out by country people until fairly recently—long after **Saint Patrick** successfully challenged the druids with a fire of his own on a **May Day**. This had always been the day for the coming of new divine generations to Ireland, be it the Tuatha Dé Danann or the early settler Partholón, who also died on a **Beltane** Monday. He would not be the last, for the custom of the **Beltane** cake (known in Scotland as *bannock*) that was shared out at the end of an evening of song and dance around the May fire makes it clear that the person who would get a specially marked piece originally used to be thrown into the fire as a scapegoat. He would be treated as such, and even as dead, for up to a year after the evening when the community went through the motions of this former sacrifice. Julius Caesar was able to observe the actual sacrifice on a mass scale in Gaul, where criminals, war prisoners, even innocent people—should other victims be in short supply—would be burned alive inside giant wickerwork dummies (like the hapless protagonist of the 1974 British horror film *The Wicker Man*) to bring its sponsors health.

The Witches of Walpurgis Night

Coming six months after **Halloween**, **May Day** was another perilous time when witches roamed. In Ireland and the Isle of Man, people thought witches took the shape of hares, and they would kill the hares they found among their cattle that day for fear they might spoil their butter. A woman who fetched fire on **May Day** was also accounted a witch. One even used to be burned in effigy in the all-night May fire in some places in Bohemia. There, as in the other Czech lands of Moravia and Silesia, brooms are now favored when it comes to "burning the witches" as part of these recently revived **May Day** customs that also involve leaping over the flames or running through the embers. As in the German lands of Saxony, Tyrol, and Alsace, this took place on the eve of **May Day**, the famous **Walpurgis Night** of Gothic novels, named after a niece of the English missionary Saint Boniface, Apostle of Germany—where she followed him. For the Church, her main feast day is February 25, the day of her death in 779 at the abbey she ran in Heidenheim. And yet, the commemoration of the transfer of her remains to Eichstätt on a May 1 close to a hundred years later has been much more widely observed, no doubt in order to bring to bear against the witches the powers displayed during her lifetime in the struggle against pagan gods. For her relics caused a miracle working oil to exude from the stone of her new tomb at the church of the Holy Cross in Eichstätt (just like those of **Saint Nicholas**, as related in a popular liturgy in honor of his December 6 feast day that provided a model for many other saints' miracle stories—and happened to be composed by a bishop of the same Bavarian town in the tenth century). This oil was sold as a cure against all sorts of ailments, so that it might have seemed only natural to invoke the holy woman's powers against those unleashed by the witches on this night, and that ill-intentioned people might channel against others through spells on fields, cattle, and humans. Like the other nations of the Balkans, Greeks believe such curses to be especially effective in bringing harm to their home, fortune, and children at the start of this month, whose name sounds like their word for magic—*ma(g)ia*. On May 3, the feast of **Saint Mavra**—whose name means "black"—women also fear that they will get black spots on their hands if they do any handwork like cutting or sewing and that cloth bleached on that day will turn out black.

All these evils of **May Day** were the demonized form of the pagan spirits of winter fighting their yearly losing—but all the more ferocious—battle against those of summer, reenacted in contrasting seasonal costumes by opposing teams of young men on horseback in German and Swedish villages until the eighteenth century. In central and northwestern Europe, the forces of winter took their last stand on the hilltops, where people still kindle fires in order to "drive away the witches." As in Ireland, a special method (albeit a different one using flint stones) was called for to light them in Sweden—the only Scandinavian country to have bonfires on that evening and to this day. Old folks in rural areas used to be able to tell by the northerly or southerly angle of the flames in the wind which way the battle of seasonal forces was going and whether the spring would be cold or gentle as a result. Even in a Swedish university town like Uppsala, on **Walpurgis**mas Eve, the students still gather by the river Fyris to simulate the ritual destruction of their old (winter) caps and then party all night before getting new (spring) caps on **May Day**. In once Swedish-ruled Finland too, a sure sign of spring and the triumph of light over the bleak darkness of Nordic winters is the appearance on city streets of these brand-new black-rimmed white velvet caps on the heads of all the students who successfully passed their comprehensive language, history, or math exams come **May Day**. In Helsinki, they all converge on South Harbor for **Vappu** (the local form of **Walpurgis**) to place a white cap on *Havis Amanda* (the nude maiden on that square's fountain), before forming a parade to go lay on the tomb of the unknown soldier the armfuls of flowers given by their loved ones. They can then proceed with their partying, around the special **Vappu** treats of *tippaleipä* ("drop bread") and *sima* (homemade yeast-fermented lemonade)—not to mention stronger drinks.

May Prince and May Princess

At some point during the month across the Gulf of Finland in Tallinn, Estonians lovingly reenact a typical example of seasonal customs once known throughout Northern and Central

Europe. They were brought in the fourteenth century by the city's German overlords, who would only allow the natives the part of onlookers in the Middle Ages, until the Swedish conquest and the Reformation put an end to these customs in the sixteenth century. Still, in Germany and Scandinavia well into the Renaissance, the May King was often escorted from the forest to the town (during **Whitsuntide** instead in some places) by armed men, as though going into battle against the forces of winter in the kind of mock combat which certain knightly competitive **games** long perpetuated. Today, it is thus dressed as the Baltic barons of old that the Estonians themselves put on the feast of the *Maikrahv*—competing in medieval sports and jousts for the honor of becoming the Earl of May (German *Maigraf*), and of getting to choose the Countess of May from the finalists in a pageant of the city's finest young girls, who also compete in parallel demonstrations of womanly skills, poise, and graces. The May Prince then takes his Princess on his horse, and the whole company of young knights, fair maidens, dignified burghers, and beautiful ladies proceed behind them in wagons from the fortifications of the upper city down its winding streets all the way to the Town Square. There, the couple is crowned by the mayor and given an official parchment letter with the keys of Tallinn, to recall the degree of sovereign power once granted them. The first criminal who threw himself at their mercy that day would be pardoned. The previous year's *Maigraf* would then throw a "Ladies' Ball" at the Great Guildhall as the final act of his tenure. The new Earl of May would also soon throw a ball—outdoors during **Whitsuntide**—to honor the ladies who made the heavy candles for the upcoming **Corpus Christi** procession and the men who would carry them along with him. He would entertain them all again afterwards as a fitting conclusion to his brief springtime reign.

While Greeks are familiar with the procession of the May Boy, wreathed with flowers, who sometimes impersonates the Peppertree as vegetation spirit, elsewhere in Europe it is more common for girls between the ages of four and fifteen to embody Spring on **May Day**. During the Renaissance, the French Court physician and famous seer Nostradamus could describe the very old custom of his native Provence of "choosing the neighborhood's most beautiful young girls, to gorgeously attire them with crowns of flowers, garlands, jewels and silk accoutrements, on elevated thrones, in the guise of young goddesses put in niches commonly called *mayes* to which all passers by, at least those of honest standing, are invited and obliged to contribute with a few silver pieces in return for a kiss" (de Benoist 1996, G/T 22, p. 11). As though to echo the ancient cult of the nymph Maia—one of the Pleiades who, according to legend, had saved Marseille soon after its foundation by Greek colonists around 600 B.C.E., this *belle de Mai* could be seen on the month's first Sunday enthroned on the city's squares or by its thoroughfares, until the early twentieth century. In Madrid since the seventeenth century, men have done the rounds of all the city's neighborhoods to appraise the charms of the *mayas* or *majas* (as in Goya's famous paintings on that theme) chosen in every parish to preside over popular balls, covered with garlands. In the valleys of the Pyrenees, there even used to be more down-to-earth "girl fairs" where young men who were ready to settle down went to "buy a wife" in May. Elsewhere in northern Spain, there were more subtle ways for boys to express romantic interest, usually involving flowers. In Asturias, for example, a boy would wait outside the church to which the girl he had his eye on had brought flowers for the Virgin Mary (who was honored this way all through that month), and he would offer her a flower as she came out.

The Maypole and the Green Man

From France (since at least 1207) to Hungary, there is a custom—now revived in certain places such as the Czech Republic—calling for young men to put a bunch of flowers, a bough, or most often a tree in front of girls' houses, using plant symbolism that varies from one region to the next to express their interest—of whatever kind. Thus, birch might stand for love and be left all month, but a cherry-tree signifying fickleness would soon get removed, as would a crooked trunk or one hung with filthy rags. (In parts of France, boys would even jokingly remove anything left outside a town's houses—bikes, lawn ornaments, and the like—and gather it all in a big pile on a public square, like triumphant springtime sweeping away all the odds and ends left over by retreating winter.) More serious "honor mays" were also put up (generally for the month) in front of inns or the houses of notables—such as elected officials in the few areas where this is still done. In colonial French Canada, peasants would put up a stripped spruce tree in front of the landlord's house and shoot at the crown on top before being treated to wine. In Nice, a pine used to be planted in front of the palace of this Provençal county's governors until Piedmont ceded it to France in 1860. There, the custom of "turning the may" has endured without interruption, and is carried out every Sunday of the month by folk dancers who circle a maypole ringed with ribbons in the gardens of the Roman arenas in the hills of Cimiez. Among other ruins of former Cemenelum, evidence has been found of the ancient brotherhood of tree-bearers who brought the pine of Attis for the **spring rites of Cybele** reenacting their ill-fated love. To this day, in the Greek island of Corfu's towns, young workers dressed in white with a red belt and scarf still carry a maypole through the streets.

It is from Southern Europe that children's ribbon dances around short maypoles were introduced to England by the art critic John Ruskin in 1888—as the "Morris dances" had allegedly been by the fourteenth-century regent John of Gaunt, according to the first mentions of these "Moorish" dances under Henry VIII,

when they took the highly ritualized forms still observed in today's Morris Clubs. With the riding of hobby-horses and dragons and the continual swinging of handkerchiefs to the playing of pipes, the beating of drums, and the ringing of bells, many folk dances in the Morris repertoire revolve around the legendary figures of Maid Marian and Robin Hood—another version of the Green Man known on **Saint George**'s Day as Green George and on **May Day** as Jack-in-the-Green. This man disguised as a shrubbery still figures prominently in such seasonal events as the Royal Festival **May Day** of Knutsford in Cheshire. He finds an echo in the May Bear made of branches and ribbons that ends up in a river in Switzerland and Germany, like Green George in Austria.

England's typical tall, permanent maypoles, first recorded in 1216, also have their equivalents in Germany, where they appear by 1225. In Bavaria, maypoles decorated with figurines representing different professional guilds embody civic pride and elicit intense competition between villages about their height and beauty—witness the frequent attempts to steal one another's poles as the new ones are being prepared in secret every year (a bit like **Whitsuntide** flagpoles in Rumania). In Great Britain, along with other **May Day** customs, maypoles were banned as heathen in 1644 by Oliver Cromwell's Puritan republic, to come back with a vengeance after the Restoration of the Stuart kings. Solemnly erected in London in 1661, a 130-feet "tall May-pole once o'erlook'd the Strand" (Pope, *Dunciad* 2:24, 1963, p. 99)—until 1718, when Sir Isaac Newton bought it as a support for the 124-feet telescope the Dutch scientist Christiaan Huygens had offered him years before, then the largest one in the world. There used to be singing and dancing around a maypole in American colleges and city schools—especially in New York, though often later in the month so as to avoid bad weather. At first suspicious of maypoles, the French Revolution rationalized them as part of its propa-

Merrymakers dance around the flower-decked maypole in Elizabethan England in an engraving from J. Nash. (Bettman/Corbis)

ganda as early as 1790, as rootless "Trees of Freedom" topped with headless Phrygian bonnets. Even Louis XVI then planted one in the garden of the Tuileries royal palace in Paris, but it was later torn down by revolutionary authorities as "withered by despotism." "Trees of Freedom" were used as a Republican symbol to defy other regimes well into the nineteenth century.

In 1890, the International Workers' Congress in Berlin adopted **May Day** as the workers' annual holiday, commemorating the Haymarket Square massacre that occurred on May 1, 1886, when mostly German-born anarchist workers were involved in a bloody confrontation with the police as they were holding a **May Day** fair in Chicago. In a transition partly engineered by labor activists such as the pioneering French folklorist Arnold Van Gennep (1873–1957), this traditional date for the end of hiring contracts took on a new dimension, as agricultural, seasonal symbolism was replaced by industrial, political allegory, and images of the coming re-

newal of the fertile forces of Nature as part of her ever-recurring cycles were overlaid by those of the coming Revolution of the productive forces of society as the end-point of historical progress. In contrast to the more moderate American and Canadian version of **Labor Day** on the first Monday in September (also initiated in the United States by the labor movement from 1882, but ratified by Congress in 1894 and endorsed by Presbyterian bodies in 1905), the initial association of International **Labor Day** with secular left-wing radicalism impelled the Catholic Church to find a less polarizing, nonconfrontational, and properly Christian alternative to its widespread observance. It therefore declared May 1 the feast of **Saint Joseph the Craftsman**—when the Pope still receives delegations from labor unions and employers' associations.

May Love and Its Taboos

The same method had been used early on by the Church to absorb rival pagan festivals that could not be suppressed, down to the early eighteenth century, when the entire month of May was placed under the patronage of the Virgin Mary. (In the Coptic Churches of Egypt and Ethiopia, May 1 had always been the feast of the **Nativity of the Virgin Mary**, celebrated elsewhere on September 8, when the sun is in the middle of the constellation of Virgo.) The Queen of Heaven took over the role of the May Queen and her symbol, the rose, along with other seasonal practices. Among them was an age-old taboo on marriage during the month of May, rooted in the yearly visitations of the evil dead in pagan Rome. They used to be placated at the **Lemuria** of the ninth, eleventh, and thirteenth and expelled during **Argei** on the fourteenth. Their noxious presence cast its gloomy shadow over many activities, especially those of a sexual nature, in which they might interfere by taking the place of the living. This was now explained in terms of Mary's virginity but had been attributed earlier still to the somewhat ominous commemoration with which the month used to begin: the May 3 feast of the **Exaltation of the Holy Cross** on which Jesus Christ was executed, later moved to September 14.

Yet in ancient Rome already, the month of May was also chastely devoted to Maia, the *Bona Dea* ("Good Goddess"), a fertile virgin who stood for the fecund power of love. She was depicted as such during the Renaissance in Sandro Botticelli's allegorical painting of *Spring*, with Eros flying above her and the May Queen at her side throwing roses from a bouquet, crowned and garlanded with flowers. It used to be only from **May Day** onward (or from **Saint George**'s Day one week before in Slavic countries) that making bouquets of cut flowers was allowed; cutting them earlier would have undercut the awakening vitality of vegetation. On the eve of **May Day** in Greece, town-dwellers go to the gardens to gather the flowers used for making the wreaths to be nailed over their front doors in order to welcome May—or buy them ready-made from the florists in the larger cities. Country people use green plants and fruits to make theirs, always adding garlic against the evil eye and thistle against enemies. They also renew all household articles, especially the jugs that hold life-giving water, which is then sprinkled around the house with a green twig, much as it is for **Epiphany** blessings on January 6. In Portugal, boats as well as houses are decorated with a bouquet called a *maio*. In many parts of France until the 1930s, branches were tied together crosswise into small blessed *croisettes* that were planted in the fields at the beginning of the month to ensure their owners' prosperity, giving rise to celebrations both on that occasion and when they were later found during the harvest.

Just as it would be unwise to cut and weave together young plants into wreaths prematurely, for humans the month of May holds out the promise of love and yet forbids its consummation. The latter is still reserved for the May Prince and the May Princess as the symbolic primordial couple of the plant and water spirits respectively. It is already found in early Rome in the sacred marriage of King Numa to the birth-favoring water nymph Egeria, and among the ancient Germans, as the union of the sky god Odin with the fertility goddess Freya, from which *Lenz* (Spring) was born on the night of **May Day**. Likewise, the pre-Islamic Turkish festival of **Hidrellez** over the night from May 5 to May 6 celebrates the meeting of Hizir and Ilyas—a couple symbolizing earth and water. This is a time to make wishes, especially for young people of marriageable age, who leave small pouches containing rings or coins hanging on tree branches until morning, so they will find the right partner and a prosperous life. Tree weddings are celebrated in May in parts of Italy, where the trunks are made to perform a love dance.

Humans, too, express erotic interest, and even serious commitments, in the often elaborate plant symbolism used in folklore to convey these tender feelings. However, acting them out in full carnal union would be premature at the delicate moment when the contrary life-giving and life-threatening forces of Nature are at the peak of their yearly struggle. A fall of tension and a collapse into fusion would hinder the clean separation of energies that is the precondition for their fruitful union. To prepare the ground, they are allowed to play themselves out and against each other in amorous battles of the sexes, as well as in peer emulation in gender-based competitions. The charged, yet innocent, atmosphere of May love—a spring awakening consonant with sublimated adolescent stirrings—has provided the setting for much of the medieval poetry celebrating a largely Platonic kind of courtly love, that was spread by the troubadours of Provence (such as Raimbault de Vaqueyras in his best-known verse *Kalenda Maya*). From this sweet bud of May, romantic love would eventually blossom as the West's ruling passion, as Swiss writer Denis de

Rougemont contended in his famous 1939 book on *Love in the Western World.*

See also Akitu; Argei; Assumption; Conception and Birth of the Virgin Mary; Corpus Christi; Days of the Dead (China, Korea, Japan); Days of the Dead (West); Elevation of the Cross; Epiphany; Matronalia; Midsummer; New Fire Ceremony; Saint George; Saint Nicholas; Samhain; Spring Festival of Cybele and Attis; Whitsuntide

References

Doleta Chapru. *A Festival of the English May.* Dodgeville, WI: Folklore Village Farm, 1991.

Alain de Benoist. *Les Traditions d'Europe.* 2nd ed. Arpajon, France: Labyrinthe, 1996.

Denis de Rougemont. *Love in the Western World.* Translated by Montgomery Belgion. Princeton, NJ: Princeton University Press, 1983.

Sinikka Grönberg Garcia. *Suomi Specialties. Finnish Celebrations, Recipes and Traditions.* Iowa City, IA: Penfield Press, 1998.

Ronald Hutton. *The Pagan Religions of the Ancient British Isles: Their Nature and Legacy.* Oxford: B. Blackwell, 1992.

Morris Ring. www.themorrisring.org.

Helen Philbrook Patten. *The Year's Festivals.* Boston: Dana Estes and Company, 1903.

Alexander Pope. *Dunciad.* Twickenham Edition. New Haven, CT: Yale University Press, 1963.

MEATFARE SUNDAY

See Lent

MEATFARE WEEK

See Carnival

MEETING OF OUR LORD

See Candlemas

MEMORIAL DAY

See Midsummer

MICCAILHUITONTLI

See Days of the Dead (West)

MICHAELMAS

See Saint George, Samhain

MID-AUTUMN (CHINA, KOREA, JAPAN)

Known in Japan as **Tsukimi** after the local adaptation of its **Moon Viewing** custom, and in Korea as **Chuseok** or **Thanksgiving**—an even bigger festival than **New Year**'s Day, **Mid-Autumn** or *Chung Ch'iu* is first of all a major Chinese harvest festival. Traditionally held toward on the fifteenth day of the eighth lunar month around the autumn equinox, it actually marks the halfway point of the fall season in the Chinese reckoning (as in the ancient Celtic one). It is also called the **Gathering Festival**, to refer to family gatherings, as symbolized by the full moon that shines brightest and closest to the earth on post-harvest feasts celebrating the unity of gods and men amid plentiful food and weather that is still fine. Certain tales are then told about the moon to account for the customs of this festival, though few modern Chinese people still follow them all strictly on this ordinary workday.

Mid-Autumn Activities

Chinese families have a five-, seven- or nine-course dinner (since these are lucky *yang* numbers), often including snails, served with wine and closing with a late dessert by the moonlight on any night between the thirteenth and the seventeenth of the eighth month, the official season for **Mid-Autumn** celebrations of the harvest moon as established by the powerful Empress Dowager Cixi or Tz'u Hsi (1835–1908). Other typical Chinese **Mid-Autumn** activities may include playing on a swing, eating lotus seeds and water chestnuts, singing folksongs, and dancing with the brightly colored lanterns that decorate shops and streets during the festival. In addition, Koreans used to wrestle—traditional *ssireum* style, do circle dances, or play the cow game or the turtle game. Today, on an even larger scale than Americans on their **Thanksgiving**, they flock from far and wide to their native areas on the three-day holiday of this **Harvest Moon Festival**, when everything is closed, highways are clogged, and train and plane tickets are booked months in advance. Koreans use grains and fruits from the new harvest in annual memorial services on the graves of their ancestors from the fifth generation and up. Their maintenance and the management of other common property is often discussed in annual clan conferences held on the occasion of these very extended family gatherings that every member is sure to attend.

That night, Chinese children are allowed to stay up late and go to high places with their families to light lanterns of many shapes (which also decorate homes) and eat cakes as they watch the moonrise shine on laurel flowers. This custom goes back to the earliest records of the **Mid-Autumn** festival, under the Western Han Dynasty Emperor Wu Di (156–87 B.C.E.), who made it a three-day celebration featuring banquets and **moon viewing** on the Toad Terrace—named after the mythical Lady Chang'e, who became a three-legged toad upon finding her new abode on the moon. In Japan, the Great **Moon Viewing** (called there *Chushu Kangetsu*) was introduced from China at the Imperial Court in 897. The habit of gazing at the full moon eventually spread from the aristocracy to the populace under the name of *Tsukimi*—"Moon Viewing." In mid-September, Japanese people eat red rice and sweet potatoes as they throw **moon viewing** parties, centering on an ancient offering of dumplings, pampas grass, and fruits. Like many Chinese communities, lovers of Japanese culture abroad (in Hawaii, for instance) may organize elaborate showcases of traditional arts and crafts on the occasion of the **Moon Viewing** and the **Mid-Autumn** season.

Among the Chinese, it is crucial that the woman of the house preside over offerings to the moon, because both represent the wet "feminine" or *yin* principle in their respective spheres, and it will only increase with the coming cold season; hence the saying that "men do not bow to the moon, women do not sacrifice to the kitchen gods." Thus, elder sisters, mothers, and grandmothers buy all kinds of round fruits (their shape evoking both the moon and family unity)—such as crabapples, grapes, honey peaches, melons, and pomegranates (as universal symbols of fertility), so they can prepare special altar plates in honor of the Moon Lady Chang'e and set them up at night in the courtyard. They used to also offer her beans or beanpods as the favorite foods of the Moon Rabbit she holds, as well as thirteen seasonal mooncakes to stand for the thirteen months of the full lunar year. In addition, the ritual can include pouring wine cups, burning incense, spirit money, and finally images of the moon legends on which these rites are based. Elders may tell children these stories after the family has then had dinner—partaking of the food offerings, among other things. In villages, adults may give children a burning incense stick for a game that allows them to become the actual mouthpieces of minor spirits of the *yin* realm. They form a circle around one or more of their playmates who sit with their faces hidden in their arms while they sing "Frog, Frog, Mother Frog! This is the fifteenth of the eighth month! Appear!" The children in the middle soon fall into a trance, jumping and croaking like the frogs that possess them (not unlike Aztec priests at the **Etzalqualitzli** festival), unless possessed by other water creatures like crayfish and shrimp. They become as wet and cold as these, so that the incense sticks can be put out on their skin without hurting them, while the adults ask the Little Frog Mother (comparable to the Moon Lady) about the rains of the coming fall season. Lifting the children from the ground—where *yin* forces dwell—brings their trance to an end.

How the Moon Got Its Own Goddess

Chinese theater originated on temple grounds as another way for the gods to become manifest through humans. Thus, the Moon goddess appears at **Mid-Autumn** when the four-thousand-year-old legend of Chang'e is the theme of shadow puppet plays and operas performed in marketplaces. The story goes that in the mythical time of Emperor Yao, there were ten suns taking turns shining on the earth—until one day they decided it would be more fun to appear simultaneously in the human realm, even though this spelled disaster for its inhabitants. The god of Heaven ordered his best archer Hou Yi to rein them in. Yet he shot down the nine extra suns instead. Both Hou Yi and his beautiful wife Chang'e were banished to earth, where the people made the archer king over them in gratitude and awe. There, too, he ignored all limits to his "masculine" or *yang* drive, as he took advantage of his position to oppress the people. To preempt any rebellion and become like a god again among ordinary mortals, he went to Mount Kunlun and secured an elixir of immortality from the Queen Mother of the West. Hou Yi had meant for both he and his wife to become immortal, but before he could drink the elixir, Chang'e drank it all up herself so as to foil his evil plan. As Hou Yi was being assassinated by a disciple he had trained in archery, the double dose of elixir caused his wife to fly up in the sky—along with her pet rabbit.

Thinking of the moon she loved to gaze at, Chang'e was instantly taken to its palace, where she joined the old alchemist Wu Gang. His own quest for immortality had taken him there due to a mistake, which the Jade Emperor of Taoist cosmology condemned him to expiate by vainly trying to cut down a cassia tree of immortality for all eternity. Like him, Chang'e, as the goddess of beauty, may be seen in the moon ever since that time, holding the misty white Jade Rabbit (sometimes seen as a form assumed by the pill of immortality she spat out) as it pounds cinnamon cloves in a pestle, vainly trying to prepare a new dose of the elixir of life for his mistress. As in many other cultures beyond China's, the rabbit happens to be a fertility symbol, so that in the lunar calendar ruling women's fertility, as well as the earth's, along the vital cycles of yin and yang, the **Mid-Autumn** moon has traditionally been a choice occasion to celebrate marriages. Girls dream of love and turn to Chang'e as a powerful intercessor who knows all their secret wishes. In versions of her story where she appears as imprudent and her husband in a more benign role, Hou Yi pursues her in the sky with his magic arrows, which Chang'e wards off from her moon palace, and he settles in a palace of his own he builds in a grove of cinnamon trees on the sun. As perfect celestial symbols of yin and yang respectively, Chang'e and Hou Yi now see each other only on the fifteenth of each month, when the sun shines brightest on the full moon.

Mooncakes

"The crusty small cake so sweet is as round as the full moon," wrote the great Taoist poet Su Tung-p'o (1036–1101) of the *yuebing,* which appeared under the Tang Dynasty (618–907), but only became popular under the Sung emperors who succeeded it. The *Annals of Yanjing* record that at **Mid-Autumn,** as it is an offering, the yuebing is sold everywhere. On top of the cake, there are drawings depicting the moon palace, the rabbit and such. The biggest yuebing can reach a foot in diameter. Some eat the yuebing after the sacrifice, others keep it until lunar **New Year**'s Eve"(Qi Xing 1987, p. 60). These widespread seasonal customs allegedly made it possible to use the yuebing to hide the tracts giving the signal for Han leader Liu Fu Tong's uprising against the Mongol Yuan Dynasty in the fourteenth century, and this clever trick has been commemorated on **Mid-Autumn** ever since (not to mention its literal use during the 1900 Boxer Rebellion against Western exploiters to once more convey the simple message to "kill the foreigners"). The mooncakes have kept evolving over the centuries into a number of regional varieties, with many different fillings

A baker makes moon cakes to be sold for the Mid-Autumn Festival in Hong Kong. He is filling them with cooked duck egg yolks, but there are several varieties of the seasonal cakes. (Earl and Nazima Kowall/Corbis)

(aside from duck egg yolk symbolizing the moon) to recall this secret message of resistance against oppression—a meaning also conveyed by the pictures on the outside evoking Chang'e's self-sacrifice. The Jade Rabbit and other classic folktale designs as well as floral motifs are also often imprinted on them with special wooden molds.

Under the Ming Dynasty (1368–1644), yue-bings were offered with wishes for family harmony. This is the lesson to be learned from the story behind the custom of gazing at the moon until the fourth watch in the hope of seeing the dragon boat in which immortals leave the moon palace on **Mid-Autumn**. In the same way that Greek village-women stay up all night on **Christmas** Eve in order to be granted any wish they make if they can see the heavens open in glory, a Chinese person who sees the heavenly dragon boat on the night of **Mid-Autumn** will have everything he or she touches turn into gold. For this is supposed to be what happened to the loom of Sixth Sister Yao when she was forced by her mother-in-law to weave seven *jin* of cotton into cloth overnight or get beaten. Mrs. Yang relented when she realized her daughter-in-law had been blessed with a heavenly visitation from compassionate immortals and promised not to mistreat her anymore.

In Korea on the night before **Chuseok**, the whole family would sit around within sight of the full moon to make *songpyeon*, a version of the moon-shaped rice cake that is filled with fruits of the new harvest like sesame seeds, beans, chestnuts, or Chinese dates, and steamed over pine needles. Unmarried young people had an incentive to make theirs as nice as possible; it was thought their future spouses would only be as good-looking as the songpyeons they produced.

See also Christmas; Dionysia; Easter; Holi; New Year (China, Korea); Rain Festivals

References

Annual Customs and Festivals in Peking as recorded in the Yen-ching Sui-shih-chi by Tun Li-ch'en. Tr. and ed. Derk Bodde. 2nd ed., rev. Hong Kong: Hong Kong University Press, 1965.

Choe Sang-su. *Annual Customs of Korea: Notes on the Rites and Ceremonies of the Year.* Seoul: Seomun-dang, 1983.

Kunio Ekiguchi and Ruth S. McCreery. *A Japanese Touch for the Seasons.* Tokyo: Kodansha International, 1987.

William C. Hu. *The Chinese Mid-Autumn Festival: Foods and Folklore.* Ann Arbor, MI: Ars Ceramica, 1990.

Qi Xing. *Les Fêtes traditionnelles chinoises.* Beijing: Éditions en langues étrangères, 1987.

▶ MID-LENT

See Lent

▶ MIDORI NO HI

See Cherry Blossom Festival

▶ MID-PENTECOST

See Whitsuntide

▶ MIDSÖMMER

See Midsummer

▶ MIDSUMMER (WEST)

Throughout Europe and the Arabic-speaking countries of North Africa, **Midsummer** fire festivals are celebrated in connection with the summer solstice, which falls on June 21 in the Northern Hemisphere. This date now marks the beginning of summer rather than its midpoint, as late June did when the term "**Midsummer**" was attached to it by the eighth century in Saxon Britain, due to the continuing influence of the Celtic calendar organized around the four midpoints between solstices and equinoxes, such as **May Day** and **Lammas Day** (August 1). Yet the June 24 Christian feast of **Saint John the Baptist** is widely favored for these pagan celebrations of solar light and growth at their annual high point—which may be a reason why French Canadians made it their national holiday. It was no doubt set on this date by the early Church in an attempt to "baptize" seasonal observances, possibly relying on the important role that water plays in **Midsummer** rites.

Solstice Symbolism and Magic

The North African bishop Saint Augustine of Hippo, however, already underlined the scriptural basis for linking the summer solstice with the Nativity of Saint John the Baptist, who is unique among the saints in having his birthday celebrated like Christ and Mary, in addition to the August 29 date of his death. Like the sun when it reaches highest above the horizon and the days are about to get shorter, John could say of his master upon baptizing him at the start of his public ministry: "He must grow greater, I must grow smaller." (John 3:30). For, as Christ told his disciples, "of all the children born of woman, there is no one greater than John; yet the least in the kingdom of God is greater than he is" (Luke 7:28), as the eternal "Sun of Justice" invisibly outshines the waxing and waning visible sun. While Christ's lowly human birth happened six months later than that of Saint John as his Forerunner, the latter's witness on behalf of the expected Messiah was the glorious final culmination of Biblical prophecy. The major feast of the **Nativity of Christ** is quietly celebrated indoors in the dead of night and the darkest of winter after the winter solstice on December 25—around the modest fire of the family hearth, from which the ashes of the **Yule** log will be taken to protect home and fields against disease and bad weather. Conversely, the minor feast of the **Nativity of Saint John the Baptist** is boisterously celebrated outdoors after the longest day that is the summer solstice—in a public place or on a height around a great bonfire, whose flames and remains also serve to dispel the same perils at this other turning point of the year and over its second half.

Midsummer customs follow the same remarkably widespread patterns, whether they are attached to the feast of **Saint John** on June 24 or alternatively to that of **Saint Peter** on June 29 as in Belgium and parts of Russia—or even to both as in Cornwall. They are always about the solstice as that time when the sun (*sol* in Latin) appears to stay (*stare* in Latin) its course—in this case, at its maximum height, the apex of its growth. So the height a bonfire's flames grow, or people can jump over them, or a **Midsummer** maypole reaches above them frequently gets correlated to how tall the harvest is going to get that year. To translate the sun's growth energy from the fire to fields, orchards, beasts, and humans, people might run through the fields with torches (as on the first Sunday of **Lent**), or jump over the fire, which was often an occasion for young couples to declare themselves publicly. They might also swing flaming wheels on heights, to reflect the sun's circular motion, or roll them downhill into the water to mirror its imminent decline.

Purifying Water

These flaming wheels were likened to fiery dragons when they were thrown into the air from a hill in sixteenth-century Würzburg. Still, according to a medieval writer, such displays of fire and smoke (long produced by burning animal bones—hence the word *bonfire*) were actually meant to drive away the foul dragons that mated in **midsummer** skies. For their noxious seed was thought to spread pestilence on the earth by poisoning rivers and wells when it fell into them. In parts of France, the brands from the bonfire were thrown into wells and fountains to keep the water pure and prevent it from drying up. In Würzburg as in a number of other German or Czech towns, this was done to keep the plague as well as eye ailments at bay. There, people also wore chaplets of mugwort and vervain as they jumped over the fire and stared at it through bunches of larkspur. (Mugwort was also one of the ingredients used to keep away the gods of plague during the **Dragon Boat Festival** around the summer solstice in China—though conspicuous fires were traditionally proscribed there at that time of year; dogwood was used for the same purpose at the **Double Nine** festival in the fall, as was chrysanthemum to preserve eyesight.) Many such herbs would be collected for use in medicine, divination, or magic at a special time before sunrise, breakfast, or lunch, having imbibed the magical properties of dew on that day. People might therefore roll in the grass, if they did not take a purifying bath in a spring, a pond, or the sea, or else simply drink that auspicious **Midsummer** water and give it to their beasts. Thus in Sweden, sick people would go to certain holy springs to take advantage of the healing virtues they acquired on **Saint John**'s Eve—which the Christian Church could quite naturally attribute to the Baptist's association with the blessed waters of the Jordan in the midst of the desert's scorching heat.

In Goa, until 1961 a colony of Portugal in India, *São João* is the *festa* of the filling up of wells and rivers by the rain upon the welcome start of the monsoon. Catholics then march to them with foliage on their heads to the sound of drums and trumpets around a newlywed couple whose crowns boys vie to remove and to whom fruits will later be offered. Many men jump in twice (as Saint John supposedly jumped twice inside Elizabeth's womb upon sensing the presence of Jesus in that of her newly pregnant cousin Mary) to fish for their prize: bottles of a local high-alcohol toddy—cashew or coconut *feni,* so spirits get higher as the day wears on.

Ancient Rome's plebeians and slaves would also get drunk on **Midsummer** as a counterpart of the winter **Saturnalia,** in a festival of the goddess Fortuna, when races were held both on foot and between some of the flower-decked boats carrying young revelers on the Tiber river. In Russia, peasants would throw pails of water on each other or even push one another into the river, as they also threw in it the figures of two Slavic gods: Kupalo (from *kupat'sya,* meaning "to swim"), made from straw with women's clothes and a floral crown and necklace, and Morena (meaning "winter" or "death"), represented by a tree with ribbons. The latter is reminiscent of the maypole central to Swedish **Midsummer** customs ever since German immigrants thus postponed their **May Day** customs to adapt them to Scandinavia's later blossoms. If Slovaks also dunked Morena after **Easter,** Russians used to bathe along with Kupalo on the feast of **Saint John,** with whom Kupalo was sometimes identified. On **Midsummer**'s Eve, as they jumped over the fire in couples, they would carry either Kupalo's effigy or a birch branch—a **Midsummer** symbol of growth that is still displayed everywhere from church altars to city buses in neighboring Finland.

The Golden Bough

For Russians as for many Europeans all the way to Britain, the night before **Midsummer** had magical properties. It was the time when ferns released their golden spores that could lead those who picked them to hidden gold, being a magical emanation of the sun's golden fire—witness the German tale about the hunter who shot at the **Midsummer** sun at its noontime height and caught three drops of its blood in a white cloth, which turned out to be fern seed. Likewise in Wales and Shropshire, the Golden Bough that the mistletoe was seen as was collected by maidens on that night, the same way the ancient Celtic druids did: by spreading a white cloth under an oak. Placing the mistletoe

under their pillow would guide them in their dreams to their future husbands, just as divining rods made from it would guide Swedes to buried treasure on **Midsummer** Eve. Throughout Western Europe, mistletoe (or else "the oil of **Saint John**" found on oak leaves in northwestern Italy) was collected on **Midsummer** Eve or morning to make decoctions that were used against either all ailments or specific ones. Among the latter was the "falling sickness" of epilepsy, since mistletoe plants do not fall from the high oak branches on which they take root. Like the sun, they have their home far above the ground, and their white blossoms also become golden as they dry after being cut. This is why the mistletoe was treated as a magical emanation of the solar fire by the Celts, and as its common substitute the fern seed, was likely collected on the great solar dates of the summer and winter solstices. This in turn gave rise to its role at **Christmas**time. Another instance of this principle may be seen in the June 24 custom of Rumanian girls of collecting certain yellow flowers (*Galium verum*), popularly called either *dragaica* or *sînziene*—the names of fairies active at **Midsummer**.

Cleansing Fires

The earthly fire of **Midsummer** also had health benefits, besides promoting marriage and fertility. Thus, older Bretons held their backs to it so they would not hurt when they worked on the coming harvest. After a formal dance before civic authorities, Basque villagers jump over the flames in turn, with younger ones taking the leap once the fire has grown small. In Bohemia at this point, each couple would hold hands as they leaped over it three times. The fire was supposed to be as high as the flax would grow. It was believed that both sweethearts would be safe from marsh fever over the year, and by the end of the year, a girl was sure to be married if she saw nine different fires that night. The same belief was found in the French provinces of Berry and Brittany; in the latter, a girl was disappointed if the boys forgot to catch her and swing her nine times over the embers (a practice known as *ober ar wakel* in Breton). As a protection from illness, babies too were rocked three times over the embers. Their naked bodies were stroked with branches instead in Manacor on the Baleraric island of Mallorca, and cattle was driven through the fires at night, as in the Ukraine. If this was done the next morning in Prussia and Lithuania, most often, separate small fires were made on convenient sites—like crossroads, fields, or courtyards—to fumigate cattle on the previous day. **Midsummer**'s Eve was therefore known in various parts of France as "the beasts' **Saint John's**." Unlike "people's **Saint John's**" on his public feast, when the fire was sometimes blessed by the priest and would usually be sanctioned by the presence of civic authorities who might officially light it, "the beasts' **Saint John's**" was private and almost secretive, since it was long discouraged as irredeemably pagan. This unofficial "profane" fire was, however, fit to be used on beasts, as opposed to the "sacred" official fire, reserved to the baptized—even though it was never the parish that put it on, but the neighborhood, in friendly competition with others in the vicinity for the nicest one.

Among the Muslim peoples of the Maghreb— be they Arabs or native Berbers—this distinction does not exist. They use the same smoke for the fumigation of people, cattle, fruit trees, and fields alike on *lansara,* as they call **Midsummer**, observing its ancient rite on June 24 of the Julian calendar they have kept from Roman times in addition to the lunar Islamic one, in which solstices have no place.

As the smoke was brought to the useful animals to protect them from witches and demons, these were often burned in the fire in the guise of the evil animals embodying them: toads, snakes, foxes, and cats. The latter were stuffed in a cage or a bag atop a pole in the middle of the bonfire in many French villages and cities right until the Revolution. In Austria, witches are still burned in effigy, and unmarried young men parade decorated poles— because these once served to avert a plague, it is said. In the village of Ciudadela on the Balearic island of Minorca by contrast, some fifty horses are trained year-round for **Midsummer** cavalcades in between which they are lifted up by the crowds.

Community-Building

In Sardinia and southern Italy, "sweethearts of **Saint John's**" exchange pots of basil, corn, or other plants that have been grown forty or more days in advance by the girls, much like the "gardens of Adonis" previously made by women at this time of year in honor of the feast of the death and resurrection of this ancient pagan god of vegetation. An obscene image of Adonis sometimes used to appear in defiance of clerical authorities on these public tokens of romantic commitment and covert symbols of natural fertility. If this was an occasion for formal, if playful, socialization for all young people, the lighting of the official **Midsummer** bonfire has often been a solemn ceremony. For this show of unity called for the participation of every member of the community, from providing fuel to collecting the ashes after the all-night dance around the fire. Like the sacred fires of the ancient Celts at other times of the year, it might even be kindled by archaic friction methods as in Hungary, or the Ukraine, or French Canada (where a priest might strike stones together to make the sparks), and the fire might be taken home to rekindle the purposely extinguished hearth, as in Upper Bavaria. Even the dead (the *anaon*) were invited to warm up on flat stones or benches set just for them near the glowing embers in Brittany. There, as in the neighboring Vendée region, deceased relatives were called by sliding one's fingers around the lubricated edge of a copper basin half-filled with water. This produced an otherworldly plaintive sound not unlike the more comical sound of the rumble-pots and other festive instruments used for a similar purpose around **New Year**'s Eve, during **Carnival** or on **Martinmas**—all times of the year when the dead draw near.

The war dead may also come to mind during the patriotic songs and speeches that are part of the celebration of *Juhannus* as Finland's **Flag Day**; the white-and-blue banner then flies all through this clearest night when the sun hardly sets, if at all. While **Midsummer** folklore usually featured wedding divination in European folklore, and the entire month of June is still wedding month throughout the West, it is also on the occasion of this civic holiday that the most weddings are celebrated in that Nordic country, namely on the Saturday between June 20 and 26. *Midsömmer* has been observed on the one closest to June 24 across the Baltic Sea in Sweden since 1950. There, the traditional **Midsömmer** meal is *matjesill*—a kind of marinated herring in sweet sauce with dill potatoes, followed by strawberries with whipped cream as a dessert. More beer is drunk then than on any other day of the year, though it is also the custom in Sweden to drink a lot on the winter solstice and near the equinoxes on **Easter** and **Michaelmas**. In Denmark too, people sing patriotic songs around the bonfires that "burn away witches" at beachside balls on *Sankthans-aften*—**Saint John's** Eve—though it is not a holiday.

June 24 was chosen as the national holiday of French Canadians in 1834, when a banquet was held on that day by the group soon to be known as the *Société Saint-Jean-Baptiste*. This nationalist organization still puts on a big parade each year in Montreal, derived from an earlier religious procession in honor of **Saint John the Baptist** going back to French colonial times. **Midsummer** was then marked with fireworks and cannon shot—as in Paris when the king lit the bonfire. The feast day still starts with a mass said by the archbishop of Montreal in the historic Saint-Jean Baptiste Church. The street celebrations that follow are more secular and inclusive on the official civic holiday that is

the *Fête Nationale* in the Province of Quebec. It comes one week before **Canada Day**—the nationwide holiday in honor of the Confederation of British colonies that gave birth to the Dominion of Canada on July 1, 1867. In addition, June 21 was declared **National Aboriginal Day** by Canada's Governor General Roméo A. LeBlanc in a royal proclamation of June 13, 1996, in honor of Indians, Inuit, and Métis, and on account of the summer solstice's "important symbolism within their cultures."

Though this symbolism is no less important for the cultures of the Old World, there, industrialization initially brought about a marked decline in **Midsummer** practices, except perhaps in Scandinavian countries, where people were always eager to celebrate the brief but spectacular Nordic summer around bonfires.

As for the United States, it has been said by their foremost expert on comparative calendrics that "our inherited puritanical mind-set, traceable all the way back to Oliver Cromwell's England, is as responsible as anything else for dousing the fires and purging the pagan rites from the summer calendar," so that "contemporary summertime ritual is remarkably free of communal holidays that even remotely resemble those our ancestors once vigorously celebrated. The days we mark in the seasonal quarter that follows the **Christmas** to **Easter** crescendo are all civic and patriotic in nature: **Memorial Day**, **Flag Day**, **Independence Day**—not a one of them has roots that tap very deeply into old tradition" (Aveni 2003, p. 104).

Yet **Midsummer** fires at least have also started to make a comeback elsewhere, thanks for instance to the campaigns of the Federation of Old Cornwall Societies in their former English stronghold since the 1930s. But there remains a big difference between traditional and revived **Midsummer** celebrations. If the former reinforced solidarity within small-scale agrarian communities when it was most vital—right before the collective effort of harvest-time, they were recently rekindled largely as an affirmation of local identity within a larger society in response to the challenges and opportunities of increased leisure time, social mobility, and mass tourism.

And then there are also the reconstructed **Midsummer** rituals observed on a mass scale in a neo-pagan or New Age spirit in such ancient sites as Chartres in France and above all Stonehenge in England. Around this prehistoric stone calendar aligned with the solstice, thousands now join self-styled "druids" to welcome the summer sun with song and dance to the beating of drums.

> **See also** Annunciation; Carnival; Christmas; Conception and Birth of the Virgin Mary; Double Nine; Dragon Boat Festival; Easter; Inti Raymi and Huarachicu; Lent; Lugnasad; Martinmas; May Day; New Year (West); Powwow; Samhain; Saturnalia; Sun Dance

References

Anthony F. Aveni. *The Book of the Year. A Brief History of Our Seasonal Holidays.* Oxford: Oxford University Press, 2003.

Anna Franklin. *Midsummer: Magical Celebrations of the Summer Solstice.* St. Paul, MN: Llewellyn Publications, 2002.

Ronald Hutton. *Stations of the Sun: A History of the Ritual Year in Britain.* Oxford: Oxford University Press, 1996.

Indian and Northern Affairs Canada. http:// www.ainc-inac.gc.ca/nad/ggp_e.html.

Jerusalem Bible. Garden City, NY: Doubleday and Co., 1968.

John Matthews. *The Summer Solstice: Celebrating the Journey of the Sun from May Day to Harvest.* Wheaton, IL: Quest Books, 2002.

A. R. Wright. *British Calendar Customs. England.* Vol. III: *Fixed Festivals -June-December, Inclusive.* London: The Folk-Lore Society, 1940.

▶ MIDWINTER (IROQUOIS)

The **Midwinter** Festival is the "**Greatly Prized Ceremony**" of the Iroquois ritual calendar. It is also called "**Most Excellent Faith**" after that

displayed through the burnt offering of a white dog to the Creator. Its symbolism centers on the struggle between Sky-Holder and his destructive younger brother on the cusp between the old and the new years and involves both thanksgiving for past blessings and wishes for the future. It is also known as a "**Festival of Dreams**" or *Honnonouaroia*, like the ones that used to be celebrated on special occasions by the Hurons—cousins of the Iroquois in the Eastern forests of North America.

A Longhouse Festival

With variations in ritual between different tribes and Longhouses, as the traditional Iroquois religious centers are called, **Midwinter** celebrations could take several weeks in the past. More recently, they have lasted six to eight days around late January or early February. Their beginning depends on both the appearance of the Pleiades directly overhead at dusk and the first new moon after the winter solstice.

On the first morning of the **Midwinter** Festival, as on that of the **Green Corn Ceremony** in August, there is a partial recitation of the *Gaiwiio* or "good word" of *Gä-no-waú-ges* or "Handsome Lake." It is the formal record of the dreams and visions through which, from 1799 to his death in 1815, this *sachem* or chief of the Seneca nation and prophet to the Iroquois received the revelation at the basis of the traditionalist revival known as the Longhouse religion. Now followed by at least a quarter of the 20,000 or so Iroquois living on reservations in Ontario, Quebec, and New York State, this religion stresses the rigorous observance of the seasonal festivals of **thanksgiving** for the bounty of the earth, as it was maintained before European contact disrupted this culture's traditional ways.

Hunter-Gatherer Rites

The first part of the rites observed at the **Midwinter** Festival is oldest in origin, being rooted in the symbolic complex of hunter-gatherer societies and their shamanistic practices. In the nineteenth century, rites of general confession of each person's sins of the last year might take up to three days in the Longhouse in advance of the appointed date of the **New Year**, in order to clear the air and secure auspicious beginnings. Two "keepers of the faith" (*ho-nun-dé-unt*), swathed in bear skins or buffalo hides and with their faces made up or masked, would go into each house twice: first in the morning, to ask that it be prepared by taking out any rubbish or impure animals and any hindrances to the coming observances, for the duration of which any mourning would have to be postponed; and then in the afternoon, to inform residents that the festival had now begun and to enjoin everyone to observe it, in compliance with the will of the Great Spirit.

> Your first duty will be to prepare your wooden blades (*Ga-ger-we-sä*) with which to stir up the ashes upon your neighbors' hearths. Then return to the Great Spirit your individual thanks for the return of this season, and for the enjoyment of this privilege. (Morgan 1901, p. 201)

The keepers of the faith thus again visit every house on the second day to carry out this ash-stirring rite first, followed by all the neighbors, before the residents can perform it themselves. The fire is later rekindled, as in the **New Year** customs of many other cultures. When the ashes are stirred in the hearth, the Iroquois burn tobacco to invoke "Sky-Holder who lives in the sky," "the nocturnal Orb of Light, our Grandmother," and "the Stars on the sky in many places," asking them to ensure the fertility of the earth in the coming year.

On the third and fourth days, small dancing parties, each with their own repertoire, would visit every house in turn. So would a "thieving party" of "Laughing Beggars" with an old woman carrying a large basket to collect materials for the fifth day's evening feast. If they felt someone was not being generous enough, they were entitled to take whatever they could get away with unnoticed. When caught red-handed, they had to give back the article on the spot, but if they had already left with it, it was considered theirs, and it could only be bought back from a public display at the end of the collection by substituting it with something of equal value. Over the first four days, celebrations thus took place at home rather than in the common ceremonial setting of the Longhouse. They included social dances at night, after the seasonal Snow-snake game, in which people betted heavily on the slithering progress of a two-meter-long polished hickory stick in the snow for up to half a kilometer.

Dreamguessing

It is also at this stage of **Midwinter** celebrations that the False Face medicine society performs many of its curing ceremonies, both for its own members and for the community in the Longhouse. This favorite society of the Iroquois probably owes its typical practices to the Hurons, among whom they were observed in the eighteenth century. Sometimes also observed on a basis of individual need, these include blowing ashes, handling hot coals, imitating hunchbacks, carrying sticks, and, most closely associated with **Midwinter**, the renewal of dreams. Those who have been cured by the medicine society over the past year sponsor dances for the members to whom they owe their recovery. The lessons and healings of past dreams are "renewed" through expression in song and dance, carrying out the guidance received through them, or acting out those they do not yet understand and seek to interpret. As the dreamguessing Ceremony of the Great Riddle begins, experts in dream interpretation are consulted in each moiety, or half-tribe, about the meaning of the dream, and the entire tribe may join in with intuitions and ideas from the public. If the dreamer finds a certain interpretation useful, the person who came up with it will get some gift or favor in return, thus creating a bond of friendship between the two parties. Once a subconscious need has thus been clarified, the tribe helps the person get her or his "dream wish." Someone who, having guessed right, is then asked to help fulfill a dream, does not see this as an obligation so much as both an honor and a vital contribution to tribal harmony and spiritual continuity. If the dream wish turns out to be antisocial or excessively unrealistic, it may still be fulfilled through symbolic gifts or psychodramas, where people play roles in each other's dreams. This kind of group therapy can also include confronting real people who have appeared in a dream in a negative role, to try to sort out and resolve any outstanding interpersonal issues this may reveal.

Beyond its serious spiritual purpose, such "dreamguessing" also has a playful side, as people vie to get attention—and satisfaction—for their own dreams by shouting, singing, and dancing. In some tribes, moieties compete against each other to guess a person's dream first, while in others, people go door to door insisting the residents "guess" what they have dreamed of on the basis of hints such as a pantomime. "Guessing" here can include interpreting, resolving, or even fulfilling the dream. In the past, once you were targeted for a riddle, this was the only way of putting a stop to the harassment of any of the temporarily demented trick-or-treaters who ran naked or in wild costumes through the streets and houses of a village, smashing or throwing down everything in sight, and throwing cold water and all manner of fluids, or else ashes and burning coals, on their victims. Old scores might then be settled under cover of the suspension of liability for this collectively sanctioned lapse of sanity into raving hysteria and unbridled license. The personal subconscious was given a free reign by society at this turning point of the year, so pent-up energies could be released and the air was cleared for auspicious new beginnings.

The Sacrifice of the White Dog

There could be no better way to begin the year than the sacrifice of a white dog to the Creator. For this animal was the faithful hunting companion of the Iroquois, and its spirit was best suited to convey to the Great Spirit their own steadfast faith in him. It was in this sense a medium of communication with the divine realm, like the smoke of tobacco offerings. An animal's whiteness already marked it as consecrated to the Great Spirit. To preserve the dog's purity from any blemish, it was strangled on the first day of the festival, taking care not to shed its blood or break its bones. Only then was it spotted with red paint and ornamented with feathers—or more recently ribbons of many colors—until the sacrifice was dropped within the last century or so. It had begun to lapse in some nations like the Oneida before being revived along with all other traditional observances with the spread of the new dispensation of Handsome Lake at the beginning of the nineteenth century. The sacrifice of a dog—usually white—was also part of the ceremonies of many other Algonquian and even Siouan cultures (not to mention Paleo-Siberian shamanistic cultures), including its hanging on a pole. In some Iroquois tribes, two dogs might be sacrificed at once—one for each moiety. But most often, only one would be left hanging for four days until it was taken down on the morning of the fifth day of **Midwinter**, to be burned on a pyre near the Longhouse by the keepers of the faith. One of these would invoke the Great Spirit and give him thanks for all his blessings, proceeding to do the same with a number of secondary spirits, from Mother Earth to the "Three Sisters"—squash, maize, and beans—as "Our Sustenance," which is also the name of one of the later dances of this festival.

The Four Sacred Rituals of Agricultural Cycles

After this long **thanksgiving** prayer, people would attend the Great Feather Dance—the first of "four sacred rituals" given by the Creator, separated by social dances from the evening feast that also belonged to the second part of the festival, that is to a more recent layer reflecting the agricultural concerns of a farming village society. The second of these "four sacred rituals" modeled after ceremonies in the sky world is the Skin or Drum Dance. A **Thanksgiving** Dance is introduced during the Longhouse religious meetings of the sixth day, and Husk Faces burst in to announce they are going to the other side of the world to till the crops. Like the False Faces, they are known for curing by blowing ashes and handling hot coals.

The third sacred ritual consists in personal **thanksgiving** chants named after the next morning's *Ah-dó-weh* council at the Longhouse, where they conclude the short speeches delivered by everyone in turn to thank a variety of beings—living or (to the modern mind) inanimate. This can take a couple of hours until everyone is done expressing gratitude for all kinds of personal and public matters. This is clearly meant to seal social harmony in order to start the **New Year** on the right foot. People can then turn to the fourth and last sacred ritual, concluding the festival (though it could also take place on the fourth day): the Peach-stone board game instituted by the Great Spirit himself, in which six of these fruit pits are thrown like dice in a wooden bowl as a ritual symbolizing human life and ethics. The small articles used for stakes are collected the day before from house to house by moiety appointees as a kind of sacrifice; they are then paired into prize packets of two items of equivalent value—one from each moiety, so that people from the winning side get back their property and double it with that of the losing side. As the Cayuga *sachem* Deskáheh could explain: "The same may be applied to life; one must give something to receive something, whereupon one goes to 'heaven' provided that in the game of life he plays straight and right. If he does not play straight he will lose all . . . The game is sacred, for it is the Great Spirit's game. It represents life, to some extent. The sacrifice, playing straight to win the reward, and the danger of losing—all teach the lesson of love, of sacrifice, and 'good' with the fun of a wholesome game" (Speck 1949, pp. 142–143). This is contrasted with the spreading addiction to secular gambling, which the Iroquois (among other North American Indian cultures) were already succumbing to when Handsome Lake tried to restrict it to its original sacred setting as part of **Midwinter** rites. The privileged place of betting in traditional Iroquois culture may then partly account for the rise of casinos as the most prosperous businesses on reservations in the northeastern states.

A Tuscarora Variant: Nu Yah

The traditionalist elements among five of the six nations of the Iroquois Confederacy—Mohawks, Oneidas, Cayugas, Senecas, and Onondagas—observe the old festivals such as **Midwinter**, while, as a rule, the Christians in these tribes keep aloof from the Longhouse—especially on such ceremonial occasions. The Tuscaroras as a nation did away long ago with their Longhouse and adopted Christianity from Baptist missionaries, who largely succeeded in counteracting Handsome Lake's traditionalist revival. As a result, they do not have the traditional ceremonies still observed by the other nations of the Iroquois Confederacy, with the exception of the raising of a chief. Otherwise, there is only one major festivity during the year that shows remnants of traditionalist elements: the **New Year** celebration that has taken over from Midwinter under the name of *Nu Yah.*

Beginning three days before January 1, the festival, as it is presently observed among the New York Tuscaroras, includes a visit to each house on the reserve to collect food for a feast, a competitive hunt for game for the latter between "old" men (that is, all fathers) and "young" (that is, childless) men, the **New Year** morning visitation of as many houses as possible—entering them without knocking but shouting "*Nu Yah!*," the offering to these (mostly young) callers of a cookie, a doughnut or a piece of cake, pie, or fruit at each house, and the lunchtime feast and evening meeting sponsored by the Tuscarora Temperance Society. From the second third of the nineteenth century, this initially mixed body of Christians and traditionalists took over the role of the traditional keepers of the faith and was instrumental in developing this acculturated alternative to **Midwinter** observances, in which Tuscaroras of all persuasions could overlook their customary rivalries and join in harmony and good cheer as one nation for a change.

Traditional customs had existed side by side with those of the **New Year** after the Tuscaroras had to leave their North Carolina homeland as a result of military defeats. When they settled for a while in Pennsylvania during this eighteenth-century migration northward, they found that their German neighbors would go visiting each other on *Neujahr,* receiving little cakes or *Festkuchen* at each house. They liked the custom and adopted it, just as New York merchants at the same time used the **Saint Nicholas** *koekjes* that were still imported from the Netherlands as part of their own British **New Year** visitation customs. As these original cookies bore the image of the patron of sailors, so Tuscarora women baked their own version of German **New Year** cookies in the shape of the animal spirit protector of their particular clan. If these clan cookies are no longer made, **Nu Yah** endures as a hybrid festivity which promises to last as long as the Tuscarora nation does. Its form is much the same today as it was in the early years, except that, with the dissolution of the Temperance Band, there is no longer a parade and musical entertainment on **New Year**'s Day. The hunt preserves a trace of the greater role it used to play until about a century ago among other Iroquois in preparation for the Midwinter Festival. Yet in contrast to them, **Nu Yah** sees no burning of tobacco, curing rites, or any other religious ceremony, and remains a secular affair, but for the grace said before the feast—now a Christian **thanksgiving** prayer.

> **See also** Busk; New Year (West); New Fire Ceremony; Saint Nicholas

References

Harold Blau. "The Iroquois White Dog Sacrifice: Its Evolution and Symbolism," in *Ethnohistory,* Vol. XI (1964), No. 2, pp. 97–119.

Barbara Graymont. "The Tuscarora New Year Festival," in *New York History,* Vol. L (1969), No. 2, pp. 142–163.

Lewis H. Morgan. *League of the Ho-De-No-Sau-Nee or Iroquois.* Vol. I. New York, 1901 (reprint New York: Burt Franklin, 1967).

Frank Gouldsmith Speck. *Midwinter Rites of the Cayuga Long House.* Philadelphia: University of Pennsylvania Press, 1949 (reprint Ohsweken, Ontario: Iroqrafts, 1987).

Elisabeth Tooker. *The Iroquois Ceremonial of Midwinter.* Syracuse, NY: Syracuse University Press, 2000.

▌ MILAAD

See Mawlid

▌ MIMOUNA

See Passover

▌ MI'RAJ (ISLAM)

Coming after four and a half months without any festival, the night of the twenty-seventh to the twenty-eighth of the month of Rajab is marked by pious Muslims with Koran readings and supererogatory prayers, in honor of the night of that date (in most accounts) in the year before the **Hegira** when the obligatory five daily prayers were ordained by God as a pillar of Islam, and forgiveness was promised to repentant sinners. For it was on the Night of the

Journey and of the Ascension (*Lailat al-Isra wa al-Mi'raj* in Arabic) that Mohammed was taken through the seven heavens to the throne of God to receive moral commandments, along with his highest mystical vision.

The Nocturnal Journey

This happened in the summer of 620, during *Umra*—the Lesser Pilgrimage to Mecca, when Mohammed was in the tenth year and the darkest hour of his prophetic mission. He had lost both his first wife and first disciple Khadija and his uncle and only political supporter Abu Talib within a couple of days of each other in the previous "Year of Sorrow" (*am-el-Huzn*), and had just been expelled from his own clan after declaring that all its pagan ancestors—even Abu Talib—were burning in hell. This was tantamount to negating the very source of all the temporal and spiritual laws of Mecca's tribal Arab society. It thus in turn negated Mohammed by making him an outcast—that is, literally a nonperson without identity or rights of any sort, at the mercy of escalating persecution, including attempts on his life. It was at this moment that the One God who put him at loggerheads with all of human society came to his aid by granting him an inner vision that clarified the scope of the Prophet's mission to create a new society in submission (*islam*) to Him alone, and gave him renewed strength to do just that against all odds.

Strictly speaking, only one line in the entire Koran explicitly refers to the event in question. It is the one with which *sura* 17 begins, giving glory to the One "who did take His Servant for a Journey by night (*isra*) from the Sacred Mosque to the Farthest Mosque" (Abdullah Yusuf Ali translation 1946). A tradition going back to Mohammed's wife Aisha would suggest that this was a purely spiritual inner journey, accomplished while the Prophet was sleeping—though "his heart was awake." But by the time it was recorded by his biographer Ibn Ishak, who died in Baghdad in 767, the Ummayad Caliphs of Damascus were anxious to have a major holy place they could control closer to home than Mecca. So, while identifying the latter's Ka'aba with the "Sacred Mosque" (*al-masjid al-haram*), they promoted a belief that placed the "Farthest Mosque" (*al-masjid al-aqsa*) in the ruins of the Temple of Jerusalem, where the al-Aqsa Mosque had already been built by Caliph al-Walid I in the late seventh century.

From the twelfth century onward, Jerusalem thus came to be regarded as Islam's third holy city, right after Medina. To explain how the Prophet Mohammed could travel from Mecca to Jerusalem and back in the space of a single night, a winged creature called Burak (variously described as being white, halfway between an ass and a donkey, and with a woman's head and/or a peacock's tail) had been introduced into the story. The Prophet was said to have flown the whole distance on its back. Muslims have given the creature's name to the Western Wall of the Temple of Jerusalem, where they say it was tethered that night. Yet they also came to credit Burak, as the mount of prophets, with Mohammed's ascension to heaven. At the Dome of the Rock—Islam's oldest surviving monument as a shrine built for pilgrims by Caliph al-Walid I between 685 and 691, they thus point to the mark of a hoof on the Temple's stone floor on the spot where it struck the ground with supernatural force as she took a great leap, propelling Mohammed skyward. In this account, the Koran's "nocturnal journey"—Isra—is the physical one, airborne on Burak from Mecca to Jerusalem, while Mohammed's **"ascension"** is **Mi'raj** proper. (A belief peculiar to Shiites is that, on his way back from Jerusalem to Mecca, the Prophet made a stop in Qom—an important pilgrimage site south of Tehran. Iranians thus celebrate this day as *Ghadir Khomm,* and it is the traditional time to marry orphans off.)

The Ascension

The term *mi'raj* also refers to the angelic ladder of spiritual progress through which the Prophet

Mohammed's nocturnal journey to heaven. From a Persian manuscript representing the Prophet's ascent to heaven, his face being masked with a veil to hide his glory. (Bettman/Corbis)

was led most of the way by the angel Gabriel. Its degrees are then called *ma'arij,* each corresponding to a particular prophet: Adam to the First, Jesus and John the Baptist to the Second, Joseph to the Third, Idris (that is most likely Enoch) to the Fourth, Aaron to the Fifth, Moses to the Sixth, and Abraham to the Seventh—at the threshold of the unknowable Godhead, where Mohammed even led them all in prayer. God encouraged Mohammed in his mission as the Seal of the Prophets by reminding him that his predecessors had endured similar or worse tribulations than the ones he had already known, or than the exodus of his own he would soon face with the **Hegira** the next year, leading

his people through the desert to freedom. In view of this and of the decisive times ahead, it is said that God gave Mohammed twelve commandments for his people to follow, along the lines of the Ten Commandments given to Moses on Mount Sinai for the Jews. On his way back down, Mohammed was asked by Moses about what had transpired. When he mentioned that God required fifty daily prayers of the Muslims, Moses insisted that Mohammed go back up to God to get this figure lowered, on the basis of his own experience trying to get the Jewish people to observe ten commandments. Mohammed dared to plead with God for a more merciful daily regimen of prayers, but

Moses made him go back several times because he always thought the number of prayers was too high. It was finally fixed at five a day when Mohammed was just too embarrassed to go and bother God with such requests anymore.

Mystical Interpretations

Yet he had also been there at some other time, says the Koran (53:14) about this summit of the human experience of ultimate reality that it calls "the Lote-Tree beyond which none may pass" (Abdullah Yusuf Ali translation 1946). According to the mystical Sufi tradition, the boundary in question is that of the Prophet's being. It holds that, seeing the Lotus-Tree as "one of the greatest signs of His Lord," he could gaze beyond it into "the Garden of the Refuge" as his own inner paradise; did he not after all once say that "he who knows himself, knows his Lord"? It would then be his own personal angel that the Prophet saw in the Archangel Gabriel— that is an epiphany of what can be revealed of an unknowable God to His creature, called to meet Him in mystical union at its own limit, on the very edge of the limitless.

But this whole question of the vision of a transcendent God has always been highly controversial in Islamic theology, where established orthodox opinion has often denied its very possibility. This is why **Mi'raj** largely remains just a popular festival without much official backing. For it is based on the stuff of legend: an apocryphal story that has become a favorite object of both mystical speculation and popular piety, in a literary genre of its own that has developed across a variety of local traditions throughout the Islamic world, from Morocco to Indonesia, largely in view of readings for the festival of Mohammed's **ascension**. It even seems to have provided a model for the classic poetic account of the medieval West's cosmology in terms of Roman Catholic spirituality: Dante Alighieri's *Divine Comedy*.

See also Ascension

References

Miguel Asín Palacios. *Islam and the Divine Comedy.* Tr., abr. Harold Sutherland. London: J. Murray, 1926 (reprint London: Cass, 1968).

Sophie Pommier. *Muhammad's Night Journey.* Mankato, MN: Creative Education, 1998.

The Prophet of Islam in Old French: the Romance of Muhammad (1258) and the Book of Muhammad's Ladder (1264). Tr., intr. Reginald Hyatte. Leiden, Holland: Brill, 1997.

Qassim al-Samarrai. *The Theme of Ascension in Mystical Writings; a Studay [sic] of the Theme in Islamic and Non-Islamic Mystical Writings.* Baghdad: National Printing and Publishing Company, 1968.

▶ MISCHIEF NIGHT

See Samhain

▶ MONDAY OF SAINT THOMAS

See Easter

▶ MOON VIEWING

See Mid-Autumn

▶ MONTH (FESTIVAL OF THE)

See KI.LAM

▶ MOST EXCELLENT FAITH

See Midwinter

▶ MOTHERING DAY, MOTHERING SUNDAY

See Annunciation, Lent

▶ MOTHERS' DAY

See Conception and Birth of the Virgin Mary, Lent

▶ MUERTOS (LOS)

See Days of the Dead (West)

▶ MULID

See Mawlid

▶ NAADAM (MONGOLIA)

The Mongolian word *naadam* means "manly game or entertainment." This is still the focus of the great Mongol festival of **Naadam**, whatever its other religious and economic functions. It even used to play an important ceremonial role in the political life of foreign dynasties of the Chinese Empire. Now, though, pastoral nomads compete over a couple of days in the traditional "three manly games"—wrestling, archery, and horseracing, in both Inner Mongolia (within Chinese territory) and independent Outer Mongolia (where **Naadam** is held near the capital, Ulaanbaatar, as the national holiday on July 11).

History

For 2,000 years, these three sports were not just entertainment, but a vital part of military training for the nomadic tribes of the steppes between Siberia and China. A thousand years ago, they became the main activities of the **Naadam** Festival, and winners soon began to receive prizes in money and other gifts. After Gengis Khan unified the Mongol tribes under his leadership in 1206, these sports were featured on the celebrations for the enthronement of khans, the triumphal return of victorious armies, and the conferring of powers onto generals in wartime.

It was Gengis Khan who put wrestling on the program of examinations which soldiers and generals alike had to undergo in Mongol armies. The expression "three manly games" first comes up under the Yuan or Mongol Dynasty established in China in 1271 by Kublai Khan, grandson of Gengis Khan. Under the Ch'ing Dynasty (the last one to rule over the Chinese Empire from the time Manchu tribes related to the Mongols took it over from the latter's indigenous Ming Dynasty successors in the seventeenth century), the word *naadam* came to refer to the banquet offered at the Imperial Court before the gathering of the Eight Banners—an organ of government derived from the military units that had allowed the Manchus to follow in the Mongols' footsteps in China after first conquering them. Chinese civil servants used to be promoted on this occasion, until the Republic of China was proclaimed in 1911, while Outer Mongolia became an autonomous monarchy under a lama, the "Living Buddha."

The Mongols' eventual conversion to a Tibetan form of Buddhism had given some religious coloring to **Naadam**. Although this aspect would have to recede under the Communist regimes of Mongolia and China, the festival also provided the setting for a great fair. It thus served as a temporary market for nomadic herdsmen, who otherwise had limited opportunities to engage in trade or meet people from other clans on a national scale. **Naadam**'s July 11 opening date was thus set as the national holiday of Mongolia in 1922 by the revolutionary leader Damdiny Sühbaatar, who thus meant to commemorate both the taking of the capital Urga on July 6, 1921, and the formation soon thereafter (on July 10) of a new independent government that would rename it *Ulaanbaatar* in honor of this "Red Hero" a few months after he died on February 23, 1923. The largest **Naadam** is now held there by the river Tuul in Nairamdal Park with its sports stadium. Gengis Khan (whose very name used to be outlawed under the Communist regime) is the wildly popular national hero—now played by an actor—who comes out on the stadium amid epic pomp and fanfare to lend his prestige to this festival of Mongol pride that he helped shape at the height of his people's golden age. It is also more modestly held at some crossroads of Inner Mongolia, where nomads raise their tents, often after weeks of trekking over vast distances for the occasion. The steppe then suddenly mushrooms with makeshift shops, restaurants, photo studios, bookstands, libraries, and drugstores—like a small town in the middle of nowhere, full of lights, bustle, and music until late at night.

Three Manly Games

The first of the "three manly games" that visiting families can attend at **Naadam** is the wrestling competition, which takes place in a solemn atmosphere. The wrestlers wear colorful copper (or silver) studded leather shorts, hats, and boleros as they enter the ring (which may be either outdoors or under a big tent) in a special dance, loudly singing: "Bring on your valiant wrestler!" The rule of the match is that whoever touches the ground with a part of his body above the knee other than the hands loses. As for the winner, he gets a colored piece of cloth pinned on his chest. The champion who is able to remain standing for the majority of

nine rounds on all three days of **Naadam** (in Ulaanbaatar) is called an "eagle"; he is loudly acclaimed by the public, having earned the enduring respect of a far-flung nomadic community for excelling at its national sport.

Both sexes can take part (with different rules) in the second "manly game" of archery, dressed in beautiful traditional costumes. The red targets are painted on 360 half-meter-high leather cubes aligned along a little wall, which reflects the evolution of this game from the hunt for marmots on the steppe. The essential hunting skills of archery were at the base of the art of war that allowed the Mongols to conquer much of the known world on their famous little horses. Indeed, archery and horseracing were both natural developments of their pastoral lifestyle.

Something of the Mongol people's past glory lives on at the crowning event of **Naadam**, in which participants from all walks of life may hope to excel. As the third "manly game," horse races may be mostly for boys, but the horses are the real stars. A peculiar Mongol style of race calls for horses to trot instead of gallop, while the riders stand very erect; yet they can run just as fast as a galloping horse. However, this is not the standard style of **Naadam** races.

For weeks in advance, the horses have been put on a diet to lower their weight, and they are trained to run faster. Prior to the competition, they practice in qualifying races. Five of these, from five to thirty kilometers each in distance, are held in the steppe by the airport in Ulaanbaatar. The greater the distance, the lighter the jockey has to be, which means that contestants retire by the age of twelve. Appearance is also important; thus, a horse's mane and tail will be especially woven into braids.

On the appointed day, vodka flows freely as Mongols loosen up in an informal setting that contrasts with that of the stadium used in the capital for the other games. Fathers see to the last details of preparing the horses, which the children riding them encourage with songs in-

Two Mongolian wrestlers at Naadam, a festival made up of three competitions: wrestling, horse racing, and archery. (The Cover Story/Corbis)

voking their strength and resilience as they ride in a ritual circle in front of the judges' elevated stand. The whole family then goes to the meeting place at the finishing line. From there, the competitors proceed way out into the steppe directly to the distant starting line, while their parents may lie on the ground eating and smoking. The jockeys, wearing multicolored turbans, bow just before the signal is given. Elders then bring each rider a silver bowl filled with fresh milk, and offer him a white scarf—a form of homage also known in the related shamanistic and Buddhist culture of Tibet. They sing words of praise both for the rider and for his horse. The hymns to the horses go on during the race to encourage the horsemen and continue after the race to celebrate the winners, as well as to cheer up the losers.

There are no stands at the finishing line, where the families remain; they watch from atop their own horses to see when the horses they have entered in the competition will come in, and if their sons will still be on them. If a son has fallen off in exhaustion, the horse is still in the race and can even win it without him, since it is the horse's performance that is being assessed. This is precisely why children aged six to ten, who can barely guide a horse, are sent to ride their families' choice mounts, so that the animals' own merit can shine through with minimal human input.

Many races take place over **Naadam**, arranged according to the horses' ages, with a fifteen-kilometer race for two-year olds and a seventy-kilometer race for older animals. At Ulaanbaatar, as many as 200 horses at a time may be racing across the plain in a cloud of dust (preceded by the jeeps of reporters and VIPs), as the youngsters who ride them (often without saddles) relentlessly spur them on with their whips. The top winners and bottom losers of every category perform the same ritual when they get off their horses: they sprinkle their head and hindquarters with vodka before gulping it from the bottle themselves—over and over again. Later on in Nairamdal Stadium, the champion will have the honor of bowing at the feet of the President of Mongolia.

See also Games (Rome)

References

Henry Field, ed. *Mongolia Today: A Traveler's Guide—Geography, Nature, Hunting, Museums, Monuments, Customs, Tourism*. Coconut Grove, FL: Field Research Projects, 1978.

Qi Xing. *Traditional Chinese Festivals*. Beijing: Foreign Language Publications, 1987.

Ya. Yunden. G. Zorig, and Ch. Erdene. *This is Mongolia*. Ulaanbaatar, Mongolia, 1991.

▶ NAA DAMBA

See Mawlid

▶ NAKED FESTIVALS (JAPAN)

In many areas of Japan, there are so-called **Naked Festivals** (**Hadaka Matsuri**). The two best known take place on Honshu Island, in the cities of Inazawa and Okayama, where, some time in February, throngs of men stripped to a loincloth compete to touch or to possess a sacred object. In all such festivals, washing and splashing each other with cold water, in a playful version of the Shinto purification rite called *mizugori*, plays a prominent part and contributes to the high spirits, even in the middle of winter.

Inazawa: The Naked Man as Scapegoat

The **Naked Festival** of Inazawa, a suburb of Nagoya, is held annually on February 5 and goes back at least 1,200 years. Having already gotten drunk on *sake* rice wine—at once to commune with the gods, fight the cold, and

have a good time—some 10,000 men wearing only loincloths and sandals race in gangs to carry their towns' written prayers (tied to long bundles of bamboo) to Kounomiya Shrine. The countless thousands of spectators cheering them on along the streets also push and shove to get a chance to touch these phallic objects, as this is supposed to bring them good luck over the coming year. The practice is reminiscent in this of ancient Rome's **Lupercalia** race of men in loincloths in mid-February.

Six hours into the event, all the runners have reached the shrine's precinct, where they continuously get splashed with freezing water. They are waiting for the arrival of the man of the day: the Naked Man (*Shin-Otoko*). He is the only one considered to be truly worthy of the title, since he has been selected to shave off all the hair on his body in a purification rite before setting out alone on the same itinerary—stark naked. The crowd roars as he approaches the shrine, for it is once he enters it that his ordeal truly begins: this man has to run, tumble, and crawl to the other side of the sea of men it contains. They in turn are all out to chase him, jump on him, and pummel him in their frantic attempts to touch him, so as to transfer onto him the evils of their community and draw from him some luck for the coming year (since he is to them what their own bamboo bundles were to the crowd outside). When the Naked Man somehow makes it in one piece past the courtyard into the sanctuary of Kounomiya Shrine, he pays his respects to the gods, puts on some clothes, and gets symbolically banished from town, from which he takes all the evil away with him. This makes him an exact counterpart of the *pharmakon*—the human scapegoat at the center of the ancient Greek festival of **Thargelia**.

Okayama: Sheer Naked Aggression

Also commonly called **Hadaka Matsuri**, the folk festival **Saidaiji Eyo** is held on the third

Saturday of February of every year at Okayama's Saidaiji Kan'nonin Temple. This regular date was set fairly recently to accommodate the crowds of tourists. The festival originally took place on the day of the first **Full Moon** (*Koshogatsu*)—that is on the fifteenth day of the first month. It was also called **Little New Year**, or even **Women's New Year**, since women would perform domestic rites of aggression with phallic rods to capture the first month's male energies and give birth to boys. Likewise, the paper amulets the priests of that temple of Kannon (China's Kuam Yon, female bodhisattva of compassion), started distributing to the faithful on that day at the beginning of the sixteenth century became so popular that they had to throw them into the crowd, and eventually replaced them with a more sturdy pair of wooden rods. The word *shingi* for these "sacred rods" of the gods used to be written with the characters for "true" and for "wood," but the first one was eventually replaced by the character for "treasure," which best describes the value ascribed to these talismans and the lengths young men will go to get them.

Today, the event begins at 7:20 on Saturday evening with a children's version of the **Naked Festival**, first for boys from the first and second grades competing for *mochi* rice cakes, then for boys from the third and fourth grades competing for an octagonal treasure tube, and finally for boys from the fifth and sixth grades competing for a rounded treasure tube. At 9:00 P.M., the Eyo Winter Fireworks are launched on the banks of the Yoshii River, while temple grounds already echo with the powerful rumble of an all-women *taiko* ensemble (since beating drums is a common way to welcome gods and call worshippers at a **matsuri**). Around 11:00 P.M., up to 10,000 men wearing only the traditional *fundoshi* loincloth begin to crowd the temple's main sanctuary. They get instructions on how to use water to purify their bodies before running around the temple precincts and paying their respects to the deities Senju

Kan'non and Go'ousho Daigongen. Only then are they allowed to press onto the grounds, where they will splash themselves and each other with cold water to become ritually pure.

This routine is repeated several times, until around 2:00 in the morning, when all the doors are closed and the lights are turned off as the head priest throws the *shingi* rods from a window into the crowd. Then pandemonium erupts as the compact mass of sweaty male bodies is convulsed by the fierce struggle for possession of the sacred symbols of Senju Kan'non and Go'ousho Daigongen. But the combination of luck, skill, and strategy that decides the outcome of the competition ultimately depends on the will of these two deities, that is on whom they favor to win their wooden passports to year-long happiness. This **Naked Festival** thus provides an excellent illustration of the principle behind the competitive sports and **games** associated with Japanese festivals: they are meant to test human beings in a way that allows the gods to have a clear and direct say in their affairs.

See also Anna Perenna; Games (Greece); Lupercalia; Matsuri; New Year (Japan); Thargelia; Yom Kippur

References

Hideo Haga. *Japanese Festivals.* Tr. Don Kenny. Osaka, Japan: Hoikusha Publishing Co., 1981.
Kodansha Encyclopedia of Japan. New York: Kodansha International, 1983.
Tamotsu Yato, ed. *Naked Festival. A Photo-Essay.* Intr. Yukio Mishima. Phot. Gan Hosoya. Tr. Meredith Weatherby and Sachiko Teshima. New York: Walker/Weatherhill, 1969.

NAKED YOUTHS (FESTIVAL OF)
See Carneia

NAMAHAGE
See New Year (Japan)

NAMING OF THE PROPHET
See Mawlid

▶ NANAKUSA NO SEKKU

See Sekku

▶ NARAK CHATURDASHI

See Divali

▶ NATALIS SOLI INVICTI

See Christmas

▶ NATIONAL ABORIGINAL DAY

See Midsummer

▶ NATIVITY (OF CHRIST)

See Christmas

▶ NATIVITY OF SAINT JOHN THE BAPTIST

See Midsummer, Conception and Birth of the Virgin Mary

▶ NATIVITY OF THE BLESSED VIRGIN MARY

See Conception and Birth of the Virgin Mary

▶ NATIVITY OF THE PROPHET

See Mawlid

▶ NAVARATRA AND DUSSHERA (HINDUISM)

Among Hindus (and to some extent Jains), the festival of the "nine nights" (that is, *Navaratra*) starts on the **new moon** of Ashvina (September–October) right after the *Pitripaksha* fortnight devoted to departed spirits. It honors the Mother Goddess Durga in her many forms as Divine Power or Shakti. As **Durga Puja**, it is therefore particularly important for Shaktas—devotees of Shiva the Destroyer who emphasize his consort or feminine energy as supreme, as well as for other Shaivas. It is also observed by Vaishnavas (devotees of Vishnu the Sustainer) but with a different emphasis on her more peaceable manifestations. However, the first three days still begin with Kali, as goddess of strength, for protection and valor, before shifting to Lakshmi, as goddess of wealth, for the next three, and ending with Sarasvati, as goddess of knowledge, on the last three days. Vaishnavas then celebrate the victory of Vishnu's avatar Rama over the demon Ravana, for which they say he called on the power of Durga—often even ascribing to him the goddess's victory over the "Buffalo Demon" Mahishasura, that Shaivas too celebrate as that of good over evil on the tenth day of **Dusshera**. The "Great Tenth Day of Victory" is also called *Vijay Dashami*, or **Dasain** in Nepal.

Pitripaksha: Hindu Days of the Dead

But just before this novena begins with the new moon of Ashvina, the waning or "dark half" (*krishna paksha*) of the month that leads up to it (which is part of Ashvina or Bhadrapada depending on the calendar used) is set aside to honor the ghostly spirits of departed ancestors or *pitris*. When performed over the two weeks of this *Pitripaksha*, because of a special grace of Yama, Lord of Death, the water oblation called *Tarpan-Arghya* that orthodox Hindus normally make for their dead relatives of many generations on every new moon, as well as the *Shraddha* ceremony they carry out every year on the anniversary of a relative's death, can both reach the pitris more immediately, and even indiscriminately. Not only can relatives who are not in the offerer's direct line of descent benefit from these rites, but all departed souls, even those without living descendants to perform them, or who suffer the consequences of a lack of charitable deeds to their credit, or whose death anniversary cannot be observed because it is not clear just when they died, or whose life was unnaturally cut short by accident or violence. Like the *lemures* on the ancient Roman **Lemuria**, such restless pitris who cannot normally be reached by standard funerary offerings during the rest

Devotees immerse an idol of the Hindu goddess Durga into the Hooghly River during Durga Puja, or Dusshera, as the culmination of Navaratra, and the biggest festival of Bengali Hindus, in the eastern Indian city of Calcutta, October 23, 2004. (Jayanta Shaw/Reuters/Corbis).

of the year can be appeased on **Pitripaksha**, except that it is by having their wishes fulfilled along with those of honored ancestors. For Yama allows all of them to come down to the homes of their descendants at the climax of **Pitripaksha**, devoted to "all ancestors" and therefore called *Sarvapitri Amavashya*. (Similarly, dead Mexicans make their way back home once a year on **All Souls** as the *Día de Muertos*.) On this great concluding new moon day, also called *Mahalaya Amavashya*, devout Hindus who have followed strict ritual rules over the two weeks of **Pitripaksha** (such as bathing three times a day and partial fasting) do the full array of funerary rites and give plenty of charity to help secure the object of their prayers: the propitiation of departed spirits so they may rest in peace over the coming year.

Ritual Readings

Then the fight against the demon begins on the first day of the **Navaratra** novena (unless the extra holy month of **Adhik Maas** happens to be inserted between it and **Pitripaksha**—as in 2001 and 2020), to last until he is defeated on the ninth day. The tale is told in the "seven hundred verses" of the *Gatha Saptashati* or *Chandi* (one of Durga's many names) culled from the *Markandiya Purana,* and said to date back to 1400 B.C.E., which must be recited from beginning to end (as Rama is thought to have done when he vanquished Ravana). For if this kind of Tantric ritual or esoteric practice peculiar to Shaivas (and certain Mahayana Buddhists) is incompletely or improperly carried out, the spiritual energies it is meant to harness may be unleashed in a harmful way. In Bengal, where Shaktism is most influential, on the first day of

Navaratra, a rite is celebrated in honor of the goddess of learning, Sarasvati, in which she is worshipped together with the sacred books of the house. Selected passages of the *Chandi* are then recited at an auspicious time determined by the almanac.

The Effigy of the Goddess

By then, an image of Durga—carved out of wood or sculpted in metal elsewhere—will have been skillfully crafted out of clay from the Ganges in Bengal. On the evening of *Shasti* (the Sixth Day), this *protima* is installed in front of a betel plant (*Piper betle*) in a *pandal*—a colorful covered enclosure that is erected in every locality. *Pandals* number in the hundreds in Delhi and in the thousands in Bengal's capital Calcutta, a city named after Kali. This divine Shakti or power is invoked in everyone present during the initial *Bodhana* or "awakening" ceremony, as the people say: "O Mother, we awaken thee for the good of the world; join us, O Mother, in our autumn festival," and the priest says the *Pranpratishtan* mantra as he touches the pupils of the *protima*'s eyes to awaken her to life. During the day, people will come to pay their respects to the goddess, surrounded under the same dais by the other deities which were initially installed along with her a thousand years ago by Bengal's King Bijoy Sen in thanksgiving for his successes against neighboring kingdoms, as part of a Hindu revival in the wake of Muslim invasions and the collapse of Buddhism in India. Among these deities are Lakshmi, Sarasvati, Kartik (god of valor), Ganesha (god of success), and his wife Kola Bou (the banana bride). Portrayed by a young banana plant with nine leaves, wrapped in a white sari with a red border and also called Navapatrika, she stands for the end of the rainy season and the beginning of autumn.

Holy Water and Sacred Dances

This plant symbolism takes center stage on the Seventh Day (*Saptami*) when the actual **Durga Puja** begins with the worship of an earthen vessel filled with water and covered with a bunch of five mango leaves with a tender green coconut on top, adorned with the image of the goddess or with a swastika and placed on a *yantra*—a mystical geometric design traced on the ground. There follows an *Anjali* ceremony in which people repeat its mantra after the priest as they crowd around the protima's dais to offer flowers and betel leaves to Durga, the goddess whose worship is most prominent in Bengal and Assam. The first night is called *Ghatsthapana* on account of the "establishing of the holy water vessel" (called *kalash*) that is put before the image of the goddess as Vedic verses are read or incantations are said to entice her to alight on the rim at an auspicious moment determined by astrologers. For nine days, neither the protima nor the kalash is to be touched, and there should be fasting of some kind, while an oil lamp (called *nandadip*) is kept burning throughout. A fresh flower garland is tied before the protima every day, and grains are sown in mud by the jug, so that, sprinkled with holy water and kept in the shade, it sprouts during **Navaratra**, and a bunch of tender plants can be put on clothes on **Dusshera.**

In Nepal, barley seeds and other grains are also sown in the cow dung designs on the kalash itself, as well as the sacred yellow *jamara* flower that adults put in their hair and behind their ears over the last days of **Dasain,** as well as on top of children's heads as a blessing from Durga. The "House of **Dasain**," or *Dasain Ghar*—the room set aside for the goddess to reside in a water jug—is off-limits to other females for the duration of the festival, when rituals are performed there daily. This is done by brahmin priests wearing red robes in her honor in wealthy homes that can afford hiring them. Groups of singing devotees go purify themselves in the waters of a different *tirtha* or sacred bathing spot on each of the nine nights "while stars are still seen in the heavens." Still dripping wet in their damp clothes, they take trays of offerings on their heads to the temples of Durga before dawn. Also on each of the nine nights, starting around midnight, male dancers impersonating the Eight Mother Goddesses (*Asta Matrika*) make their way through the narrow streets of Patan to perform old traditional dances by torchlight at the local temple of *Mahadevi,* the Great Goddess whom the eight all manifest with a final afternoon performance on the tenth day at the shrine of another one of her forms—Taleju, patron of Nepal's ruling dynasty. This is located in the former royal palace.

In many parts of India during **Navaratra** and especially on **Dusshera,** following the monsoon rains, women and girls in their best attire carry pitchers from house to house and dance around the *garabi* or *garb*—a pot decorated with flowers and betel leaves, its mouth covered with a coconut, containing offerings that are hung in the doorways. Such joyous dances in which they clap their hands in rhythmic movement are especially associated with Gujarat, but others like them are known elsewhere in the country, as in Tamil Nadu and Rajasthan, and they are also performed at the **Holi** spring festival, though mostly in honor of Krishna.

Solemnities and Entertainment

All through the festival, many people visit temples of the Goddess, usually located on the outskirts of a town or village, or else on high mountains. In some places, special food is prepared for the Goddess every day, and brahmins, married women, and young girls are invited for dinner. On the last evenings, an *arti* service is celebrated with great solemnity by a priest who traces a circle of light before the *protima,* while burning incense and ringing bells. In Bengal, wherever their sound and that of the traditional *dhak* drum reaches, people feel that the Great Mother protects them from harm. On the seventh to ninth days, there is also *puja* and *anjali* in the morning, followed by a community lunch and an afternoon of sports and games for young and old. Among other activities often featured are film showings, theater (including the recently revived *jatra* or folk plays, and music performances of all kinds) from street entertainment up to the Carnatic classical music festival started by Maharaja Swathithirunai at Sree Padmanabha Swami Temple in Thiruvananthapuram in Kerala. There and elsewhere, dolls of gods and animals are artistically arranged by young girls alongside toys and trinkets in tiered displays reminiscent of Japan's **Doll Festival.**

Among Shaivas, some Vedic rites such as the *homa* or butter oblation to the sacred fire are integrated into services that remain essentially Tantric—as a kind of high magic, like the Shondhi Puja performed in Bengal at an auspicious hour of the night to usher in the ninth day. Following a public reading from the *Chandi,* 108 lamps are then lit and as many blooming lotuses are offered to the goddess to mark the exact moment of her killing of Mahishasura.

Sacrifices

In many places in India, buffaloes, goats, and pigs have been sacrificed in this connection, but Nepal remains unsurpassed in the scale of this seasonal bloodletting. Vegetarian Vaishnavas there prefer to hack a pumpkin to pieces instead, and the majority Newar people of Kathmandu Valley break duck eggs over an idol and may drink the yolk as *prashad* or a blessing gift from Durga. The meaning is the same as that of countless temple sacrifices in which merit is directly proportional to the height to which the blood spurts upon slitting an animal's throat. In Kathmandu's Taleju temple, if the blood fails to reach one of the upper tiers, it should at least wash over the kalash inside, or else its efficacy is lost. The royal family's own kalash would have been brought over the day before (which is called *Fulpati* after the sacred flowers and leaves covering the sacred object) with dazzling pomp and circumstance from its ancestral seat in

Gurkha to the royal **Dasain** *Ghar,* in an inner chamber of the same Hanuman Dhoka palace where the dynasty's ancestral patron Taleju has her main temple in the capital.

During the "Black Night" (*Kalratri*) of the "Great Eighth" (*Mahashtami*), while goats, sheep, chickens, and ducks by the hundreds may be sacrificed elsewhere, only buffaloes are slaughtered there, following exacting Tantric ritual prescriptions. Durga prefers the blood of black, uncastrated water buffaloes, most like the Buffalo Demon she slew in mythical times. But within living memory, she was not above accepting human sacrifices, such as the ones long legal at Dakshin Kali near Farping, where her terrifying image is bathed in blood on this Black Night. Rumors are even perpetuated among the people of secret sacrifices of this kind that might still be performed by some sects at certain temples, which are said to account for mysterious cases of missing children. Be that as it may, the animals sacrificed on such occasions as **Dasain** are actually privileged, since they are thought to be reincarnated as human beings. As for their remains, the severed head, tail stuffed in its mouth, is left facing the idol in the temple, and the keeper can later have it, while donors get to take the body home as prashad, parts of which will also be distributed as a blessing from Durga to relatives and friends after the family has feasted on it that evening.

The next one is *Nawa Ratri*—the Ninth Night of a day Kathmandu's Newars call *Syako Tyako,* because "the more you kill, the more you gain." Among prayers, gifts, and sacrifices to the Mother Goddesses on this "Great Ninth" (**Mahanavami**), there is one they particularly like to perform on this occasion. It is that of a goat whose head is cut into eight specific parts and sewn back together with a reed to be taken to the home of the paternal house or its equivalent, where eight men seated in order of seniority will get their respective part, as a way to reassert ancestral bonds.

Specialized Blessings

Early that morning, dozens of black buffaloes are slaughtered at the armory across from Hanuman Dhoka in front of high officials and the troops in full dress uniform, as bands play and cannons boom. Each beast is to be decapitated in one stroke before a display of regimental colors that will be imprinted with an official's blood-soaked hand, in order to secure Durga's blessings as goddess of victory and power. Because officers who used to attempt this execution themselves and happened to botch it had reason for concern at such a bad omen, the task is now left to soldiers who are adept at it, while civil servants from the warrior caste stand at attention holding merely symbolic *khukuri* sabers. Again, the carcasses will be consumed later in regimental feasts.

Along with spirits, flowers, rice, and red powder, blood from the gaping throats of sacrificial beasts is also used that day to bless vehicles of all kinds (including every plane of Royal Nepal Airlines), especially if it is an offering to Bhairab, Durga's bloodthirsty male counterpart and means of transportation to the gods. A goat or a duck is sacrificed to their Great Carpenter Vishwa Karma, patron of arts and crafts, drenching in blood the tools of people's trade in factories and workshops, which are closed for the occasion. Flowers, incense, and flaming wicks are also used to bring the blessings of this god or of the Goddess Durga on the implements used in all professions, from the weapons of warriors and hunters to the instruments of craftsmen and doctors, as well as students' books.

This literate kind of implement is particularly emphasized by Vaishnavas, with their reliance on Vedic scripture, in their version of these observances over the last three days of **Navaratra**, which are devoted to Sarasvati, goddess of learning. In Kerala, all of **Mahanavami** is dedicated to her with pujas performed in the morning and evening, and a range of vegetable offerings slightly larger than that already featured at the *Pujavaipu* ceremony the night before—the night of *Durgashtami* ("Durga's Eighth"), also known therefore as **Sarasvati Puja**. It is done in temples and households with a reputation for learning (like those of brahmins), opened for the occasion to the public, among whom the offerings will be distributed afterward. The ceremony takes place in a decorated room where an image of Sarasvati is set in front of an arrangement of books and scriptures, as well as weapons and implements too sometimes. Studies and all skilled work would have been suspended all day, to resume on the morning of the tenth with the removal of books and tools as part of the breakup of the puja or *Puja Eduppu*, marking an auspicious new beginning for work and learning. As in **New Year** customs in Japan or ancient Rome, skilled workers then do a symbolic amount of work with the tools of their trade, and people who can will write the alphabet on sand and read a few sentences from sacred scriptures. Children are taught how to write the alphabet on sand or rice as an initiation into the world of knowledge called *Vidyarambham*. Only then are they actually entitled to read and write.

The Start of the War Season

The following Tenth Day (*Dusshera*) also used to be the day to worship weapons, as the hero Arjuna did on this day when he took back those he had hidden in a hole in a *shami* tree, once he came out of a year's retreat in the forest and set out to fight the good fight against a rival divine clan, as related in the *Mahabharata*. This is one reason why the feast of **Dusshera** is of special importance for the princely kshatriya warrior caste, since it used to mark the beginning of the war season as the time for *simollanghan*, when kings crossed over their borders to fight against neighboring kingdoms. When the military situation did not allow for the regular performance of the appointed *puja,* prayers and sacrifices would still be made to invoke the blessings of Durga on this day of her own victory over

Mahishasura. In Mysore, Karnataka's second largest city after Bangalore, it is still celebrated with a pomp and pageantry reminiscent of the days when, there as in other princely states, the Maharaja would come out of the royal palace on a state elephant, preceded and followed by cavalry and infantry, in a procession of nobles and officials, with trumpets blaring and war drums sounding, to go perform these rites at a sacred site outside city gates. In the afternoon of **Dasain** day, several quarters of Kathmandu hold a "Sword Procession" (*Kharga Yatra*) where Buddhist priests in a trance wear costumes to represent the deities possessing them as they each hold up a sheathed sword quivering on its own with the energy of Durga's power, which it symbolizes.

Final Processions

On this day in India, images of the warrior goddess are taken out in jubilant processions to nearby bodies of water to be immersed in them. In the morning, married women first bid farewell to the goddess by applying *sindar* or vermilion to the parting of her hair, her bangle, and her feet, and putting a sweet in her mouth. Then, instead of a puja, there is a Tantric ritual called *Darpan Visharpan,* where a mirror that has reflected her feet is plunged in a basin of water. In the afternoon, some of her weapons and adornments are removed from the protimas before they are taken on trucks (formerly ox carts) to a gathering point on the banks of the water. There may or may not be a final *arti* before they are put on a boat and immersed amidst shouts of joy and triumph. People can now go home to an empty *pandal* for *Shanti jal,* that is, to receive a sprinkling of the "water of peace" that signals its advent with the final victory over evil. The sacred water vessel and its shrine are also dismantled and the offerings ceremonially disposed of as a brahmin says the Vedic prayer: "Give us peace, O Goddess, preserve peace, and give peace to the earth and the whole universe."

The Play of Rama

In North India, where Vaishnavas associate **Dusshera** primarily with Rama's victory over the demon king Ravana, the *Ram Lila* (or "Play of Rama") is the highlight of this festival of the Tenth Day. For the war led by the seventh avatar of Vishnu to recover his wife Sita from her abductor also lasted for ten days. The tale, as told in the great *Ramayana* epic, is played in different episodes on successive nights by young actors in elaborate costumes and masks. In Delhi, many amateur troupes perform plays, recitations, and music based on the life of the legendary hero Rama. Athletic tournaments and hunting expeditions are often organized too. On the tenth day, there is a procession to the Ram Lila grounds, where huge cracker-stuffed effigies of the demon-king Ravana and his brother and son explode and burn to the cheers of thousands of spectators (as at the burning of King **Carnival** in the West). In the Kulu valley in the Himalayas, villagers in colorful costumes also form a procession of local deities to the sound of pipes and drums. In remembrance of a divine rain of gold in Rama's kingdom of Ayodhya (during the reign of his ancestor Raghu), rewarding the guru Kautsa—who distributed it to the people—on this day there is also a custom of picking the leaves of *apati* trees, which people give each other as *sone* (that is, "gold").

Seasonal Visitations

Across the border in Nepal, the red *tika* dot worn by goddesses on their forehead was a mark of victory and power often bestowed to warriors on their way to battle in the past as it is nowadays as a general blessing of good fortune on all elders on **Dasain**. It is vital to visit all of them in rising order of seniority to put some red paste on each one's hand and forehead. For not to do so would be tantamount to severing relations. On the contrary, all disputes must be laid to rest and goodwill should pre-vail during the time allotted for going through this rite with all of one's senior relatives. **Tika Puja** is the name of this five-day period between **Dasain** and the "full moon of Kartika" (*Kartik Purnima*). This may also be reckoned as the midpoint of Ashvina. In Bengal, it is called **Lakshmi Puja** (like the third day of **Divali** elsewhere), and the period of mutual visits where people offer sweets, which extends from the "Tenth Day of Victory" (that is, **Vijay Dasami**) until **Kali Puja** at the end of the month, which is known as **Bijoya**, for it is a continuous celebration of victory—that of spirit over matter, of the divine self over base desires, of the light of wisdom over the darkness of ignorance.

Related Festivals

Also in Bengal, the month-long autumn festival of **Durga Puja** used to be echoed by another one when the image of the Goddess was similarly worshiped, but it now appears to be declining. It was called **Basanti Puja** to mark the spring equinox. In some regions of India, there is likewise another springtime novena or **Vasanta Navaratri**, culminating on *Rama Navami*—"Rama's Ninth" of the waxing, bright half of the month of Chaitra (March–April). The miraculous birth of Rama (as a result of the performance for a childless king of the ancient Vedic *ashvamedha* horse sacrifice) is then widely celebrated in his temples. The *Ramayana* is first ceremonially recited and expounded upon there in between concerts over the eight or nine days of **Ramayana Week** since the official **New Year**'s Day of India's 1957 calendar reform, much as in those leading up to the Vaishnava version of **Dusshera,** celebrating the exploits of a mature Rama.

> **See also** Carnival; Days of the Dead (West); Divali; Games (Rome); Holi; New Year (Japan); New Year (West); Sekku; Vaishakha and Vaisakhi

References

M. Amanullah. *Dashera of Bastar.* Photographs by Ashok Pagnis. Bhopal, India: Vanya Prakashan Tribal Research and Development Institute, 1988.

Sauresh Ray. *Durga Puja,* [*s.l.*]: R. M. E. Press, "Living Festivals" series, 1990.

Richard Schechner. *Performative Circumstances, from the Avant-Garde to Ramlila.* Calcutta: Seagull Books, 1983.

▶ **NAVA VARSHA**

See Vaishakha and Vaisakhi

▶ **NAVU VARSH**

See Divali

▶ **NAW RUZ (ZOROASTRIANISM, BAHÁ'ISM)**

Celebrated near the spring equinox, on March 21, the ancient Persian festival of **Naw Ruz** survives today as the **New Year** celebration of two world religions: Zoroastrianism and Bahá'ism. It also remains a vital part of the cultural identity of the mostly Muslim populations of the Iranian plateau and of adjacent areas in Iraq, Afghanistan, Pakistan, Uzbekistan, Tajikistan, the Caucasus, and Turkey, but above all of the Parsis of India, who have kept the flame of Zoroaster's faith alive in exile after Persia became Muslim.

An Ancient Persian Festival of Creation, Redemption, and Spring

Naw Ruz (also known as **Noruz** or **Nevroz**) means "New Day," referring to the seventh day of Creation, the one when mankind appeared, in the Zoroastrian account. In Persian mythology, the primordial couple arose out of the semen of the cosmic human archetype Gayomart after he was killed by the Devil, called Ahriman in Persia. Preserved and purified in the sun, this seed then fell to earth, where it sprouted as rhubarb forty years later, on the first day of spring: **Naw Ruz**, in the shape of two intertwined figures, one with a man's face and the other with a woman's. The Lord breathed life into them and named them Mashya and Mashyani.

In 538 B.C.E., the benevolent first world-emperor or King of kings who founded Persia's Achaemenid Dynasty, Cyrus the Great (for whom the prophet Isaiah first coined the title *Mashyakh*—the Messiah or "Anointed One" of the Lord—for freeing the Jews, along with other communities, from their Babylonian exile) changed the time of the **New Year** from the autumn equinox to the spring equinox. He was thus following the pattern of **Akitu**, the festival of divine and royal enthronement centering on the sky god Marduk and his earthly representative that Babylonia's last king Nabonidus had been neglecting for some time when his capital surrendered to Cyrus the year before. This was widely seen as a result of his failure to ceremonially reassert divine protection over his realm—a lesson that was not lost on the victorious new Shah, acting as viceroy of the One God of Creation. "It appears almost certain that it was Cyrus himself who imported this foreign practice to secure his seat on the throne, establishing it in the process as the signature of Iranian nationhood" (Kriwaczek 2002, p. 203) even to this day, when the poet Ferdowsi's national epic **Shahnameh** (1010) about Persia's pre-Islamic glories is constantly referred to around **Naw Ruz**. On the occasion of this festival, where the king appeared as a killer of the dragon responsible for the dry season, ambassadors and suppliants from numerous peoples within and without this first multinational empire used to come bearing gifts and tributes to the majestic palace complex of the ceremonial capital Persepolis built by Cyrus's Achaemenid successors Darius the Great and Xerxes I. Their **Naw Ruz** procession is vividly sculpted along the lower walls of its imposing ruins.

Naw Ruz is celebrated on the first of five intercalary *Gatha* days. Named after the five divisions of the Gathas (Zoroaster's hymns), they separate one year from the next at the end of the month of Âbân and are devoted to the souls of the dead or *fravashis*—hence this period's name, *Farvardine*. Initially, **Naw Ruz** was the festival of the creation of mankind by God, but it was later also devoted to Rapithwin, who personifies noontime and summer. Nevertheless, for a long time, **Naw Ruz** was celebrated twice, following both the lunar and solar calendars. In fact, the **New Year** is still celebrated twice but for different reasons, except by the Fasli sect of Iran; the other two sects (the Qadmis and the majority Shenshais) observe the anniversary of their landing in India as another **New Year**'s Day around July 21 and August 23 respectively. Celebrations of the standard Jamshedi **Naw Ruz** (said to go back to King Jamshid of the ancient Peshdadian Dynasty) used to begin on the last Wednesday of the old year, followed by a weeklong holiday, after which they would come to a close on the thirteenth day of the **New Year** (much as **Akitu** did at the same time in ancient Babylon). Though this remains a day for picnicking in the countryside and playing seasonal outdoor games, the **Naw Ruz** holidays with their mutual visits and gift exchanges (be it only of treats and trinkets, extending to colleagues, acquaintances, and even strangers on the street) have otherwise been scaled down to two days. Still, Iran remains plunged in giddy chaos for some ten days before and after March 21, as people travel from one end of the country to the other to spend time and have fun with their families, so that hotels are booked long in advance, and heavy traffic on all roads makes them even more dangerous than usual.

As in many other traditions, the Persian **New Year** is a time to chase evil spirits and invite good energies by cleaning the house and wearing new clothes. In Bombay, Parsi men wear their traditional white coats and *pugree* hats to the fire temple. There, they take part in most of the liturgical rites typical of the six seasonal **Gahanbar** festivals to be joyfully observed by all Zoroastrians: Midspring, **Midsummer**, Harvest time, the Time of Prosperity, **Midwinter**, and the spring equinox as the last one. Its **Naw Ruz** ritual thus includes the *Afringan* hymns of praise, the *Baj* prayers to angels and guardian spirits, and the *Yasna* offering of the *haoma* drink of immortality, while the *Pavi* prayers to God and his spirits give way to the *Fravardigan* and *Satum* prayers for all the dead. Purity laws need to be observed with special care, as their souls are thought to come out of heaven and hell to partake of the offerings set aside for them at their living relatives' ritual banquets. This reunion prefigures the joy of the resurrection of the body and the restoration of the Creation of Ahura Mazda (the "Wise Lord" of Avestic scripture) to its initial goodness after Ahriman's final defeat. Such an eschatological spiritual vision of cosmic redemption overlaps with the seasonal experience of nature's liberation, central to the ancient Persian **New Year** festival, when the king was seen as the slayer of the dragon ruling over the dry season. A political meaning can even be discerned in the epic story that plays the same role in Kurdish seasonal songs about a humble blacksmith's successful struggle against a tyrannical ruler. The celebration of **Nevroz** among Kurds, long semiclandestine under the repressive regimes of Iran, Iraq, and Turkey, can now openly feature traditional festive meals with their symbolic foods.

Persian New Year Customs

Like **New Year** festivals from Britain to Japan, **Naw Ruz** has its **carnival** king in the comic figure of Haji Firouz—a wild tambourine-man in blackface and red pants, which goes back thousands of years. In ancient times, a few days before **Naw Ruz**, the king and his harem would wait for Haji Firouz and his followers to come and dance for them at the palace. Having received a handful of coins from the king to distribute to his followers, Haji Firouz would lead them out of the palace in a procession to the houses of all the worthies of the capital to repeat their performance and demand gifts in the name of the king. These could even include slaves and girls for his harem. Haji Firouz might also carry a rope, which he would throw over the wall of a garden. On the other side, the home's owner had to tie to it the object nearest at hand, so Haji Firouz would predict his future from whatever he retrieved when he pulled back the rope. For instance, pastries heralded a sweet **New Year**, but a broom announced a rough year ahead. The procession did its rounds until the thirteenth day, when the value of all the presents collected was tallied; if it was above 40,000 *riyals*, the man playing Haji Firouz was given an important position at court, but below that amount, he was banished from the capital. Today, few Parsis and Iranians suspect the long history behind the trick-or-treating mummers who still go from door to door on **Naw Ruz** in the guise of Haji Firouz.

From the remaining Zoroastrian areas of Iran (like Kerman and especially Yazd—a favorite **Naw Ruz** tourist destination) to the periphery of Persian lands (as in Kurdistan), there is also a custom that goes back at least to the prophet Zoroaster's time and finds many parallels in the folklore of the Old World. It is that of jumping over **New Year** bonfires and chanting: "My yellow to you, your red to me"—yellow standing for disease and impurities, and red for the purifying energy of fire, at the heart of Persian religiosity.

Unlike other **New Year** festivals however, **Naw Ruz** does not begin at a fixed time of day like midnight or sundown, because it follows strictly the ancient solar calendar devised under King Jamshid and called the *Taquim-e-Nowrooze-e-Sheheriyari*, which knows no leap years and always lasts precisely 345 days, five hours, forty-five minutes, and forty-five seconds. In the past, canon shots would mark the exact moment of the **New Year**, but today it is

A family gathers for a ceremony celebrating Naw Ruz, the Iranian New Year. The ceremony goes back to pre-Islamic times. (Paul Almasy/ Corbis)

announced on the radio—unless, that is, the "rolling egg" method is followed, which consists in placing an egg on a very smooth surface and waiting for it to move ever so slightly on its own, just when the bull holding the world on its horns annually flips it from one horn to the other! At that point, family members have been waiting around a table, clutching coins or green leaves as symbols of the prosperity they hope for over the coming year. To greet its official arrival, the younger ones get up and kiss the hands of their elders, who give their juniors and social inferiors seasonal gifts called *eidi*—either cakes, flowers, or cash (preferably gold coins), much as in the lucky money pockets also offered by seniors in response to **New Year** greetings in China. In Iran and among Parsis, older people stay home to receive the homage of younger guests, who soon arrive for their gifts, since young people go visit their seniors in other households and also get gifts from them. All this can also be traced back to the ancient court practice of making formal gifts to the king, as the high priest, called the *Mobed mobedan*, would present him with twelve items symbolizing wishes for the **New Year**. They were: a slave boy, a stallion, a falcon, a sword, a bow and arrow, a ruby ring, a pen and inkpot, and, finally, a golden cup of wine, which he would put in one hand, and a tuft of barley, which he would put in the other hand along with some gold and silver coins. Likewise, Persian people today hold on to coins and green leaves while they await **Naw Ruz**.

When guests arrive at a house on **Naw Ruz**, they are welcomed by a *thoran* garland above the door. They then walk over intricate chalk designs on the floor to make their way to the *Sofrah Navrozi* table that awaits them inside with all kinds of delicacies, such as *sev* (vermicelli floss candy), hardboiled eggs, curd, and *falooda* (a seasonal milk and rose syrup drink that is a favorite with youngsters). On this table are also laid a number of symbolic objects, in addition to a Koran that provides a thin veneer of Islamic piety: candles, milk, and a mirror, among other things, but above all, as the centerpiece, a white cloth on which are arranged seven species of flowers, seven kinds of dry or fresh fruit, and seven twigs from different fruit-trees, adding up to twenty-one items so as to coincide with the twenty-one letters of the ancient *Yatha Ahu Vairyo* prayer. Though the items included may vary from one place or one era to another, they all have to be things that start with an "s"—as in *surkh* for "red." (So anything will do that is of that ubiquitous color of the Chinese **New Year**.) Hence the name *Haft Seen* ("Seven S's") for the most important domestic ritual of **Naw Ruz**, whose origins are as remote as its meaning is obscure. Yet, all places of business have a *haft seen* table on display and are usually hung with bunches of cypress, myrtle or rue—plants that all have Zoroastrian symbolism.

Throughout the day, Parsis greet one another with the rite of *hamazor*, where one passes his or her right hand between the palms of the other before they exchange good wishes for the **New Year**. They also call it *Pateti*, after the *Patet* seasonal prayer of repentance for past misdeeds, expressing commitment to right action in the future. In Bombay (recently renamed Mumbai) where most of them live, they flock to the shops that sell seasonal treats and to the theaters that show Parsi plays in the evening.

Naw Ruz under Islam

Naw Ruz has endured in Iran (as Persia is called nowadays) as the main, solar **New Year**—beside the season-neutral Islamic lunar calendar, despite recent efforts on the part of Shiite fundamentalist authorities to discourage the observance of pre-Islamic customs like gift exchanges and thirteenth-day outings amidst a newly verdant nature. During this favorite time for weddings, the Islamic prohibition on alcohol does not even prevent many Iranians from taking out a secret supply of wine—even if (possibly to avoid suspicion) it is made from pomegranates and honey rather than from grapes. **Naw Ruz** also came back with a vengeance in Afghanistan after the fall of the Taliban who had banned it outright, even though it is the country's traditional **New Year**. For such is this festival's irresistible appeal that Islam's Sixth Imam Ja'far al-Saadiq, less than a century after the Muslim takeover of Zoroastrian Iran in 632, could still praise it as follows to a devout Arab visitor: "**Naw Ruz** is the Day when God made an Alliance with the souls of His servants that they might recognize Him as the One and follow His Messengers and His proofs. It is the Day when the Sun shone on the world, when the breeze rose to fertilize the plants and the earth became verdant" (Mavaddat 1987, p. 23). The Shiite holy man went on to relate to **Naw Ruz** every past, present, and future event of Islam's history.

The Bahá'í New Year

Derived from messianic forms of Shiite Islam, the Bahá'í faith (which arose in Iran in the nineteenth century and is now professed by five million people throughout the world) has adopted **Naw Ruz** as its own **New Year** from the days of its forerunner the Bab in 1844. In the Bahá'í nineteen-month calendar that, he then introduced the nineteen-day month of fasting known as 'Ala (modeled on Islam's **Ramadan**) lasts from March 2–20. **Naw Ruz** immediately follows it on the twenty-first as the New Day at the start of the month of Baha of the spring season and of the **New Year**, all pointing to the even larger temporal dimension of the new dispensation for a united world which Bahá'u'lláh brought to his disciples. For, in the words of his eldest son Abdul-Bahá, they are to "make of this world a New World, so that the old earth disappears and another sphere is born, and that old ideas make way for a new way of thinking" in a kind of spiritual spring.

> It is the **New Year** that is the complete turn of a cycle of the year. A year is the expression of a solar cycle; but now is the beginning of a Cycle of Reality, a New Cycle, a New Age, a New Century, a New Time, and a **New Year**. That is why it is most holy. (Mavaddat 1987, p. 22.)

See also Akitu; Carnival; Days of the Dead (West); New Year (China, Korea); New Year (Japan); New Year (West); Nineteen-Day Feast; Purim; Ramadan; Rosh Hashanah; Vaishakha and Vaisakhi

References

Mary Boyce. *Zoroastrians. Their Religious Beliefs and Practices.* London and Boston: Routledge and Kegan Paul, 1979.

John Ebenezer Esslemont. *Bahá'u'lláh and the New Era: An Introduction to the Bahá'I Faith.* Wilmette, IL: Bahá'i Publishing Trust, 1980.

Threety Irani. "Navroze," in P. N. Chopra, ed. *Festivals of India.* New Delhi: Government of India, Ministry of Education and Social Welfare, 1977, pp. 40–45.

Paul Kriwaczek. *In Search of Zarathustra. The First Prophet and the Ideas That Changed the World.* New York: Knopf, 2002.

Naw-Rúz = New Day: A Compilation. Los Angeles: Kalimát Press, 1992.

Rochan Mavaddat. "À propos de 'Naw-Rúz'," in *Bahá'i France,* Nos. 9–11, January–March 1987.

▶ **NEMEAN GAMES**
See Games (Greece)

▶ **NEMESIA**
See Days of the Dead (West)

▶ **NENOHI NO EN**
See Sekku

▶ **NERONIA**
See Games (Rome)

▶ **NESTEIA**
See Thesmophoria

▶ **NETJERYT**
See Khoiak and Heb-Sed

▶ **NEUJAHR**
See Midwinter

▶ **NEVROZ**
See Naw Ruz

▶ **NEW FIRE CEREMONY (AZTECS)**

For the Aztecs, the end of time came every fifty-two years, when the two calendars they used finished on the same day. This meant the sun god Tonatiuh might have to submit to the returning culture hero Quetzálcoatl (the "Feathered Serpent") instead of the supreme air god Tezcatlipoca as usual. So as to allow time to start anew, in imitation of the sacrifice of two primordial deities who had thrown themselves into the fire of creation to give rise to the sun and moon, Aztecs would first let all old fires go out and then hold a **New Fire Ceremony** (*Toxiuhmolpilia*), also known as the "**Binding of the Years**" (*Nexiuhilpilitzli*), the greatest and most solemn of their public festivals.

When Two Calendars End at the Same Time

The Aztecs shared a combination of two calendars with other Central American peoples like the Mayas. The ritual calendar used in divination, called *tonalpohualli,* comprised all possible combinations and permutations of twenty named days with thirteen numerals, adding up to a 260-day year. The civic solar calendar, called *xiuhpohualli,* regulating agriculture and business, grouped *tonalpohualli* days into eighteen named "weekly" periods of twenty, adding up to a 360-day year (not unlike the nineteen "weeks" of nineteen days of the 361-day Bahá'í calendar). To reach 365 days, five intercalary days, (or *nemontemi,* (the Nahuatl word for "hollow" or "superfluous") were added, separating the last month of one year from the first month of another and considered inauspicious as a time of instability (just like the five days of the epact bridging the lunar and solar years in ancient Egypt). Solar years were in turn grouped into cycles of fifty-two, since this is the interval at which the solar and divinatory calendars would be completed on the same day, as part of a "calendar round" of the 18,980 possible combinations of the two sets of dates. This is reflected in the thirteen turns that four flying acrobats dressed as macaws—the sun's sacred birds—have to swing around a pole on the end of ropes rotating at the top in the *volador* game still played at Mexican *fiestas,* since thirteen times four equals fifty-two solar revolutions.

A Brush with Doom

The entire cycle always ended on a 1 *Malinalli* (a Nahuatl word for "grass") in the divinatory *tonalpohualli* calendar. To avert the possibility that the world might end with it, certain precautions were called for on that date. To prevent pregnant women from turning into wild animals, they were shut up inside the granaries, while children were kept awake lest they turn into rats. Fear kept people awake all through that night anyway. As in much **New Year** folk-lore, there was furious sweeping and cleaning of everything in sight. All Aztecs then threw away into water, burned, or broke their possessions, casting out the old to make way for the new—be it idols, furniture, mats, pestles, or hearth stones. In this way, dumps of pottery have been able to provide a neat clue to the chronology of Aztec styles. This holds even more clearly for temple pyramids, as they were rebuilt for every new fifty-two-year cycle, like the one at Tenayuca, enlarged at regular intervals in 1299, 1351, 1403, 1455, and 1507.

Rekindling the Fire

Most importantly, the fires in all Aztec dwellings and temples were allowed to go out with the old cycle. People waited with baited breath for the outcome of the **New Fire Ceremony** that alone could rekindle them if the world was allowed to go on for another fifty-two-year period. In order to perform it, priests marched in solemn procession up the Hill of the Star on a peninsula near Culhuacán to wait for the star Yohualtecuhtli (either Aldebaran in the Taurus constellation or the Pleiades as a whole) to get past its zenith, which would show that the world was allowed to get past this point in time. Having ascertained this, they would tear out the heart of a sacrificial victim and kindle a flame in a small wooden hearth they placed inside the hole left in his chest. Just as in many similar new cycle fire rituals the world over, the priests used an archaic drill method to generate this sacred flame. It was then carried to all corners of the land on pine sticks to light the fires anew in every hearth, including the sacred braziers of perpetual fire, that numbered over 600 in the capital alone. With the conclusion of this **Binding of the Years**, the Aztec world came out of the shadow of dread to find a new lease on life, which the people celebrated with feasting.

See also Busk; Easter; 8 Monkey; New Year (West); New Year (China, Korea); New Year (Japan); Nineteen-Day Feast; Samhain

References

Anthony Aveni. *Empires of Time. Calendars, Clocks, and Cultures.* Rev. Ed. Boulder: University Press of Colorado, 2002.

Alfonso Caso. *The Aztecs. People of the Sun.* Norman: Oklahoma University Press, 1958.

Brian M. Fagan. *The Aztecs.* New York: W. H. Freeman, 1984.

George C. Vaillant. *Aztecs of Mexico: Origin, Rise, and Fall of the Aztec Nation.* London: Allen Lane, 1975.

▷ NEW MONDAY TO NEW FRIDAY

See Easter

▷ NEW MOON

See Rosh Hodesh

▷ NEW YAM FESTIVAL (EWE)

Throughout the yam-growing areas of tropical West Africa, where its greatest civilizations (Ashanti, Dahomey, Ife) have arisen, one of the most important festivals is still the annual blessing of a new harvest of this indigenous staple. Its main outline may be discerned by focusing on the Ewe-speaking peoples that settled in southern forests and close to coastal areas from Benin to Ghana. They now know it as *Tedudu* ("yam-eating"), though older generations preferred to call it *Dzawuwu* ("purification"); these two names reflect twin aspects of the festival.

The Timing of a Unique Harvest Ritual

In Ghana, only those Ewe who live in the interior of the Volta Region have a festival for yam—while their other crops (which include corn, rice, and cassava) are not singled out for one. This is because growing this tuber requires the most attention and work, and the help of gods and spirits is therefore acknowledged by presenting its **first-fruits** to them—or else they

might not be so helpful the next year. In many other cultures, chiefs or village elders consult with ancestral spirits to determine the exact date of the **New Yam Festival**, but among the Ewe as in most of Ghana, it is traditional calendar experts such as the head fetish priest who calculate it and inform these local authorities. Depending on the place, the Ewe **New Yam Festival** can begin as early as August 12 and last as little as two days in Tsome, or fall as late as September 27 and last for over a week as in Nyangbo, not to mention a few spots where it has been absorbed by the November commemoration of a tribe's migration to its current home, as in Kpedze. In view of the many local variants in the details of the rites involved, it is mainly the Ewe of Peki near the lower Volta River that will be considered here.

Welcoming Worthies

The Pekis, who once belonged to the sphere of influence of the Akwamu branch of the Akan peoples, have kept the calendar common to them to calculate the start of their own yam festival in the first half of September, following one of the **Adae** forty-day cycles that begin on a Sunday (**Akwasidae**) as opposed to a Wednesday (**Awukudae**). Like those of many tribes on a **New Yam Festival**, the paramount chief of Peki invites the other local chiefs for **Akwasidae**. He then slaughters three sheep to serve to them, along with wine brewed from the sap of palm trees that elders have ritually felled in a sacred grove on an auspicious day. Some unfermented wine is sent to the priest for his initial offerings in the fetish house. The chief's senior spokesman pours wine as a libation to pray for the welfare of the assembled chiefs and their subjects—whose elders will also be invited for drinks by the chiefs once they return to their respective villages. On this first day, there is drumming and dancing in all of them before the town crier announces that the next Tuesday will be the day of general cleansing and purification.

Expelling Evil

After sunset that Sunday, each home is swept clean by the housewife, and all fires are extinguished so hearths too can be cleaned and the ashes taken out of town. There, the men meet the fetish priest, and they put together the various plants and animals gathered for a ceremony in which the priest ties up evil spirits and witches (symbolized by a chicken and a frog) to a branch. (In Ghana's Ho district—famous for its yam festivals—a young oil palm leaf is used instead.) He then drags them in a procession to the ash heap. They are left there after prayers meant to ensure that no evil gets any nearer than this point. In some places, the roads are either magically sealed (as in Wodze) or physically barricaded (as in Kpeve) to prevent evil from entering a village. The cassava crop even used to be thrown out of town with much abuse as undesirable at this point in Agate's purification rites, because of the plant's exotic origins. In all Ewe fetish houses, sacred objects—such as the ceremonial stools in which ancestral spirits dwell—are ritually cleansed too. On this Tuesday in Peki, those people who have been widowed over the last year are supposed to quit their mourning, and there is no funeral (only a summary burial) for those who die between the town's purification and the actual harvest celebration on Friday.

The Offering of First-Fruits

In preparation for this offering, Pekis go dig up their yams on Thursday, only to hide them in the bushes outside of town, since they should not be brought in before sunset. More importantly, to prevent evil from entering the area, the **first-fruits**, specially grown in a special plot tended by the priest (as is also the practice among Nigeria's Ibo) should first be offered by him—in this case at a forest shrine of the war god Tato, along with corn flour, wine, and water. Nine times over (to square the sacred number three), he can then apply a slice to the tongue of a harvester and then a slice of the largest yam of the new crop to his own tongue in the fetish house. This special yam is often grown in a corner of the house from the head of a yam planted there on the previous year's **New Yam Festival** Friday, in advance of the regular February planting season. The priest also pours fermented wine, egg yolk, and ram's blood on three spirit stools, before villagers come to kneel before them in **thanksgiving**, while sweet wine is being poured.

Only then can they proceed to harvest their own tubers. If anyone tastes the yams prematurely, he faces serious punishment and fines, as this is thought to jeopardize the village's survival and well-being by leaving it open to wrathful or evil influences. This taboo on eating (or even bringing home) the **new yam** before a certain point is a common feature of all versions of this festival, from Ivory Coast to Nigeria. It distinguishes this harvest festival from others in the same region, such as the **Homowo** of the Ga around Ghana's capital Accra.

Yet it is no longer observed as literally as it once was, since food is grown out of reach of urban masses and brought in from far and wide by modern means of transportation. This makes it impossible to keep track of where a crop comes from and ensure that no one eats it before it is blessed. With this blurring of local patterns of sacred space and time and the general secularizing impact of modernization, many yam festivals are by now maintained largely as mere social occasions, without strictly observing this premise of their propitiatory ceremonies.

A Week-Long Holiday

In Peki's **New Yam Festival** early on Friday morning, every village chief sends a chicken and two yam tubers to the fetish priest. He uses them to prepare a communal meal of yam *fufu* in front of the fetish house, where all are welcome to partake of it. In Ho on the first Sunday market in September, it is prepared in the house of the paramount chief, to make sure he is first (after the fetish, that is) to have his share of the **new yam**. Much as elsewhere in Eweland, some of it is also divided into two portions, one of which is dyed red with a mixture of egg yolk and palm oil. Both are then scattered around the house, as well as on the ground—as an offering to the implements used to harvest the precious crop.

There follows a big parade of new yam tubers in front of the assembled chiefs and priests. In some places, this has turned into an agricultural show since German colonial rule in Togo. Where Christian missionary influence has prevailed, a preacher's sermon or a church service may also precede the drums signaling that every household can now have its own yam-based festive midday feast, with yam *fufu* and chicken or fish as the main course. After lunch, people call on the other families of the neighborhood to bring them best wishes for the **New Year** if, for instance, the Akan calendar applies. All the while, the fresh crop of yam tubers is proudly displayed in every peasant's home. Drumming, dancing, and all manner of rural fun and games can also begin. They will go on almost unabated for about a week of well-earned rest from a difficult harvest, for as the Ewe saying goes: "If you labor for something, you must enjoy its sweetness." The way the holiday comes to a close in Peki is fairly typical: a male family member takes a firebrand from the hearth to chase evil spirits from every corner of the house and all the way out of town, before throwing it into the branches of a tree.

See also Adae; Busk; Situa

References

C. A. Ackah. "The Historical Significance of Some Ghanaian Festivals," in *Ghana Notes and Queries,* No. 5, 1963, pp. 16–27.

E. Y. Aduamah. "The New Yam Festival Among the Ewe: A Comment," in *Ghana Notes and Queries,* No. 12, June 1972, p. 31.

D. G. Coursey. "The New Yam Festival Among the Ewe," in *Ghana Notes and Queries,* No. 10, December 1968, pp. 18–23.

Geoffrey Parrinder. *West African Religions. A Study of the Beliefs and Practices of Akan, Ewe, Yoruba, Ibo, and Kindred Peoples.* 2nd ed. London: Epworth Press, 1961.

▶ NEW YEAR (BALI)

See Nyepí

▶ NEW YEAR (CHINA, KOREA)

The celebrations of the Chinese **New Year** take place between **New Year**'s Eve and the **Festival of Lanterns** on the fifteenth day of the first lunar month, usually falling between January 19 and February 23. They combine festive observances of many types: seasonal, mythical, and religious. Their common theme is clean endings and auspicious beginnings. Like the season's foods, they come in endless local variations. Among the basic customs are: welcoming a new Kitchen God, displaying **New Year** prints and Spring couplets, setting off firecrackers, visiting family and friends, giving lucky items, hanging red lanterns, enjoying Lion Dances and other performances, and the like.

Place in the Calendar

The **New Year** has been known by many names over more than 2,000 years as a Chinese national holiday (though 2002 corresponded to the Chinese year 4700 in a traditional count that comes into effect on the winter solstice or **Dong Zhi**). Among them are *Yuan Zheng* ("**Beginning of the Month**") and *Yuan Shuo* ("**First Day of the First Month**"). This first lunar month starts toward the end of winter, when Chinese peasants have time and food enough to spare, with nothing better to do than wish for the best over the coming year, by consuming the fruits of the past one and disposing of its undesirable residues. Then on February 5 or 6 comes the first of twenty-four divisions—*Jie Qi*—of the peasants' solar calendar, called the "Beginning of Spring"—*Li Chun*. The **New**

Year has been named after it: the **Spring Festival** (*Chun Jie*), ever since the Republican Revolution of 1911 brought the adoption of the Gregorian calendar the next year, as well as the dating of Chinese years from the accession in 2698 B.C.E. of the legendary Yellow Emperor (said to have instituted the traditional calendar on March 8, 2637 B.C.E.), instead of from the beginning of the current emperor's reign or his own declaration of a new era, as had been customary until the abolition of the monarchy. Under this name, the lunar **New Year** was distinguished from January 1 (the official start of a **New Year**) by referring to its approximate solar date. The use of the Western calendar was more strenuously imposed after the Communist Revolution of 1949, with the result that the Chinese **New Year** was long celebrated less extravagantly on the Chinese mainland (with the exception of Hong Kong) than it was (and still is) in Taiwan as well as in Chinese communities in other Asian countries. There, every business and public institution closes for what remains the biggest event of the year, which is something like American **Christmas** and **Thanksgiving** rolled up into one. As for people of Chinese background in the West, they often have to make a conscious effort to hold on to this essential part of their heritage instead of just following local holiday customs, at the same time as it is gaining new visibility in the general population through the schools, the media, and many shops. The **New Year**'s Day of some other Far Eastern cultures, such as Korea's **Seol**, Vietnam's **Têt**, and Tibet's **Losar**, is also celebrated by largely following local versions of China's calendar and customs.

New Year's Eve

On the sixteenth day of the twelfth month, by the festive meal following the old year's final sacrifice to the Earth, all old things (such as clothes) have to be either gotten rid of or renewed. Since lunar **New Year**'s Eve is a time to take care of loose ends, work contracts, mar-riage promises, and other pending affairs have to be settled by then, and the last day of the year is considered auspicious to make sure they are and that any quarrels are resolved. This includes settling debts (an aspect also known in Western and Korean **New Year** customs), so as to be able to start the **New Year** with a clean slate. In Taiwan, those who cannot pay sometimes take refuge in the front seats of theater performances given in temples on this day, so that their creditors will not dare come after them to pay up in full view of an indignant holiday audience. If people need to clean up the house and take out the garbage before the **New Year**, it is not only in order to make a fresh start, but also because it is believed that the year's wealth would be thrown away with the trash if this was done during its first two days. They sweep every corner of the house, as a way to clear it of the accumulated evils of the past year. (This is done by torchlight in Korea, in order to prevent new demons from coming near.) It is important not to sweep outward through the threshold, as this would also sweep away the family's luck, just as using knives and scissors would cut it off, so that people have to get haircuts a few days in advance. The same thing would happen if they failed to hide their brooms afterwards (much as, in the West, looms should be put away during the **Twelve Days** of **Christmas**). Witness the merchant Ou Ming of a **New Year** cautionary tale: when he tried to brutalize again the beautiful servant girl he had been given by a wizard along with lots of jewels, Ru Yuan disappeared with them inside a broom, leaving its careless owner a pauper.

But with the **New Year** also come new evils, slipping through the crack between two cycles of time. It is in order not to lay themselves open to the attacks of demons and misfortune that Chinese people make sure they at least give the impression of being happy and wealthy, by putting on their best and newest clothes for instance. This is also why they ring in the **New**

Year by letting off rounds of firecrackers day and night. This scares off evil as it did the one-footed little people haunting hilltop bamboo groves in ancient times. It was said that they came down once a year (when one year ended and another began) looking for things to eat and spreading disease to the mortals they met. Yet, they could not stand the crackling noise of bamboo tubes as they burst in the fire, which firecrackers have been imitating ever since. Likewise in Greece, the loud bursting noise of certain wild plants when they are thrown on the burning **Yule** log never fails to drive away the pesky little people called *kallikantzaroi,* who poison food and can only come up from the bowels of the earth to roam it over the **Twelve Days** of **Christmas**, hinging on the **New Year**. And just as ancient Athenians surrounded their temples with a red thread to prevent them from being polluted by such evil spirits during the festival of **Anthesteria** in February or March, the lucky color red—seen everywhere around the same time of year during Chinese **New Year** celebrations on account of its *yang* associations with the fiery brightness of the sun and the life force of blood that demons cannot stand—is the one thing that is sure to prevent the ogre Nian (whose name means "year" in modern Chinese) from coming to devour humans on **New Year**'s Eve. For he might get tempted to return to his bad habits of a long time ago, before a wise old man convinced him to prey on other monsters instead. This is said to be the reason why, before every **New Year**'s Day, people started to hang red paper bands with wishes for happiness to enter the house above their front doors, as they would eventually begin writing auspicious words in gold ink on parallel sheets on either side.

However, these Spring couplets have a more likely source in the peach-wood talismans that were put up from about 3,000 years ago on the first thirty days of the year. While the peach is a phallic symbol that can drive off evil and confer immortality, the talismans represented Shen Tu and Yu Lei as kings over ghosts and demons. It was believed the two gods had subdued them on the orders of the God of Heaven, because they had been gnawing at the peach trees of the Peach Capital Mountain in the East China Sea, the first island to catch the light of the rising sun every day. These fierce protectors thus came to be associated with the peach trees they stood guard over. At first sculpted in peach-wood, they were later simply evoked in writing on parallel peach-wood boards that people would hang on both sides of a double door. Emperor Meng Shang of the Later Chou Dynasty (951–960) once asked some scholars to compose auspicious verses to put on the boards on either side of his bedroom door on **New Year**'s Eve. Unhappy with the results, he came up with his own, and this began a trend. Under the Sung Dynasty (960–1279), members of the Imperial Academy put Spring couplets on paper and hung them at the gates of the Palace. Then Hung Wu, founder of the Ming Dynasty (1368–1644), told all nobles and ministers to imitate him in hanging parallel sentences (*duizi*) on the front doors of their residences for the **New Year**. The custom spread to every home in China.

There had long been a similar custom of hanging pictures of two guardian gods (*Men Shen*) on double doors, and of repainting them in bright colors every **New Year.** The pair became specifically identified with generals Qin Shubao and Yuchi Jingde, who had stood guard before the bedroom of Emperor T'ai Tsung (626–649) to prevent the ghost of the Dragon Lord of the Jing River from haunting him in his sleep for having failed to prevent his execution by the heavenly Jade Emperor. To allow them to also get some sleep, the monarch had their images painted on the Palace gates, and common people put up reproductions on their own front doors. *Men Shen* were but one in a range of favorite themes illustrated on *nianhua*—hand-painted woodblock prints that became immensely popular in late Imperial

China to decorate houses on **New Year**'s Eve. Some nianhua represented exorcists, who played the same defensive role as door gods. Others jointly evoked the pantheon of China's "three religions"—Confucianism, Taoism, and Buddhism—to bring down their respective blessings. Others still brought luck by depicting the objects of wishful thinking—plentiful crops, male heirs, worldly success in affluence and prestige, and colorful scenes of the idealized home life of the well-to-do—or from famous plays, stories, and legends. With the industrial production of such prints as China's version of season's greeting cards, their imagery and symbolism may have been simplified, but hundreds of millions are still made and distributed every year.

On **New Year**'s Eve, humans also have to actively relate to the higher realms, by performing the appropriate ritual, for good fortune to come down. Families have to get together for this, so China's trains are overflowing with people trying to make it home for the "year change" (*guonian*). At nightfall, the doors of houses are supposed to be shut and locked. Tables are put up for the gods in front of their home altars. These hold dishes of three main meats (pork, chicken, and fish), lucky red tangerines (which visitors also bring with their leaves intact to symbolize a lasting and secure relationship), and rice cakes, as well as spirit money. Prayers begin as the incense sticks are lit, while the gods are offered wine so as to put them in a festive mood. When the incense is half burned and the gods have had their meal of the food offerings, they are ready to receive offerings of spirit money. Like ordinary money, it symbolizes worldly goods, except it is meant to be burned as a way to transfer this wealth to the other world in payment of a debt of gratitude for divine gifts. After this has been done, the tables are moved to the left of the gods' altars to make offerings to the ancestors' altars. Aside from rice in which red paper flowers have been stuck (which symbolize the household's abundant supplies, although nothing is supposed to be left of the old year but these festive offerings), the ancestors, having seniority, first feast on the aromatic essence of all the food and rice wine before leaving the tasty substance for the **New Year**'s Eve dinner of their living descendants. This is the most copious meal of the year, at its most auspicious when it comprises eight courses, because that number sounds like the verb "to grow" in Chinese. If a family member happens to be missing for this all-important gathering, an empty chair may be set at the dinner table with the person's clothes on it. Under the round table, a heater (or *lu,* the same word as for "incense-burner") adorned with a string of coins symbolizes family unity, life, and luck. Like the different kinds of fresh flowers (normally associated with funerals during the rest of the year) and the miniature prosperity tree that adorn the home as a promise of spring, all dishes have a symbolic meaning as a wish for luck. Fruits with many seeds like peanuts stand for the wish to have children in the coming year. Sweets stand for all good things, greens for growth, fish for surpluses, dumplings for money, and such.

This is just the beginning of *chuxi,* which means "spending the night"—from **New Year**'s Eve to the next morning—in order to usher in the **New Year**. Oil lamps and red candles are put in every corner of the house to expel evil spirits lurking there. The entire family stays up long after the eating winds down. Children refuse to go to bed even though they are dozing off, and the longer they stay awake, the longer their elders are supposed to stay alive. (As a prank based on folklore, Korean children even get their eyebrows painted white if they do fall asleep.) Men chat; women are busy in the kitchen preparing more food for **New Year**'s Day or more spirit money for the ancestors. For these will be attended to again at daybreak, with offerings to their tablets or their portraits (just as in the Korean *charye* ceremony). It is also at dawn that the men of the house will welcome back the Kitchen God, Zao Wang. This male guardian of home fires was sent off to Heaven on the twenty-third or twenty-fourth day of the twelfth month to make his annual report to the Jade Emperor on the behavior of all members of the household. Offerings on that occasion were meant to bribe him into hushing up anything negative and even included sticky sweets or glutinous rice that would literally keep his mouth shut or garble his report. His image had been burned in the courtyard with spirit money amid firecracker bursts, which will also welcome him back when the new image of the god is put in its frame on **New Year** morning. When such images are "bought," it is important to say the god is "invited" and avoid using words that make him sound like a commodity, as he might get offended.

Nowadays, three quarters of the Chinese mainland's population actually spend **New Year**'s Eve watching a four-hour-long **Spring Festival** variety special on the China Central Television network—a tradition of sorts since 1982.

New Year's Day

On the "First Morning of the Year"(*Yuan Dan*) at the start of the "First Day" (*Yuan Ri*) as the "Time of the Beginning"(*Yuan Chen),* it is vital to make auspicious first moves, as on **New Year**'s Day anywhere. Since killing is out of the question, this is considered a vegetarian day. Traditionally, the whole family would put on new clothes (often with a touch of red), pray to its ancestors, and look up in an almanac an auspicious time and direction to move toward for its first walk outside the house. After arranging offerings to the God of Happiness, all would carry lanterns and set off firecrackers to drive away disease and secure peace, stopping at every temple on the way to burn joss sticks and pray the returning gods for a good year ahead.

Later that day, Chinese people may have their fortunes told. In any case, as in most cultures, they still try to visit their relatives and acquaintances to give them their best wishes for the **New Year**—an activity known as *bai nian, zou chun,* or *tan chun.* A prominent member of the community with too many people to visit all might just send them his name card instead or a card bearing the character *fu*—for "prosperity." Group visits between palaces on **New Year**'s Day started under the Ming Dynasty some six centuries ago and eventually became widespread in all of society. When a Chinese person gives **New Year** greetings to somebody senior (typically unmarried children to their elders), in return, he or she gets some lucky *yasui* money in a lucky red pocket (called *lai see* in Cantonese and *hong bao* in Mandarin) as a kind of birthday gift—since everyone is now deemed to be a year older. For Chinese children kneeling before their elders (as French Canadians also once did before their father for his **New Year** blessing), this used to be the only money they could spend freely, without parental hindrance, to buy candies, melons, and especially the ubiquitous lucky "red" oranges and mandarins. In Taiwan today, thousands line up to receive about $6 of lucky money from the President, but many may be turned back when pockets run out. As in Indian **New Year** customs, gambling and betting are allowed in order to test one's luck for the coming year. But the general idea is that "giving and receiving lucky money signifies good luck for all. Those who give will in turn receive" (Gong 2005, p. 15), according to the basic principle of the gift and the obligation to return it by a counter-gift that regulates premodern social exchanges, as typified by the Native American **potlatch** in anthropological literature since Marcel Mauss's *Essay on the Gift* (1924).

In Hong Kong, there is a **New Year** parade of one to two dozen floats through the streets of Wanchai quarter. In Indonesia, 2003 was the first year when the lunar **New Year** could be observed as a public holiday by the relatively rich but resented and mistreated Chinese minority.

In Korea on the **New Year**, *sebae* (a formal bow of respect to one's elders) is followed by *seongmyo* (bowing to the ancestors' graves, as one would if they were alive). Bowing to the dead or the living used to be just as important in traditional etiquette.

Second Day

In China, the second day of the **New Year** is also devoted to making visits, with a special focus on married women, who go back to their parents' home and see their siblings again, bringing their own children, along with some gifts. In return, they are given sugarcane and lettuce to bring back home as blessings of sweetness on their families. Visitors get tea and cigarettes. Members of a clan used to have a **New Year** reunion (*tuan nian*) at their common ancestral shrine, where they would congratulate each other, chat, have some food, and play games. At home, this is the day to "attract wealth and draw in treasures" by displaying pictures of the God of Wealth (Cao Shen). Somebody often dresses up to play his part and hand out money and sweets to children, like **Saint Nicholas** in the West. At night, families set lanterns afloat on a body of water.

Third Day

No visits were made on the inauspicious third day of the **New Year**, the "loyal dog day" of staying home and "sending away poverty." This took the form of cleaning the house and taking out the trash to be burned in the fields. Other ways of keeping filth and poverty at bay and bringing in happiness and wealth included prostrations to Cao Shen, setting off firecrackers, and lighting incense sticks and candles. However, lanterns had to be put out early, and people did not stay up late, so they would not disturb the rats as they came to feed on the grain and salt scattered on the floor for them. For this was an auspicious day for animals (the birthday of all dogs or that of pigs, and the day when rats got married), country people said.

Fourth Day

It is on the fourth day that all deities formally come back to earth. To invite them, their pictures and those of their guards are burned with spirit money and incense, food is offered, and firecrackers are set off. In order not to offend possible latecomers from the celestial realm, the welcoming ceremony only takes place in the afternoon. During this **New Year** period on the hinge of time, when the eternal gods come down to mix with lowly mortals, people refrain from using needles, for fear they might inadvertently prick their invisible guests. They also ought to make some noise before entering the bathroom to use the toilet, so the gods have time to slip away in case they should happen to be in the room and are not made to witness anything unsightly and offensive. This is considered to be the birthday of ducks and sheep.

Fifth Day

The next day is that of "Breaking the Five" (*Po Wu*). All five elements combine, as an ordered cosmos, on the birthday of the gods of the five directions, when they are inspecting the human realm in person. (This is also the birthday of cows.) People then pray for good fortune and prosperity, having removed previous offerings. Businesses offer the gods red cloth and hang some on their storefronts, as they reopen after the one long holiday of the Chinese year. The fifth day's weather is supposed to be an indication of the weather to be expected in the year ahead—much as on **Candlemas** at the same time of year in the West.

Sixth Day

It is around the sixth day (the birthday of horses) that Lion Dances begin. Since there were no lions in ancient China, they had the same mythological status as dragons and unicorns and the same magical power to chase away evil spirits. It is as a kind of exorcism that seven to ten uniformly dressed men perform their elaborate dances, holding up the fanciful shape of a lion. The same goes for the smaller lions that may be seen doing the rounds of all the houses of a Chinatown, as if trick-or-treating, from January through April. They chase away demons and bring good fortune to homes and businesses by dancing amid the crackle and smoke of firecrackers, once they have been fed treats dangling at the end of ropes from sticks hand-held out of doors and windows.

Seventh Day

The seventh day of the year commemorates the seventh day of Creation, when (much as in the Persian account or on the sixth day of Genesis) the goddess Nü Wa shaped humans out of mud into her own likeness. Chinese women perform similar gestures a night in advance to prepare *dim sums* for a meal of seven symbolic dishes with seven candles. They have to first make peace among themselves and keep children out of the kitchen, for fear that careless talk might dispel the lucky harmony symbolized by dim sums, causing them not to cook well, or worse, to burst in the boiling water. This would spell trouble for the whole year, while counting them would bring poverty. The same applies to the *jiaozi* dumplings that are renamed *yuanbao* in Northern China at this time of year, after the ancient gold ingots they are shaped as, symbolizing fortune along with the eight specific lucky items inserted in one of each of the eight kinds of yuanbao to be mixed into the batch; they can then function much as fortune cookies to indicate to the family members who find them what blessings they may expect over the coming year.

Eighth Day

The eighth day is reserved for paying homage to the stars—praying to their god, making nocturnal offerings to them, attending temple fairs, walking to high places, viewing flowers. It is also the birthday of rice.

Ninth Day

The ninth day is the turn of the Jade Emperor or Mister Heaven (*Tiangong*, in popular parlance). On the birthday of this head of the Chinese pantheon, people make an effort to avoid offending Heaven by losing their temper and disturbing mutual harmony. This is also the birthday of fruits and vegetables.

Tenth Day

This is the birthday of grains.

Season-Long Activities

During the first ten days of the lunar year in Korea, each house hangs a fortune mesh dipper on the wall, to hold taffy, matches, or money. In China's country villages, drum and gong bands are heard from **New Year**'s Eve to the end of the **Spring Festival**. Throughout Southeast Asia, raw fish salad or *yu san* is a seasonal meal enjoyed between these two dates, even beyond Chinese communities. Among these, other seasonal activities include opera performances, walking on stilts, dragon-lantern processions, bamboo merry-go-rounds, and Boat Dances, culminating on the fifteenth day of the **New Year** with the **Festival of Lanterns**.

> *See also* Candlemas; Christmas; Dionysia; Divali; Dong Zhi; Epiphany; Holi and Vasant Panchami; Laba; Lantern Festival; New Year (Japan); New Year (West); Nyepi; Saint Nicholas; Vaishakha and Vaisakhi

References

Patricia Bjaaland Welch. *Chinese New Year*. Hong Kong: Oxford University Press, 1997.

Wolfram Eberhard. *Chinese Festivals*. London: Abelard-Schuman, 1958.

Rosemary Gong. *Good Luck Life. The Essential Guide to Chinese American Celebrations and Culture*. Foreword by Martin Yan. New York: HarperResource, 2005.

William C. Hu. *Chinese New Year: Fact and Folklore*. Ann Arbor, MI: Ars Ceramica, 1991.

▸ NEW YEAR (INDIA)

See Divali, Navaratra and Dusshera, Paryushana and Dashalakshana, Vaishakha and Vaisakhi

▸ NEW YEAR (ISLAM)

The Islamic year begins on the First of Moharram, which is the first month of the Arabic lunar calendar, with the **Day of the Hegira** (*Hijra*)—the Prophet Mohammed's trek from Mecca to Medina, marking the beginning of the Muslim era. But this relatively late addition to the Muslim cycle of celebrations may coexist with other **New Year** observances not specific to Islam.

Alternate New Year's Days

For in some Muslim countries, **New Year**'s Day (*Ra's el'aa'am* in Arabic) is not only the First of Moharram. It can also be the first day of another calendar—a solar one, like **Naw Ruz** on March 23 in the Persian calendar as in Iran, or **Yanayer** (January 1) in the Julian calendar still used in the Maghreb since Roman times for economic activities. Thus in Tunisia, the Julian **New Year** (called *Ras el'aa'am el-'aajmi* as opposed to *Ras el'aa'am el-'hijri*—the *Hijra* **New Year**) is celebrated thirteen days after the Gregorian **New Year**, since the modern Western calendar has official status throughout the Maghreb as in Turkey; this means that Tunisia celebrates **New Year**'s Day three times! But regardless of the increasing role of the Gregorian calendar and Western **New Year** observances, the First of Muharram has remained sacred for all Muslims since the early modern Ottoman era as the **Day of the Hegira**, marking the birth of Islam as a community of believers in One God and in His Prophet Mohammed.

The Day of the Hegira

The term **Hegira** (from the Arabic *hijra* for "leaving, breaking away") refers to the miraculous escape of the Prophet Mohammed and his companion Abu Bakr from the plots of their pagan enemies in Mecca. It relates more specifically to the moment they reached Quba, the southernmost tip of the oasis of Mecca, on the eighth of Rabi'al-Awwal in the Arab calendar—a date corresponding to September 4, 622. Mohammed and his Companions had recently concluded the Pledge of War with those who were now their Helpers—the people of the Nawfal clan of Medina who had come to Mecca for the annual pilgrimage (which had been performed by Arabs since time immemorial before becoming one of the five pillars of Islam). This new alliance that reached beyond tribal clan allegiances allowed the Prophet to join them in an indissoluble union based on his new creed, which took precedence over blood ties such as his own with the Quraysh clan of Mecca. This was an even more radical step for Arabs than the adoption of monotheism (indigenous forms of which had long coexisted with their traditional polytheism).

This is the meaning of *Hijra*—not just an emigration, but a painful break with the past, and specifically from communion with a well-known lineage of dead ancestors and living relatives on which Arabs based their personal and collective identities up to that point. These family ties were left behind along with Mecca's idolatry of many gods, just as Abraham had left Ur of the Chaldeans and his father's idols on God's command to establish His chosen people in the Promised Land of Canaan. Likewise, it was in the second holy city of Medina that Muslims shifted their allegiances from the local tribe to the universal *Umma*, which, as one community for all believers of whatever background, now reflected among men the supreme unity of a transcendent God. This is why they eventually started to count years from the one of this turning point, the **Hegira**. Yet they did not start with its actual date but with the first day of that year, corresponding to July 16, 622. It was adopted as the official start of the Muslim era, from which its years were now to be counted, under the second Caliph or successor of Mohammed after Abu Bakr: Umar ibn al-Khattaab (581–644).

On the eve of the First of Moharram, an important assembly is held in mosques to commemorate the historical **Hegira** and reflect on its spiritual meaning. Beyond that, the Muslim **New Year**'s Day is also marked by seasonal greetings and the telling of edifying stories about the founders of the faith.

See also Naw Ruz; New Year (West)

References

Mahmood Ahmad Ghazi. *The Hijrah, Its Philosophy and Message for the Modern Man.* Lahore, Pakistan: Islamic Book Foundation, 1981.

Zafarul-Islam Khan. *Hijrah in Islam.* London: Muslim Institute, 1997.

V. V. Tsybulsky. *Calendars of Middle East Countries: Conversion Tables and Explanatory Notes.* Moscow: Nauka Publishing House, Central Department of Oriental Literature, 1979.

▶ NEW YEAR (JAPAN)

Traditionally in Japan, the **New Year** holidays, mostly known as *Shogatsu,* are a time to expel demons, give thanks to the gods, and welcome ancestral spirits, in order to secure good fortune over the coming year. The celebrations of this quiet, yet vibrant, season are associated either with the first day of the year (*Oshogatsu*) or the year's first full moon (*Koshogatsu*), the latter following the native Japanese peasant lunisolar calendar, and the former the Chinese lunar calendar officially adopted in the sixth century, which was replaced by the Gregorian solar calendar after the Meiji Restoration of imperial power, ushering in rapid modernization in the late nineteenth century. The four different dates of **New Year** celebrations—the first day and first full moon of the solar and lunar calendars—varied a lot until the latter's were then fixed on February 1 and 15.

Year-End Preparations

Come December, popular year-end parties reminiscent of **Christmas** office parties and known as *bonenkai* are held in pubs and restaurants by all kinds of Japanese associations and companies, though participants usually pay their own share of expenses. Seasonal decorations are sold at temples and shrines at year-end fairs called *toshi no ichi.* The word *toshi* means both "rice" and "year," because the peasants' solar calendar used to revolve around the planting and harvesting of this staple crop before the official adoption of the Gregorian calendar in 1873. In some rural areas, the old calendar is still used to determine the date of **New Year** celebrations (which may fall there anywhere between January 20 and February 19).

Whatever the date used, the **New Year** is preceded by a period of purification starting in the last days of the old year with a ceremonial housecleaning. At the very least, home altars are then dusted off. Set on the thirteenth day of the twelfth month by the official calendar of the Tokugawa shoguns (who ruled Japan in the Emperor's name from 1603 to 1868), the Sweeping of Soot (*Susuharai*) was even then observed at a later date in practice. To this day on **New Year**'s Eve, called *omisoka* in Japanese, just before midnight, Buddhist temples all over the country begin a countdown of bell peals known as *joya no kane.* The bells are struck 108 times to symbolize the purification of this canonical number of earthly desires (*bonno*). From 774 onward, on the imperial court calendar of **annual events** (*nenchu gyoji*) of the Heian Period, the nineteenth, twentieth, and twenty-first days of the last month were devoted to *On-Butsumyo*—the General Confession of the sins committed over the closing year. Different Buddhist priests held services each night in private residences and in the palace. There, a statue of the merciful female deity Kannon was set up along with painted screens depicting the horrors of hell. They

Young women at a Japanese New Year celebration throw beans to drive away evil spirits for the year, ca. 1950. (Hulton-Deutsch Collection/Corbis)

served as a reminder to courtiers of the need for penitence.

On the last night of the year from 706, officials from the Ministry of Central Affairs would join the Masters of Yin-Yang to recite special spells in a Service of Expulsion called *Tsuina.* One of the Imperial Attendants was selected as Devil Chaser (*Hososhi*). Wearing a golden mask and a red skirt, accompanied by twenty assistants, he would do the rounds of every building and courtyard of the Palace. He was supposed to expel all evil spirits prior to **New Year** rituals proper, by twanging his bowstring, shooting arrows into the air, and striking his shield with a spear. By the eleventh century, the Devil Chaser tended to get confused with the devils he was chasing. It therefore became customary for the gentlemen of the Court to shoot arrows at him and his assistants. (Chroniclers have not bothered to specify if the unkindly targeted exorcists were ever actually hit.) Similar steps were taken in the private households of notables.

In parts of northeastern Japan—especially on the Oga Peninsula in Akita Prefecture—all households where small children or a new bride are to be found are invaded by a pair of demons (played by local boys) who come to threaten them on **New Year**'s Eve. Reflecting the duality of "rough" and "gentle" or "blessing" aspects in Japanese deities, one of these **Namahage** is red and carries a stick with Shinto's sacred white paper tassels, and the other is blue and wields a butcher's knife, beating a wooden bucket with it. When the intruders eventually settle down, the master of the house, who is formally attired, comes with wine and food to entertain them as he assures them that his bride is a good housewife and the children are not crybabies. This ancient practice is reminiscent of the holiday questing and mummering customs that abound in various parts of the West, especially around the **New Year** from **Saint Nicholas** to the **Twelve Days** of **Christmas**.

Spring Cleaning

The eve of the old solar **New Year**'s Day is when "spring begins," according to its Japanese name: **Risshun.** Many **New Year** customs confirm this original link with the expected coming of spring as a time of rebirth. Among them are the bright green, yellow, and pink colors of the plant-shaped rice cakes with which are decorated the branches hung from the ceiling of all the houses of Ojiya in Niigata Prefecture. One year in three, **Risshun** used to precede the main, lunar **New Year**'s Day— **Ganjitsu** or **Gantan** ("**Day of Origin**"). Since the coming of spring or **Setsubun** was scheduled on the third or fourth day of the second month, some of the observances traditionally held on this day still take place between February 3 and 5, even though this is the coldest period of winter. The best known is the ritual of opening the doors and windows of houses and expelling bad luck and demons by tossing beans into the air while saying, "*fuku wa uchi, oni wa soto*" ("fortune in and demons out"). Health is secured by eating the number of beans equivalent to one's age, and it is dignitaries of the same Chinese astrological sign as the current year who throw soybean packets from special wooden boxes at the crowds gathered outside Buddhist temples for this Bean-Scattering Ceremony or *Mame-Maki*. The practice is reminiscent of the ancient Roman fertility rites of the **Floralia**, when beans were also thrown at the people, as well as of the domestic exorcism of the **Lemuria**, in which the master of the house tossed beans over his shoulders to drive away restless spirits. Likewise, the **Mame-Maki** used to be performed at the Imperial Court on the last day of the lunar year, only to sweep away the spirits of winter cold and gloom and welcome springtime cheer with the **New Year**.

In a similar vein, the Great Purification (*Oharai*) services to cast out evil influences were not only conducted on lunar **New Year**'s Eve from remote antiquity, but also on the last day of the sixth month (another crucial point dividing the two parts of the Japanese year), as well as in times of special need like epidemics. In all cases, having attained ritual purity by fasting and abstinence, princes and officials would gather by the main gate of the Imperial Palace to perform a Shinto service purging the emperor's subjects of their impurities and sins. The sins of the monarch were removed by washing his life-size effigy (*mi-agamono*) in a river. Today still at the **Gion Okera Festival** in Kyoto, a sacred fire of the medicinal herb *okera* (*Atractylis ovata*) is kindled in Yasaka Shrine on **New Year**'s Eve. It is then distributed on lengths of special rope until the early hours of the **New Year**. Visitors can thus take the fire home to cook their first meal of the year with it, in the hope of remaining free of illness throughout the year. A very similar fire purification ceremony is also held at Omiwa Shrine in Nara Prefecture. The principle seems to correspond to that of the **Yule** log and other sacred fires of the **New Year**, to be found since ancient times in many traditional cultures all over the world.

Auspicious Beginnings

This practice is also a good illustration of the principle that still draws millions of Japanese people (and all of them in the past) to their places of worship on the first day of every year. It is then that the native gods, the *kami*, are revitalized. **New Year**'s Day is therefore the best day to seek their blessings, because the kami are at the peak of their power and efficacy. Letting this opportunity go by would be inauspiciously starting the year on the wrong foot, with a deficit of energy, thereby inviting misfortune. Whether good or bad, the kind of fortune met with during the crucial first days of the year makes of its first month the **Standard Month** (*Shogatsu*) that is representative of what is to be expected of its other eleven months.

First recorded in 642, the initial ceremony of the **New Year** among Japan's ruling élite used to be the Obeisance of the Four Directions (*Shihohai*). It has been observed regularly from the reign of Emperor Saga (809–823) to this day. When Kyoto was the capital in the Heian era (794–1185), the Emperor would go before dawn to the Eastern Garden of his Residential Palace to call upon his guardian birth star from among the seven stars of the Big Dipper. This was in accordance with the astrological usage of China's Tang Dynasty. He would look to the Great Ise Shrine and make obeisance to the heavens and the earth in the four directions, as well as to his parents' graves. He then prayed gods and ancestors in turn for a prosperous reign and the subjugation of evil spirits. After doing similar rites in their own mansions, nobles would go to pay their respects at that of the foremost of their kind, the powerful head of the Fujiwara clan and Chancellor of the Realm (*kampaku*). They were later admitted to the Imperial Audience Chamber for the Lesser Obeisance. This was introduced as *Kochohai* around 850, to replace the more elaborate Tang-style *Choga* ceremony.

Still observed today (albeit in modified form), the **New Year**'s Day Feast (*Ganichi no*

Sechie) arose in 649 from the practice of giving tributes of food, clothes, and services in honor of the **New Year**. Until the third day, from about 815, various types of spiced wine were prepared as an elixir of longevity by the Palace Medicinal Office and tasted by specially appointed virgins. They were given to the Emperor as **New Year** Medicinal Offerings (*O-kusuri),* in addition to lucky foods like melons, radishes, and mirror-shaped rice cakes. This ceremony was known as the "Tooth Hardening" (*Hagatame).* It was meant to ensure the monarch's good health ("hard teeth") over the coming year. Nowadays, Japanese people pray to obtain this blessing for themselves, as they toss coins in the offertory box of the first of the local Shinto shrines and Buddhist temples they are supposed to visit on January 1—a custom called *Hatsumode.* But the main purpose of the visits used to be to pray for good crops and the household's safety over the coming year. They were traditionally made to Shinto shrines located in a "favorable direction" from home.

Among the most visited Shinto shrines during the first week of the **New Year** are the Meiji Jingu Shrine in Tokyo, the Sumiyoshi Taisha Shrine in Osaka, and the Fushimi Inari Taisha Shrine in Kyoto, while the Kawasaki Datsiti Temple in Kanagawa Prefecture and the Naritasan Shinshoji Temple in Chiba Prefecture are the most popular Buddhist temples for Hatsumode.

On **New Year**'s Day before sunrise (which crowds still gather to watch, with ceremonial hand-clapping as to a deity in certain rural areas), all family members would traditionally put on their best outfits. Having drawn the first water of the year (*wakamizu*), the head of the household or its firstborn son would then pour the water into a basin for all other family members to wash their faces (as in some Greek **New Year** customs). They would then gather in front of the home altar to light candles and offer rice cakes to their ancestors, and proceed to exchange formal **New Year**'s greetings around the table, before drinking the ceremonial wine poured by the head of the family and eating a bowl of the traditional *zôni* rice paste soup. Aside from vegetables, the chief ingredient of this soup is *mochi* glutinous rice, the staple of the holiday season; countless round cakes are then made from this paste. Other seasonal dishes include sweet black beans, mashed sweet potato with chestnuts, rolled seaweed, and above all, fish. This is boiled to a paste, made into a salad, mixed into egg rolls, dried as a candy, or seasoned, as in the case of herring. These foods remain available for family and guests until January 20.

Over this festive period and on the first day in particular, Japanese people make a point of visiting each other and exchanging gifts—a **New Year** custom also found in China and Europe since ancient times. In Japan, it still serves to underline the expression of appreciation that is the key principle of the rules governing all social interactions. This even extends to inanimate objects, such as the working tools that farmers and fishermen decorate during **New Year** celebrations to show their gratitude for the indispensable part these play in their livelihood. Starting on **New Year**'s Day and throughout the holidays, people receive greeting cards or *nengajo* from relatives, friends, and acquaintances. More than four billion *nengajo* were sent annually for the **New Year** at the turn of the twenty-first century. Over the holidays, children receive special gifts of spending money—*otoshidama* from their parents and relatives, often amounting to several tens of thousands of yen in the case of high school students.

On the year's second day, at home or in public, young and old execute in fine calligraphy their first formal writing of the year or *kakizome.* It is a reminder of the time when the second day was the one when arts and crafts could ritually commence for a New Year (being taboo on **New Year**'s Day as in ancient Rome). But nowadays, January 4 is the First Business Day (*Goyo Hajime*).

The fifth day of the year used to be set aside for the Bestowal of Ranks, or *Joi,* at the early medieval Heian Court. The Chancellor and the Great Ministers would do this while very formally seated at the emperor's Residential Palace and then pass on a cup of *sake* wine.

On the year's first Day of the Hare (*u*)—which was the fourth day of the duodecimal cycle—the *U* Staff (*Uzue*) ceremony was performed from 689 onward. Japanese courtiers would give bundles of staves to the Emperor, to the Crown Prince, and to one another. These were meant to ward off evil spirits and attract divine blessings. *Uzue* spread beyond the Court to Shinto shrines in the medieval Kamakura and Muromachi Periods, and to the people of Osaka and what is now Tokyo during the early modern Edo Period. The ceremony is said to be based on the one designed by the usurper Wang Mang, who ruled over the Chinese Empire from 8 to 23, to signal with a pole the disgrace of the legitimate Han Dynasty. But Uzue is more closely related to other Japanese folk practices once observed at Court. One of them that has spread throughout society since the Edo Period consists in decorating doorways with pine boughs and bamboo, so as to attract and shelter benign deities and the returning souls of dead ancestors for the **New Year**. As symbols of stability, these ornaments are woven together with bamboo, representing righteousness, in *kadomatsu* bouquets that are placed at both sides of the entrances of dwellings and businesses, and they play a similar role as the tall *sasatake* bamboo pole with streamers on **Tanabata no Sekku**—the summer **Festival of the Weaver**. Another traditional door decoration combines elements that also stand for specific **New Year** wishes: a small bitter orange for the family's longevity, a lobster more specifically for that of its currently living members, a bit of seaweed for happiness, and a piece of fern for purity and fertility, all of which hangs on rice straw rope that stands for unity. Oversized, elaborately woven *shimenawa* sacred ropes of

this kind, meant to keep out evil spirits, also appear hung on their own over gateways, and some shrines and temples are famous for the monstrous proportions of theirs.

Women's New Year

The **New Year** kami's temporary dwelling places are ceremonially burned on the fifteenth of the first month in what is called *Tondoyaki* in eastern Japan and *Sagichô* in western Japan. In some areas, sacred "year (or rice) wood" (*toshigi* and *toshi* meaning both "rice" and "year") is still cut to be burned, as it was at the Court on this day in a Kindling (*Miramagi*) ritual first recorded in 675. Thus, in Niigata Prefecture's *Sai-no-kami* or **New Year** Deity Send-Off, children heap old rice stalks over pine branches gathered from the mountains to form the Fort of the God. They then place their offerings at its feet before setting the teepee-like structure on fire and waving farewell to the deity, who from heaven will stand guard at the gate for the arrival of the following year. Until then, one may be saved from catching a cold by eating rice cakes toasted in its burning dwelling.

The fifteenth of the first month also used to be the day of the first **Full Moon of the New Year** (*Koshogatsu*). Survivals of this archaic Japanese **New Year**'s Day in farming villages focus on imitative magic like the making of rice cakes in the shape of fish and flowers to encourage fertility and an early spring, and may include the ritual planting of rice in the snow (unique to Japan) during the second week of January. On this **Little New Year** or **Women's New Year** (*Onna Shogatsu*), women would chase each other and playfully whack one another with the elder-wood sticks used to stir a special Full-Noon Gruel (*Mochigayu*). This was thought to magically promote the birth of male children, especially since the first month was dedicated to the Shinto deities of the male element. But this practice was also common among the upper classes, and it thus appears in the classic *Pillow Book* written by Court Lady Sei Shonagon around 1002. At the Court, the Imperial Water Office would prepare the same gruel to offer it to the Emperor.

On the following day, the sixteenth of the first month, the Ceremony of Beating Time to a Song (*Toka no Sechie*) would be held at the Palace. These dances were originally performed in the eighth century by Chinese expatriates, following a Tang Dynasty custom. By the ninth century, they had become amalgamated with the *Utagaki* folk festival and were now done by a group of forty ladies-in-waiting to accompany a poetry recital. During that same Heian Period, a shell-matching game (*kaiawase*) popular among aristocrats developed into a seasonal card game called *uta karuta* that involved swiftly matching the initial three lines of any of the classic *One Hundred Poems by One Hundred Poets* (*Hyakunin isshu*) to the next two from another 100-card set. For generations thereafter, young men and women would socialize on the occasion of the **New Year** by playing this game that helped them learn classical poetry. It is still played in period costume on January 3 in Kyoto's Yasaka Shrine. A kind of backgammon called *sugoroku* also used to be popular at this time of year. Until modern forms of entertainment started to compete seriously with seasonal games, small boys would fly kites and be more likely to spin tops than little girls, who alone played shuttlecock (*hanetsuki*) with battledores elaborately decorated as effigies of historical warriors, kabuki actors, movie stars, and other celebrities.

From 860 onward, **New Year** celebrations were concluded at the Court on the eighteenth day of the first lunar month with the Bowmen's Wager (*Noriyumi*) between officers of the Inner Palace Guard and the Middle Palace Guard. This archery contest was followed by a banquet, where Court dances were also performed competitively, and there was a prize for the winning team and cups of defeat for the others. In contemporary Japan, the festive season closes with the January 15 national holiday known as **Adults' Day** or **Coming-of-Age Day** (*Seijin-no-Hi*), in honor of people who have reached their twentieth birthday over the past year. In this government-sponsored rite of passage, young people are officially bestowed the right to drink, smoke, vote, marry without needing their parents' permission, and contribute to the National Pension Fund. Along with many older people, they make offerings for a successful adult life at their neighborhood shrines and temples (although in Tokyo the Meiji Shrine is favored by all). For this, they put on their best traditional clothes, especially the women. This long used to be the **Women's New Year** after all!

See also Christmas; Days of the Dead (West); Floralia; Gion Festivals; Kasuga Festivals; Khoiak and Heb-Sed; New Year (China, Korea), New Year (West); Saint Nicholas; Sekku

References

Reiko Mochinaga Brandon and Barbara B. Stephan, eds. *Spirit and Symbol: The Japanese New Year.* Honolulu: Honolulu Academy of Arts and University of Hawaii Press, 1994.

Takutaro Sakurai. *Japanese Festivals: Annual Rites and Observances.* Tokyo: International Society for Educational Information Press, 1970.

Tal Streeter. *The Art of the Japanese Kite.* New York: Weatherhill, 1974.

Yoshiko Yamamoto. *The Namahage: A Festival in the Northeast of Japan.* Philadelphia, PA: Institute for the Study of Human Issues, 1978.

NEW YEAR (NEPAL)

See Vaishakha and Vaisakhi

NEW YEAR (TIBET), NEW YEAR (VIETNAM)

See New Year (China, Korea)

NEW YEAR (WEST)

Though steeped in folklore, in the Western world, **New Year** celebrations do not have the official religious status they possess in other traditions. Yet this was the case of January 1 in the ancient Roman calendar, now in universal use in its updated Gregorian version. This reformed calendar was adopted in 1582 by Catholic countries, while others only gradually followed suit—from Scotland in 1660, through Germany and Denmark around 1700, to Sweden and England in the early 1750s. Though William the Conqueror had already switched the date of the **New Year** in the latter country from December 25 (the day he was crowned after his Norman invasion in 1066) to January 1, later on Great Britain had joined the medieval Western European norm in taking the year to begin with spring on March 25 (as had been decreed for Rome by Julius Caesar in 45 B.C.E.). The climax of **New Year** celebrations came a week later on **April Fools' Day**—a time for pranks reminiscent of the year-end **Feast of Fools**, and, like it, originally a French custom. (Similar practices characterize India's **Holi** festival by the end of March.) At the time of Rome's foundation, a primitive ten-month year used to begin in March there. These former springtime **New Year** celebrations went on being observed in Rome long after the year was made to start in January (just as in Japan today the **Little New Year** of an archaic calendar survives on January 15 beside the official Gregorian **New Year**).

Fire and Water

Folk traditions of pagan origin have long surrounded January 1 as **New Year**'s Day, even though some customs (like children begging for money from door to door) shifted to or from **Epiphany** as the peasants' **Great New Year** on January 6, or to or from **Christmas** and the winter solstice. In the latter case, the reason is that days start growing longer at the darkest time of year, when the year itself grows short, and a **new year** will soon be in the upswing. On both **New Year**'s Day and the winter solstice, the waning of something that is on its way out overlaps with the waxing of new beginnings.

This kind of pagan light symbolism is still explicit in Rio de Janeiro's ***Réveillon*** (a French word for a late-night holiday party), which is the most spectacular **New Year** celebration of its kind in Brazil, even though it actually follows the summer solstice in the Southern Hemisphere. From dusk to dawn, devotees of the Afro-Brazilian Umbanda religion (widespread in the country's urban centers) lead about a million white-clad people in a procession to the beach, where they launch tiny candlelit boats into the sea as *macumbas* (offerings) to their chief goddess Iemanjá, who is patterned after the Virgin Mary. (She is also identified with Saint Barbara, patron of seamen, who head out to sea with their own offerings to promote the success of the coming year's catch.) To have their wishes fulfilled, the devotees have to jump over three waves and throw flowers into the sea. They keep on praying and dancing to music from big loudspeakers well after midnight, when splendid fireworks are launched from all the hotels along the beach. In their original European context, like the related **Carnival** practice of burning winter in effigy, **New Year** fireworks are a common way of marking the triumph of new light over all that dies away in darkness, and one method among others to make a racket that will scare away the demons of winter. Another one may still be observed in North America in some remote subarctic communities like Fort Chipewyan, Alberta, where all shotguns fire thunderously into the air for fifteen minutes at the stroke of midnight on **New Year**'s Eve— much as they did in colonial Manhattan.

Many folk customs, however, emphasize the delicate formal transition between a dying fire and a new fire. This was a central feature of the Celtic **New Year** celebration of **Samhain** on what is now **Halloween**. In many northern locations of Great Britain, there is still a custom of "burning the old year out" in a civic bonfire.

A related pattern of lighting thirteen fires or thirteen candles often appears in **Epiphany** customs of the British Isles. It may be likened to the traditional thirteen desserts of the **Christmas** Eve dinner in Provence, especially in Nice. There, the **Nativity** is still called *Calèna* in the local dialect of the Occitan language—a clear reference to the **calends of January**, that is **New Year**'s Day in the ancient Roman calendar. In both cases, the number thirteen, accounted for by folklore in terms of Jesus Christ and his twelve disciples, is more likely to be pure **New Year** symbolism, standing for the sun and the year's twelve months.

In ancient Egypt, the religious **New Year** that began on the first day of the month of Thoth (marked by the rise of the brightest star Sirius in conjunction with the sunrise around mid-July) was solemnized by lighting a taper with **new fire** in Karnak's sacred precinct. Outside it, friends and relatives exchanged wishes and small gourds of the water drawn at dawn (to repeat divine creation at the dawn of time) by priests who would distribute it at the conclusion of the procession of the supreme sun god Amon's huge and precious water jar, as a magic symbol of the flooding of the Nile just starting in the south. Likewise in Great Britain, "**New Year** Water" drawn from a town's public water supply (a well, spring, or river) was widely presumed to bring good fortune to all it touched, be it people, beasts, or implements. Competition was sometimes fierce between families to be the first to get the water at dawn on **New Year**'s Day; they might camp all night around a well and fight for access to it in the morning. This water was often kept in bottles all year long, like the water blessed on **Epiphany** by Orthodox priests or that drawn from the local fountain on the dawn of **Christmas** (when it was not holy water from the September 14 **Holy Cross** service) in Greece in order to make the yeast needed for baking bread over the coming year. There, the distinct rite of the "renewal of water" is also observed on January 1 as

Saint Basil's Day. All containers in the house must be emptied of water and replenished with "Saint Basil's water" obtained from the well that morning, following rites that usually involve food offerings to the Nereid water spirit dwelling in the spring or fountain. Thus, in Aetolia, corn is thrown into this body of water by a child who then says, "May riches flow as water flows" but is not to utter one word, neither on the way to fetch the "speechless water" nor on the way back home, where all will drink from it and wash with it. On account of its reputed curative properties, water was also drawn in strict ritual silence from brooks and fountains on **Easter** morning in folklore ranging from Germany to French Canada, where it is even bottled by mineral water plants to be sold in drugstores, with profits going to charities. If such **New Year** magical practices sometimes ended up on **Christmas** or **Easter**, the Western Church had long projected **Easter**-like sacrificial symbolism onto **New Year**'s Day by making it the feast of the **Circumcision**, honoring the first shedding of Christ's blood eight days after his **Nativity**, as Jewish law demanded of male infants.

Shapeshifting and Gift-Giving

But the Church did not tolerate as easily other age-old pagan **New Year** customs. Christian authors consistently condemned **New Year** deer and bull masquerades, especially after their religion became official in the Roman Empire. For putting on an animal's head meant playing at being the god it stood for and overwriting the image of God in man as restored in Christ as God-Man. This did not stop most people, even though they were baptized believers, from going through the motions of their Celtic ancestors' rituals that made them one with the deer-god Cernunnos. He was known in Britain as Hern or "Old Hornie"—hence the word "horny," originally referring to the sexual energy of a beast as displayed in the yearly renewal of its horns. (The reason for **New Year** kissing under the mistletoe is also that this plant is a fertility symbol, since it is still green and growing white fruits in the middle of winter.) Identifying with the deer made sense as the seeds of a **New Year** were sown. But access to the Kingdom of God beyond time depended on personal faith, not on biological reproduction over time. As Saint Maximus of Turin put it around the turn of the sixth century in his Sermon No. 64 (p. 156): "How then are you able to celebrate the Lord's **Epiphany** religiously when, with your greatest devotion, you have also celebrated the **kalends of Janus**?" The first resolution of a Church synod held in Auxerre in Burgundy in 603, renewing canon 23 of the Synod of Tours that had officialized the *Dodecahemeron* or Twelve Days of **Christmas** in 567 (the better to control pre-Christian survivals), was to ban both the wearing of masks and the exchange of **New Year** gifts on January 1.

Generally consisting in money (referred to as "*stips*" in this festive context), these seasonal gifts were called *strenae* in ancient Rome, where, for instance, schoolmasters expected them from their pupils, by courtesy of the parents. Derivations of this old Latin word are still quite common in modern Romance languages, with the same basic meaning of **New Year** or **Christmas** presents. From its French form *étrenne* has come the verb *étrenner,* to refer to the tentative and playful, yet solemn, first use of a new object. This was just the point of the Roman *strenae:* to ensure auspicious beginnings so that good fortune would spread over the coming year from its highly sensitive first day.

Starting the New Year on the Right Foot

Presents were part of a whole range of ways of starting the **New Year** on the right foot. Tripping on the threshold of the house when setting out on a journey was a bad omen at any time of year. But January was the month of Janus, the god of thresholds—like those between different realms: the divine and the human, past and fu-

ture, the old year and the new. The poet Ovid portrayed the god Janus explaining to him in these terms various January 1 customs. On this holiday, people did not just rest; they also made a symbolic show of attending to their daily occupations, since being inactive on the first day of the year might make them lazy all year. Thus, the judges would sit without giving out sentences, the troops would be gathered with their insignia, peasants would put a hand to various tasks. The latter would invoke Janus first in their sacrifices to Mars to purify their land, since he was the mediator between mankind and the gods, the *Janitor* at the door, as well as the god of beginnings. Not only prayers, but all words, had their full weight on this day when the gods' ears were open like the doors of their temples. So Romans tried to avoid quarrels and idle talk and wished each other well as a good omen—the origin of our season's greetings. They offered sweets so that the whole year might keep the sweet taste of its beginnings, from the three traditional gifts: dates, figs, and honey, given in a white jar.

This is also why Greeks still break a pomegranate over the threshold on **New Year**'s Day. They always make sure the dinner table is laden with fruits, honey, olive branches, and other symbols of happiness. These include many cold and hot dishes as a good omen for the year (not unlike the *Sofrah Navrozi* table in Iranian homes on **Naw Ruz**, the ancient Persian **New Year** that is celebrated on the spring equinox), as well as the dead relatives' portion of "**Saint Basil**'s colybes"—corn cakes that keep away evil and spells. Conversely, coffee should not be drunk or ground, as it could give its bitter taste to the year. Greek housewives still offer buns, cakes, nuts, or coins to children on this day when they are joined by the grown-ups in going from door to door singing *kalandai* (carols) as on **Christmas**. But this time, they all convey their wishes by tapping every member of the family on the back with a green rod, among other symbolic actions they may perform to secure the household's happiness and prosperity over the coming year, in addition to each carrying an auspicious object: an apple, an orange, a paper ship, or a paper star. In some parts of Greece, windows and doors are left open all day for all comers to get a piece of cake. Front doors are hung with wild lily (brought on the way back from getting "speechless water" to touch the head of everyone in the house with wishes for a happy **New Year**) around Marathon, with wild hyacinth in Athens, but most often with olive or laurel branches, as used to be done in Constantinople. This former Eastern imperial capital relayed to the Greek populations of northern Turkey an ancient Roman custom of replacing the old olive branch over the fireplace with a fresh one.

As a sign of joy and ritual purity, it was dressed in white that the Romans went to Capitol Hill to attend the inauguration of the new consuls. The consuls wore the new purple robes of their office as they sat for the first time in their ivory chairs, which had just been carried separately in a procession to the temple of Jupiter. There, young bulls, raised in sacred enclosures and free of the stain of labor, were sacrificed to please the gods, after the omens about the coming year discerned on the dawn horizon by an official augur had been announced to the people. Saffron was burned in the gilded temples of the Capitol, and the golden reflections of the crackling fires were also very auspicious. Senators, knights, and commoners who could afford it brought money to the Emperor, with which he bought statues of the gods. Poor plebeians ("clients") would offer their wealthy patrician protectors ("patrons") a bronze coin of the lowest denomination—the *as* with which the Roman currency started, and which appropriately bore the two-faced effigy of Janus. No matter the value of the money offered, the idea was that, as a gift, it was a favorable omen of good fortune.

This principle was called "saining" in British folklore, and translated into many superstitions also embedded in Far Eastern **New Year** customs (except that, as on the summer solstice **Midsummer** and **Dragon Boat festival**s, the Chinese thought it more auspicious to refrain from activity than to add to the upsurge of seasonal energies). Among these are the need to sweep the house by midnight so none of the dirt of the old year is carried over into the new on its first day, when nothing should be thrown out so fortune does not decrease over the year, and nothing should be washed or else a family member may be washed away, just as bills should be paid and debts settled by then so the year is not marked by a deficit. The same concept applied in Great Britain as in Greece and other countries to the "First Foot," the first visitor to cross the threshold of a private house on New Year's Day. Because his or her identity was also an omen for good or ill over the coming year, the visit of a neighbor or a friend was often arranged in advance so as to avoid the bad surprises that blind luck might otherwise bring. The visitor was warmly received, as he or she was supposed to bring small gifts for every person in the household, often replaced by flowers, mistletoe, or holly (or even a stone in Greece, where the resulting heap is thrown away after eight days). Such **New Year** visitation customs were entrenched in colonial Manhattan, where **Christmas** was a purely religious festival, as in England. This pattern endured until fairly recently in Scotland and France, and even in French Canada. There, **New Year**'s Day was the high point of holiday season revelry in large family gatherings, though it began on a solemn note with the (grand)father's formal blessing of his kneeling children, young and old. The grownup ones who had moved out would rush to his feet to receive it as soon as they entered the house. Only later would one think of the *étrennes*, but soon thereafter groups of men would start dropping in on their rounds of **New Year** visits, kissing the ladies, taking a drink, and giving their wishes before leaving their cards.

Whereas in many parts of continental Europe, the Protestant Reformation and Catholic Counterreformation had often shifted **New Year** presents and other customs to **Epiphany**, Anglicans eventually blended them into their pious observance of **Christmas**, regarding **New Year**'s Day as a pagan affair. In the newly independent United States of America, the kind of riotous urban street revelry out of which Philadelphia's **New Year**'s Day Mummers' Parade later evolved was still frowned upon in respectable circles. There was long some hesitation in these quarters about the most suitable date for a gentrified revival of Manhattan seasonal customs: **Christmas** or **New Year**'s Day? **Christmas** won out in its current form due to the wide popularity of Clement Clarke Moore's poem *A Visit from* **Saint Nicholas**, the work of an Episcopalian, shaped by Anglican tradition.

A Springtime New Year's Day

In ancient Rome too, the attributes of the winter solstice and **New Year**'s Day were somewhat interchangeable, due no doubt to the close analogy between the shortening, then increasing length of days and the diminishing, then rising number of days. When Ovid asked Janus why the **New Year** began in winter, the god's answer pointed to the winter solstice. "Winter has the first new sun and the last old one: So Phoebus [the sun] and the year begin the same"(*Fasti* 1:163–164, p. 8). Ovid had been arguing that springtime would have been a more obvious starting point for the year, as it had been for his distant forebears. He saw as evidence that the Roman year used to begin at the *calends* of March the practice still observed in his day of putting new laurel trees and removing the old in front of the ancient Curia and Regia temples on March 1. Laurel had purifying properties as the symbolic plant of Phoebus-Apollo, the sun god. The Roman names of the months we still use today, when they include a number, are obviously counted from March, two months later than January. Thus, Septem-ber is not the seventh month its name implies, but the ninth, and so on to the "tenth"—December—in twelfth place. It had been so for centuries when Ovid was writing his *Fasti* at the beginning of the Roman Empire. Yet the "**New Year**" inauguration of consuls had only been set on January 1 since 153 B.C.E.; before that, starting in 222 B.C.E., it had been performed on the fifteenth of March (the ides) and for a while in the fourth century B.C.E., on the first of March (the calends). To this day in parts of Switzerland on what is called *Chalanda marz,* young people crack whips and sound bells of all sizes, like hellish **carnival** music in the chaotic gap between two years.

This "old" March 1 **New Year** was the one that the Vestal Virgins had always observed in their temple on the Forum, by putting out the sacred fire they kept on its hidden altar, to then rekindle it by the archaic method of rubbing two pieces of wood from certain auspicious trees. Likewise in parts of Greece, there was until recently a custom of lighting a new fire on March 1 after putting out the old fire the previous day. In ancient times, the druids used a method similar to that of the Vestals (not to mention the Aztecs at their **New Fire Ceremony** every fifty-two years) to rekindle their sacred fires, and from them, all the fires of Celtic lands; only they did it two months later on **Beltane**, the feast of Bel, their version of the sun god Apollo, who is triumphant on **May Day**. Conversely, the humble Christ Child, as the "Sun of Righteousness," was later welcomed in British, French, and Balkan homes in the darkest night of winter with the solemn lighting of the **Yule** log, recalling old springtime fire rituals long connected with the **New Year** in Rome.

See also Annunciation; Beautiful Festival of the Valley; Carnival; Christmas; Conception and Birth of the Virgin Mary; Dragon Boat Festival; Easter; Elevation of the Cross; Epiphany; Feast of Fools; Holi; Lupercalia; Matronalia; May Day; Naw Ruz; New Fire Ceremony; New Year (China, Korea), New

Year (Japan); Nyepí; Panathenaea; Saint
Nicholas; Samhain; Saturnalia; Vestalia

References

Edwin Oliver James. *Seasonal Feasts and Festivals.*
New York: Barnes and Noble, 1961.

Raymond Montpetit. *Le Temps des fêtes au
Québec.* Montreal, Canada: Les Éditions de
l'Homme, 1978.

Stephen Nissenbaum. *The Battle for Christmas.*
New York: Knopf, 1997.

Ovid. *Fasti.* Tr. A. J. Boyle and R. D. Woodard.
Harmondsworth, Middlesex, UK: Penguin
Books, 2000.

Max L. Raab. *Strut!* (Documentary film
about Philadelphia's New Year's Day
Mummers' Parade.) Max L. Raab
Productions, 2002.

The Sermons of Saint Maximus of Turin. Tr.
Boniface Ramsey. New York: Newman Press,
"Ancient Christian Writers" No. 50, 1989.

NEW YEAR FOR ANIMALS, NEW YEAR FOR KINGS, NEW YEAR FOR TREES, NEW YEAR FOR YEARS

See Tu bi-Shevat

NEXIUHILPILITZLI

See New Fire Ceremony

NGURLMAK

See Kunapipi

NIGHT OF ONIONS

See Khoiak and Heb-Sed

NIGHT OF POWER

See Ramadan

NIGHT OF SHA'BAAN

See Ashura

NIGHT OF SHIVA

See Mahashivaratri

NIGHT OF THE PRINCIPLE

See Lantern Festival

NINETEEN-DAY FEAST (BAHÁ'ISM)

Recurring on the first day of all nineteen weeks
of a 361-day year (plus four extra intercalary
days called *ayyám-há* to match the solar year),
the **Nineteen-Day Feast**, or **Bahá,** is central to
the practice of the Bahá'í faith, and it is the
touchstone and model of its humanitarian vision of religiously guided direct democracy. It
fulfills both a spiritual and administrative function at the grassroots level of the local assemblies that have to be constituted wherever at
least nine Bahá'ís are living.

Principle

The **Nineteen-Day Feast** was instituted by the
Bab, the Forerunner of the Bahá'í faith, and ratified by its founder Bahá'ullah in his holy book
the *Akdas,* so that his followers would meet and
express friendship and love, thereby manifest-
ing the divine mysteries. According to Bahá'ullah's son Abdul-Baha, the goal of the festival is
to establish concord, uniting hearts by frater-
nization in mutual help. These are at the basis
of society, because human beings cannot exist
without a tangible link between them. Cooper-
ation and mutual help are the preconditions for
the progress of any important movement, and
this is why the **Nineteen-Day Feast** was described by Bahá'ullah as the very foundation of
the new world order he came to build, even
though, strictly speaking, it does not constitute
an obligation like temperance, the three daily
prayers, or the annual week of fasting, **'Alá**
(which is derived from the Moslem holy fast
month of **Ramadan**).

Symbolism

Monthly units are replaced by nineteen-day
weeks in the Bahá'í calendar, similar in this to
the traditional calendars of Central America

and Indonesia. What is unique to it, however, is the perfect symmetry between the weekly and yearly cycles, since the nineteen weeks of the year have the same names as the nineteen days of the week, of which 'Alá is the last, immediately followed by Bahá, the first day of another week, when the Nineteen-Day Feast is held. There might then be readings from the *Béyan,* the holy book of the Bab, organized in strict parallel to the calendar he devised, in nineteen-chapter sections called *vahid,* as are nineteen-year Metonic cycles (numbering exactly 235 full moon cycles), nineteen of which add up to a *kull-i-shay,* a cycle of 361 years of 361 days. Similarly, if the nineteen sections of the *Béyan* had been completed as planned, the number of chapters in the Babi holy book would have added up to 361, "the number of all things" following which God is supposed to have organized Creation, since it is the square of nineteen as the number of unity. But it was probably chosen because it "most closely approximates 19.1113, the square root of the total number of days in the solar year, 365.2422. In other words, the Bahá'is' nineteen-day weekly cycle is the closest approximation of the square root of the annual cycle. By introducing it, they have managed to establish the most symmetrical relationship possible between the week and the year, which no one else throughout history has ever managed to accomplish" (Zerubavel 1985, p. 49).

Practice

The Nineteen-Day Feast that makes this grand unified rhythm of Bahá'í time a concrete regulator of believers' lives should unfold in three stages, of which the first two appear to owe a lot to the Friday sermon at the Muslims' Day of Assembly. The first part, entirely spiritual in character, is devoted to readings from Bahá'í and other sacred scriptures such as the Bible and the Koran. The second part is reserved for a general consultation addressing the business of the local community as well as national and international concerns of the faith. It is through the channel of the Nineteen-Day Feast that individual believers can forward their suggestions and recommendations to the National Spiritual Assembly, provided they have first been approved by their own community and submitted to the Local Assembly. The National or Local Assembly's answer to these resolutions is then conveyed to the local community at the next Nineteen-Day Feast.

The third part of Bahá observances consists in informal socializing, usually around some snacks and nonalcoholic beverages, though the Bab insisted that sharing a glass of water could even be enough, because the main thing is to preserve and manifest the spiritual imprint of the first part of the festival. Purity is of the essence, or else the holy festival is profaned. This should be expressed by physical cleanliness and more importantly by a clean heart, which does not have any room for the seeds of discord in idle worldly talk but instead radiates generosity in friendly faces and courteous demeanor. On this condition, Bahá'ullah could say he would always be in the midst of his disciples as long as he could breathe this aroma of friendship at their assemblies. His successor Abdul-Baha said the same thing about his own postmortem presence at the Nineteen-Day Feast, going so far as to suggest it had the same spiritual efficacy for Bahá'ís as the Lord's Supper for Christians at Sunday worship.

Responsibilities

In view of these spiritual benefits and the responsibilities they entail, it is said that Bahá'ís should consider this festival as the crucible of their activities, of their participation in the mystery of holy utterances, of their oneness in a universality that leaves far behind all limitations of class, race, nationality, religion, or personality. It is thus incumbent upon every Bahá'í to regularly attend the Nineteen-Day Feasts, except if he or she is ill or traveling out of town. Bahá'ís from other localities may also attend, as well as minors who have made their declaration of faith and have already started to study the teachings. The believers who are entitled to partake in this religious experiment in grassroots democracy are expected to arrange their personal schedule accordingly, in compliance with the Bahá'í calendar.

See also Day of Assembly; New Fire Ceremony; Nyepí; Passover; Ramadan; Sunday

References

Hushmand Fathea'zam. *The New Garden.* New Delhi: Bahá'í Publishing Trust, 1962.

National Spiritual Assembly of the Bahá'ís of Australia. *Local Spiritual Assembly Handbook.* Mona Vale, Australia: Bahá'í Publications Australia, 1996.

Eviatar Zerubavel. *The Seven Day Circle. The History and Meaning of the Week.* Chicago: University of Chicago Press, 1985.

▌NINTH DAY

See Sekku

▌NINTH OF AV

See Tisha be-Av

▌NORUZ

See Naw Ruz

▌NOUMENIA (GREECE)

Throughout the Greek world, every month began with a festival meant to coincide in principle with the appearance of the first visible sign of the **new moon**, after which it was known as a **Noumenia**.

Monthly Festivals

Most of the other days of the first decade of any month, while the moon was waxing, were actually festival days in Athens. That of the second day was dedicated to *agathos daimon,* the "good demon" or genius of the earth. The third day was Athena's birthday, and the fourth was that of Heracles, Hermes, and Aphrodite, when her companion Eros was also honored. Aristotle's disciple Theophrastos noted (*Characters* 16) that, on that same day, the superstitious also made offerings to the androgynous god Hermaphroditus born of the two deities combined in their name. There was no festival on the fifth day, but, in all of Greece, one was dedicated to the moon goddess Artemis on the sixth as her birthday, as was another to the sun god Apollo on the seventh. Athens' founding hero Theseus was honored on the eighth day, along with his father the sea god Poseidon.

The Holiest of Days

While no other deity but Apollo ever had its festival concurrently with his birthday on the seventh, no annual festival whatever included the **Noumenia**. The philosopher Plutarch (*Moralia* 828A) could therefore refer to it as the "holiest of days." A quarter of attested financial transactions in the historical record for Athens occurred on monthly festival days (as opposed to a handful during annual festivals). It should therefore come as no surprise that a big market was held in the city on the first of every month. Men would still find the time to practice athletics at the palaestra, as well as to hold banquets. Back home, frankincense was to be placed on the statues of the gods as a regular part of the routine of private religious rites.

See also Rosh Hodesh

References

Benjamin Dean Meritt. *The Athenian Year.* Berkeley: University of California, 1961.

Jon Mikalson. *The Sacred and Civil Calendar of the Athenian Year.* Princeton, NJ: Princeton University Press, 1975.

H. W. Parke. *Festivals of the Athenians.* Ithaca, NY: Cornell University Press, 1977.

▌NUNTARIYASHAS

See KI.LAM

NU YAH

See Midwinter

NYEPÍ (HINDUISM)

As the purification of the whole island around the spring equinox, **Nyepí** is Bali's most important annual festival. It is also the only one of island-wide significance in the lunisolar *saka* ("monthly") calendar of Hindu origin—as opposed to the acosmic *wuku* ("weekly") calendar of Javanese origin, counting 210 days (that is all possible combinations of the five-, six-, and seven-day weekly cycles out of nine overlapping cycles of two to ten days), the one most used for Bali's exceptionally complex sequence of ceremonies. Fundamentally different from them in being seasonal rather than occurring at wildly divergent points of Nature's cycles from one time to the next (much more so that in the case of the 354-day Islamic lunar calendar followed by most Indonesians outside the last Hindu stronghold that Bali remains), **Nyepí** is considered to be **New Year**'s Day. And yet, it actually comes on the first day of the tenth month, called Kadasa, that is **Vaishakha** in the particular Hindu calendar it comes from, though its Balinese version is one month ahead in the names used, so this one would correspond to Chaitra (March–April) in parts of India.

Sweepings of the Year

Lasting a couple of days, **Nyepí** really begins at the end of the previous month with *Tilem Kasanga,* the "new moon of Kasanga," which is the Balinese equivalent of the Hindu month of Chaitra. This is when Yama, Hindu Lord of Hell, sweeps it of devils and ghosts. These evil spirits fall on Bali with a great din, so that the entire island and every village is unsafe and needs to be purified. Since people will therefore try to stay indoors and put out fires and lights on **Nyepí** itself, the food for that day needs to be prepared in advance. This keeps the whole community busy on the days leading up to **Nyepí**, when there are also processions to take the gods to bathe in the sea. At the crossroads where demons congregate, scaffolds need to be built for priests, along with altars for the offerings they will make to both gods and demons in a great purification called *metjaru.*

Offerings to Demons and Gods

On this day, there is unrestricted gambling in connection with the universal cockfighting that is intimately related to this ceremony, since the land is cured by the spilling of blood over impure earth, which feeds and appeases demons as the metjaru does. Countless dead roosters can be taken home afterwards to serve as the next day's **Nyepí** meal, while in Bali's capital Denpasar, children are offered decorated trays of cakes and sweets by the officials of each ward or *banjar.* Before sunset, the demons have to be lured by their share in the great offering in order to then be expelled by the powerful curses of the priests. This offering is set nearer to the ground than the high platforms bearing offerings to the high gods of the Hindu Triad as well as to deified ancestors. Offerings to the sun god Surya are placed on an even higher platform to the east, and a somewhat lower one is set across from them for the eight *pedanda* or brahmin priests, who officiate with chants and bell-ringing facing the direction of the rising sun. When he is not seated alongside them on his own smaller, lower platform, the *sengguhu,* or lower-caste priest dealing with evil spirits, faces north toward an image of their master Batara Kala, drawn in rice flour on the ground and surrounded by a little bamboo fence to keep dogs away. A low fence of woven palm leaves also protects the manifold offerings symbolically arranged according to color-coding among the eight points of the compass. They might include money and utensils, all sorts of alcoholic drink, meat from all the beasts of Bali, along with samples of all the fruits and seed found on the Indonesian island, held by hundreds of banana leaves. It takes months to collect all these ingredients, so that the majority are wilted and decomposed by the time **Nyepí** arrives—reflecting a certain contempt for the coarse lower beings who accept such offerings laid on the ground for them to absorb in this earthy fashion. Once the ceremonies are over, the poor are allowed to loot the money and any other offerings that can still be of use to humans.

From Pandemonium to Sabbath

But first, consecrated rice, holy water, and sacred fire to light every hearth anew (as in many a similar **new fire ceremony** elsewhere on the globe) are distributed to the *klihans banjar* or ward heads for them to pass on to every head of a household in turn. In some places, small boys then fight with fire in imitation of former battles of this kind between banjars. Everywhere, firecrackers are set off and people run through the streets in groups, their faces and bodies painted, carrying torches on the end of long poles and beating drums, gongs, and cans (not to mention the trees and the ground) as they yell over and over again, "*Megedi!*"—that is, "Get out!" As in many **New Year** customs from China through Russia to Scotland, all this racket is meant both to imitate and scare away evil spirits—in this case, the ones that have been purposely attracted by the offerings, only to be ritually expelled at the "great offering," wherever they may still lurk. This pandemonium may go on well past midnight on the eve of "bringing the land to silence"—which is the meaning of **Nyepí**. For a bit like the **Sabbath**, this is supposed to be a day of absolute stillness, when people stay at home, road traffic is normally forbidden, no light or fire is permitted (not even to light a cigarette), no work is to be performed, and no sexual activity is allowed, while the bodies of the recently deceased need to be removed from the house (unless they happen to have received the consecration to read the holy scriptures like the brahmins). But there are plenty of local variations in these observances, and many exceptions to their rules. In Denpasar, people go about doing their **New Year** visits, and there are certain seasonal outdoor games between boys and girls. In some villages, walking outside is allowed as long as nothing is carried, while in others, as in Western **carnivals** or year-end festivals, all sexual restraints are lifted at community picnics in the rice paddies. This is probably a local method to promote their fertility by imitative magic.

The Ritual Pacing of Rice Planting

Yet normally, no one may enter the rice fields on the special **Nyepí** days of "restriction" observed in every village, on pain of heavy fines. This is a time to reaffirm boundaries between villages and their respective fields, be it in space (as at ancient Roman **Terminalia**) by stretching lines or erecting gates over the roads where they end, or in time. Official pacemakers are responsible for setting **Nyepí** as the holiday preceding the twenty-day period within which all planting has to be done, also on pain of heavy fines for transgressors and those who abet them. (However, certain transplanting rites need to be performed along with offerings to rice deities on the eve of **Nyepí**.) Strict enforcement is not only necessary to maintain work discipline and efficient division of labor, but also for ecological reasons having to do with water, disease, and pest control. The vermin infestations unleashed by state-sponsored attempts to increase productivity by having several planting cycles a year have proved the soundness of the traditional wisdom regulating the yearly agricultural calendar of every village, as enshrined in the religious ceremonies surrounding **Nyepí** in Bali.

See also Carnival; Feast of Fools; May Day; New Fire Ceremony; New Year (China, Korea), New Year (Japan); New Year (West); Nineteen-Day

Feast; Rogations; Sabbath; Saturnalia; Terminalia; Vaishakha and Vaisakhi

References

Miguel Covarrubias. *Island of Bali.* New York: Knopf, 1973.

F. A. Liefrinck, et al. *Bali: Studies in Life, Thought and Ritual.* Dordrecht, The Netherlands: Foris Publications Holland, 1984.

David Suzuki with Amanda McConnell. *The Sacred Balance: Rediscovering Our Place in Nature.* Vancouver, Canada: Greystone, 1997.

O-BON
See Days of the Dead (China, Korea, Japan)

OCTOBER HORSE
See Games (Rome)

ODWIRA
See Adae

OENACH
See Lugnasad

OKEEPA
See Sun Dance

OKHI DAY
See Protection of the Mother of God

OKUNCHI
See Sekku

OLD CHRISTMAS
See Epiphany

OLENZARO
See Christmas

OLYMPIC GAMES
See Games (Greece)

OMER
See Lag ba-Omer

ON-MATSURI
See Kasuga Festivals

ONNA SHOGATSU
See New Year (Japan)

OPALIA
See Saturnalia

OPET
See Beautiful Festival of the Valley

ORIGIN (DAY OF)
See New Year (Japan)

ÒRUNMILÀ (FESTIVAL OF)
See Òsun Festival

OSCHOPHORIA
See Dionysia

OSHOGATSU
See New Year (Japan)

OSIRIS (FESTIVAL OF)
See Khoiak

▶ ÒSUN FESTIVAL (YORUBA)

A major goddess of the Yoruba people that makes up one-eighth of Benin's population and over a fifth of Nigeria's, and whose cult was brought by slaves to the Caribbean and South America, **Òsun Sèègèsí** (pronounced "Oh-shun Sheh-geh-see") or "**Òsun** who owns the beaded comb" has her traditional yearly festival in the western Nigerian town of Òsogbo (a contraction of the Yoruba *Oso Igbo* for "spirit of the forest"), by the river bearing her name. It has also been observed by Yoruba religious lineages active in the United States since the late twentieth century, normally some time in August. Devotees of **Òsun** flock to a sacred riverside grove to ask favors of or give thanks to this elegant amazon, mistress of the *àjé* (ambivalent "powerful beings"), who controls childbirth.

Mythical Beginnings

Many *orisa* (pronounced "oh-ree-shah") or "head guardians" (that is, Yoruba deities or deified ancestors) have **Òsun** as a name. It refers to the "seeping out" of a source, usually because, in their myth, they turn into a river, and they have their seat at some point along the **Òsun** River in the state of the same name created in southwestern Nigeria in 1991. But **Òsun** Òsogbo is considered to be the real goddess **Òsun** of the river along which she is most widely worshipped, as it was heard to say Òsogbo (pronounced "oh-shog-boh")—that is, "all my pots of indigo dye have been broken"— when two refugees from a drought affecting their respective homelands in the eighteenth century felled one of the trees of her sacred grove of dye-producing plants into the water. They agreed to move their new settlement to the marketplace where their heirs' palace now stands in the town therefore known as Òsogbo. It is the center of her cult, attracting devotees and tourists every year in the rainy season, around early August, when the river's flow is abundant, fresh, and sweet to the taste, for the great festival of **Òsun**.

At an appointed time after the festival of **Òrunmilà** (one of **Òsun**'s two husbands, in addition to the thunder god Shango), Òsogbo's traditional ruler: the Atáója, summons this god's priest or *babaláwo* ("father of mysteries") to his palace to perform divination that will reveal the specific date and particular sacrifices **Òsun** has in mind for her upcoming festival day. The festive season leading up to it officially begins once the Atáója, as her representative, makes her wishes public at the end of the first of many solemn royal processions—to her shrine at the market in this case. There, he accepts on her behalf communal gifts of food and drink that will be shared among visitors at his palace later that day. Lesser local rulers also come with gifts—of money as well as in kind— to renew their allegiance to the Atáója and the goddess he stands for. Because she is known for promoting childbirth, women who have had a baby since the last festival carry them in the procession, in which the many children who have likewise been devoted to her also figure prominently. Women and children especially wear the golden colors of **Òsun**'s divine authority, delegated to the Atáója by the covenant his ancestors made with the local goddess—possibly in the guise of an earlier lineage of female rulers.

The Lighting of the Sixteen Lamps

Four days after the announcement of the festival's proceedings, drummers in the palace courtyard lead worshippers in calling upon the spirits of **Òsun** and other orisa to join in its official opening. They are trained in the elaborate *Ifá* divination method central to Yoruba life and sacred lore. Yet it is the gift of Òrunmilà (mediator between heaven and earth) to his wife **Òsun** of a simpler alternate method just for women that is being commemorated with the Lighting of the Sixteen Candles (*olójùmérindínlógún*), namely the sixteen-cowrie divination now spread from Africa to the New World. It also reflects the sixteen palm nuts used instead of these shells in standard Ifá divination, the sixteen major divisions of the Ifá corpus of texts, and the sixteen primordial orisa who came down from heaven to organize the world for human life. Their plans went awry at first because, being males, they neglected to include **Òsun** in them, as she was just a woman, and they failed to realize the vital role she had to play in world order as leader of the *àjé* ("powerful beings"). The Supreme Being Olódùmarè himself, who had given her this role, had to advise the sixteen major orisa to consult with the Great Mother **Òsun**, who demanded initiation for herself and "women like her" to make up for the earlier slight and restore the cosmic balance of energies.

To celebrate women's knowledge and power as a divine gift, thousands of people gather around a brass column holding sixteen receptacles in which cotton and palm oil are kept burning from dusk to dawn. **Òsun**'s clergy—of all ranks and both genders—goes back and forth between the sixteen lamps and the secret rituals it performs indoors, out of sight of the uninitiated. The Atáója and the Iyá **Òsun**, or chief priestess, also come out of their adjacent dwellings three times to lead the people in joyous invocation of deities and ancestors by dancing around the lamps behind their respective musicians before returning inside to worship. Hunters open their path by firing into the air, in a kind of reenactment of the way Òsogbo's two founding fathers were led to their new home by an elephant hunt.

The Òsun Festival Proper

Eight days later, a virgin chosen from the ruling family, the Arugbá, carrier of the sacrifice, assisted by the Àwòrò (an administrator of **Òsun**'s clergy) after early morning public prayers inside her shrine on palace grounds, takes the offerings to her sacred grove by the **Òsun** River. They will renew the covenant between its goddess, her representatives, and Òsogbo Township. The Atáója, as "He who

feeds the fish with his own hands" (the meaning of his title), is the one who officially pours the offerings into the river, along with the Iyá **Òsun** and the Àwòrò, in thanksgiving for the past year's blessings and to secure them again over the coming year. He does this after performing certain rites with them and other high clergy in the seclusion of a sacred precinct whose walls are guarded by a few sitting babaláwo. But first, he addresses his people and visitors from his temporary throne in the grove, having entered it in full regalia with his court along a ceremonial path cleared by trumpeters and drummers under general acclaim.

While he is out of view, worshippers and lower clergy carry on with their festive song and dance. The tone is set by troupes of musicians and dancers representing a variety of orisa, whose worshippers gather around their statues set at the base of trees, while those of **Òsun** are covered with palm fronds (unlike on previous days). Among the performances that stand out are the colorful and acrobatic *Egúngún* masquerade, embodying the ancestors' power to sanction departures from the Yoruba way, and the parade of *omode Òsun*— "children of **Òsun**," sent to their mothers because they made proper sacrifices for this blessing on the goddess's previous festivals. Such offerings typically consist of corn meal, bean-loaves, and pounded yam with the Yánrin vegetable, but snails and guinea-corn are among some other things she cannot even stand. Each year, women loudly promise the gifts they will bring this fertility goddess if she helps them have children, and those whose wish has been granted are also vociferous in their thanksgiving. The ones who used to be barren before this divine intervention go back to the river to perform special rituals with the Iyá **Òsun** and the Arugbá. Other people wash their faces in the river or drink its water after it has been blessed by its resident deity's acceptance of the yearly solemn sacrifice by king and clergy. Many in the wading multitudes on the riverbank fill containers with sacred water to use it over the year—either for ritual purposes or for its power to heal the sick.

All the while, people continue to gather outside the decorative walls of the sacred grove's entrance. Some rest between it and the nearby vending area, where fried fish or beans and other street foods are sold along with refreshments ranging from soft drinks to palm wine, while others seek out friends and relatives to chat and have fun with them. Many have their photograph taken. It is common for devotees to join in the dance of a passing troupe. Crowd control, including the creation and maintenance of passageways, is one of the tasks of the *olose* (pronounced "oh-loh-shey") or "whipping boys." But they also challenge each other with their whips in groups of two, four, or six; this staged fight, symbolizing the struggle against malevolent forces, keeps them at bay during the proceedings. They may yet face the concrete opposition of devout Muslims who object to the joyful pagan displays that only end that night at the palace across the street from the mosque.

See also Adae; Kokuzahn

References

J. Omosade Awolalu. *Yoruba Beliefs and Sacrificial Rites.* London: Longman, 1979.

Diedre Bádéjo. *Òsun Sèègèsi: The Elegant Deity of Wealth, Power, and Femininity.* Trenton, NJ and Asmara, Eritrea: African World Press, Inc., 1996.

William Bascom. *Sixteen Cowries: Yorùbá Divination from Africa to the New World.* Bloomington: Indiana University Press, 1980.

OUR LADY MESOSPORITISSA, OUR LADY POLYSPORITISSA

See Presentation of the Virgin Mary

OUR LADY'S HERB DAY, OUR LADY'S THIRTY DAYS

See Assumption

◗ PAI-PAI
See Matzu's Birthday

◗ PALIO
See Games (Rome)

◗ PALM SUNDAY (CHRISTIANITY)

Coming at the apex of the main fasting season on the last weekend before **Easter**, **Palm Sunday** (together with its Eastern forefeast **Lazarus Saturday**) is a joyful prelude to this celebration of Christ's Resurrection, prior to the intervening **Holy Week** of his Passion and death on the Cross. Its devotional focus is the Redeemer's brief moment of earthly triumph—the Entry of Christ into Jerusalem—where the palms waved at him by the crowd have become the pretext for many popular celebrations of springtime greenery. An ancient procession held on this feast fell into disuse in the Eastern Church at the turn of the second millennium of the Christian era, just when the Western Church took it up almost until the third.

Place in the Calendar

The Roman liturgy of **Holy Week** starts with the blessing of palms and a procession on Sunday. The previous week is known to Catholics as **Passion Week**, after Passion Sunday as the former name of **Palm Sunday** in Rome. For, until the tenth century, this last Sunday of **Lent** only commemorated the imminent Passion of Christ, rather than the Entry of Christ into Jerusalem that formed a joyous prelude to it. Matthew's version of the story of Christ's Passion has thus been solemnly read in its entirety on that day ever since the fifth century. For all of that time, across all changes of emphasis, it has been called in Latin by the ancient and ambivalent name of *Dominica in Palmis de Passione Domini*. **Passion Week** and **Holy Week** together form **Passiontide** in the Western Church.

The week leading up to **Palm Sunday** is called Palm Week in the East. It is also called **Dumb Week** in Greece, since no service is held in church except for one on the eve of **Lazarus Saturday**. In the Orthodox Church, **Palm Sunday**, along with its forefeast **Lazarus Saturday**, stand apart from both **Lent** and **Holy Week**. As the hinge between the longer fasting season and the short, but intense, final stretch to **Easter**, they are a semifestive break before renewed ascetic efforts.

Lazarus Saturday

In the Eastern Church, **Palm Sunday** is closely linked and intermingled with the commemoration of an episode that immediately precedes the triumphal Entry of Christ into Jerusalem. The previous Saturday is named after the beloved disciple whom Christ resurrected in Bethany, which was the starting point for his journey to Jerusalem the next day. This was a kind of prophecy of the agony awaiting him there, as well as of the ultimate triumph of his own resurrection. For the resurrection of Lazarus at the command of Jesus heralded the universal resurrection at the end of days. If, as a man, Jesus cried over his friend's death and wanted to undo it, as God himself, Christ would actually have had it in his power to call him back to life.

In Greece, **Lazarus Saturday** is popularly known as the **First Easter** on account of the disciple's death and resurrection, which not only prefigured Christ's, but also echoed those of the youthful gods Adonis and Attis in pagan springtime rituals, as evidenced in the ancient practice of the impersonation of the dead Lazarus by a child, which is still to be seen in Cyprus. All around Greece, it is evoked by other, usually pictorial, means in children's door-to-door funeral processions as they sing *Lazarakia* hymns, for which each child is given a special *lazaros* bun. Such buns are still baked by some Greek communities in the New World, even if the processions have failed to cross the ocean. In Bulgaria, it is girls who go singing and dancing in the homes of acquaintances on **Lazaritsa** (as this day is known there), as a women's rite of passage from childhood to maidenhood.

The Entry of Christ into Jerusalem

News of the resurrection by Jesus of his friend Lazarus, crowning all the other miracles he had performed, brought crowds to cheer him as he entered the holy capital city, joyfully welcoming him as the long-awaited Messiah who would restore the Kingdom of Israel. Christ came seated on a young donkey as the prophet Zechariah had foretold of the future king, the

way King David himself had once victoriously entered the city. In the Biblical equivalent of a ticker-tape parade, the people of Jerusalem waved palm and olive branches to show their allegiance to Jesus as this victorious king. They even threw their garments in the way of this Son of David, much as they had done centuries earlier when they acclaimed Jehu as King of Israel (2 Kings 9:13). But the Kingdom of God Jesus came to establish was not to be confused with the temporal power the Jews expected to see restored and turned against foreign rule, as it was not of this world, consisting in Christ's victory over death through his obedience unto death. As they come with palms to celebrate the earthly triumph of Jesus as a prefiguration of his eternal victory, Christians are supposed to recall that they are heirs to the Kingdom of God only insofar as they are willing to go with Christ all the way through the dark tunnel of the Passion on the Cross, so as to come out the other end in the light of **Easter**.

Palms, Evergreens and Pussy Willows

Palm Sunday is a very festive occasion, one when the fasting rules of the season are relaxed. On Moscow's Red Square, there even used to be a toy and candy fair where the wealthy would show off. In France and Spain, it had become customary by the eighth century to imitate the Jews' acclamations of "Hosannah!" (an Aramaic expression of praise to God that also happens to be the word for a palm leaf) at Christ's coming, and by the ninth century the practice of bringing branches to church had spread in the West as in the East. Churches are decorated with palms in sunny regions, unless it is with olive or laurel branches where they are more available, as in certain parts of Mediterranean countries. Substitutes such as box-tree branches are used in northern climes, or even pussy willows as the first blossoms of spring in Russia, where this is **Pussy Willow Sunday**. Flowers and evergreens may also be used. Wherever they appear, palm leaves are often woven into different shapes, especially crosses. In Greece, a small cross is handed to each parishioner together with a myrtle or bay branch by the priest at the door of the church after the service. This bunch is called a *vaya* and will be propped with the family's holy images at home, as the pussy willow is in Russia, and its equivalents elsewhere. In many **Palm Sunday** customs, the blessed boughs should never be stuck with a sharp object, as doing so would cut their power to ward off evil and disease and to promote fertility in all living things, from trees and fields to barnyard animals and young brides, and even improve the productivity of inanimate objects such as boats and windmills.

Palm Sunday foliage is often brought to the tombs of the dead in Greece as in many parts of France. In the latter country, a 1961 survey showed that **Palm Sunday** stood alongside **All Saints** Day as the time of year when the largest number of people came to the cemeteries to pray for their dead. There, as in other Latin countries, they would plant box-tree branches blessed on **Palm Sunday** on their loved ones' graves and would often insist on being buried holding one in their hands as a token of the life hereafter. As an evergreen plant, the box-tree has been ascribed this funerary symbolic meaning since pre-Christian times, when it was dedicated to underworld deities Hades and **Cybele**.

In Russia and Central Europe, people had to eat the willows' pussies on **Palm Sunday** in order to avoid summer fevers. From Carelia, a largely Orthodox region of Finland straddling Russian territory, a related custom has spread to the rest of this mostly Lutheran Nordic country: asking people if they want to be touched with a pussy willow while saying a magic formula for health, in exchange for a reward from that person on **Easter** morning. This may be a traditional chocolate egg containing a ring or the more recent effigies of the **Easter** witches of folk tales and copper coffee pots for them to drink from. Healing properties were also ascribed to branches from the maypole made by the children in eastern Slovakia for the procession of **Flower Sunday** (as **Palm Sunday** is also known in Eastern Europe). People would throw their expensive garments or small boughs in its path, and give money or an egg or two to every child who offered them a wreath when they answered the question: "Do you wish for a new summer?" Such maypoles are decorated with flowers in Poland, with dry flowers and grain in Lithuania and Latvia, and with apples, oranges, and pretzels in Austria. In Germany, **Palm Sunday** is called **Green Sunday** because of all this greenery.

Palm Sunday Processions

Children of all ages already figured prominently in the festive procession observed in Jerusalem on **Palm Sunday** by the presumably Spanish pilgrim Etheria in the fourth century. Late in the afternoon, they would all run to the site of the **Ascension** outside Bethany, near the starting point of Christ's final progress toward Jerusalem, and the little ones would be held by their parents as the crowd, waving palm and olive branches, slowly escorted the bishop back to the city for the last evening service of a long day of celebrations. From Jerusalem, the practice of **Palm Sunday** processions spread to most Eastern Churches. Yet it somehow fell into disuse in Constantinople about a thousand years ago, being reduced in the Byzantine liturgy to an indoor procession after the Eucharist at the end of the service. At this point, the priest just carries around the church the icon depicting both the Resurrection of Lazarus and the Entry of Christ into Jerusalem.

Around the same time, the Roman Church was moving in the opposite direction in adopting and expanding upon the practice. Since the Middle Ages, **Palm Sunday** processions have taken place on the way to church, with the blessing of the palms being performed before Mass. Among Catholics, this used to be an elaborate ritual including a solemn procession just

In El Salvador, children hold palm leaves to celebrate Palm Sunday, the beginning of the Holy Week. (Reuters/Corbis)

outside church doors to symbolize the entry into the Heavenly Jerusalem made possible to the faithful by Christ's sacrifice on the Cross. For a long time, only the clergy went outside, but the people was included in the procession after 1955, before the whole affair was made less solemn and optionally more discreet in 1970. Despite a revival of some of these traditional rites in the Anglican and Episcopalian Churches since the nineteenth century, most Protestant churches do not observe them at all.

Likewise, a beloved and spectacular variant of the **Palm Sunday** procession has long been eliminated in all but a few Austrian and Alsatian hamlets, though there have recently been isolated efforts to revive it: the *Palmesel*—"Palm-Donkey." In the Rhineland and southern Germany, there used to be (since at least the

tenth century) a live reenactment of the Entry of Christ into Jerusalem on a donkey. Initially, the bishop himself might take the place of Christ on the donkey—or more often than not, on its wooden substitute on wheels, which, in many cases, included a wooden sculpture of Christ riding it. This vehicle eventually became a sacred object in its own right, and the Christ figure was often decorated with wreaths, sausage rings, and pretzels. This was eventually frowned upon by clerical authorities, especially after the Protestant Reformation banned the practice, while the Catholic Counterreformation discouraged it, and the "enlightened despotism" of Emperor Joseph II forcibly put an end to it in its last stronghold of Austria in the eighteenth century. In this process of repression, many Palm-Donkeys, which had been lovingly carved as a focus of civic pride, were publicly destroyed. Some museums and churches now cherish the few survivors as precious medieval artworks.

See also Ascension; Days of the Dead (West); Easter; Elevation of the Cross; Holy Week; Lent; May Day; Spring Festival of Cybele and Attis

References

Eileen Elizabeth Freeman, ed. *The Holy Week Book.* San Jose, CA: Resource Publications, 1979.

Mary Paloumpis Hallick. *The Treasured Traditions and Customs of the Orthodox Churches. A Fascinating Study of the Richness of Traditional Orthodox Religious Customs.* Minneapolis, MN: Light and Life Publishing Company, 2001.

Hugh Wybrew. *Orthodox Lent, Holy Week, and Easter: Liturgical Texts with Commentary.* Crestwood, NY: St. Vladimir's Seminary Press, 1997.

▶ PANATHENAEA (GREECE)

The greatest festival of ancient Athens was that of the city's patron goddess Athena Polias of the Erechtheion temple, celebrated every year on her birthday on the twenty-eighth of Hekatombeion, the first month of the Athenian calendar, toward August. A distinction arose under Pisistrates (600–527 B.C.E.) between the annual Lesser **Panathenaea** and the Greater **Panathenaea** this tyrant instituted in 566, held every four years with great pomp (to rival Pan-Hellenic **Games** like the **Olympics**) from the twenty-first to the twenty-ninth or thirtieth of Hekatombeion.

The Games

In this larger format, the **Panathenaea** began with a musical contest in the Odeon, built especially by the democratic statesman Pericles (*c.* 495–429 B.C.E.) as a venue for this substitute for the rhapsodies traditionally excerpted from epic poems to be recited on this occasion. Those of Homer had been collected and edited under the sponsorship of Pisistrates, who probably made a point of showcasing them in this festive setting in the first place. Among other innovations due to Pericles were song performances with flute or cithara accompaniment, as well as dithyrambs (poetic eulogies) sung by choruses as they circled the sacrificial altar. The award for the music event consisted in a gold wreath with a cash prize.

Next came the sporting events (many of them not **Olympic**), which were eventually concentrated in the Panathenaeic Stadium, built in the second half of the fourth century B.C.E. Gymnastic competitions were arranged by age and degree of difficulty and included wrestling, boxing, pancratium (combining the latter two), the pentathlon, and much racing. Equestrian contests of a military nature followed, be it on chariot (like the daredevil *àpobates* race testing the ability to dismount from one at full speed) or on horseback (like throwing a javelin at a target). The prizes, of which the first was worth five times the second, consisted in jars of oil from the Academy's olive trees. Many examples and imitations of these Panathenaeic prize amphoras have come down to us, with an image of Athena on one side, and a depiction of an athletic contest on the other. An ox was the prize for the sponsor and leader of the best group to perform a Pyrrhic war dance of Spartan origin, which had been introduced in Athens in the time of the tyrant Pisistrates. To commemorate his dynasty's demise, a muster of men was later held, as the city's ten tribes sent their strongest, most dashing warriors in teams to make a good impression in a kind of male beauty pageant. Such a gathering of armed citizens was a democratic demonstration, as it would not have been allowed under the tyranny. Like other contests, this was a liturgy, in the original Greek sense of the term, meaning "working for the people," since the festive event was voluntarily sponsored and organized by a wealthy citizen as a public service. Another example of a liturgy was the torch-race, where the winners earned their sponsor a water-jar. It coincided with a big "night festival" (*pannychis*) celebrated by choirs of boys and girls on the eve of the most important part of the Greater **Panathenaea**, the procession, as famously depicted on the friezes of the Parthenon, the grand temple of Athena Parthenos ("Virgin"). Like the "All-Athenian" festival itself, it testified to Athens' devotion to its patron, as well as to civic pride in the powerful and well-organized political unit it had fashioned out of many local tribes over a fairly large territory for a city-state.

The Procession

The greatest procession of the year assembled on the twenty-eighth of Hekatombeion before sunrise at the Pompeion, near the Dipylon Gate at the north end of the city. It set out through the Ceramicus cemetery, and then the agora or public square, on its way toward the Acropolis, in a neat cross-section of Athens's most important places. Priests and prophets, magistrates and treasurers, and the superintendents of sacrifice opened the march before generals, colonial envoys, and delegates of allied cities with offerings. As the future mothers of Athenian citizens, the city's maidens of marriageable age carried sacrificial vessels, censers, and baskets of cakes for offerings (hence their designation as *kanêphoroi* or "basket-carriers"), as they escorted the centerpiece of the procession (probably only taken out for the Greater **Panathenaea**): the new saffron-dyed robe for the *xoanon*—an ancient wooden sculpture of Athena in the Erechtheion temple, named after the mythical ancestor of Athenians, who was thought to have instituted their great civic festival. Athena's robe was suspended like a sail on the yardarm of a ship gliding on rollers, and spread out so that all could admire the workmanship of the embroidered depiction of the battle of the gods and the giants. Many women had put all their skill in completing the garment first begun by two of the *arrèphoroi* (girls aged between seven and eleven whom the chief magistrate would choose from noble families to perform certain religious functions as helpers of the priestess of Athena Polias over the course of a year). These women were to be found among the citizens' families following this display of their handiwork. Folding seats and parasols were held at their disposal by the daughters of resident foreigners. The latter, called metics, had the honor of bearing honey cakes and fruits on flat dishes, among other offerings, with jars of the wine needed for sacrificial rites. Next came the sacrificers leading oxen and sheep, followed by citizens too old for military duty, carrying knotted sticks, who bore olive branches. The four-horse chariots from the equestrian competitions led the way for a display of cavalry in travel gear that took up the largest portion of the procession. It wound up with an infantry parade, while musicians played their flutes and citharas as they marched.

Having turned eastward to the Eleusinion, north of the Acropolis, the endless procession made its way around to the hill's western ascent. There, the robe known as *peplos* was taken off the rolling ship so as to be folded and carried through the covered gateway of the Propylaea and a long plaza to the Erechtheion, the temple of Athena Polias ("Civic"). Her wooden statue was dressed with it by one of the archons or magistrates who exercised the ancient religious functions of a king. On an altar in front of this temple, along with the client cities' sacrifices of a cow and two sheep each, the hecatomb that gave the month its name was offered. In this most solemn sacrifice, a hundred oxen were slaughtered, and their entrails were examined to ascertain whether that offering was agreeable to the goddess. Certain parts would be burned on the altar, and the rest was to be divided at the Ceramicus between the clergy and the various demes or local groupings of the people, in a plentiful banquet. Sacrifices were also performed on the Areopagus hill where the supreme court met, as well as to Athena Hygeia just inside the Propylaea. Just as public meetings were cancelled at the end of that month, all court proceedings were dropped if they had not been concluded by the time of this civic **New Year**, when the appointment of new magistrates was announced, as part of the general reaffirmation of the political order.

At the close of the festivities, a regatta was held in the Piraeus (the port of Athens), where, as in the other contests, it was tribes rather than individuals which competed for a substantial prize of 300 drachmae, with more funds to cover the winners' festive banquet. The budget for all these contests came from the treasury of the temple of Athena Polias, and they were organized by ten judges appointed for four years. Except for occasional public fundraising, the sacrifices were supplied by ten superintendents appointed annually by each of the tribes to prepare and manage the proceedings of the city's most splendid festival.

See also Dionysia; Geerewol; Games (Greece); New Year (West); Saturnalia; Thargelia

References

Ian Jenkins. *The Parthenon Frieze.* Austin: University of Texas Press, 1994.

Jenifer Neils, ed. *Worshipping Athena: Panathenaia and Parthenon.* Madison: University of Wisconsin Press, 1996.

Spyros Piblis. *Panathenaea: The Greatest Festival of Ancient Athens.* Athens: Classical Editions, 1970.

PANCAKE TUESDAY

See Carnival

PANCHAK YAMA

See Divali

PANHELLENIC GAMES

See Games (Greece)

PARDON (CHRISTIANITY)

Celtic Brittany's most typical religious and folkloric ritual, the *pardon*, is the feast day of the saint to which a church is dedicated. The people of that parish and others in the area then come, often in fulfillment of a vow or penance, to perform pious acts that are meant to secure divine forgiveness and practical favors such as healing, the safety of sailors, the protection of cattle, and abundant crops. Held from March to October but mostly in the summer, **pardon**s are big social events for Bretons, who wear their best folk costumes.

Some places have two **pardon**s a year: a small one for the local people, where devotion is still most sincere, and a big one as a regional pilgrimage attracting believers (including handicapped beggars) from far and wide on account of the favors already granted by that church's particular saint—often the Virgin Mary or her mother **Saint Ann**. In either case, beyond local variations, a **pardon** normally begins the night before the feast with an invocation of the saint in question in the church or chapel dedicated to him or her, in preparation for the solemn morning mass, followed in the afternoon by vespers at a consecrated place, which can be a holy well. It is reached at the end of a singing procession (for example, a flotilla of small boats across a bay between Concarneau and the chapel of Sainte-Anne de Fouesnant on the saint's July 26 feast) bearing relics, crosses, statues, gold-embroidered banners, and *ex-votos*—such as models of ships saved from danger. That shrine is decorated with flowers and offerings of different kinds, depending on the place: it could be skeins or beeswax, grain or wool sacks, white hens or pigeons (as at Sainte-Anne de la Palud) or ox and cow tails (as in Saint-Herbaut). These gifts reflect the kind of protection expected from a given **pardon**, as at specialized ones like the horses' **pardon** of Baye, where the beasts are taken before the priest at a certain crossroads out in the fields to be blessed with a sprinkling of holy water.

It used to be once the sacred ceremonies were over that the **pardon** turned into a local fair or a profane village feast, warily tolerated by the clergy; for these were rare occasions when boys and girls could socialize openly. Nowadays though, if the **pardon**s that survive are sometimes little more than tourist events; the *fest-noz,* or "feast-night," on a **pardon**'s eve has become very popular as a party where Bretons get to practice their complex folk dancing steps—an activity meeting with renewed interest among all generations. It should also be said that the *Tro-Breiz* annual pilgrimage (a 548-kilometer "tour of Brittany" to the tombs of the seven bishops who brought Christianity from Great Britain) has recently been revived with some success, after a long, three-century lapse, attesting to a revival of traditional faith and customs on the **pardon** circuit.

See also Kermis; Lent

References

Frances M. Gostling. *The Bretons at Home.* Intr. Anatole Le Braz. New York: R. M. McBride and Company, 1925.

Pierre-Jakez Hélias. *The Horse of Pride: Life in a Breton Village.* Tr. and Abr. June Guicharnaud. New Haven, CT: Yale University Press, 1978.

Anatole Le Braz. *The Land of Pardons.* Tr. Frances M. Gostling. New York: The Macmillan Company, 1906.

▶ PARENTALIA

See Days of the Dead (West)

▶ PARILIA

See Fordicidia and Parilia

▶ PARTY

See Potlatch

▶ PARYUSHANA AND DASHALAKSHANA (JAINISM)

Paryushana is the Sanskrit name of an eight-day festival of the Shvetambara sect (named af-ter its "white-clad" ascetics) of the ancient Jain religion of India, which knows it as *Pajjusana* in the Prakrit language of its sacred scriptures. It takes place from the thirteenth day of the dark half to the fifth day of the bright half of the month of Bhadrapada (August–September). Just after it is over, the rival Digambara sect (named after its "sky-clad," or naked, male ascetics) begins to observe its own ten-day version of the most crucial Jain festival: **Dashalakshana**.

Abiding in Fasting and Forgiveness

One of the meanings of *Paryushana*, "Abiding," is to stay in one place for the duration of the monsoon season. For it is the auspicious climax of *chaturmas*—the "four-month" rainy period during which wandering ascetics settle down to take shelter among laypeople, who will strive to imitate them by fasting or restricting their diet, and even temporarily becoming a monk or nun for at least twenty-four hours. They are actually supposed to observe this practice called *posadha* twice a month but are mostly content to try it at the end of the year. They have the option of a partial fast called *daya* or *samvara,* allowing one food and boiled water at will over the course of a retreat, though they all have to forego even these on the very last day of the year, called *Samvatsari,* meaning "annual."

Paryushana also means abiding in devotion and moral exertion through service and pacification. Thus, to ensure that no quarrel is carried over into the new year, people ask each other to forgive their misdeeds of the past year, conscious or not. This too they are supposed to do all through the year, but they get the opportunity to do it communally on the last day (rather like Eastern Christians on **Forgiveness Sunday** as they enter **Lent**), at the end of a temple service where pardon is also sought from all living beings for injuries of any kind. In this spirit, Jain communities (especially in Gujarat where they are mostly concentrated) are sometimes able to get local authorities to ban the slaughter of animals for food temporarily. Jains also privately send year-end letters to all friends, acquaintances, and business associates, Jain or not, to ask them forgiveness for any possible or hypothetical wrongdoing.

Worshipping Words and Images

On the last day of the festival, Jains give alms to the poor and take out the image of a *Jina,* or spiritual "conqueror," of detached omniscience in a procession through the streets, headed by an ornamental pole called *Indra-Dhvaja* (the "Staff of Indra"). For it was this ancient Vedic god, patron of warriors, who received in his hands all the hair cut off as a sign of renunciation by Mahavira (599–527 B.C.E.), founder of Jainism. **Mahavira's Birthday** (which is also a festival in its own right for Jains of all sects on the thirteenth day of the bright half of the month of Chaitra—in March or April) is underlined the day before with a procession of his cradle, as well as the decoration of temples with flags as on any other birthday of a *tirthankara,* or "fordmaker" across the ocean of rebirths. The Sthanakvasi subsect is an exception, as it frowns upon such image-worship.

One of the original features of Paryushana is the recitation by monks of the *Kalpa-Sutra,* a part of the Prakrit canon devoted to the lives of the Jinas. The example of their ascetic strivings was supposed to inspire and bind together the monastic community as it waited out the rains amidst the lay population. Eventually, it too was allowed to attend on the fourth to eighth days of the festival, though few people avail themselves of this privilege until the last day, when they all show up. On the previous days, it is actually a basic Gujarati commentary that is read (sometimes by specially trained young laymen in the absence of monks), following a custom that may go back a couple of centuries. For a breakdown in monastic tradition then left leadership in the hands of simple clerics who lacked the basic skills to interpret canonical texts written in ancient languages.

Yet even the few people who know Prakrit among the crowds present on the final day while two monks (sitting on a dais) alternate reading from the original text cannot possibly follow its meaning, as it is gabbled at a breakneck speed rivalling that of a Western cattle auctioneer. That is why a designated young layman has to rely on prompts from one of the monks to show the worshipful audience miniature paintings from an illuminated manuscript of the *Kalpa-Sutra,* illustrating as they come up events of Mahavira's life as well as stories from medieval commentaries. The sight and sound of the holy book (as of the Gujarati commentary read out at the same rate on the fourth to seventh days) are actually what is most meritorious on this and other days of the festival. On the fifth day, the right to touch and garland silver images of the fourteen dreams announcing Mahavira's birth to his mother, lowered from the ceiling of the monks' lodgings as they read the corresponding passages, is actually sold to the highest bidder—as is often done with such ritual privileges. As Paul Dundas has pointed out:

> This bidding represents one of the most public activities which a Jain layman can perform within the community and serves as a means by which his moral and financial status can be established, while at the same time the idiom of the activity, which is that of the marketplace, acknowledges the centrality of business in Jain society. (Dundas 2002, p. 198)

Celebrating the Ten Religious Qualities

Just as a communal meal on **New Year**'s Day, breaking the strict fast on its eve, concludes Paryushana among Shvetambaras, Digambaras are about to launch upon their own equivalent of it, based on a rival set of scriptures called ***Dashalakshana**-Parvan.* This "Festival of the Ten Religious Qualities" has one day devoted to each in turn. These qualities are forbearance, gentleness, uprightness, purity, truth, restraint, austerity, renunciation, lack of possessions, and chastity; the reading of the corresponding chapters of the *Tattvartha-Sutra* is accompanied by sermons from the congregation. Toward the end, the most auspicious day is *Ananta-Chaturdashi* ("Endless Fourteenth"), celebrating the Fourteenth Tirthankara Ananta in a *puja* (service) with fourteen flowers. There is also general fasting and veneration of images. As with the Shvetambaras, the final day is one of "Asking for Pardon," or *Kshamapana.*

See also Lent

References

Paul Dundas. *The Jains.* 2nd ed. London: Routledge, 2002.

Jyoti Prasad Jain. *Religion and Culture of the Jains.* 2nd ed. New Delhi: Bharativa Jnanpith Publication, 1977.

Margaret Stevenson. "Festivals and Fasts (Jain)," in James Hastings, ed. *Encyclopaedia of Religion and Ethics,* Vol. V. New York: Charles Scribner's Sons, 1912, pp. 875–878.

▶ PASCHA

See Easter, Lent

▶ PASSION WEEK, PASSIONTIDE

See Palm Sunday

▶ PASSOVER (JUDAISM)

The festival of **Passover** is celebrated in March or April on the fifteenth of the Jewish month of Nisan. It is preceded on the fourteenth by the **Fast of the Firstborn**—those of Israel who were "passed over" by the last of the seven plagues of Egypt. It is the first of three **pilgrim festivals** mentioned in the Pentateuch as requiring Jewish males to come up to Jerusalem especially to observe them. **Passover** lasts seven days in Israel (and for Reform Jews) and eight in the Diaspora, where the Last Day is repeated and the second is treated as a full festival day

rather than as one of the **intermediate days** (***hol ha-mo'ed***) of rejoicing when work is forbidden, weddings are discouraged, and mourning is restricted. This is a feature shared by **Passover** with the **pilgrim festival** of **Sukkot.** Among Moroccan Jewry the world over, **Passover** is immediately followed by a more relaxed folk festival of brotherly love and community harmony, called **Mimouna.**

Two Festivals in One

The Hebrew name of **Passover** is **Pesah**, derived from a verb for "protecting," "having compassion," or "passing over." It is also known as the **Festival of Unleavened Bread**, the only kind of bread allowed for the week. The festival of **Passover** (***Hag Haposah***) and the **Festival of Unleavened Bread** (***Hag Hamatzot***) were originally two different festivals. The oldest one was **Passover**, the animal sacrifice of nomadic herdsmen who slaughtered a small head of cattle at the time of lambing and the change of pastures in order to secure the health of the rest of the herd. The Hebrews made sure none of its flesh was left the next day, since it could not be preserved on the road; hence the requirement that any uneaten portion be burned. The **Festival of Unleavened Bread** was an offering of the first sheaf of barley made by the sedentary peasants the Hebrews had become after having settled in the Promised Land of Canaan. Before they were exiled from it to Babylon, the latter, agricultural festival had been united with the former, pastoral one as part of King Josiah's religious reforms of the late seventh century B.C.E., standardizing and centralizing Jewish rites around the capital Jerusalem. It was set on the day after **Passover** proper, that is on the fifteenth of a month then known as Abib, meaning "ears" (of grain), and in post-Exilic times as Nisan, from the Akkadian *nisannu* for "beginning," denoting that this was an archaic **New Year** ritual of springtime renewal. Hence the requirement that this **Spring Festival** (***Hag Haaviv***) be celebrated only after the spring equinox, on the basis of which an extra lunar month is added to the year seven years out of the nineteen it takes for the lunar cycle and the solar cycle to coincide, so that it does not get out of step with the rhythm of the seasons as reflected in the latter. It is from this *omer* sacrifice of the new barley, originally meant to authorize consumption of the new grain crop, that the forty-nine days of **Omer** are still counted to determine the date of **Shavuot,** the next **pilgrim festival** in the summer, held on the fiftieth day (hence its Greek name of **Pentecost**). Yeast was associated with the corruption of mould and was therefore to be cleared from the premises of a dwelling, in order for them to be pure and to afford its inhabitants a fresh start in a new life, free from the restrictions of winter.

The Festival of Unleavened Bread

The historically based Feast of **Unleavened Bread** was eventually grafted onto this agricultural nucleus, so that the week-long ban on leaven is explained by the Bible in terms of the Hebrews' haste to leave the shackles of slavery in Egypt to find freedom (an event set in springtime): they did not have time to wait for the dough for their bread to rise. In honor of their zeal to heed the call of liberation, after which **Passover** is also known as *Hag Haherout* (the **Festival of Freedom**), there is such a taboo on yeast-based foods that any Jew who eats any during the festival may be cut off from the people of Israel. Still, the original concern for ritual purity at the first full moon of a **new year** is clearly in evidence in the stringent rules for the removal of all traces of *hametz* (leaven) from the house. Thus, a Hasidic wife has to clean it thoroughly and clean all dishes that have been in contact with *hametz*, if she does not ritually sell them to repurchase them later. Then, on the eve of **Passover**, the husband, holding a candle, goes from room to room in search of crumbs of anything fermented in water. Some have been deliberately hidden so he can find them and sweep them with a feather into a large wooden spoon to put them in a paper bag that will be burned the next morning. From that day on, and normally for all the time the festival lasts, the only bread Jews are supposed to eat is the unleavened kind known as *matzoh,* used in sacrifices involving bread. For every head of a Hebrew household was required to come and make one at the Temple of Jerusalem on the second day of **Passover** once major observances had been centralized there. The host used by Roman Catholics for the Christian sacrament of the Eucharist since the ninth century is also of this type, as it is directly derived from the **Passover** sacrifice.

The Sacrifice of the Paschal Lamb

The custom of offering a lamb to God on the first day of **Passover**, on which the sacrificial symbolism of **Easter** and the Christian liturgy is based, has been preserved in amended form by the Samaritans. This is a dissident community of Jews who claim to have been spared the fate of the ten lost tribes of Israel deported and assimilated after the Assyrian conquest of their Northern Kingdom in 721 B.C.E. By now barely 500 strong, they still collectively roast dozens of their fattest sheep at their ancient holy place at the foot of Mount Gerizim, about forty kilometers north of Jerusalem. Other Jews had to give up the regular performance of their own sacrifice after the destruction of the Temple, where it had been taking place ever since the centralizing reforms codified in Deuteronomy.

Until this happened in 70, the head of every Jewish family was supposed to come to the Temple of Jerusalem with a Paschal lamb to be slaughtered on Friday evening by the priests. They would splatter the altar's horns with its blood, instead of the lintels and doorposts of the family home or the pole at the entrance of a tent, as had originally been the case. This was done in memory of the sign the Hebrews painted on the front of their dwellings with the blood of the lambs they sacrificed in the Biblical account of the original **Passover**, following the command given to Moses by God, so the Exterminating Angel would know which houses to pass over as he went over the land of Egypt bringing death to the firstborn male of every family, as a display of the wrath of God and of His mercy to His chosen people. This memorial was so central to the descendents of these chosen few that, for those who may have been prevented from presenting their sacrifice at the Temple because they found themselves abroad or in a state of ritual impurity (due to touching a dead body), there was even a "Second **Passover**" (*Pesah* Sheni or **Pesah** Katan) on the fourteenth of the following month of Iyar, when a little **unleavened bread** was eaten.

The Semitic concept of a sheep as a substitute for a human sacrifice, also echoed in the last minute replacement of Abraham's son Isaac by a ram as an offering to God, can be traced back to a Sumerian liturgical text of the fourth millennium B.C.E. To this day, Muslim Bedouins observe ritual prescriptions similar to those followed by Jews at **Passover** since Biblical times when they sacrifice a lamb: its flesh has to be entirely consumed in a meal or by fire, its blood may not be spilt on the ground, and it is normally roasted so that none of its bones is broken, or else the entire herd might get maimed. Conversely, it was a common belief in ancient cultures that an unbroken bone could become the seed of the resurrection of the whole being it had belonged to. It was therefore doubly significant that, as Christ's beloved apostle John underlined in his Gospel, the Roman soldier who went around breaking the legs of the men crucified on Golgotha to hasten their death chose not to do it to Jesus but to pierce his side instead— much as the prophet Isaiah had foretold in identifying the Messiah, as a passive "man of sorrows," with the Paschal lamb. This allowed Christians to see in Jesus a divine-human substitute for the animal sacrifice by virtue of which the firstborn of Israel were spared when Moses was set to lead his people to freedom in the thirteenth century B.C.E.

The Seder Meal

By the Common Era, this Biblical story of the Exodus had long been recounted as part of the ceremonial meal for which ten to twenty pilgrims to Jerusalem would gather in a decorated room after the lamb was brought back from the Temple on Friday night. Unfolding along the lines of the prescriptions found in Chapter Twelve of the Book of Exodus, this religious meal known as the *seder* (a Hebrew word for "order") is still served in Jewish homes on the fifteenth and (except in Israel and in Reform communities) sixteenth days of the month of Nisan. It is meant to allow every participant to personally relive as a spiritual event the defining moment of the history of the people of Israel that was the Exodus. For as is written in the Mishnah's second-century *Pesahim* tractate (*Babylonian Talmud* 1938, 10:5, 116b), which describes and explains the order of this meal, coming out of Egypt means passing "from bondage into freedom, from sorrow into joy, from mourning into festivity, from darkness into great light, and from servitude into redemption."

The head of the family first puts on a white ritual gown called a *kittel,* and then proceeds to sanctify the holiday with a benediction or *kiddush* said over a cup of wine, before explaining that the unleavened bread on the table stands for the "bread of affliction" that was the lot of the Hebrews while they were slaves in Egypt. All wash their hands before being presented by the master of ceremonies with *maror* (bitter herbs also meant to recall the bitterness of slavery); lettuce, celery, or other raw vegetables may fit the bill, once they are dipped in vinegar or salt water.

After the host has mixed the second cup of wine and water, the guests sing the first two Psalms (113 and 114) of the so-called "Egyptian Hallel" (from the Hebrew word for "praise") initially recited at Temple sacrifices during **pilgrimage festivals**. Exceptionally on **Passover**, the first of the benedictions normally

A Jewish family holds a Passover seder, commerating the Hebrews' escape from slavery in Egypt. (Ted Spiegel/ Corbis)

preceding and following recitations of the Psalms is skipped. One or two of the symbolic items on the seder plate are then removed: a shank bone, standing for the Paschal lamb which would have just been roasted at home in the days of the Temple, often along with a hard-boiled egg representing either the destruction of the latter or God's loving kindness (depending on the tradition). Once the second cup of wine has been poured, the youngest child asks the following standard questions about the unusual ceremonies: "Why does this night differ from all other nights? For on all other nights we eat either leavened or unleavened bread; why on this night only unleavened bread? On all other nights we eat all kinds of herbs; why on this night only bitter herbs? On all other nights we need not dip our herbs even once; why on this night must we dip them twice? On all other nights we eat either sitting up or reclining; why

on this night do we all recline?" All this symbolism is explained in the stock answers recited in unison in fulfillment of the Biblical injunction (Exodus 13:8) to pass on the story of Israel's liberation from bondage from generation to generation.

An annual high point of Jewish life, this ritual retelling is known by the Aramaic word for "lore," as the *Haggadah*. The allusions to reclining in the Haggadah would suggest that the custom of **Passover** toasts may have been derived from the Greek and Roman banquets of the time when the Talmud took shape. A fine example of a *midrash* or compendium of scriptural interpretations, the Haggadah was largely drawn from it in the same era, but the earliest complete text that has come down to us was put together in the tenth century by the Kabbalist philosopher Saadiah Gaon. Other versions are still used in various Ashkenazi and Sephardic communities, as the Haggadah has been diffused through an enormous number of editions, some of which are famous for their calligraphies and illuminations. Many new liturgical passages (such as homilies on the unbroken spirit of the captive Hebrews, on the ten plagues of Egypt, and on the parting of the Red Sea) have found their way into the Haggadah during the Middle Ages.

After the second cup of wine has been drunk, and the **Passover** sacrifice has been explained, all present again wash their hands before consuming *matzoh* and *maror* dipped into a mixture of crushed fruits and wine called *haroset,* in order to convey that suffering and sacrifice are eventually rewarded by freedom and spiritual progress. This signals the start of the meal, formerly centering on the lamb. A third cup of wine is poured once grace has been said afterwards, to express thanksgiving to God, and a fourth after the reading of the bulk of the Hallel, consisting of Psalms 115–118, previously read in part, to acknowledge God's loving Providence. (A so-called "half-Hallel," the one used on every **New Moon** and limited to Psalms 113–114 and 117–118, is read during the last six days of **Passover**.)

In some communities, a fifth glass is poured for Elijah, and an extra seat is left empty, in case the prophet should show up on this occasion to announce the Messiah's arrival, as a Kabbalistic tradition insists he will one day. The door is even left open for a while during the seder dinner as Biblical verses are read in order to welcome Elijah. When he does come, it is said he will resolve all the controversial issues having to do with the interpretation and application of the Law. Thus at **Passover**, the seder dinner does not only look back to the historical redemption of the people of Israel from the bondage of Egypt, but also looks forward to its coming redemption in the days when the prophet Elijah and the promised Messiah will appear in close succession at the end of history. In the meantime, before this final judgment of

the living and the dead, Jews like to insert the names of dead relatives in the medieval *yizkor* (Hebrew for "may He remember") prayers recited after the reading of the Law and before the Torah scrolls are put back in the holy ark on the final day of **Passover**.

While Ashkenazi communities read the Bible's Song of Songs during **Passover**, the folk songs that conclude the seder meal most often go back to the Middle Ages. Among them is a poem designed to entertain children and keep them awake on that special night, entitled *Had Gadya* (Aramaic for "The Lamb") and first found in a Haggadah produced in Prague in 1590. Some commentators see it as an allegory of the Jewish people's destiny among the nations; others, as a description of the soul's experience of embodiment, from birth to final judgment. The song's explicit point that everyone finds somebody else who is stronger, but that above all stands God, has parallels in English and German literature, and even in the Christian story of Saint Christopher, as the mightiest giant in the world, who carried travelers across rivers and yet is said to have faltered under the weight of the Christ Child.

A Post-Passover Celebration of Moroccan Jewry: Mimouna

Upon the close of the **Passover** holiday at sundown on the Last Day, Sephardic Jews of Moroccan background begin a more light-hearted celebration all their own, called **Mimouna**. In contrast to the seder night, when Jews hurry home from the synagogue to start the Haggadah, after **Passover**'s last evening service, they take time to greet each other with wishes for success (*terbah*) and special **Mimouna** blessings, and to have a drink before visiting people in their community in hierarchical order from the rabbi's family on down to their own relatives, friends, and neighbors, whom they will also welcome at their open house around a festive table. Set on a white tablecloth and decorated with flowers and stalks of wheat, this is a display of symbolic foods (reminiscent of Persian **Naw Ruz** customs): milk or buttermilk, flour, eggs, honey, butter, fruits, nuts, yeast cakes, sweets, five dates, five coins, five beans, wine, and plain yeast. Women wear their embroidered caftans to prepare a rich menu of dairy delicacies, such as stacks of *muffaleta* crepes. Grilled fish is also on the menu when engaged couples are invited for dinner by the fiancée's parents, on a night when other singles look for a prospective marriage partner as they mingle under their family's watchful eye, among the people of all ages who go out on the streets to socialize.

Early on the morning of **Mimouna**, families head to the local wells, springs, rivers, swimming holes, or to the seashore, where they splash their faces with water and step barefoot into it. This appears to reenact the crossing of the Red Sea, which is supposed to have taken place on the last day of **Passover**, and is associated with both spiritual and worldly freedom and bounty. These two meanings are intertwined in the feast's name, in addition to an allusion to the medieval religious philosopher Maimonides' father (more explicit in the alternate name **Maimuna**). Maimon is said to have died on the day of this feast, which also originated in the Moroccan city of Fez he happened to be from. On the one hand, *Mimouna* comes from the Hebrew and Aramaic word *mammon,* which means "riches" or prosperity, suggesting these are determined on this day for individuals and the nation—as on a **New Year**'s Day such as **Rosh Hashanah**, or the ancient **New Year for Kings** on the first of Nisan, identified in Exodus 12:1 as the first month of the year on account of the birth of the Jewish nation with its liberation from Egypt on **Passover** on the fifteenth. On the other hand, *Mimouna* also contains the Hebrew word *emunah* for "faith," referring specifically to the belief that the final redemption will occur in the month of Nisan, just like the Hebrews' liberation from Egyptian bondage on **Passover**. Given these patriotic and messianic

overtones, it may not be entirely surprising that Israeli politicians have taken to using helicopters to descend upon the various outdoor settings of picnics where Moroccan-rite Jews pitch tents, play music, dance, and make merry in a holiday spirit of community harmony and peaceful relaxation on **Mimouna** Day. As a result of such politicized gate-crashing, these massive gatherings now often turn into confrontational electoral meetings instead.

See also Akitu; Easter; Eid; Holy Week; Naw Ruz; Nineteen-Day Feast; Rosh Hashanah; Rosh Hodesh; Shavuot; Sukkot; Sunday; Tu bi-Shevat; Whitsuntide

References

The Babylonian Talmud. Part 2: *Seder Mo'ed,* Vol. 2. Tr. Rabbi Dr. H. Friedman. London: Soncino Press, 1938.

Baruch M. Bokser. *The Origins of the Seder: The Passover Rite and Early Rabbinic Judaism.* Berkeley, CA: University of California Press, 1984.

Paul F. Bradshaw and Lawrence A. Hoffman, eds. *Passover and Easter: The Symbolic Structuring of Sacred Seasons.* Notre Dame, IN: University of Notre Dame Press, 1999.

Ronald H. Isaacs. *Every Person's Guide to Passover.* Northvale, NJ: J. Aronson, 2000.

"Mimouna. A Festival of Brotherly Love," webpage on *The Sephardi Connection* (http://www.sephardiconnect.com/pesah/mimouna.htm), 1998–2000.

The Mishnah. Tr. Jacob Neusner. New Haven, CT: Yale University Press, 1988.

▌ PENTECOST
See Shavuot, Whitsuntide

▌ PERCHTENTAG
See Epiphany

▌ PERIOD FESTIVAL
See Matsuri

▶ **PERIODIC GAMES**
See Games (Greece)

▶ **PESAH**
See Passover

▶ **PFINGST**
See Whitsuntide

▶ **PHALGUN KRISHNA PRATIPAD**
See Holi

▶ **PI MAI**
See Water-Splashing Festival

▶ **PIG FEASTS**
See Carnival

▶ **PILGRIM FESTIVALS**
See Sukkot

▶ **PITCHER FEAST, PITHOIGIA**
See Dionysia

▶ **PITRIPAKSHA**
See Navaratra and Dusshera

▶ **PLEBEIAN GAMES**
See Games (Rome)

▶ **PLYNTERIA**
See Venus Verticordia

▶ **POKROV**
See Protection of the Mother of God

▶ **PONGAL**
See Thaipusam

▶ **POILA BAISHAKH**
See Vaishakha and Vaisakhi

▶ **POSEIDONIA**
See Saint Nicholas

▶ **POTLATCH (PACIFIC NORTHWEST)**

The peoples of the Northwest Coast of the American continent have applied the word "**potlatch**" (meaning "to feed, to consume" or "to give" in their common trading lingo the Chinook jargon) to a kind of festival and fair that has long been central to the area's indigenous cultures. In the twentieth century, social scientists have also come to use it to refer to a wide range of institutions and practices the world over, from the earliest times to the recent past. This is because they all show traits of the rituals of competitive giving best exemplified in the **potlatch**, as this Native American festival fully reveals the logic of the anti-utilitarian principles governing much of premodern social and economic life.

An Economy of Festive Giving

In the strict sense, the term "**potlatch**" refers primarily to elaborate festivals combining feast and fair, political assembly, and religious initiation, that were repeatedly held all through the long winter months by the native cultures of the North Pacific coast: first and foremost, by the Amerindians of the province of British Columbia and the states of Oregon, Washington, and Alaska: Kwakiutl, Tsimshian, Haida, Tlingit, Nootka, Coast Salish, Bella Coola (or Nuxalk); to a lesser degree, and under the influence of the latter two, by many Dene (or Athapaskan) groups of the interior up to southern Yukon; also to some extent among Alaskan Eskimos and, across the Bering Strait, all the way to the Asian continent with the Chukchis and Koryaks of the Siberian Far East.

Like similar institutions in the southwest Pacific and elsewhere, the Amerindian **potlatch** involves the constant circulation of goods in the form of gifts exchanged between rival social groups, such as clans and brotherhoods. In the highly ceremonial setting of the **potlatch**, they would lavish the wealth accumulated during the fair season upon their guests. The latter were obligated to reciprocate within a reasonable amount of time, "on pain of private or public warfare" (Mauss 1990, p. 5), by inviting their hosts to another **potlatch** where they would outdo them in generosity. This would launch another round of competitive giving, made possible by nature's bounty in fish and game under the warm rains of the Pacific. Whenever successful whaling or fishing expeditions brought in a sizable surplus, people seized the opportunity to throw a feast for their neighbors. An orator would extol the wealth of the chief's domain as demonstrated by the generous entertainment of his guests. They might even compete in eating and drinking contests.

The Politics of the Potlatch

These feasts eventually came to be overshadowed by large-scale **potlatch**es, when average families were no longer able to afford them. For a process of reckless escalation was triggered by trade with British and American newcomers some 200 years ago in some northern groups like the Kwakiutl, through the influx of consumer goods and the advent of wage earnings. Yet the **potlatch** practices of southern groups like the Nootkas and Salish remained largely immune to the notorious excesses that became synonymous with the **potlatch** and gave official authorities a pretext to ban it, under pressure from missionaries, government agents, and teachers. They were all concerned that the **potlatch**es were impoverishing the tribes, since chiefs tried to outdo their rivals by giving away hundreds of blankets, or even furniture, canoes, and motor boats. Canada's federal government first enacted legislation prohibiting the ceremonies in 1884, but since it was difficult to enforce because of the vagueness of the wording, the law was later revised, and the **potlatch** went underground to evade prosecution. Despite a number of high profile trials, it was still held in remote fishing camps, or even in stormy weather so federal agents could not reach them,

until 1951, when the Indian Act was revised and Section 149 was dropped.

The deeper reason for the Westerners' repression of the **potlatch** no doubt had to do with its running counter to the assumptions prevailing by then in their own culture about economic activities, where thrift was valued and waste was frowned upon. For in spite of its economic importance, the **potlatch** was not about trade in the usual sense of the word, since each village was normally self-sufficient as far as useful goods were concerned. In their original context, Northwest Coast native communities had two ways of interacting: one was war for sport, glory, revenge, booty, slaves, and ceremonial access to the various supernatural powers governing natural resources, and the other was collaboration in view of the careful organization needed for the spring and summer fisheries. The latter were carried out under the leadership of warrior-entrepreneurs who were able to bind together for this task large work forces of their relatives and associates from far and wide. In addition to providing them with the necessary equipment and temporary lodgings, this was done by throwing impressive **potlatch**es for them, and obliging them to give something back in the process. It was at these **potlatch**es that prestige was secured and ranks were assigned within and between neighboring communities, as reflected in the strict hierarchy of seating arrangements and the quality and quantity of food and gifts offered to variously distinguished guests (all of which also typified the Celtic **Samhain** festivals of Ireland). The most honored guests ate their meal in the host's elaborately carved wooden feast dishes—family heirlooms bearing the clan's crest.

Whether they were held outdoors or inside large longhouses, locally by commoners or intertribally by noblemen, **potlatch**es were the occasion for a host to promote or uphold his status in society, to establish or reassert his claims to economic and ceremonial privileges, or to formally transfer them to heirs. For this was the way for aristocrats to demonstrate that they were effectively one in glory with the mythical ancestor from whom they claimed descent. The wealthiest among them could seize upon just about any pretext to shower guests with gifts and show off their clan's treasures, masks, and dances. In most cases though, **potlatch**es were held on the same pattern, but on a more reasonable scale, to mark a significant event in the family, such as somebody's initiation in a secret society, the birth or naming of a child, a daughter's first period, a son's marriage, or a memorial for the dead.

Clan Parties and Basketball Tournaments

Nowadays, these "**parties**" (as they are sometimes called) still commemorate such important events in an extended family's or a clan's collective life, and may include in addition baby showers, anniversaries, special birthdays, and graduations. **Potlatch**es used to last several days, but parties now take place over the weekend, so people need not worry about missing work. These events can require a year of advance planning, and they easily cost several thousands of dollars in meals, snacks, and drinks for hundreds of guests, as well as in gifts for each of them in cash or in household goods like laundry baskets, towels and handkerchiefs, cups and glasses, plates and cutlery, pots and pans, and the like, not to mention colorful umbrellas. Much as in Plains Indians' **powwow giveaways**, honored guests, such as elders or community leaders, are publicly acknowledged as they get both cash and expensive gifts like baskets, blankets, comforters, and artwork.

The role of the **potlatch** as social binding agent has partly been taken over in recent decades by the All-Native Basketball Tournament (because basketball is an indoor sport—a vital consideration in a rainy climate, where even a small community is sure to have its own gymnasium). It allows teams from all the coastal nations of Alaska and British Columbia to compete for prestige, as they once did in periodic warfare as well as at **potlatch**es. Much like the latter, it makes the host town a temporary, yet self-sufficient, hub of bustling social exchange, where traditionally festive and modern economic activities constantly overlap. These range from dances and parties to fundraising activities. Lasting eight days, the event has an even higher profile than the **Christmas** holidays. Front-row seats are precious family heirlooms, handed down from one generation to the next (like inherited names and titles at a traditional **potlatch**). Tribal solidarity with the young players and regulated intertribal rivalry between teams are still two sides of the same coin of social integration, the common currency of the **potlatch**es of old.

Waging War or Wasting Wealth

In a similar way, larger loyalties used to emerge thanks to the **potlatch** as an alternative to war that continued by other means the same fierce struggle for prestige and power; displaying wealth was just one of the methods used. If conspicuous consumption is still around in modern societies to show that this remains the case, it is in a very different sense than that of the **potlatch**. For there, it was not enough to accumulate wealth; holding on to it and showing any reluctance to part with it was worse than lacking it. Just as failure of nerve in laying down one's life in battle, or failure to perform a ritual properly, appearing mean-spirited in this way would mean losing face—quite literally, losing your soul along with your honor, like a slave. Forcing a guest into a position where he could hardly reciprocate was the supreme weapon. In order to thus "flatten" one's rival, it was legitimate to deliberately destroy valuable property, whether movable or immovable. This could include clubbing slaves to death or even giving away wives and children—not to mention burning grand pianos, canoes, or boxes of precious candlefish oil. This oil, as a food staple, skin medicine, and ceremonial substance, is

Tlingit dancers pose in traditional ceremonial attire during a potlatch at the village of Chilkat (Klukwan) in Alaska, 1895. (Museum of History and Industry/Corbis)

central to the traditional culture and economy of coastal peoples and used to be traded with the peoples of the interior against other luxury goods like fur, copper, amber, and precious stones. If it may still be poured on fires at Kwakiutl **potlatch**es, most of it is now given to the guests in bottles. The giant wooden ladles carried by the costumed dancers are reminders that pouring away this liquid gold is the quintessential gesture of the feast.

Personal Prestige and Social Bonding

These are all ways of keeping the memory of the host's mythical ancestors and animal protectors alive and powerful, along with the formal speeches often heard during **potlatch**es. The host's *persona* of social recognition through acknowledged gratitude was traditionally embodied in the totem pole depicting the clan's mythical animal ancestors. It was also represented by beaten-copper shields with their

owner's coat of arms. These would appear at a **potlatch** mainly for show, and be given only on loan, or else very reluctantly. However, other copper objects served as a kind of money (known as "the bringer of property") for the purposes of the **potlatch**. Luxury items distributed to the guests as a display of affluence would also have included multicolored *chilkat* blankets, otter skins, war clothing, axes, and carved boxes, not to mention massive quantities of food. If many of these goods had some practical use, the less they had, the better; coppers had none whatsoever, although they were worth hundreds of chilkat blankets and might be purposely destroyed for this very reason: to show that one could afford such outrageous waste. As actual or potential gifts, each with their own history of being given back and forth, such precious items were felt to be different in kind from utilitarian objects. Yet thanks to the networks woven by this prestige economy, wealth would accumulate and trickle down the social ladder. It was first gathered under the chief's aegis (to use an ancient Greek expression in its related original sense as the protection of his shield), but only to be pledged on the honor of his name on the day of the **potlatch**. Then, with the full power of the clan concentrated in his person, as demonstrated by his splendid generosity, he was free to make contracts on the clan's behalf. "To contract debts on the one hand, to pay them on the other, this constitutes the **potlatch**," according to the American anthropologist Franz Boas in his 1898 *Report on the North-Western Tribes of Canada*. "This is done publicly with much ceremony, and is like a notarial act . . . Those who receive presents at this festival, receive them as loans that they use in ongoing enterprises, but after a few years they must be given back with interest to the donor or his heir" (Mauss 1990, p. 111 n31).

The Potlatch Principle around the World

The study of the **potlatch** has thus led some social thinkers to argue that, contrary to the received wisdom of economists about the origins of trade, relationships over time within a given community are more basic than the instant exchange of goods of equivalent value for individual use; that is to say, credit precedes barter. The utilitarian paradigm that modern Western societies now take for granted only became widespread relatively recently. Previously, the "festive" principles of social organization so dramatically illustrated by the **potlatch** used to structure the institutions and the mental habits of all other cultures in history. In his landmark essay on "The Gift, and especially the obligation to return it" (1924), which has lately become an object of renewed attention and debate across the range of the humanities, the French anthropologist Marcel Mauss claimed to have "uncovered a quite considerable number of intermediate forms between those exchanges comprising very acute rivalry and the destruction of

wealth, such as those of the American Northwest and Melanesia, and others, where emulation is more moderate but where those entering into contracts seek to outdo one another in their gifts. In the same way we vie with one another in our presents of thanks, banquets and weddings, and in simple invitations" (Mauss 1990, p. 7). Aside from the now prevalent tradesman morality, "there still remain people and classes that keep to the morality of former times, and we almost all observe it, at least at certain times of the year or on certain occasions" (Mauss 1990, p. 65).

Without reaching the fever pitch and elaborate ritual of the Pacific Coast **potlatch**, socialization in many cultures was also concentrated in a winter festive season. Around the Northern Hemisphere, from China to French Canada, the cold or snowy season that put a stop to months of hard work in the fields or at sea was filled by a succession of extended family gatherings and visits to relatives. As a class, feudal aristocracies all over the world have always been shaped by codes of behavior and forms of contract embodying principles of honor and generosity, as well as a preoccupation with rank and etiquette. These noble pursuits and that holiday spirit, sharing the same roots, have equally found their ultimate festive expression in the **potlatch** of Northwestern warriors.

See also Candlemas; Christmas; Lugnasad; New Year (China, Korea), New Year (West), Powwow; Samhain

References

Margaret Anderson and Marjorie Halpin, eds. *Potlatch at Gitsegulka. William Beynon's 1945 Field Notebooks.* Vancouver, Canada: University of British Columbia Press, 2000.

Barb Cranmer, dir. *T'lina: The Rendering of Wealth.* (Hour-long video documentary.) Montreal: Nimpkish Wind Productions Inc. in coproduction with the National Film Board of Canada, 1999.

Aldona Jonaitis. *Chiefly Feasts.* Seattle: University of Washington Press, 1991.

A Northwest intertribal powwow in Cashmere, Washington. (Mike Zens/Corbis)

Marcel Mauss. *The Gift: The Form and Reason for Exchange in Archaic Societies.* Tr. W. D. Halls. London: Routledge, 1990.

▶ POTS (FEAST OF)

See Dionysia

▶ POWWOW (NORTH AMERICA)

The most widespread public gathering of North American Indians is the **powwow**, an intertribal celebration of Native culture centering on dance competitions and **giveaways**.

History

The Eastern Algonquian (possibly Pequot) term *pahwayaw* originally referred to a medicine man or shaman in southern New England, but early British settlers applied it as a verb to the curative ceremonies performed by such Na-

tive American religious specialists, and eventually to all Indian meetings involving public declamation. Such was the case of summertime intertribal visits like the adoption ceremony called the **Calumet** by French explorers that spread from the Pawnee to the Ottawa and the Sioux, and featured warriors' dances, since they were an occasion to forge military alliances. Later, in a typical pattern, with the spread of a certain men's society across the Plains, songs and dances of the peoples involved were exchanged, borrowed from, adapted, given, or bought and sold in kind between the reservations on which they were resettled in the second half of the nineteenth century. Like the feast dances of a number of religious, hunting, agricultural, healing, craft, and policing organizations, this society's dances had largely outlived their original function. Shorn of their more openly warlike features so as not to arouse the suspicion of federal Indian Affairs agents, they were gradually amalgamated, and took on a more secular, purely social character as the Omaha Dance of the Teton Sioux. It also functioned as a repository of elements of various dances drawn from other organizations. By then, such social dances were held on reservations on the occasion of ration-distribution days or of national holidays like **Independence Day** on July 4 in the United States or **Dominion Day** on July 1 in Canada. These dances eventually recovered some of their martial features as both countries recruited Indians to fight in foreign wars and as their entertainment value for the general public was recognized.

In the late nineteenth and early twentieth centuries, Indian cultural exhibitions were sponsored off-reserve by non-Indians, sometimes in conjunction with other events such as the Calgary Stampede or as separate events like the touring Wild West Show. There, Indian performers were encouraged to "fancy up" their dancing for the sake of entertainment. Regalia made of colored feathers and more vigorous, rhythmic steps thus brought out warlike features that were banned as seditious on federal reserves, but which slowly found their way back to them under the guise of the Fancy Dance. This emerged as a standard dance category in the late 1920s in Oklahoma (the former Indian Territory where most expropriated tribes had been deported).

Their constant interaction within a relatively small territory made of Oklahoma (which became a state in 1907) the crucible of the modern **powwow** as part of a revival of Native American culture. The latter was favored by U.S. Indian Affairs Commissioner John Collier's Circular 2970, which, in 1934, reversed the American government's repressive assimilationist policy by forbidding any further "interference with Indian religious life or ceremonial expression," thus paving the way for the spread of the Oklahoma-style **powwow** to all Indian groups (Young and Gooding 2001, p. 1011). Previously, federal authorities in western Okla-

homa had even resisted using the word "**powwow**" for dance events, and tried to replace Gift Dances and Ghost Dances with "picnics" and "fairs." Yet by the 1920s, the term, first spread in this sense through the popular press at the turn of the twentieth century, had started being used regularly (if still disparagingly) by Indian Affairs agents.

During World War I, some agents had even given their blessing to dances held to send off soldiers, raise money for the war effort, or welcome veterans home—thus lending a new official legitimacy to the long suspect Indian warrior ethos. As they returned from World War II, Indian veterans were greeted with victory dances and homecoming celebrations that figured prominently in local fairs and holidays. These **powwow**s were now often held in the urban areas where many of them had moved after leaving the reserves with their families, encouraged by federal relocation policies. There, Indians found themselves too few and far between to practice their specific tribal ceremonies but could still find much of their spirit in generic intertribal **powwow**s. A Pan-Indian identity, emergent among Native American soldiers during the Second World War, thus became prevalent in the second half of the twentieth century, having found its main channel and most vibrant expression in the post-war **powwow**, whether small and tribal or large and intertribal, in a format that developed on the Plains and spread elsewhere.

Dance Styles

Still quite distinct before the war, the **powwow** styles of the Northern Plains and Southern Plains peoples have converged since then. Many Northern Plains dance styles combined to form the standard Traditional Dance and Grass Dance (with colored ribbons standing for the old grass bundles), and along with the typical Northern falsetto and fast tempo, they became widespread on the Southern Plains. Likewise, the North adopted the latter's Fancy

Dance and large drum played by male singers seated on the ground around it. By the 1960s, women's versions of the Traditional Dance and Fancy Dance had become accepted, aside from their own Jingle Dance in the North (of Great Lakes origin, performed in dresses covered with small metal cones) and Cloth Dress and Buckskin Dress in the South. In the Switch Dances of the Northern Plains, men's and women's styles are even performed by the other gender. The mixed Round Dance often leads the Grand Entry of all dancers in an evening program that may include a **powwow** princess pageant, or the warrior society **Gourd Dance** in street clothes. The latter has been revived in recent years around Oklahoma specifically to honor veterans and is often held as a separate event. Some dancers can now make a living on the **Powwow** Trail of over a thousand major events a year (some with a cast of thousands) throughout North America, from Florida to Alaska, competing for money in the various style, gender, and age categories represented. Yet many dances remain open to all dancers (even from the audience) since they are not choreographed but are actually solo performances done as a group by freely following a basic style to the accompaniment of warriors' songs. Such open dances are therefore called War Dances, though they are also referred to as Intertribals at some **powwow**s.

The Sacred and the Profane

Photographs are not allowed when one dancer starts playing eerie tunes on an eagle-bone whistle during an Intertribal and the others crowd around the singing drum group for an impromptu public, yet secretive, ceremony. For an element of sacrality occasionally still manifests at these traditional festivals, even though they are not thought of as specifically religious in nature. Tobacco may be sprinkled on a **powwow** ground as part of a blessing ceremony, and cigarettes are often distributed because the smoke of this sacred substance helps prayers to rise and spirits to descend. Nonetheless, though liquor is banned at most **powwow**s, people can still get a little wild in a festive atmosphere conducive to gambling and flirting.

Powwows may now be held in big city gyms, arenas, or convention centers instead of outdoors on reserves, as was still the rule in the 1980s. In the third quarter of the twentieth century, the Southern Plains **powwow** kept many of the elements of its forerunners and of earlier fairs and homecomings, like a campground, rations for the dancers, displays and sales of Indian foods, arts and crafts, baseball, football and other games, in addition to rodeos. These were also found at Northern Plains **powwow**s (including their imitations beyond the Plains, as among Iroquois and Hurons) along with running events and even canoe races, though other games were favored, such as golf and softball tournaments. Then there were recreational and competitive hand games of ancient origins, in which two teams took turns trying to guess in which hand someone was hiding an object to rhythmic accompaniment, with the most successful team getting to take home the goods wagered by the other.

Giveaways

A more formal public redistribution of goods with roots in indigenous social and religious rituals now most often takes place at **powwow**s. Like the **potlatch** of the Northwest Pacific Coast, the Plains **giveaway** is used to share out wealth as well as to publicly announce and validate a new status in the community. It can function as a rite of passage to mark a birth, a child's first participation in a **powwow** as a dancer, a graduation, marriage, or a wedding anniversary, leaving or returning from military service, retirement, recognition of an award or public service, or a memorial for the dead. It may also formalize adoption into a family, tribe, or society, entitling one to its distinctive ceremonial privileges, as at the **Calumet** ceremonies of colonial times, or when a woman from a Cloth Dress tribe is adopted into a family or clan of a Buckskin Dress tribe like the Kiowa or the Comanche and can henceforth perform the type of dance associated with this outfit at **powwow**s. On the Southern Plains, organizers of a two or three-day weekend **powwow** work a **giveaway** into the afternoon schedule, on the grandest scale when it is held to honor an individual. The items given away may then include (especially if they bear Indian patterns) fringed shawls, blankets, sheets, towels, household goods, antiques, or other objects specifically associated with the person or family being honored.

On the Northern Plains, **powwow**s are frequently interrupted in the evening by a half-hour **giveaway** hosted by a specially selected master of ceremonies. After stating the purpose of the occasion over the public address system, he asks the honored person and his or her family to parade around the arena (with a framed portrait in the case of a memorial) during the traditional tribal anthem and honoring songs and dances, while spectators either stand or join in the dance. The latter are acknowledged through a receiving line, before individuals, families, and groups are called out by name to receive gifts from the honored person's family, members of which go on handing out gifts (in money or in kind) among the audience until nothing is left. Among the Teton Sioux in the nineteenth century, a family would be highly regarded for giving away all of its belongings at the one-year anniversary memorial for a dead relative and holding an extravagant feast afterwards. Finding itself destitute as a result, it might, however, expect to be provided for by the community, including by the **giveaway**s of other families. The custom of giving away all the deceased's belongings on this anniversary developed into that of holding a specific kind of **giveaway** each year that followed his or her passing, so that the shawls and quilts to be given away started being made or ordered right after the death. Blankets, bedding, cloth,

kitchenware, jewelry, and a variety of knick-knacks are now also given away after the eulogies and the loud weeping of female mourners on such occasions on the Northern Plains, mostly during **powwow**s. When the **giveaway** is held as an independent event though, a feast is finally served to all present, who may number in the hundreds.

See also Potlatch; Sun Dance

References

Adolf and Beverly Hungry Wolfe. *Pow-Wow.* Skookumchuck, Canada: Good Medicine Books, 1983.

Lee-Ann Martin and Bob Boyer. *The Powwow: An Art History.* Regina, Canada: The Mackenzie Art Gallery (exhibition catalogue), 2000.

Michael Parfit. "Powwow: A Gathering of the Tribes," in *National Geographic,* Vol. 185, No. 6, June 1994, pp. 88–113.

Drew Hayden Taylor. "Rhythm of Nations," in *Canadian Geographic,* Vol. 124, No. 4, July/August 2004, pp. 54–64.

Gloria A. Young and Erik D. Gooding. "Celebrations and Giveaways," in Raymond J. DeMallie. *Handbook of North American Indians,* Vol. 13: *Plains* (Part 2). Washington, DC: Smithsonian Institution, 2001, pp. 1011–1025.

▶ PRESENTATION OF CHRIST IN THE TEMPLE, PRESENTATION OF THE LORD IN THE TEMPLE

See Candlemas

▶ PRESENTATION OF THE VIRGIN MARY (CHRISTIANITY)

The November 21 feast of the **Presentation of the Virgin Mary** is also known in the Eastern Church where it originated—as the **Entry of the Mother of God into the Temple**. It marks the day the mother of Christ is said to have been taken there as a child to be consecrated to God, who would later take flesh in her womb as

Jesus—as Christians believe. This feast therefore celebrates the prelude to the salvation of mankind worked by God's Incarnation. It also marks a turning point in the agricultural calendar of Greece.

History

The **Entry of the Mother of God into the Temple** was adopted relatively late as one of the Eastern Church's **Twelve Feasts** (aside from **Easter**, in a class of its own as the "Feast of feasts"). It seems to have originated in Jerusalem. Thus, it is probably no coincidence that the Church of Saint Mary the New was dedicated there, in the holy city of the former Temple of Israel, on November 20, 543. This happened to be the eve of the **Presentation of Mary at the Temple**.

The feast itself though was actually first mentioned in the late seventh and early eighth centuries in sermons on its occasion by Saint Andrew of Crete and Saint Herman of Constantinople. It was eventually adopted by the Roman Catholic Church as well while the Pope was in exile in Avignon in the south of France, in 1374 under Gregory XI. During the Counterreformation, the feast was suppressed by Pope Pius V (1566–1572) on account of its complete lack of historical credibility, but Sixtus V re-established it upon his accession to the Holy See in 1585. In thanks for the deliverance of Venice from a plague in 1630, November 21 henceforth became the date of a yearly pilgrimage over a bridge of boats across the Grand Canal to the baroque Church of Santa Maria della Salute.

Soon thereafter, the **Presentation** was adopted as the special feast day of the French clergy. This was initiated at a time when the training of priests in a new seminary began, as the teaching order of Saint-Sulpice was founded in Paris by Jean-Jacques Olier (1608–1657). In his writings, Olier takes Mary's consecration as a virgin to dwell in the Temple as a symbol of the priest's dedication to celibacy in the exclusive service of the Church, partly on the basis of medieval typology. This was a stock set of perceived correspondences between events in the New Testament and their prefigurations in the Old Testament. Thus, the prophet Samuel who anointed Israel's first kings was offered to God while still a child by his mother, just as Mary was taken to the Temple at three in fulfillment of her parents Joachim and Ann's vow to give her to God, who had miraculously removed the shame of their childlessness. Once there, it was on her own that she unhesitatingly went up the fifteen steps leading to the holocaust altar outside the sanctuary, which traditionally corresponded to the fifteen "Psalms of the degrees" sung by the Hebrews as they came up to Jerusalem for **pilgrimage festivals**. These fifteen steps thus became a symbol of the priest's own progress up the stairs of the altar at his ordination in early modern French piety.

Theology

The rich symbolism of the Temple for spiritual life and theological understanding was one important reason why the festival was enshrined in Church tradition on the sole basis of apocryphal accounts of Mary's life such as the Book of James. This was in spite of the patent impossibility of its premise that a girl could be kept in the Temple of Jerusalem along with some companions (as though they were **Vestal** virgins in a Roman temple), let alone be admitted into the Holy of Holies where the High Priest alone could go once a year on **Yom Kippur** with fear and trembling. Of course, by then even rabbinical tradition held that "five things which were in the first temple," built by Solomon, "were no longer in the second," built by Zorobabel— among them the oil of anointment used for kings, the Ark of the Covenant between God and man, and the Holy Spirit. But as the Eastern Church points out in its liturgical texts for the feast, the Virgin Mary is presented in the Temple as the living ark of a New Covenant whereby God is united to the very nature of man in the person of Jesus Christ, whose name means the "Anointed One," born of the Holy Spirit when it dwelt in her as it once did in the Temple. His mother is also compared in these texts to the royal door through which he will come in the Temple, and to the throne on which he will sit. The Virgin Mary is actually preparing to become herself "the Temple of His Body" at the **Annunciation**, by constantly praying within the Holy of Holies.

Indeed, progress in prayer through the three stages of moral purification of the soul, clear contemplation of God, and intimate union with God has long been described by the Church in terms of the three courts of the Temple of Jerusalem, each corresponding to one of the three Biblical books attributed to its builder King Solomon as another fruit of his supreme wisdom: Proverbs, Ecclesiastes, and the Song of Songs. This journey of the Christian soul to God is reflected in Orthodox icons of the feast of the **Entry of the Mother of God into the Temple** by her own progress through these three parts to its very center. The chosen Virgin's preparation from infancy to receive the Messiah into the world, mirroring the chosen people of Israel's long expectation of his coming, is underscored by the place of the feast of her **Presentation** in the calendar: after the start of **Advent**, a season of looking forward to the **Nativity of Christ**. Many **Christmas** hymns are already sung on this day.

An Age-Old Greek Winter Sowing Festival

In the north of Greece, the November 21 date of the feast of the **Entry of the Mother of God into the Temple** has always been significant for agricultural reasons. In Macedonia, there is a belief that if seed is sown before that time, it will sprout after a day or two, but that if it is sown any time later it will take at least forty days to sprout. In Aetolia, it is thought that the weather will remain unchanged for forty days if the sky is clear enough to see the setting of the constellation of the Pleiades. This event was already taken to mark the beginning of winter by the ancient Greeks, who also believed that seed sown later on would take a long time to germinate. This is why a farmer must have sown at least half of his land by November 21, so that the feast of the **Entry of the Mother of God into the Temple** is often called that of **Our Lady** *Mesosporitissa* or "Mid-Sowing." It is also known as the feast of **Our Lady** *Polysporitissa* or "Varied Sowing," because several varieties of corn boiled in a large cauldron provide the dish of the day, plates of which are sent to relatives and neighbors with good wishes for the crops. There is a related custom in Aetolia of throwing a handful of grain (wheat, maize, beans, and the like) into the family's well or fountain with the wish: "As the water flows, so may riches flow," before taking a glass of water from it into the house.

This custom is known mostly as *polysporia*, meaning "many seeds," and in some places as *panspermia* for "all sowings," which was already the name of a similar one in ancient Greece. There, by early March, people would offer such an assortment of seeds to earth deities and to the dead on the third day of the Athenian festival of **Anthesteria**, in honor of Dionysus. A couple of weeks before the current date of the **Presentation** though, toward late October, the **Pyanopsia** festival of the sun god Apollo also included a distribution of broad beans, which still figure among the grain used for panspermia. Referring to this ancient feature of the folklore of the **Presentation** (with other harvest festivals and **days of the dead**), the Swedish historian of Greek popular religion Martin Nilsson could thus write:

> Very seldom can the continuity of a cult usage be followed through the ages like this one can. These popular customs, which belong to the oldest and, as some say, the lowest stratum of religion, are the most long-lived of all. (Nilsson 1961, pp. 31–32)

See also Annunciation; Christmas; Days of the
Dead (West); Dionysia; Easter; Thargelia;
Vestalia; Yom Kippur

References

William E. Coleman, ed. *Philippe de Mézières'
Campaign for the Feast of Mary's Presentation*
(from *Bibliothèque Nationale manuscripts
Latin 17330 and 14454*). Toronto, Canada:
Pontifical Institute of Mediaeval Studies, 1981.

Martin P. Nilsson. *Greek Folk Religion*. New York:
Harper Torchbooks, 1961.

Pierre Pourrat. *Father Olier, Founder of St. Sulpice*.
Tr. W. S. Reilly. Baltimore, MD: The Voice
Publishing Company, 1932.

PRIESTS' DAY

See Christmas

PUDU

See Days of the Dead (China, Korea, Japan)

PURULLI

See KI.LAM

PRINCIPLE (NIGHT OF THE)

See Lantern Festival

PROPSONÎ

See Carnival

PROTECTION OF THE MOTHER OF GOD (CHRISTIANITY)

The **Protection of the Mother of God** is a Marian feast peculiar to the Eastern Church. It
commemorates an apparition of the Virgin
Mary on October 1, a day also devoted to the
memory of **Saint Romanos the Melodist**.
However, while it is particularly solemn in
Slavic Churches, the Church of Greece has
shifted the observance of this feast to October
28, on account of the role attributed to Mary in
the country's firm stand against Italian Fascist
aggression on that date in 1940.

The Vision of a Holy Fool

In contrast to the Western Church, where apparitions (those of Mary in particular) have
had a high profile from the Middle Ages down
to the present time, the Eastern Church has
known comparatively few spectacular apparitions and has generally made little fuss over
such phenomena. The exception that proves the
rule is the **Feast of the Veil** or the **Protection of
the Mother of God**. Both words are translated
as **Pokrov** in Russia, where many churches have
been named after this feast since it was introduced in that country around 1160. Yet it origi-
nates in Constantinople, in the church of
Blachernes, where the Virgin's veil (known as
the Holy Mamphorion) was preserved as a precious relic, famous since about that time for the
"Weekly Miracle" of its levitation from the Friday night vigil service to Saturday's matins. The
July 2 feast of the **Deposition of the Most Pure
Veil of the Holy Mother of God of Blachernes**
already commemorated its arrival from the
Holy Land in 458. Whenever the city was under
siege, dipping this veil in the waters of the
Golden Horn could raise a storm so as to shipwreck the enemy fleet and save the situation.

In the first half of the tenth century, at such
a moment when the imperial capital was
threatened by barbarians at the gates, Saint
Andrew, called "the Fool in Christ"—as the
Orthodox Church terms mystics who special-
ize in simulating madness for humility's
sake—and his disciple Epiphanius were attending a vigil service in this church when, at
about four in the morning, they both saw
Mary advancing majestically from the sanctuary, flanked by Saints John the Baptist and
John the Evangelist, and followed by a number
of other saints. The Virgin Mary knelt and
prayed in tears for a while in the middle of the
church and then again in front of the altar,
where she finally rose, took off the shining veil
she was wearing, and held it above her head;
from there, it miraculously extended over the
whole congregation. All present felt wonder-

fully protected, although the two holy men were the only ones to see the Mother of God spreading her protecting veil. The threat of an invasion subsided soon thereafter.

According to another version of the story, it was Saint Andrew who, looking up while he was praying, and seeing the Virgin Mary overhead holding her shining veil, sprang to the sanctuary and took her actual veil out of the reliquary. He then spread it himself over the crowd of worshippers, where it was miraculously held aloft in midair and extended to cover them all. The thing that matters for the celebration is that the apparition, whatever its details, was a powerful display of Mary's intercession with her son Jesus Christ, extending protectively over the entire universe. In the words of the kontakion hymn (tone three) of the feast:

> *The Virgin is today present in the church:*
> *With the choirs of saints*
> *she prays God invisibly for us.*
> *Angels and bishops prostrate themselves,*
> *apostles and prophets rejoice:*
> *For the Mother of God intercedes for us before*
> *the eternal God.*

(Ouspensky and Lossky 1982, p. 151)

The Gift of a Singing Saint

In the center of the feast's icon, the Mother of God holds her veil, or else angels hold it above her. Below her, at the bottom of the composition, **Saint Romanos the Melodist** holds the famous **Christmas** hymn in her honor that was the first of many he composed in sixth-century Constantinople. He is shown there because he was commemorated on October 1 long before the Virgin Mary appeared at Blachernes, but also because of his special relationship with her, since his hymn-writing talent was a miraculous gift he owed to the Mother of God. It is therefore fitting that this Marian feast also be about **Saint Romanos**.

The Day Greece Said No

Yet it is now celebrated several weeks later in Greece. For obscure reasons, it had never had much of an impact in the Greek Church, despite appearing on its calendar for October 1. In 1960, in a clever move to make it more relevant, it was therefore transferred to October 28, so as to give credit to the decisive **protection of the Mother of God** for modern Greece's finest hour. A civic holiday already commemorated that date in 1940, when the country faced an ultimatum from Benito Mussolini to surrender without a fight to Fascist Italy's invading armies. The dictatorship of General Metaxas responded with a firm "No!" ("*Okhi*") in Greek, so that this holiday is commonly known as **Okhi Day**. The Greek counterattack was remarkably successful, so much so that Nazi Germany was compelled to send troops to take over from the Italians in invading Greece. Since Hitler's planned invasion of Russia was thus postponed long enough to prevent it from achieving the required decisive objectives before the winter of 1941–1942, it may well be then that Greece's resistance made a big difference in the outcome of the Second World War, resulting in the final defeat of the Axis.

As a patriotic holiday second only to the **Annunciation**, which is observed on March 25 as the main national holiday, the **Protection of the Mother of God** is also observed with great pomp on October 28, wherever there are Greeks. But in their Church, it has found added significance as a divine blessing on the determination of human beings to stand up for their own dignity as well as their brethren's as children of God, in the face of all attempts to deny it by the use of raw force.

See also Annunciation; Lent

References

Charles Cruickshank. *Greece, 1940–1941*. Newark: University of Delaware Press, 1979.

Leonid Ouspensky and Vladimir Lossky. *The Meaning of Icons*. Tr. G. E. H. Palmer and E.

Kadloubovsky. Crestwood, NY: Saint Vladimir's Seminary Press, 1982.

Hugh Wybrew. *Orthodox Feasts of Jesus Christ and the Virgin Mary.* Crestwood, NY: St. Vladimir's Seminary Press, 2000.

▶ PURE BRIGHTNESS (FESTIVAL OF)

See Days of the Dead (China, Korea, Japan)

▶ PURIFICATION OF THE VIRGIN MARY

See Candlemas

▶ PURIM (JUDAISM)

Known in English as the **Feast of Lots**, the minor and relatively recent Jewish winter festival of **Purim** is a joyful commemoration of the foiling of a plot to exterminate the Jews living in Persia around the fifth century B.C.E., as related in the Bible's Book of Esther. The role of **lots**, and so of sheer luck, in the plotter's reversal of fortune and the Jews' sudden triumph after they came within an inch of annihilation have likely contributed to **Purim**'s carnival atmosphere with its playful antics and social inversion.

The Story of Esther

The story behind **Purim** is found in the Book of Esther, which is read at the synagogue on the eve of the feast. It relates how the beautiful Esther, who won the heart of the Persian king Ahasuerus, was therefore able to save her people. Her foster father Mordecai had incurred the enmity of the prime minister Haman by refusing to bow down before him, as called for by one of the king's laws. Incensed, Haman then succeeded with a bribe in persuading Ahasuerus to order the execution of all the Jews in his empire. After Esther pleaded for the Jews and denounced Haman's plotting at a banquet that she had taken the unheard of and dangerous initiative of suggesting to the king, he was upset and went out in the garden. Ahasuerus came back to find Haman pleading for mercy with the queen, just at the moment when he was throwing himself upon her couch in a frantic gesture, which was misinterpreted by the king as an assault on his wife. The king decided on the spot to have Haman hanged and replaced with Mordecai who, with Esther, obtained permission for the Jews to kill Haman's descendants and attack all their enemies throughout the empire on the thirteenth of the month of Adar, the date that Haman had originally chosen to kill them by drawing **lots**. This is why the fourteenth is now known as the Day of **Lots** (*Purim* in Hebrew), because Haman's luck turned, and it was he who died instead of the Jews.

Variants and Constants of Purim

The festival day reenacts the celebration after danger had passed, while the **Fast of Esther** (*Ta'anit Esther*) on the thirteenth of Adar itself recalls the public meeting called by the queen after she learned of the imminent peril to her fellow Jews. They now gather that evening at the synagogue to hear the reading of the Book of Esther, except in the cities of Israel that already existed in ancient times; there, the festival itself is called *Shushan Purim* (after the Iranian city of Susa) and is observed a day later than elsewhere, on the fifteenth of Adar. However, in leap years, the Jewish calendar has two months called Adar. Whenever this is the case, the main festival is celebrated in the second month of the name, and the corresponding date of the first Adar is celebrated as a minor **Purim** (*Purim Katan*) with less exuberant rejoicing but still without any fasting or eulogies allowed. Other minor **Purim**s are specific to individual communities (ranging from Algiers to Vilnius) or to particular families (from Brandeis to Segal) on the anniversary of their being saved from imminent peril due to natural or man-made disasters. All minor **Purim** observances are modeled on the main **Purim** ones: sharing a festive meal, giving alms, and reading the story of the specific providential rescue.

Hidden Meaning and Obscure Origins

The story of Esther is taken in Jewish tradition as a sign of God's providential care working behind the scenes of history through what appears to be chance and not just through spectacular miracles and revelations—as when the Hebrews were led out of Egypt on **Passover**. That is why in Kabbalistic and Hasidic literature, which are both interested in the hidden sides of Jewish faith, **Purim** is especially honored as a day of joy and friendship, precisely because there is no specific reference to God in the entire story. This strange omission led to a long controversy before the Book of Esther was included in the canon of the Hebrew Bible, among the five Scrolls of the *Ketubim*. The twelfth-century philosopher Maimonides could then even hold it as second only to the Five Books of Moses in importance among all those that make up the Bible.

Another difficulty was raised by the question of the tale's historicity. Although a whole section of the Mishnah was devoted to the observance of **Purim** in the second century, claiming that the festival was instituted by Esther's uncle Mordecai after he replaced Haman as Ahasuerus's prime minister, there is no evidence of **Purim** in Jewish literature until the first century B.C.E. It is also hard to place Ahasuerus in Persian history, since the only king to be known to have had a Jewish consort is Yazdegird I of the Sassanian Dynasty in the fourth century, whose queen was referred to as Shushan-Dokht—"Daughter of Susa." As if all this were not enough, modern scholars have pointed out that in this book (one of the earliest novels, in the same tradition as the Persian tales of Princess Scheherezade in *The Thousand and One Nights*), the names of Esther and Mordecai are none other than those of the major Baby-

lonian gods Ishtar and Marduk—hence "*Marduk khai!*" for "Marduk lives!"

The Jewish Carnival

Such considerations have not affected the great popular appeal of Esther's story. While it is being read at the synagogue (often from a colorfully illustrated scroll called the *megillah*), the usual decorum of the liturgy is set aside. The congregation boos at every mention of Haman's name, and the children of the congregation wave special holiday rattles. Often, they will have already acted out the story of Esther as a school play earlier that day, so that they are familiar with it and feel very involved by the time of the service at the synagogue. On the basis of the Book of Esther, it is the custom to give charity to two people at least and to give two gifts of food to a friend and receive two in return. A special evening meal includes boiled beans and peas, as well as triangular pies known as "Haman's ears" or "pockets" (*hamantaschen*). Hard drinking is not only allowed but encouraged, following the Babylonian teacher Rava's call on every man to have so much wine on **Purim** that he no longer knows whether he is cursing Haman or blessing Mordecai. It is thus hardly surprising that all sorts of sanctioned wrongdoing and social inversion take place on **Purim**, as at any **carnival**.

This carnival atmosphere of **Purim** was probably emphasized in the Middle Ages in imitation of the Christians' **Carnival** just before the **Lent**en fast, starting around the same time of winter. Dressing up and even cross-dressing also figure prominently on **Purim**, as in Tel-Aviv's Adloyada **Carnival** (which may have set the stage for the city's notorious transvestite scene). In many communities, even the sacred texts legislating every detail of Jewish life used to be the object of parodies, frivolously reversing the commandments in a special **Purim** Torah. A **Purim** rabbi recited this Torah, acting as an arbitrary Lord of Misrule or **Carnival** king for a day.

A tradition of improvisational theater known as *Purim*-*shpil* developed from family entertainment at the **Purim** meal, and enhanced the festival in the Ashkenazi communities of Eastern Europe from at least the sixteenth century until the Second World War. The *Purim*-*shpil* was clearly derived from the German *Fastnacht*-*spiel* ("**Mardi Gras** play"), with disguised actors and jesters, led by a narrator, making the rounds of every home. They would perform a humorous short play based either on biblical or on local material, drawing heavily on obscenity and profanity for its effects.

See also Akitu; Carnival; Feast of Fools; Naw Ruz

References

Encyclopedia Judaica. New York: Macmillan, 1971.

Philip Goodman, ed. *The Purim Anthology.* Philadelphia, PA: Jewish Publication Society of America, 1960.

Hayyim Schauss. *Jewish Festivals. A Guide to their History and Observance.* Tr. Samuel Jaffe. New York: Schocken Books, 1996.

PUSKITA
See Busk

PUSSY WILLOW SUNDAY
See Palm Sunday

PYANOPSIA
See Dionysia, Presentation of the Virgin Mary, Thargelia

PYTHIA, PYTHIAN GAMES
See Games (Greece)

QING MING

See Days of the Dead (China, Korea, Japan)

QOYLLUR RITI

See Corpus Christi

QUADRAGESIMA, QUARESIMA

See Lent

QUASIMODO

See Easter

QUINQUAGESIMA

See Lent

QUINQUATRUS (ROME)

In ancient Rome, various professions honored Minerva during her March festival called **Quin-quatrus**, and flute-players, in particular, had their own Lesser **Quinquatrus** in June.

Minerva's Several Shrines and Constituencies

The name of the **Quinquatrus** festival was said by Ovid to refer to its five-day length and by Varro to mean that it started on the fifth day after the ides of March (or March 20). But modern authors have suggested an Etruscan origin like that of the goddess Minerva it honored on her birthday, taken to be the date when her temples had been dedicated on Aventine Hill in 263 or 262 B.C.E. and on the Caelian Hill in much more ancient times.

At the foot of Mount Caelius stood the small shrine of Minerva Capta. This statue was put there after it was taken back as a prisoner from Falerii, a major center of the cult of Minerva, after the city was destroyed by the Romans in 241 B.C.E. However, Minerva Medica had her shrine on Esquiline Hill, and it was there that the healing professions would pay her homage on **Quinquatrus**.

It was forbidden to shed blood and to fight with weapons on the first day of **Quinquatrus**. The other days featured gladiator fights, since "the war-hungry goddess loves the drawn sword." (*Fasti* 3:814, p. 79) But this trait was much less prominent in the Romans' Minerva than in the Greek Athena, with which she was identified. Especially around her Aventine shrine, where some professional guilds seem to have been based, Minerva was seen more as a patron of weaving as well as of dyeing, and of the trades calling for either a chisel or a pen. **Quinquatrus** was thus a school holiday, and teachers, who were very poorly paid, received a seasonal bonus called *Minerval.*

How Pipers Got to Play Their Own Tune

Another trade was however so crucial to the religious life of Rome that it got to celebrate its very own Lesser **Quinquatrus** on June 13, following a famous strike in 311 B.C.E. The flute-players (*tibicines* in Latin) were an essential part of all temple services, funerals, and civic **games**, and Minerva was said to have invented their instrument. When they left Rome for what is now Tivoli to protest legislation limiting their numbers and canceling their traditional banquet in the temple of Jupiter, the Senate eventually relented and arranged for their return, for fear that the gods might be offended by their sudden absence. The ban on temple banquets was lifted, and the flute players were now allowed to roam the streets of Rome in parade costumes for three days, making music in Minerva's praise.

See also Games (Rome)

References

Georges Dumézil. *Archaic Roman Religion, with an Appendix on the Religion of the Etruscans.* Tr. Philip Krapp. Baltimore, MD: Johns Hopkins University Press, 1996.

William Warde Fowler. *Roman Festivals of the Period of the Republic. An Introduction to the Study of the Romans.* Port Washington, NY: Kennikat Press, 1969.

Ovid. *Fasti.* Tr. A. J. Boyle and R. D. Woodard. London: Penguin Books, 2000.

▶ RAIN FESTIVALS (AZTECS)

Festivals in the Aztec *xihuitl* solar calendar normally occurred at twenty-day intervals on each of the eighteen "weeks" whose name they shared. Several of them were meant to attract the Tlaloc rain gods as clouds of rain for the crops. This was often accomplished by means of sympathetic magic, playing on the imagined connection between analogous phenomena of the human and the natural world (seen as the divine world), such as that between smoke and clouds or tears and rain.

Gifts to the Gods

The Aztecs believed that the gifts of nature's bounty required on the part of humans a commensurate counter-gift in order to be repeated from one season and one year to the next. Otherwise, the capricious deities who controlled such phenomena as the weather might withhold them and seriously jeopardize people's livelihoods and their very survival. The offering of humble daily tasks did not even come close to matching the munificence shown by nature on a regular, yet wholly contingent, basis, since the return of the conditions humans counted on at certain given times of the year was never really guaranteed. To put all chances on their side, the Aztecs thought it was a small price to pay (not to mention a great honor) to have to sacrifice even a child, in comparison with the blessings granted to the entire family by the spirits who protected the harvests.

A New Year Child Sacrifice

This reasoning applied to the case of the child especially chosen in every village and every town quarter to be sacrificed at the end of February to the old Toltec rain god Tlaloc, once a **new year** began in the month **Atlcaualo**. The child was taken on a symbolically decorated palanquin to a nearby river, where he or she would be beaten until he or she cried, and all onlookers would strike one another so they too would wail and weep. This was thought to induce rain deities to look upon mortals with overflowing pity, which would materialize in tears raining from the clouds—the Tlalocs, children and agents of the rain god. By way of an invitation, the hoped for storm clouds were imitated by the black smoke of the rubber balls burned on that day, as on other rainmaking ceremonies. Though a rainy period was actually around the corner, its coming was not seen as a regularly recurring natural phenomenon, but as a direct result of the people's impression of rainfall: the abundant tears they all shed when the small victim was thrown into the water to drown.

A month later came the time for **Tozoztontli**, a prayer for rain offered to its gods the Tlalocs and to the Earth-Mother Coatlicue, which lasted from late March to mid-April.

Bean Food and Frog Priests

Then the end of May and the first half of June was the time "When they eat bean-food," the meaning of the name **Etzalqualitzli**, for a period of semifasting during which people ate mashed beans as they implored the gods for rain. Many human sacrifices were made at mountain altars and at artificial ponds, where large cemeteries awaited their remains. The priests would plunge into a lake and start to swim around and croak like frogs, because these rites were aimed at both Tlaloc and his wife Chalchihuitlicue (the "Emerald Lady") who was usually depicted as a frog. The divine couple was thought to inhabit the Popocatepetl and Teocuinani volcanoes; on the latter, Tlaloc had a temple where his image was carved in green stone, in his standard pose: lying on his back with head and knees raised as he holds a disk on his chest. In towns during **Etzalqualitzli,** young people would run through the streets and take away objects that were not solidly secured (as they also do on festive occasions such as **May Day** in some parts of France), as a symbol of the picking of maize cobs that Aztecs were already looking forward to in the autumn.

That was when the great celebration of the Tlalocs would take place after the September harvest. It was called **Tepeilhuitl**, the "**Festival of the Mountains**," because races to the mountains were organized (as at the **Huarachicu** rites of passage of the Incas). Images of the god were covered with amaranth paste that was later eaten.

End-of-Year Smoke and Tears

Watchmen were posted to herald the coming of the winter solstice in December, when offerings were made to the gods of the hearth on **Atemoztli**, the "**Falling of the Waters**." This festival was named after the desired effect of the rite of putting up poles hung with rubber-coated paper strips and setting them on fire. The black clouds of smoke thus produced were thought to bring on the big storm clouds of the coming rainy season.

They would soon show up on **Tititl**, a time of storms following the winter solstice, when the rain was encouraged to fall even more vigorously by generating as many tears as possible. The methods used (in addition to the usual human sacrifices) included beating up children with bags of flour and women clawing their own faces to shreds until they sobbed profusely. All this was thought to secure good luck for the rest of the year.

See also Inti Raymi and Huarachicu; Izcalli; May Day; Mid-Autumn; Whitsuntide

References

Cottie Burland and Werner Forman. *The Aztecs.* London: Orbis Publishing, 1975.

J. Eric S. Thompson. *Mexico Before Cortez. An Account of the Daily Life, Religion, and Ritual of the Aztecs and Kindred Peoples.* New York: C. Scribner's Sons, 1933.

A. Hyatt Verrill. *Old Civilizations of the New World.* New York: The New Home Library, 1942.

▶ RAISING OF THE CROSS

See Elevation of the Cross

▶ RAKHI BANDHAN, RAKSHA BANDHAN

See Divali

▶ RAMA NAVAMI, RAMAYANA WEEK

See Navaratra and Dusshera

▶ RAMADAN (ISLAM)

As a way to mark the **Night of Power** (*Lailat-ul-Qadr* in Arabic) when the Koran was first revealed to the Prophet Mohammed, fasting (*seeyam*) every day during the ninth month (**Ramadan**) is one of the five pillars of Islam. Another one is the annual Poor Due (*Zakat*). It is usually given on the occasion of the end of **Ramadan**, along with the *Zakat-ul-Fitr* specific to this time for solidarity and asceticism, ensuring that the equivalent of a meal is provided to a Muslim who cannot afford one when the annual fast is about to be broken on *Eid-al-Fitr*.

The Night of Power

By the end of **Ramadan**, any Muslim will have experienced firsthand what it feels like to know hunger and thirst most of the time and will be genuinely inclined to relieve the burden of the poor for whom this is a permanent plight. A Muslim's fraternal awareness of the whole community of believers (*Umma*) should have increased over the month as a result of training to forego the gratification of his own desires, since he or she (along with all fellow believers) will have been radically curbing them for twenty-nine to thirty days in a row. This discipline frees the spirit from its habitual patterns and reminds it of God's sovereignty and provident mercy. As self-mastery for God's sake, it is an inner holy war (*jihad*) against temptations, where valor is shown through endurance (*sabr*) against Satan and the strengthening of faith. But it is first and foremost an act of pure submission (the literal meaning of the word *islam*) to God's command, given in the *sura* (chapter) entitled *Al Baqarah* in the Koran (2:185). This is the only passage where a month is mentioned by name, with instructions to fast throughout the month in which the holy book was first "revealed as guidance to man and clear proof of the guidance, and criterion (of falsehood and truth)" (*The Koran*, Ali tr. 1992).

This was during the **Night of Power** when Mohammed (ca. 570–632), then in his fortieth year, while meditating in the Cave of Hira, was suddenly ordered by the Angel Gabriel to take his dictation from God. It is known from a sound *hadith* (a traditionally handed-down saying) of the Prophet that this took place on one of the odd-numbered nights of the last ten days of **Ramadan**. According to his wife Aisha, he then used to exert himself in devotion more than at any other time of the year. These nights of **Ramadan** are therefore held to be particularly conducive to fruitful prayer and meditation—more than a thousand months of supplications in the case of the **Night of Power** itself. The Prophet Mohammed is reported to have said that "when the Night of Power comes, Gabriel descends with a company of angels who invoke blessings on everyone who is standing or sitting and remembering the Most Great and Glorious God" (*Islamic Correspondence Course* 1982, p. 47). In the absence of reliable evidence to decide which one of those nights is the actual Night of Power, it is commemorated with solemn prayers on the night from the twenty-sixth to the twenty-seventh for convenience's sake.

The Poor Due

The time between sundown on the twenty-ninth and the next morning's **Eid**-al-Fitr communal prayer for the breaking of the fast of **Ramadan** is set aside for special *takbir* prayers of *Allahu Akbar* ("God is Most Great") said in common in a number of variants, as well as for giving Zakat-ul-Fitr, the seasonal poor due which the head of the family has to donate on behalf of all of its members to the corresponding number of needy Muslims. These are defined as believers who do not have enough for a meal to celebrate the breaking of the fast along with the rest of the community, which must therefore look out for them in this way, at the rate of about one U.S. dollar per person. If such people are not to be found in the local Muslim community, the Zakat-ul-Fitr is to be sent to one where there are. If it is given after the **Eid** prayer, it only counts as an ordinary gift and can no longer ensure in the same way as the Zakat-ul-Fitr the purification of all the sinful actions of those who have just fasted. The regular yearly Zakat is also given then, amounting to 2.5 percent of a Muslim's liquid assets.

The Fast

According to a saying of the Prophet Mohammed, "he who fasts during **Ramadan** with faith and seeking reward from God will have his past sins forgiven" (*Islamic Correspondence Course* 1982, p. 46). Provided he has faithfully formulated the right intention (*niyya*) in his heart before beginning his fast on any day, a human being then takes on the "color" of God, by analogy to His attribute as "the Creator of the heavens and the earth, who nourishes all and is nourished by none" (*The Koran*, Ali tr. 1992, 6:14). The fast therefore regulates the entry into the body of all foreign substances, be it food, drink, smoke, or medication (including injections) as well as the issue of bodily fluids, through intentional vomiting and of course any kind of sexual activity—ranging all the way from full intercourse to a kiss (which may be replaced by patting between spouses). All of these are banned as a rule between the first glimmer of dawn, up to a couple of hours before actual sunrise, until the sun has completely set, at which time all these exchanges between inside and outside become licit again—in due course. These two moments of the start and end of the daily fasting period are signaled by cannon shots during **Ramadan** in the cities of many Islamic countries, such as Cairo in Egypt.

Just after sunset and the *iftar* prayer for the breaking of the fast has been said, it is usual to have a light snack, such as one or three dates as was the Prophet's custom; this evening breakfast is experienced as a kind of sacrament of brotherhood. Once the daily evening prayer has been completed, a full dinner may be had—obviously none too soon. In this context, a festive atmosphere overtakes Muslim neighborhoods as friends visit each other's families. Near bedtime, extra *tarawih* prayers for **Ramadan** follow the daily night prayer at home or at the mosque. In the Maghreb, both kinds of buildings are whitewashed with lime. Staying up all night is not uncommon, be it to chant from the Koran at the mosque or to mix in the joyous bustle of the streets. There, a lame old man, called the *tabbal,* will make his rounds to announce the time for a light predawn meal or *suhoor,* consisting in this case of *mesfouf,* a very fine and sweet raisin couscous, which is the children's special incentive not to go to bed. Whether or not people have been sleeping, this meal precedes the day's formal statement of the intention to fast, and devout Muslims may use the time left before the daily dawn prayer for pious reading and meditation.

Inadvertently putting something in one's mouth or embracing a family member will not invalidate the day's fast, but breaking it in any other way means that one will have to make up for it at a convenient date of the coming year, that is before the next **Ramadan**. The same goes for health reasons preventing or invalidating the fast, which for women include periods, pregnancy, confinement, and nursing. People who have to travel during **Ramadan**, including soldiers, may also postpone to a more suitable time of the year the observance of the affected days of prescribed fasting. Given human frailty, keeping one's initial intention to fast on any given day may prove impossible due to a specified number of tolerable reasons, in which case this particular day will have to be made up for at a later date. However, if the intention, once taken, is deliberately broken without valid reason, including in every case of daytime sexual relations, this day of broken faith can only be expiated in one of three ways: the release of a slave, two extra months of fasting, or giving sixty needy people the equivalent of a meal each or the corresponding amount of money, in that order. Aside from the accommodations and exemptions mentioned above, failure to fast for the entire month of **Ramadan** can never be made up for, even by a whole year of fasting, according to a *hadith* or saying of the Prophet. It must be added that the obligations

A Muslim Palestianian mother and her children enjoy traditional foods at home after a day of complete fasting during the Muslim holy month of Ramadan. (Annie Griffiths Belt/Corbis)

of **Ramadan** do not apply to people who are not of sound mind or yet of age, though children are encouraged to try to follow them for a few days as they approach puberty. For every Muslim believer, fasting during the month of **Ramadan** should preferably be accompanied by at least one complete reading of the Koran, and as much charity and as many good deeds as possible. One should also refrain from being rude, backbiting, quarreling, and from seeing indecent shows, movies, programs, and the like.

Breaking the Fast: The Moon of Eid

After a month of ascetic exertion, Muslims watch out for the **new moon** of *Eid-al-Fitr* (the festival marking the end of the month of **Ramadan**) with a great deal of excitement. The day before its expected appearance, men spend the day at the mosque and women take the children to the cemeteries to visit the family dead.

(Among the Tuareg nomads of the Sahara, both men and women visit their dead on the first of **Ramadan** instead.) The **new moon** must be sighted between the sunset of the twenty-ninth and the break of dawn on the following day, or else a thirtieth day of fasting is added. The same method is used at the end of the previous month of Shaban in order to determine the actual beginning of **Ramadan**. Whenever there is any doubt about a sighting or when poor weather conditions altogether prevent the making of any sighting, both the months of Shaban and **Ramadan** may be rounded out to thirty.

Modern communications have made local observations less critical, since the first valid nighttime sighting can be reported and applied to all areas where the night is not over yet. But in practice, different methods and many observers often lead to an embarrassing situation, where the many independent ethnic or sectarian communities of a non-Muslim country may start or break the fast of **Ramadan** at different times, up to a couple of days apart. On the other hand, the Islamic lunar calendar, beginning eleven days earlier each Gregorian solar year, ensures that the month of **Ramadan** will fall during all seasons of the year in turn. It has done that several times over since the time of Mohammed, when the root *r-m-d* in the month's name referred to the heat of summer. Thus, regardless of which time of year happens to present favorable conditions for fasting in a given place, no Muslim community will have it easier on a permanent basis due solely to its geographical location.

> **See also** Eid; Lent; Nineteen-Day Feast
>
> **References**
>
> Mario Buitelaar. *Fasting and Feasting in Morocco: Women's Participation in Ramadan.* Oxford: Berg Publishers, 1993.
>
> Rhonda Fabian, dir. *Ramadan.* Schlessinger Video Productions (Library Video Company), 1996.
>
> *The Koran.* Tr. Ahmed Ali. Princeton, NJ: Princeton University Press, 1992.
>
> Dianne M. MacMillan. *Ramadan and Id al-Fitr.* Hillside, NJ: Enslow Publishers, 1994.
>
> Muslim Students' Associations of the United States and Canada. *Islamic Correspondence Course.* Kuala Lumpur: International Islamic Federation of Student Organizations, 1982.

RANGOLI BIHU

See Vaishakha and Vaisakhi

RAS EL'AA'AM EL-'AAJMI, RAS EL'AA'AM EL-'HIJRI

See New Year (Islam)

RED-LETTER DAYS

See Whitsuntide

RED THURSDAY

See Holy Week

REED DANCE (SOUTHERN AFRICA)

KwaZulu-Natal, which is one of the smaller provinces of South Africa, and the Kingdom of Swaziland it borders to the south, which is the smallest country in Africa, are both known for holding a centuries-old **Reed Dance** festival. It gathers all the maidens of the land in late August or early September to put their virtue, talent, and beauty on display in allegiance to the King and to the Queen Mother, as potential wives or a labor tribute, respectively.

The Frail Reed of Women's Virtue

The Royal **Reed Dance**, called *Umkhosi woMhlanga* in the Zulu language and just *Umhlanga* by the Swazis, developed out of the old custom known as *umcwasho* among the latter, whereby all young girls had their place in a female age grade. When they reached a marriageable age, they had to perform labor service for the Queen Mother, ending with dancing and feasting. But if any girl fell pregnant out of wedlock, her family paid a fine of one cow to the local chief. In today's ceremony, young girls still set out to cut reeds that will be used for the restoration of windbreaks and walls in the enclosures or kraals at KwaNyokeni Palace in Nongoma, former capital of KwaZulu ("the place of the Zulus"), early every September, and some years in late August too at Ludzidzini Royal Residence, Swaziland's administrative capital, twenty-three kilometers southeast of the official capital Mbabane. Just as this reinforcement of the Queen Mother's fence is a symbolic strengthening of all Swazi womanhood, the **Reed Dance** is a show of allegiance to her, both as queen and as custodian of the rainmaking medicine. The dancers' good morals are acknowledged by the King who, as part of the ceremony, can select one of the maidens as a girlfriend. She may later become a fiancée (*liphovela* in Swazi), and even a wife.

Some girls, though, are compelled to take part in the event, because otherwise local chiefs may exact from their families a fine of one cow, several goats or chickens, or at least fifty rands in cash. The parents who can afford it would often rather pay the hefty fine than expose their daughters' virtue to the perils of an event at which cases of serious sexual abuse are reported each year. Many unwanted pregnancies also result from the girls' casual encounters with the many men who have come especially for this pageant of all the beauties of the land. Still, girls who are caught misbehaving may be lashed by the male guards appointed by each chief to chaperone the delegations of a couple hundred of them by chiefdom. In recent times, however, both Swazi and Zulu authorities have used the **Reed Dance** festival as an opportunity to educate the people about sexual morality and safety, in an attempt to prevent teenage pregnancy and halt the spread of sexually transmitted diseases—especially HIV/AIDS, which is rampant in the region.

This is sadly ironic, since the **Reed Dance** gives the nation's maidens the opportunity to display their chastity to the world. For only virgins are supposed to take part in the festival from about age ten, to make sure they are ritually pure. In Zulu mythology, if a young woman who is no longer a virgin takes part in the **Reed Dance** ceremony, her reed will break and embarrass her in front of everyone. Even today, an expectant hush falls on the crowd as the Zulu royal princess who has been chosen to lead the realm's maidens through this rite of passage leads them in choosing a reed. Shouts of joy and celebration greet her as the reed remains intact. It is also with bated breath that each of the young women in turn will now also pick her reed by the riverbed.

Inaugurating the Reed Harvest

Aside from a girl's virtue, the reed symbolizes the power of nature as well as national origins, since Zulus believe their common ancestor emerged from a reed bed, and Swazis think the first human beings came from a primordial reed, split lengthwise with a long knife. The dance is convened when the river reeds are ready for cutting, which thus begins as a communal task, symbolic of social solidarity. In Swaziland, as the more active counterpart of one of its daughters, the royal family appoints as captain (*induna*) of the girls one of the best dancers—a commoner maiden who is also knowledgeable about protocol—to announce the ceremony's dates over the radio. Other subjects are not supposed to cut reeds for their own homes prior to the ceremony.

During the first three days, the girls of Swaziland first gather at the Queen Mother's palace in the Ezulweni valley and take a ritual bath in the nearby river and hot springs. They can then walk to a river of the King's choosing (from ten kilometers away for the eight-to-thirteen age-group to forty or more kilometers for the senior teenage and early twenties class) to harvest reeds with their symbolic long knives. After spending a couple of nights there to complete the task, they walk back to the Palace with a bundle each. These bundles are tied with grass plaited into rope by traditionalists, while strips of plastic bag will do for most. They arrive after dark both times "to show they travelled a long way." In KwaZulu, to the accompaniment of joyful singing and dancing, the procession winds its way up the hill to the palace entrance where the King awaits with his retinue. The chief princess leading the group of young women kneels down before her father and presents him with a reed to mark the occasion, before joining the young women in a joyful dance of tribute to the sovereign. Among Swazi girls, who have returned by the fourth evening and spent the fifth day preparing their elaborate costumes for dancing, this occasion is also a kind of dress rehearsal for the singing and rhythmic dancing scheduled for the late afternoon of the sixth and seventh days at the Royal Village. Assisted by Court officials, they drop their reeds outside the Queen Mother's compound before they move to the arena and dance

Zulu virgins select reeds for the traditional Reed Dance, where they will be presented to the king. (Ed Kashi/ Corbis)

in their own groups—all singing different songs simultaneously.

Seasonal Crafts

Photography is permitted at the **Umhlanga**, provided a permit is first obtained from the Tourist Office. After many months of preparation, the **Reed Dance** is an opportunity for the young women to show off not just their singing and dancing, but also their beadwork. KwaZulu's beadwork is renowned as the finest in Africa. The colors, patterns, and styles of the beadwork worn by the young women as both ornaments and clothing attest to the distinctive regional origin of the craftwork, which is also available as souvenir items. In Swaziland, the girls wear metal-studded, fringed puberty aprons, with beadwork in symbolic colors: red for fertility, white for purity or transition, and black for

wealth and marriage. The color coding of the tassels on the flashy yarn sashes they wear also denotes whether the maidens are already betrothed to be married or are still available to be courted by the eligible men ogling them along their procession. Strands of dried seed pods tied around the ankles enhance the beguiling cadence of their steps.

Royal Courtship and Final Sacrifice

On the second and last day of dancing, the girls parade into the stadium past the King, Queen Mother, Queens, ministers, and diplomats, in addition to hundreds of spectators from around the world. Speeches and performers entertain the Zulu royal family and their guests, as well as the local chiefs and their subjects. As the ceremony draws to a close, the King joins in the dancing and singing. He walks out to the girls with some of his retainers to appraise them and pay homage to those he finds most beautiful—by doing the *giya* courtship dance in Swaziland, and by kneeling in front of them in KwaZulu. There, members of the Royal Guard, who have been sitting around the edge of the stadium barely containing their excitement, eventually run to revere the girls in similar fashion. But when Swazi King Mswati III rises from the royal podium at the Ludzidzini arena, it is his choice of a new girlfriend and potential new wife he indicates by going over to one whose beauty or dancing has caught his eye, wielding his golden battle axe with his right hand, and placing his shield briefly at her feet as a sign of admiration. Clan diplomacy will determine the final choice of new concubines and wives over the course of the year. Because Swazis see it as a king's duty to have as many wives and children as possible, the current monarch's father Sobhuza II had sixty-five wives and over a hundred children over the course of his sixty-one-year reign. By contrast, Zulu King Zwelithini only takes advantage of this opportunity to choose a new wife every few years, as in the case of the fifth one in 1993. That year also saw the token participation of two young white girls, who wore red skirts and tops tied in a knot in the front, in contrast to the customary topless outfits of other maidens.

Led at first by royal princesses, the girls, numbering some 10,000 in KwaZulu and up to 25,000 in Swaziland, perform a number of dances for their king. By paying tribute to their respective kings in this way, the Zulu and Swazi nations, represented by the young women, bestow on them the symbolic authority to legitimately rule over their loyal subjects over the coming year. In return, the Zulu king makes a sacrifice to the royal ancestors on behalf of all the young women and their communities across the land. It is the chief princess, wearing the *inyongo* (the gall bladder of the main sacrificial beast, which is an important symbol of purity in any Zulu ritual), who leads the procession from the palace. To show his gratitude to the girls, the Swazi king orders some twenty or so heads of cattle to be slaughtered on the eighth and final day of the festival. The girls can then collect their pieces of meat and go home.

References
C. T. Binns. *The Warrior People: Zulu Origins, Customs and Witchcraft.* Cape Town, South Africa: Howard Timmins, 1974.

Hilda Kuper. *The Swazi: A South African Kingdom.* New York: Holt, Rinehart and Winston, 1963.

Brian Marwick. *The Swazi: An Ethnographic Account of the Natives of Swaziland.* London: F. Cass, 1966.

Brian Roberts. *The Zulu Kings.* London: Hamilton, 1974.

REMEMBRANCE DAY
See Martinmas, Rosh Hashanah

RÉVEILLON
See New Year (West)

RICE-TRANSPLANTING FESTIVAL
See Matsuri

RIDVÁN (BAHÁ'ISM)
In the Bahá'í calendar of nineteen weeks of nineteen days, there are nine holy days (mostly devoted to anniversaries of founders of the faith) on which believers ought to refrain from work. The first of them is the Persian **New Year**, **Naw Ruz**, on March 21. A month later begins the twelve-day festival of **Ridván**, during which elections are held in local assemblies. The first, ninth, and twelfth days of **Ridván** are the holiest, as they mark the anniversary of the **Declaration of Bahá'ullah's mission** as the Promised One of the Babi movement—and hence of all world religions according to the Bahá'í faith, since he was destined to bring a new universal

religion that finally fulfilled their promise of peace for a unified world.

Twelve Days in the Garden of Paradise

This took place in the so-called "Garden of Paradise" that the Persian name *Ridván* (pronounced "rez-vahn") refers to, located on the edge of the Tigris river in Bagdad, where Bahá'ullah's mostly Babi supporters came to say farewell to him during the twelve days he stayed there between April 21 and May 2, 1863 (hence the twelve days of the festival). He was about to leave for the imperial capital Constantinople (today's Istanbul), because Ottoman authorities had bowed to pressure from the government of his native Persia to remove him farther away from the borders of that country, as his prophetic activity was still causing some unrest there. After five years in Andrinople (present-day Edirne in Turkey), he would spend the rest of his life in detention in Palestine, where he died at 3:00 A.M. on May 29, 1892. This day is commemorated by Bahá'ís as that of his **Ascension**. It comes nearly a week after the anniversary of the **Bab**'s **Declaration** of his own mission on May 22, 1844, two hours and eleven minutes after sunset. Since sunset marks the end of a day in Bahá'í practice, Bahá'ís celebrate it on May 23, and the month of **May** for them is therefore like one big festival!

Other Festivals of the Prophets

As for the year 1844, it is also the first of the Bahá'í reckoning, since it was the one when the Bab acknowledged before an emissary of the Shaykhi movement of Shiites, who was looking for the *Mahdi* or Messiah of a new age, that he was himself the Door (the meaning of his name) to a new prophetic dispensation of the Truth. For Bahá'ís, this Door opens onto the Divine Manifestation of the prophet Bahá'ullah, an early follower of the Babi religion, that he would later reshape into their own.

This is why the **Bab**'s **martyrdom** at noon on July 9, 1850, and his **birth** on October 20, 1819, are commemorated on a par with **Bahá'ullah**'s **birth** on November 12, 1817, and his **Ascension** on May 29, 1892. But Bahá'ís prefer to downplay the dimension of mourning implied in the festivals of their two founders' parting from this world, deliberately wishing to avoid the penitential excesses displayed in the Shiite festival of **Ashura**, honoring Imam Hussein's martyrdom.

Moderate Merriment and Philanthropic Projects

The best way to show one's loyalty to Divine Manifestations who have gone back to their Source is to further the plan for a new world that they came to reveal. This is true for all Bahá'í festivals, which are not just an occasion for merrymaking; indeed, excesses in this direction are as strongly discouraged as ascetic extremes. Festivals are above all the best time to start new philanthropic projects such as schools and hospitals, or for individual good deeds and resolutions. In Iran, whenever persecution by the authorities does not prevent their public observance, **Ridván** and the other joyful festivals of Bahá'ism are nonetheless celebrated by picnics, playing music, singing verses from holy scripture, and making appropriate speeches. This pattern is followed and adapted by Bahá'ís outside Iran, in a number of countries second only to that of the ones where Christianity is present.

See also Ascension; Ashura; May Day; Naw Ruz; Nineteen-Day Feast

References

The Ascension of Bahá'ulláh: A Compilation. Los Angeles: Kalimát Press, 1991.

J. E. Esslemont. "Bahá'í Calendar, Festivals and Dates of Historic Significance," in *The Bahá'í World* (Haifa, Israel: The Universal House of Justice), Vol. 13, pp. 749–758.

Peter Smith. *The Bahá'í Religion: A Short Introduction to Its History and Teachings.* Oxford: G. Ronald, 1988.

RISSHUN

See New Year (Japan)

ROBIGALIA

See **Rogation**s

ROGATIONS (CHRISTIANITY)

In the West, the Sunday before the feast of the **Ascension** of Jesus Christ on a Thursday and the intervening three weekdays are known as **Rogation**s, a festival of public prayers and processions (often involving dragon floats in towns) to call God's blessing on the fields and the beasts and to consecrate rural boundaries.

Rogationtide Processions

It was Saint Mamertus who, either in 470 or in 474 (the year of his death on May 11), in thanksgiving for the end of the natural catastrophes that had lately been besetting the Alpine French town of Vienne of which he was bishop, made a vow to have solemn **Rogation**s (from a Latin word for "prayer') accompanied by fasting on the three days prior to the **Ascension** from that year onward. After mass, the people would go in penitential processions in the fields while singing the so-called "Gallican litanies" attributed to Saint Mamertus. The celebration of **Rogation**s was officially extended to all Frankish churches by the First Council of Orléans in 511 and soon spread to the rest of Europe. Pope Leo III adopted them at Rome around the time he restored the Western Roman Empire by crowning Charlemagne in 800. From then on, it was officially forbidden to work during the *triduum*, which is the Monday, Tuesday, and Wednesday of **Rogation**s. This prohibition was long applied by folklore to kneeding and washing.

About a century earlier, Pope Saint Gregory the Great had already instituted the more urban (and initially more strictly liturgical) processions of Major litanies on April 25, alongside the rural Minor litanies before **Ascension** that had made **Rogation**s so popular overnight, as they took over from pagan processions such as those of the late May **Ambarvalia**. In this ancient Roman festival, the god Mars had used to be invoked in purification rites and processions around the boundaries of arable land, as Rome's best protection against all aggressions from hostile forces beyond the pale of the city's culture and the country's agriculture alike. Though the name of the god Mars already finds an echo in the name of **Saint Mark** who has his feast day on April 25, the main reason for having a Major **Rogation** procession on this date, in view of obtaining God's blessing on the crops just planted, was more likely to supersede an older festival in the pagan calendar of Rome, called the **Robigalia**. It featured games with adult and junior races and a procession outside city limits to the fifth milestone of the Via Claudia. There, the priest of Quirinus sacrificed a red dog and a sheep in order to preserve the crops from the blight of "wheat rust" by appeasing its deity Robigo (as the disease was known in Latin). The Christian procession in Rome therefore followed the same itinerary as the pagan procession (up to a certain point, where it turned around and went back to Saint Peter's basilica for a mass).

Originally, Minor **Rogation** processions would do the grand tour of parish territory, with stops to rest and snack. Later on, they were scaled down to a small tour of the most important or sacred spots. The faithful would follow the priest in a very specific order of social categories (such as men, women, boys, girls). Temporary altars decorated with flowers and greenery were set up at every stop, where the priest would bless the fields and the beasts as the faithful sang the litanies. The blessings would be aimed at a specific harvest for each day, with the parish's major crop usually singled out on Wednesday as the final day of **Rogation**s. In 1969, as part of a general move away from such largely folkloric practices, the Roman Catholic Church shifted the focus of Minor **Rogation**s

Early in each farm season, Rogation Days are observed at the Mt. Loretto farm school in Colorado. This 1996 procession is led by priests who are blessing the flocks for a fruitful year. (Bettmann/Corbis)

from the processions to votive masses, to be observed in accordance with the guidelines set by local Churches. Of the few parishes that have kept on organizing traditional **Rogations** processions, some are found in parts of France, such as Burgundy, while in Switzerland, others take crosses and banners as they join the regional pilgrimage to Maria Sonnenberg chapel, where, since 1589, penitents bring petitions or leave *ex-votos* to the Virgin on *Kreuzmontag,* or "Cross Monday," before the **Ascension**.

Beating the Bounds

Having spread to England in the eighth century, **Rogation**tide is still known in its northern counties as the **Ganging Days**, after an Old English word for "going, walking" in the season's processions. Banned in many Protestant countries (though in some places the Lutheran Church has kept them before **Pentecost** and/or in May), **Ganging Days** were tolerated by the Anglican Church on account of the vital social role played by this collective "perambulation"

led by the clergy, which until the nineteenth century allowed villagers to publicly ascertain that no boundary markers delimiting property had been moved and that contracts had been respected. To this day in Leicester, such a bound-beating ceremony (reminiscent of the ancient Roman festival of **Terminalia**) is held every three years on **Ascension** Day in the presence of the city's notables and the cathedral's dean, who proclaims: "Cursed is he who removeth his neighbour's landmark!" Similar customs are known in other places in England, like Oxford.

They also occur during either **Rogation**tide or **Ascension**tide (the ten-day period between the feasts of the **Ascension** and **Pentecost**) in other countries such as Switzerland, Austria, and Bavaria. In these southern German lands, the beating of the bounds of parishes is often done on horseback. Sometimes, the horses are first made to witness the sacrament of the Eucharist at the parish church, which somehow establishes a mystical connection between the blood of Christ and the soil they are going to trample ritually to protect it from hail, in what is called a *Blutritt* or "Blood Ride." (This may perhaps help explain the resonance that slogans like *Blut und Boden* or "Blood and Soil," coupled with constant marching to establish territorial claims, could find in the national consciousness of Germany under Nazi rule.) In Hungary among other places, equestrian contests allow young people to display not only their skill, but also their manly vigor at this time of year, thereby communicating it to the ground as they trample it and jump on it. This fertilizing virtue of cavalcades may also have something to do with the famous Holy Blood procession and medieval pageant still held in Bruges every year—traditionally on **Ascension** Day, or now on the first Sunday after May 2; it centers on the display of a vial reputed to contain a drop of Christ's blood, which, since the Crusades, has become the city's palladium or totem and Belgium's most sacred relic.

Taming the Dragon

In France and Belgium, processional dragons often used to be led in triumph during **Rogation**tide in urban centers and were fed by the crowd along the way. In Paris, for instance, children would put small breads, pastries, and fruits in the mouth of the wickerwork dragon of Saint Marcel as it went through the streets; the food collected would then be given to the sick in the hospital. This particular parade disappeared around 1730. However, such dragons would also crop up in the giants' parades still known in many towns of Northern France, Belgium, and England, but they are much older than them and have probably inspired the fashion for oversized characters in these picturesque parades, which are literary more than folkloric in origin. The dragons themselves go back at least to the twelfth century and have their roots in the paganism which they came to represent in Christian legend. **Rogation**tide dragons (which would often come out again on **Ascension** Day itself—to say nothing of the role of dragons in Provençal and Spanish **Corpus Christi** processions) are usually associated with the particular local holy man who vanquished and tamed them. Yet, they do not represent evil as such, so much as the ambivalence of the forces of nature, particularly regarding the water supply vital to the crops, which they were universally thought to control. This is why they received offerings of the fruits of the earth in order to placate their power over its fruitfulness. But it also extended over humans in the discreet form of a custom found in parts of Burgundy, where the first girl to adorn the statue on the village fountain on **Rogations** would most likely get married over the year.

See also Ascension; Corpus Christi; Terminalia; Whitsuntide

References

Joyce Bazire and James E. Cross, eds. *Eleven Old English Rogationtide Homilies.* Toronto: University of Toronto Press, 1982.

Alain de Benoist. *Les Traditions d'Europe.* 2nd ed. Arpajon, France: Éditions du Labyrinthe, 1996.

Bernard of Clairvaux. *Sermons for the Summer Season: Liturgical Sermons from Rogationtide and Pentecost.* Tr. Beverly Mayne Kienzle and James Jarzembowski. Kalamazoo, MI: Cistercian Publications, 1991.

A. R. Wright. *British Calendar Customs. England, Vol. I: Movable Festivals.* London: The Folk-Lore Society, 1936.

ROIS (FÊTE DES)

See Epiphany

ROMAIA

See Fordicidia and Parilia

ROMAN GAMES

See Games (Rome)

ROSALIA, ROSARIA

See Easter, Whitsuntide

ROSH HASHANAH (JUDAISM)

The Jewish **New Year**, called **Rosh Hashanah**, is a fall celebration of the Creation of the world, of God's kingship, and of His future **Day of Judgment**—in view of which it opens a ten-day penitential period culminating at **Yom Kippur**. It features the solemn sounding of a horn called the *shofar,* recalling the ram substituted for Isaac in Abraham's sacrifice.

The Day of Creation

The Biblical term *Rosh Hashanah*, meaning "head of the year," did not originally refer to the fall festival now celebrated by Jews any time between September 6 and October 5 as their **New Year**'s Day on the first and second days of Tishri. This month used to be the seventh in the Babylonian calendar, which started in the spring. It was kept in this position by the rabbis of the early Common Era, even as they gave it a

Boy in prayer shawl for Rosh Hashana—the Jewish New Year—in New York City, 1911. (Library of Congress)

Babylonian name whose root *seru* means "to begin," on account of a festival that marked the beginning of the business year with the sale of the late crops, so that the Jewish **New Year** was eventually transferred to its date. Before it became **Rosh Hashanah**, the festival was already known in the Bible as **Yom Teru'ah** or the "**Day of Blowing the Horn**." Yet, the holy book does not tell us the reason why a horn was blown on this particular occasion, in addition to others like the weekly **Sabbath**, the monthly **New Moon** or **Rosh Hodesh**, and the anointing of a new king (a practice revived for the inauguration of Israeli presidents). According to a homily for the **Sabbath** of Repentance in the *Sefat Emet* collection of the Hasidic teachings of Rabbi Yehudah Leib Alter (1847–1905), there is "no need to sound the shofar on the **Sabbath**," since it was instituted in Eden by God's grace after Adam repented from his sin, as an actual

"return of Creation to Oneness, with no admixture of evil" necessitating divine mercy and human repentance. By contrast, in the mixed conditions of historical time, if "on each **Rosh Hashanah** the Creation is renewed," it is only "in accord with the consciousness and willingness of the people of Israel to accept His blessed kingdom," since "the shofar sound is meant to arouse this Oneness, as Scripture says: 'Make yourself two trumpets of silver . . . when the community is assembled, you shall sound them' (Numbers 10:2,7)" (Green 1984, p. 396).

Amid the music of drums, lyres, and harps, "sound the **New Moon** trumpet, at the full moon, on our feast day! This is a statute binding on Israel, an ordinance of the God of Jacob," sings the Psalmist (81:3–4). During the period of the Second Temple (515 B.C.E.–70 C.E.), because it was crucial that all Jews, wherever they were, begin the year at the same time, **Rosh Hashanah** came to be celebrated over two days (as ordained in the Jerusalem Talmud, *Erubin III*), so as to allow for delayed news or discrepancies between sightings of the **New Moon** of Tishri, as the signal to open the festival (except for a few exceptional cases that call for it to be postponed to the next day or the one after). Although a reform of the calendar in 359 had made it possible to observe the feast on the first of Tishri alone in Palestine, the two-day span of the feast eventually prevailed as standard practice both in the Holy Land and abroad, under the influence of twelfth-century Jewish scholars from Provence (who were also shaping the early Kabbala at this point). In this, **Rosh Hashanah** differs from other festivals that include a second day only in the Diaspora—that is, in Jewish communities outside the land of Israel. Unlike these other second days, that of **Rosh Hashanah** is considered part of the first and so does not permit a relaxation of the laws governing *nolad*, the creation of something that was not there before. This would be especially out of place on the day that the liturgy identifies with the Creation of the world—from which Jewish years are counted, being traditionally held to have taken place in 3761 B.C.E., on the twenty-fifth of the month of Ellul. The first of Tishri actually commemorates the sixth day of creation, when the primordial human couple of Adam and Eve was made to crown God's work.

The Day of Judgment

The opening of the books of life and death is another prominent theme on this **Judgment Day**, or **Yom ha-Din**, and is closely related to the theme of God as King. According to the historian of religion Sigmund Mowinckel in a classic study of *The Psalms in Israel's Worship* (1962), many psalms point to a pre-Exilic Hebrew **New Year** festival held in the fall. God was then enthroned as King in a way that recalls the enthronement of the sky god Marduk in the Babylonian pantheon on the **Akitu New Year** festival, in which this event had been moved from fall to spring. But as their religious scholars like to point out, instead of trembling like the heathens when they appear for judgment before their dread lord, the Jews rejoice in their trust in God's Providence, looking out for them over the year to come. During the **Rosh Hashanah** service, they recite ten Biblical texts proclaiming God's kingship, ten about His remembrance of His people (hence the day's name **Yom ha-Zikkaron** or "**Remembrance Day**"), and ten more about the means of this remembrance: the ceremonial shofar horn, made from any animal's horn except a cow's. It is sounded after each set of prayers: six times ten blasts after each plus forty at the end of the service, adding up to a hundred on both days—unless one falls on the **Sabbath** when even the horn cannot be used. Medieval commentators suggest that this is not only to express God's majesty and as a reminder of His glorious revelation on Mount Sinai (both evoked by the long and strong initial and final note), but also as a call for the soul to wake up, repent, and come back to the practice of the Law as given there to the chosen people of Israel (with trepidation over the process of judgment expressed in the short and somber middle notes). Since post-Biblical times, a ram's horn is preferred, in memory, it is said, of Abraham's submission to God's will, that eventually spared him the sacrifice of his son Isaac after it was first ordained by God. His obedience is also symbolized by the horn's curvature, since Abraham bowed completely before God. This was "a day of trumpet blast and battle cry" for the prophet Zephaniah (1:16), when "the whole world passes before God like a herd of sheep" in a striking image from Talmudic tradition (Malka 1989, p. 111). "Human beings are judged as individuals and as part of a group, as individual 'sheep' and as a 'flock,'" in a month that is seen as corresponding to the zodiac sign of Libra, the scales of justice. This symbolism also points to the dual quality of anxiety and elation of this festival:

> According to the sages, the patriarchs Abraham and Jacob were also born on **Rosh Hashanah**. Just as many bad events occurred on **Tisha be-Av,** so many happy events occurred on **Rosh Hashanah**. Three barren women (Sarah, Rachel, and Hannah) were made fertile, enabling them to bear children: Isaac, Joseph, and Samuel the Prophet. Jewish slave labor in Egypt stopped on the first day of Tishri. (Kanon 2002)

The Quality of Mercy

On the one hand, according to the Mishnah (a philosophical law code canonized by the second century), the awesome sounding of the shofar at the synagogue on **Rosh Hashanah** announces the Lord's Days of Judgment over all mankind. Yet on the other hand, a *midrash* or Bible commentary attributed to Rabbi Josiah also makes clear that "Israel is the people which knows how to win over their Creator with the blasts of the shofar, so that He rises from His throne of judgment to His throne of mercy and is filled with compassion for them, and turns

His quality of judgment into the quality of compassion" (Lev. R. 29:4, in "Rosh Ha Shanah" 1971, p. 309) For this to happen, His people must first return to Him by the way of repentance (*teshuvah*), over the course of the ten-day penitential season heralded by the shofar, leading up to atonement at **Yom Kippur**. This is why the thirteen attributes of divine mercy taught to Moses by God (Exodus 34:6–7) are central to the penitential prayers called *selihot* that are recited before the morning service of each of the ten days, and even in the preceding days of preparation for this period of heightened mindfulness of the Law.

Realizing what is really at stake, Jews then wish each other to be inscribed in the book of life for another year and many more. On the first night of the New Year, they prepare delicacies to offer each other for luck. At the festive meal of the second night, they dip pieces of bread and apple in honey so as to underline this hope that the quality of mercy will prevail and the new year will keep the sweet taste, expressed in the prayer they say before eating them: "May it be Thy will O Lord our God and God of our father, to renew unto us a good and sweet year" ("Rosh Ha Shanah" 1971, p. 305). But fortunes can still rise and fall over the coming year, as the ladder shape of a special seasonal bread reminds members of some Jewish communities. Pomegranate and fish evoke prosperity, and dates represent God's good care of Israel in thwarting the schemes of its enemies. However, nuts may not be eaten, because their Hebrew name is numerologically equivalent to the word for "sin," and as Jews pray to God at the *Tashlikh* ceremony after the prophet Micah: "to the bottom of the sea throw [*ve-tashlikh*] all our sins" (Micah 7:19). For this, they gather near a body of running water to recite appropriate Bible verses and *selihot* on the first afternoon of **Rosh Hashanah** (or the second afternoon if it falls on a **Sabbath**). The lidless gaze of the fish from below the waters is traditionally said to reflect God's ever-merciful looking out for his creatures from above the heavens.

See also Akitu; Conception and Birth of the Virgin Mary; Naw Ruz; Rosh Hodesh; Sabbath; Tisha be-Av; Tu bi-Shevat; Yom Kippur

References

Max Arzt. *Justice and Mercy: Commentary on the Liturgy of the New Year and the Day of Atonement.* New York: Holt, Rinehart and Winston, 1963.

Philip Goodman, ed. *The Rosh Hashana Anthology.* Philadelphia, PA: Jewish Publication Society of America, 1971.

Arthur Green. "Teachings of the Hasidic Masters," in Barry W. Holtz, ed. *Back to the Sources. Reading the Classic Jewish Texts.* New York: Summit Books, 1984.

Jerusalem Bible. Garden City, NY: Doubleday and Co., 1968.

Sharon Kanon. "Celebrating the World's Birthday," in *Western Jewish Bulletin,* September 6, 2002, http://www.jewishbulletin.ca/archives/Sept02/archives02Sept06–11.html.

Victor and Salomon Malka. *Le Petit Retz du judaïsme.* Paris: Retz, 1989.

Mishnah Tractate Rosh Hashanah with the commentary of Rabbi Ovadiah MiBartinura. Tr. Jeffrey R. Cohen. Brooklyn, NY: Tanna v'Rav Publications, 1981.

Allan Rosengren Petersen. *The Royal God: Enthronement Festivals in Ancient Israel and Ugarit.* Sheffield, UK: Sheffield Academic Press, 1998.

"Rosh Ha-Shanah," in *Encyclopedia Judaica.* New York: Macmillan, 1971.

ROSH HODESH (JUDAISM)

The day of the **New Moon** marks the beginning of a month in the Jewish calendar, hence its Hebrew name *Rosh Hodesh,* meaning "the head of the month." It should be observed with rejoicing like a festival, though some sects keep a **Yom Kippur**-like fast on its eve.

Biblical Prescriptions

This is because **New Moon** feasts are put on a par with other festivals in the Bible's Book of Numbers (10:10), and on account of verse 24 of Psalm 118, always recited on this occasion: "This is the day made memorable by Yahweh, what immense joy for us!" Fasting is therefore forbidden, and funeral services are kept to a minimum, as is domestic work. On the contrary, it is recommended that every family hold a festive meal or *zebah* as in the Book of Samuel (1:20). This sacred feast is concluded with the special prayer "*Ya'aleh ve-Yavo*" in the grace said afterwards. As on the last six days of **Passover**, an abbreviated "half-Hallel" (omitting parts of Psalms 115 and 116) is read on the **New Moon** at the synagogue.

According to the Bible, on the **New Moon** people would go on a pilgrimage to see a holy man (2 Kings 4:23), and members of a family who lived in different places would come together at their birthplace for a festive sacrificial meal. At the royal court, this feast was also held on the following day, and ritual purity was a prerequisite for being allowed at the table (1 Samuel 20). The law set down in Numbers (28:11–15) also required three special public sacrifices: a burnt offering, a grain offering, and a libation, preceded by a sin offering in order to ensure ritual purity.

For all these reasons, one of the main functions of the old Sanhedrin religious High Court into the Common Era was the sacred proclamation of the first day of the new month: the *kiddush ha-Hodesh* or "sanctification of the month." It was made by an official called the *Beth-Din* after he had waited through the night and day of the thirtieth for the detailed reports of the first eyewitnesses of the appearance of the **New Moon**'s faint crescent, called the *Molad*, which, once ascertained beyond any shadow of a doubt (a task so vital it overruled **Sabbath** restrictions on human activity), marked the start of the first day of the corresponding month; if they failed to appear, it was automatically proclaimed for the second half of an extra thirty-first day. This is why **Rosh Hodesh** is actually celebrated over two days: the thirtieth of the old month and the first of the new, except after twenty-nine day months, when only the latter is observed, unless it is after the month of Ellul, since the **Rosh Hodesh** of Tishri happens to be **Rosh Hashanah**.

A Minor Day of Atonement

It is said to be in memory of the *Beth-Din*'s *kiddush ha-Hodesh* that, since the destruction of the Temple of Jerusalem in 70, the solemn announcement of **Rosh Hodesh** at the synagogue on the previous **Sabbath**, the *birkat ha-Hodesh*, is recited while standing before the *Musaf* service, where the former additional **New Moon** sacrifice used to be; it starts with the words: "The beginnings of the months Thou didst assign unto Thy people for a season of atonement throughout their generations." On this basis, a minor day of atonement called **Yom Kippur Katan** has been observed on the eve of the **New Moon** by Kabbalists since the sixteenth century, under the influence of the school of Isaac Luria in Safed, in the mountains of upper Galilee.

A Day of Rest for Women

If business transactions were to be avoided on the **New Moon** in Biblical times (Amos 8:5), work is still allowed when it comes up today, though women may take the day off or do only light tasks, like sewing as opposed to weaving. This is meant as a reward to Jewish women for not having given up their jewelry to be used in making the golden calf while Moses was away on Mount Sinai.

From Monthly to Weekly and Yearly Cycles

Before a permanent calendar was established in the fourth century, a month officially began when beacons were kindled on the Mount of Olives. They were then relayed by other fires all over the Holy Land and even in the Diaspora, so as to notify all Jews that the members of the High Court or *Sanhedrin* had sanctified the **New Moon** on the basis of the sightings of two reliable witnesses, as mentioned earlier. But messengers had to be dispatched to faraway communities whenever confusion was created by the misleading beacons of the heretical Samaritans. In such cases, the **New Moon** was sometimes observed on both the thirtieth and thirty-first days of the month.

Over time, the increasing importance of the **Sabbath** made the **New Moon** relatively less significant, as a weekly rhythm of observances gradually took precedence over the monthly cycle of the lunar calendar. The **New Moon** of the seventh month, that of Tishri in early fall, was an exception, since it heralded the main **pilgrimage festival**—the **festival of ingathering**, or **Sukkot**. This was done by sounding the *shofar* horn on this particular **New Moon**, which eventually became the way to ring in the Jewish **New Year**. While ordinary **New Moons** receded into the background, one **Rosh Hodesh** was thus raised above the others as **Rosh Hashanah**.

> **See also** Noumenia; Passover; Rosh Hashanah; Sabbath; Sukkot; Yom Kippur

References

Encyclopedia Judaica. New York: Macmillan, 1971;
Bruce M. Metzger and Michael D. Coogan, eds. *The Oxford Companion to the Bible.* Oxford: Oxford University Press, 1993.
Judith Y. Solomon. *The Rosh Hodesh Table: Foods of the New Moon. Jewish Women's Monthly Festivals.* New York: Biblio Press, 1995.

▮ ROYAL ENTRY
See Conception and Birth of the Virgin Mary, Corpus Christi

▮ RUNNING OF THE BULLS
See Games (Rome)

▮ RUSALII, RUSHAJET, RUSICAT
See Whitsuntide

▶ SABBATH (JUDAISM)

The **Sabbath** is the last day of the Jewish week, ordained by God as a day of rest like the seventh day of Creation, when He rested after all His work. Strict rules curtailing any creative activities on the part of His chosen people of Israel are there to make sure that all its members do the same and turn to God as the uncreated source of all creation.

History

The observance of the **Sabbath** is not attested before the eighth century B.C.E., but Israelite legal traditions as recorded in the Book of Exodus (23:12, 34:21) suggest an earlier date. Yet, despite its inclusion among the Ten Commandments, it is unlikely to go all the way back to Moses himself, as it presupposes a move from nomadic and pastoral ways to sedentary agricultural ways. It does not seem to have been very strictly enforced before the exile in Babylon, where it may have been influenced by the local custom of holding the seventh and last day (called *shabattu*) of every quarter of the twenty-eight-day lunar month to be inauspicious for most human endeavors and activities, since it was ruled by the planet Saturn and its genius Ea, inducing sluggishness in mind and body. The masters refrained from work as a taboo on Saturday and also made it a day of rest

for their slaves. From there it was but a short step for Hebrews among these slaves to hallow *Shabbat* as their own special day. For it set them apart from the idolaters around them as the basis for a unique seven-day week, distinct from the quarters of the moon that regulated Babylonian religious life and therefore independent of natural cycles in its hallowing of time itself at fixed numerical intervals to face the utterly transcendent Creator of all things. It remains the only day to be named in the Jewish week, the other six being simply numbered—one half as leading up to the **Sabbath** (Wednesday to Friday), and the other half as coming after the **Sabbath** (Sunday to Tuesday).

In the days of the Temple of Jerusalem, the twelve showbreads, arranged on a table next to the Holy of Holies to stand for the twelve tribes of Israel, were changed by the priests on every **Sabbath**. With its destruction by the Babylonians in 586 B.C.E., the Synagogue Period began, named after a building deliberately designed to hold a weekly congregation. Replacing the spatial center provided by the Temple, the temporal structure of a pulsating week defined by the **Sabbath** as its peak (and long identified with the week as a whole by a common name, as it still is by the Armenian *Shapat*) rested on the new institution of the synagogue, where the Jewish people could gather anywhere in remembrance of God. It was therefore known as the "**Sabbath** house" until as late as the first century B.C.E., when the **Sabbath** was about to be permanently identified with the day of Saturn (a planet they therefore named Shabtai) in the astrological sequence of seven planetary days that had already gained wide currency in Greco-Roman culture on the basis of Babylonian lore, which and is still reflected in the number and names of the days in most European languages. Regulations and prohibitions for this weekly holiday had proliferated after the return of the Hebrews to the Holy Land. When they later spread through the Hellenistic world and the Roman Empire, their superstitious Gentile neighbors may have come to view this day as an unlucky one when it was best to do as little as possible (much as the Babylonians had done before them). This may be why they too easily associated it with Saturn, the god and the planet of restrictions and downfall.

Turning from Creatures to the Creator

The **Sabbath** is traditionally thought to owe its name to a Hebrew word for "bringing to an end," with reference to the seventh day of creation in the first chapter of Genesis, when God rested in the satisfaction of six days of work on the world, making it a day of completion. According to a *midrash* or Bible commentary, if God, who knows no exertion, can "write about Himself" that he rested, how much more ought man to rest, since it is said that he was born to toil. This day of rest is therefore at the heart of the Jewish religious and national identity, on the basis of God's explicit commands to remember it and hallow it by ceasing work after six days (Exodus 20), and to observe it in memory of Israel being delivered from slave labor in Egypt by God's mighty deeds (Deuteronomy 5). These two commands are symbolized by the two candles that the mistress of a Jewish household will light

an hour before nightfall on Friday, to herald the **Sabbath** about to begin, as it lasts from sundown to sundown. During this time, no more fire may be kindled or extinguished, and no creative activity may be undertaken. This includes buying and selling, writing, and traveling more than half a mile beyond city limits. It ensures that attention shifts from particular lights to the Source of Light itself, from creatures to the very fact of Creation, and to the Creator who acts through it for His chosen people. According to the Jewish theologian Abraham Heschel, "the meaning of the **Sabbath** is to celebrate time rather than space. Six days a week we live under the tyranny of things of space; on the **Sabbath** we try to become attuned to *holiness in time*. It is a day on which we are called upon to share in what is eternal in time, to turn from the results of creation to the mystery of creation; from the world of creation to the creation of the world" (Heschel 2003, p. xviii) and to its ultimate end, when Creation will have been redeemed from all evil and restored to oneness in God. For when Jews observe the **Sabbath**, their faces are said to glow with the radiance of *neshamah yeter*—an "additional soul" that enters the lives of mortals as the primal light Adam and Eve enjoyed in Eden, allowing them to see the world in the pristine glory which will suffuse it again in the messianic time. Meanwhile, the **Sabbath** is also a day of much needed physical rest from hard work, to which not only Jews are entitled, but also their beasts of burden, their slaves, and the foreigners in their midst (Exodus 23:12).

By extension, under Mosaic law, the land itself was allowed to rest every seventh year as a sabbatical year when little work was done, the social hierarchies largely determined by labor were relaxed, and all accumulated debts were cancelled. Every fifty years, the one following seven such sabbaticals was the jubilee as ***Shabbat** shabatton* (meaning something like "**Sabbath** of **Sabbath**s"), when the land was redistributed equally between all the clans of Israel, restoring an "original" state of social justice.

Sabbath at the Synagogue

It has been a challenge for Judaism to translate some age-old customs, devised to honor the holiness of the **Sabbath** since the days of the Patriarchs, to the modern context of the technological world that has made basic creative procedures so casual. Both electricity and the internal combustion engine involve the kindling of fires. This can be gotten around in the case of electrical appliances by the use of time-switches set in advance. Automobile travel is forbidden by Orthodox Judaism and allowed by Reform, while Conservative Jews may use their cars to go to the synagogue.

There, Psalms 95–99 about God's kingship as a present fact are recited before the Friday evening service called *Kabbalat* **Shabbat** ("Welcoming the **Sabbath**") and dating back to the Middle Ages. The Song of Songs is added in Sephardic communities, where the Moroccan poet Shimon Levi's song in memory of the early Talmudic master Bar Yohai is also sung at home. The practice of singing the hymn *Lekhah Dodi* (composed around 1540 by the Kabbalist Rabbi Solomon ben Moses ha-Levi Alkabetz) at the start of the Friday evening service was initially confined to the Sephardic rite, but it is now also standard in the Ashkenazi tradition of Northern and Eastern Europe. Its opening lines, from which the title is taken, set the stage for sexual imagery drawn from the Bible's Song of Songs to evoke the encounter of the **Sabbath** (as the crowning seventh day of Creation) with her Lord (who had her in mind from before Creation) as a prefiguration of the reunion of opposites in the messianic final days (bringing Creation back to the Creator):

> Come, my Beloved, with chorus of praise.
> Welcome **Sabbath** the Bride, Queen of our days.

> Come, let us all greet Queen **Sabbath** sublime,
> Fountain of blessings in every clime.
> Anointed and regal since earliest time,
> In thought she preceded Creation's six days.
>> (Wigoder 2002, p. 473)

In Israel, where it originated like the psalm recitation among Isaac Luria's Safed circle of Kabbalists, this poem used to be sung while the faithful literally went out in the courtyard of the synagogue or into the fields around town to meet the **Sabbath** at sunset, and to meditate on the mystical inner meaning of this sacred moment. As a relic of this custom, today all eyes turn toward the door of the synagogue while the *Lekhah Dodi* is being recited.

The Saturday morning service includes the weekly Torah readings (while those of the following weeks are previewed in the afternoon service). The Torah scroll is first retrieved from its cabinet (called "the ark" to recall the Ark of the Law in the Holy of Holies of the Temple of Jerusalem), taken around the synagogue and unveiled. It is then read by at least seven members of the congregation (though some may prefer to follow on the scroll as another reads from it). Their ascent to the podium (called *aliyah*) is the moment to announce or celebrate important turning points in the life of individual members, be it times of crisis with prayers for the sick and thanksgiving for a rescue from peril or happy occasions like marriages scheduled for the coming week and the birth or naming of babies. The best known such occasion is a rite of passage called Bar Mitzvah, when a boy (or a girl, in the case of the Bat Mitzvah, also to be found in many Conservative and Reform congregations) who has turned thirteen over the past week assumes adult religious responsibilities before the community by doing one of the readings from the Torah. He (or she) may sometimes additionally chant the *Haftarah*, a thematically related excerpt from the Prophets that is read out on feasts and fast days.

Special Sabbaths

There are a number of **Special Sabbaths** throughout the Jewish calendar, featuring liturgical variations, particular customs, or commemorations of events or themes. They are sometimes named after a key word in the additional Torah reading that then replaces the *Maftir,* the last portion of the assigned one, as in the case of the "four readings" (*Arba' Parashiyyot*), each with their own special *Haftarah* as well. Concentrated in springtime, they are named **Shabbat** *Sheqalim* (after *shekels,* a monetary unit, from Exodus 30:11–16) just before the month of Adar (or the second one of this name in a leap year), **Shabbat** *Zakhor* (after "remember," from Deuteronomy 25:17–19) before **Purim**, then **Shabbat** *Parah* (meaning "red heifer," from Numbers 19:1–22) and *Ha-Hodesh* (or "the month," from Exodus 12:1–20) in immediate succession leading up to **Passover**. While the **Sabbath** just before **Passover** is called **Shabbat** *ha-Gadol* ("great **Sabbath**"), the one that takes the most place in liturgical life is **Shabbat** *Mevarekhin,* recurring all through the year, since it immediately precedes a new month; the name of the month is then formally announced along with the day of the **New Moon** on which it begins. In many Ashkenazi communities where women did not usually attend **Sabbath** services, they would come on this "**Sabbath** of the Blessing," named after the special **Rosh Hodesh** petition composed by Rav, which asks for life, peace, gladness, salvation, and consolation for the house of Israel.

Domestic Rites

It is in any case up to women to make sure that distinctive food is prepared in advance for the **Sabbath** and that the table is specially set when the head of the household returns from the synagogue. There will then be two candles and two loaves of white **Sabbath** bread (in contrast to black weekday rye bread, just as **Sabbath** fish is different from regular salt her-

ring), to recall the double portion of manna provided by God to the Jews on their journey through the wilderness, so that they would not have to work to get their food on the **Sabbath**. These *hallot* are covered by decorative cloths (traditionally embroidered by women since the seventeenth century) during the abridged *kiddush* blessing said by the husband over a cup of wine, so that the precious life-giving bread does not take offense at the special treatment of the festive drink. The children of the house will first have been blessed by both parents. Special table hymns called *zemirot* are chanted at the day's festive meals, where it is better to also have guests. In Hasidic communities, the courses are the same from one week and one household to the next, since this is not a meal where a wife's particular human gift for cooking should get special notice and risk detracting attention from the general divine gift of the occasion itself. The **Sabbath** concludes on Saturday evening with the *Havdalah* blessing, thanking God for separating the sacred from the profane—like day from night and the **Sabbath** from weekdays, blessing over spices so they can cheer up the soul after the holy day's departure, and a blessing over light so that fire may be kindled again. The special **Sabbath** clothes one should wear can then go back to the separate **Sabbath** half of the wardrobe, since the Talmud insists on the cultivation of a distinctive "**Sabbath** look" contrasting with profane weekday garb, which includes a requirement that women wear special jewelry.

Borderline Cases

According to the pioneering sociologist of time Eviatar Zerubavel (1989, p. 116),

> The ancient Talmudic ruling that travelers who lose count of the days of the week should nevertheless keep observing the **Sabbath** every seventh day despite the likelihood of its being the "wrong" day makes it quite clear that at the

A Jewish family prays before the Sabbath meal. (Dave Bartruff/Corbis)

very heart of the institution of the **Sabbath** lies the periodic alternation between the sacred and the profane along a 6–1 pattern. This structural feature is far more central to Judaism than the actual temporal location of the sacred within historical time.

In another significant ruling, Rabbi Akiva ben Joseph (50–136), one of the four great masters of the Mishnah, held that the **Sabbath** was only desecrated if a proscribed act was performed even though it could have been done before or after. If there was no choice, there was no offense, so that for instance a midwife could freely ply her trade if a woman came into labor on the **Sabbath**. However, healing people, as Jesus Christ insisted on doing on the **Sabbath**, would not have fallen into this category. There were also those who stuck to the strict letter of the prohibitions, such as the Essene sect based in Qumran, who would not help a wounded animal or one giving birth if it happened to be the **Sabbath**. However, studying the Torah for a while is allowed, with due moderation on this divinely ordained day of rest for all Jews, pious or not. It is also a preferred time for conjugal lovemaking. In the State of Israel, the **Sabbath** is the official day of rest on which all businesses must be closed, the only question being the legal definition of a business.

See also Day of Assembly; Nyepí; Passover; Purim; Rosh Hashana; Rosh Hodesh; Sunday

References

Eviatar Zerubavel. *The Seven Day Circle. The History and Meaning of the Week.* Chicago: University of Chicago Press, 1985.

Abraham Joshua Heschel. *The Sabbath: Its Meaning for Modern Man.* Boston: Shambhala Publications, 2003.

"Lekhah Dodi," in Geoffrey Wigoder, ed. *The New Encyclopedia of Judaism.* New York: New York University Press, 2002.

Yehoshua Noivirot. *Shemirath Shabbath: A Guide to the Practical Observance of the Sabbath.* New York: Feldheim, 1989.

Adin Steinsaltz. *Miracle of the Seventh Day: A Guide to the Spiritual Meaning, Significance, and Weekly Practice of the Jewish Sabbath.* San Francisco: Jossey-Bass, 2003.

▶ SACRED HEART (CHRISTIANITY)

On the heels of **Corpus Christi** comes another Eucharistic feast instituted by the Roman Catholic Church on the basis of the private visions of woman mystics: the feast of the **Sacred Heart** of Jesus, focusing on forgiveness for sins against his real presence in the bread consecrated at Mass and for ingratitude for this saving sacrifice of his body.

From the Wound on Christ's Side to the Heart Inside

It was only from the eleventh century onward that, in the Western Church (as opposed to the newly separate Eastern Church), devotional attention gradually shifted from the wound on Jesus' side, out of which came his blood in Passion narratives, to the wounded organ inside, in the private meditations and mystical visions of a growing number of contemplatives. This theme was eventually taken up by certain religious orders, like the Franciscans who were propagating a devotion to the Five Wounds on Christ's crucified body, as part of which the image of the wounded heart of Jesus was widely circulated—all the more so when the Jesuits made it their emblem, appearing on books and buildings alike. By their time in the Counterreformation, various ascetic writers had helped make this devotional theme familiar to a broader public. In 1641, the Jesuit-educated Norman preacher Saint John Eudes founded the Congregation of Jesus and Mary on the basis of the intertwined cults of both their hearts, that of the Virgin still being more specifically revered on account of the spreading belief in her **Immaculate Conception**. He wrote the first liturgical services for each of these cults, and was then able to devise a distinct feast of the **Sacred Heart** of Jesus, which was celebrated for the first time in 1670—on August 31 in Rennes and on October 20 in Coutances. It is still observed on the latter date by Eudist Fathers.

A Penitential Twist to Eucharistic Piety

Yet such a feast would only become popular as a result of a series of divine apparitions to Saint Margaret Mary Alacoque (1647–1690), a humble nun of the recently founded Congregation of the **Visitation of Holy Mary**. (The name refers to Mary's visit to her cousin Elizabeth, six months pregnant with Saint John the Baptist. This Gospel episode is itself the object of a minor feast since the fourteenth-century Council of Basel; it was revived in 1863 as a way to promote the newly proclaimed dogma of the **Immaculate Conception**, and switched from July 2 to May 31 in 1969.) Saint Margaret Mary maintained that Christ had requested to be honored under the guise of his heart of flesh and that a feast should be established for this purpose on the Friday after the octave of **Corpus Christi** (during which this "great apparition" took place around June 16, 1675). This was to be done in reparation for all sins against the Eucharist, as a most grievous instance of the ingratitude for Christ's love already displayed by men at the Passion it stood for, and ever since then. She was also instructed to turn to Father Claude La Colombière, superior of the Jesuits in the same Burgundian town of Paray-le-Monial. He readily consecrated himself to the **Sacred Heart** and used Saint Margaret Mary's written account to promote this new cult, which could soon count for this on the Jesuits and Visitandines as well as the Eudists.

From a Small Order's Mass to a Feast for All Mankind

Though the cult of the **Sacred Heart** rapidly spread to other religious communities, the Holy See was still lukewarm and only granted the feast for the exclusive use of the Visitandines with the Mass of the Five Wounds in 1697. The cult became common among the general population when several cities in the south of France followed the example of Marseille, which had publicly worshipped the **Sacred Heart** and consecrated itself to it in 1720 to seek relief from a plague. In the face of this growing momentum, the French Church as a whole was finally allowed to observe the feast in 1765 and, maintaining the pressure on the papacy, was able to obtain from Pius IX its adoption by the Catholic Church as a whole in 1856, as a double major. It was upgraded to the double rite of first class in 1889, but in the meantime, more and more groups, congregations, and states had been consecrated to the **Sacred Heart** (not to mention the massive basilica built between 1879 and 1910 atop Montmartre in reparation for the revolutionary excesses of the Paris Commune of 1871). On Sunday June 11, 1899, all of mankind was solemnly consecrated to the **Sacred Heart** by Leo XIII, in what he called "the great act" of his pontificate, inspired by the visions of Sister Mary of the Divine Heart (née Drost-zu-Vischering), a nun of the Good Shepherd in Oporto, Portugal. She had happened to pass away two days before, on the actual date of the feast of the **Sacred Heart**, that is on the third Friday after **Pentecost**. An office and the mass *Cogitationes* were added to the service in 1929, and three series of three readings in 1970. Like **Corpus Christi**, the feast of the **Sacred Heart** has a strong visual focus on a vivid symbol of Christ's sacrifice, to foster pious meditation and religious feeling—here: compassion for his sufferings for the sake of mankind and reliance on their efficacy to make up for the latter's lack of mindfulness of them.

See also Corpus Christi, Whitsuntide

References

The Catholic Encyclopedia. New York: Robert Appleton Company, 1912 (Online Edition: Kevin Knight, 1999).

Raymond Jonas. *France and the Cult of the Sacred Heart: An Epic Tale for Modern Times.* Berkeley: University of California Press, 2000.

New Catholic Encyclopedia. New York: McGraw-Hill, 1969.

▷ SACRIFICE (FEAST OF)
See Eid

▷ SAD-HALDA
See Divali

▷ SAIDAIJI EYO
See Naked Festivals

▷ SAINT ANN
See Pardon

▷ SAINT BASIL THE GREAT
See Epiphany, New Year (West)

▷ SAINT BRIDE, SAINT BRIDGET
See Candlemas

▷ SAINT CATHERINE
See Saint Nicholas

▷ SAINT DASIUS
See Saturnalia

▷ SAINT DEMETRIOS
See Saint George

▷ SAINT DISTAFF DAY
See Epiphany

▷ SAINT ELIGIUS, SAINT-ÉLOI
See Martinmas

▶ SAINT FERMIN

See Games (Rome)

▶ SAINT GEORGE (CHRISTIANITY)

April 23 marks the feast of **Saint George**, one of Christianity's most popular saints, since he has something for everyone: commemorated at a turning point of the pastoral year, this martial protector of states in general and agriculture in particular is chiefly known for saving a princess from a drought-causing dragon.

A Military Saint

The least dubious piece of information we have about Saint George's largely—if not entirely—legendary life is that he was apparently beheaded for his faith during the last great Roman persecution of Christians, under Emperor Diocletian on April 4, 304, in Lydda—Lod in present-day Israel. There were pilgrimages to his grave from the sixth century to the eighth, when the Muslim conquest of Palestine made them more difficult—even though local rulers have kept respecting any church dedicated to this native son. His story as put together in the twelfth and thirteenth centuries states that he was born there in 280 and, walking in his father's footsteps, became a high-ranking officer in the Roman army. He fought gallantly on the Empire's frontiers, at first in the East against the Persians, and then serving in the West on the staff of Emperor Constantius Chlorus in York. This episode would later cause him to be associated with Glastonbury, the holy city of Arthurian romance, and contribute to making him the model of the Christian knight. As such, he became the patron saint, not just of England (replacing King Edward the Confessor since the 1222 Council of Oxford), but of countless European towns and several Christian nations, starting of course with Georgia in the East all the way to Portugal in the West, and including the former kingdoms of Sicily in Italy and Aragon in Spain.

A Book and a Rose on Saint George's Day

Also part of Spain, Catalonia has made of the feast of its patron **Saint George** a day to reaffirm its nationhood against the central state's attempts to suppress it after its side lost in the War of the Spanish Succession of the early eighteenth century. A custom arose of lovers exchanging a rose (since in Catalan folklore roses instead of blood streamed from the dragon's neck after the brave knight **Saint George** freed a princess by cutting it with his sword) and a book (since April 23 happened to be the date on which Spain's greatest writer Miguel de Cervantes is traditionally said to have died in 1616—though historians favor April 22 as the actual day). In 1923, it was officially sanctioned as a double gift to loved ones by the Catalan Chamber of the Book Trade. In 1995, foreign publishing and media personalities were invited to Barcelona to witness the very popular social event that this practice had allowed the yearly opening of the book publishing season to become. They were so impressed that UNESCO promptly declared April 23 to be World **Book Day**. Jointly with the Catalan government, it then launched a successful worldwide campaign to have book trade organizations of a now growing list of countries observe **Saint George**'s Day by encouraging its customs there, with bookstores giving out roses and free books to shoppers.

Saint George and the Dragon

In Eastern Christianity, **Saint George** is honored as a "Great Martyr," and his intercession is asked for in the matins of his feast on behalf of "those who suffer various tribulations" in order to "free them from all oppressions." This is also why, for example, South Indian pilgrims (Christian or not) flock by the thousands to make offerings of money or *ex-votos* to miraculous statues of **Saint George** on the occasion of the patronal feast of two great Catholic churches dedicated to him in Kerala, among the most popular festivals in that state. Both last eleven days (the one at the ancient Forane Church in Edapally from April 23 to culminate on May 4 and that of Edathua from April 27 with its climax on May 6), and feature the ceremonial hoisting of **Saint George**'s flag, the procession of his statue, colorful historic costumes, the illumination of the church, and spectacular fireworks.

As the martial champion of the oppressed, **Saint George** was depicted riding a white horse on the banners and pennants of the Byzantine Empire, and still is on the regimental flags of the Greek army, as its patron saint. He has always been seen as the Christian embodiment of the classical Greek heroic ideal. Hymns written in his honor have thus incorporated many features of tales from pagan mythology about demigods, like Cadmus who killed the dragon guarding a spring, sowed its teeth in the earth and reaped a harvest of armed men: the *Sparti* ("Sown"), noble founders of Thebes in Boeotia.

Another example is the famous story which appeared around the tenth century, about how George fought against the dragon who was terrorizing a city and demanding human sacrifice as tribute, or else he would cut its water supply. **Saint George** volunteered to kill the dragon and save the king's daughter who had been designated as the next victim, on the condition that he and his people would accept baptism into the Christian Church. This is usually said to have happened in the Libyan city of Selena, but in other versions the story it is set in England near a hill known as Arthur's Table (*Bwrydd Arthur*), and in others still in Joppa (present-day Arsuf) on the coast of Palestine. The latter happened to be the place where Perseus was supposed to have killed the sea-monster to which the local king's daughter Andromeda was being offered, so it would stop devastating the country with floods. This Greek myth was thought by Robert Graves to have been born of a reinterpretation of the iconography of Philistine coastal shrines of Astarte, showing the

Akkadian god of heaven and order Bel killing the female sea-monster Tiamat, thereby subduing chaos in Babylon's creation myth. This cosmological theme, echoed in the Bible, is vividly conveyed in the imagery of **Saint George** and the dragon as the triumph of good over evil.

Green George

Yet no less important is the connection between the dragon and water, as shown at the climax of the celebration of **Saint George**'s Day as the patronal feast of Arachova near Mount Parnassus in Greece. The village's water supply having been cut off earlier, it is restored again when the dancing old men who sing the popular Greek folk song about **Saint George** come to the line saying: "Dragon, set the water free that revelers may drink." As part of a mythological pattern to be found from Europe to China, **Saint George** represents the typical Western instance of the warrior hero who protects agriculture by regulating the flow of water, sustaining it, and he generally promotes vegetation and growth: his Greek name after all means "he who works the earth." That is why he appears on his April 23 feast as Green George in much European folklore and is often identified in Britain with the Green Man of **May Day** customs, themselves derived from **Beltane**, the ancient Celtic feast of the light principle Bel. Such is the case in the Cornish town of Padstow, where the **May Day** Hobby-Horse goes through the streets and enters every house singing: "Oh where is **Saint George**? Oh where is he, Oh?"— no doubt as a way to invite fertility in. In the Belgian city of Mons, the *combat de Lumeçon* attracts large crowds every year as a ritual performance of the fight of **Saint George** on horseback (accompanied by people on foot in bizarre costumes impersonating his hunting dogs and horses) against a wooden dragon carried by "wild men" wearing foliage. In eastern Slovakia, as part of a **Palm Sunday** maypole procession, children sang: "**Saint George** calls, the earth will open,/All forms of flowers will come, roses and violets./Grandmothers be merry, we bring you summer,/Pretty green rosemary, indeed a grove, a green **May**" (Mihalek 2000, p. 3). Unlike other Eastern European peoples, Slovenes did not always accept substitutes for a real Green George to throw into a body of water after the foliage-clad figure had led the young people's joyful **Saint George**'s Day tree procession. Serbs used to rise before dawn and swim in a river before a communal breakfast picnic in the fields or the woods, on this the official start of the campaign season for the haiduks (partisans who for centuries kept up a guerilla struggle against the Turks occupying their country). In Tyrol, children would "ring the grass" to chase away the evil spirits that might hinder growth. In parts of Russia and the Ukraine, the priest would go out into the fields to bless them before young married couples rolled several times over the sprouting crop to promote their growth. Alternatively, he himself might be rolled over the fields willy-nilly by the women, so the holy powers ascribed to his person would imbibe the ground and allow the corn to grow for all—including the priest, as the parishioners were quick to point out when he dared to complain. Conversely, a Serb or Croat woman who was unable to have children used to place a new chemise overnight on a fruitful tree on the eve of **Saint George**'s Day and knew her wish would be fulfilled within a year if she then found some bug had crept into it. In many Slavic lands until the mid-twentieth century, mothers would wake up their children that night by sprinkling them with a wet nettle, which they all tried to sting each other with all day, as an injection of the plant's vigor. Since evil spirits also happened to be particularly active overnight, throughout Central Europe, greenery would be put on the fronts of houses and stables to counter their influence.

Saint George's Flock

Saint George's Day on April 23 was a critical turning point of the year in other respects. It was often the counterpart of the feast of another warrior saint six months later—be it **Saint Demetrios** on October 26 in Greece, **Martinmas** on November 11, or **Michaelmas** (in honor of the Archangel Michael) on September 29 in Western Europe, as days when contracts ended, and the herds were brought in for the winter (as on the **Nativity of the Virgin** on September 8). Thus, **Saint George**'s was a time for country fairs where servants and shepherds were hired and land dues were paid, as well as to get the herds out of their folds and up to their summer pastures. On this occasion, a Russian prayer recalls the dragon slain by **Saint George** in asking for his protection against "sly beasts" threatening them on the way there. In the Carpathian mountains of Rumania, the ewes are first milked, and then all the sheep are purified by making them jump through a "living fire" that is kept up all summer long (much as ancient Roman shepherds would themselves jump over a fire on the April 21 festival of **Parilia**). And just as their distant forebears drank milk and ate cake as part of these dawn protection rites, after a tree procession like that of Slovenian peasants, Rumanian shepherds made a point of having dairy products at the joyous meal with which they concluded their *Sambra oilor* ("Sheep Society") ceremonies on April 23.

Greek shepherds also share with relatives, friends, and other villagers a copious meal having as a centerpiece the "lamb of **Saint George**" along with yogurt, cheese, and milk pies, sometimes keeping the shoulder for the priest who has to visit every sheepfold in turn, and making sure there are no leftovers. Lambs are also sacrificed or offered to the church by all those who have made a vow to the saint to this effect at a time of need, like losing sheep, so that he would help them through it. Elaborate rules specifying the victim's color and gender, the place and ritual of the sacrifice, and divinatory observations to be made vary from town to town, but the meat, raw or cooked, is always distributed to the villagers. The procession, headed by the icon of **Saint George**, is often preceded or followed by dances, games, and athletic contests, such as a horserace between the young men with a large loaf of bread at the finish line, which the winner must cut up and share with the other competitors. For if **Saint George** (as the timeless hero riding a white horse) wins the prize, it is not after all for fame and fortune, but for the glory of God, and in view of ensuring the free flow of nature's bounties for the general welfare of the entire community.

See also Akitu; Conception and Birth of the Mother of God; Elevation of the Cross; Martinmas; May Day; Palm Sunday; Samhain; Terminalia

References

Sir E. A. Wallis Budge. *George of Lydda, The Patron Saint of England: A Study of the Cultus of Saint George in Ethiopia. Translations of the Ethiopic texts as found in the manuscripts from Makdala now in the British Museum and an introduction.* New York: AMS Press, 1978.

Fairs and Festivals of Kerala. Trivandrum, India: Department of Public Relations, Government of Kerala, 1991.

Sir James George Frazer. *The Golden Bough. A Study in Magic and Religion.* One-Volume Abridged Edition. New York: Collier Books, 1985.

Robert Graves. *The Greek Myths.* London: Penguin Books, 1960.

Richard Mihalek. "Easter in Drahovce," April 30, 2000, in *Eastern Slovakia—Slovak and Carpatho-Rusyn Genealogical Research* (http://www.iarelative.com/easter/mihalek.htm.)

SAINT JOHN

See Christmas

SAINT JOHN THE BAPTIST (BEHEADING OF)

See Conception and Birth of the Virgin Mary

SAINT JOHN THE BAPTIST (CONCEPTION OF)

See Annunciation

SAINT JOHN THE BAPTIST (NATIVITY OF)

See Midsummer

SAINT JORDAN'S DAY

See Epiphany

SAINT JOSEPH

See Lent

SAINT JOSEPH THE CRAFTSMAN

See May Day

SAINT KNUT

See Epiphany

SAINT LUCY (CHRISTIANITY)

In many parts of Europe, the feast of **Saint Lucy** on December 13 has inherited characteristics of pre-Christian winter solstice festivals of light, on the basis of its date, of this martyr's name, and of the role of eyesight in her legend. This often makes it a time when beings from the beyond can become manifest to humans in ambivalent forms. A romanticized version of this festival is still observed throughout Swedish society, and to a lesser extent in Finland and Norway. In all Scandinavian countries, children experience *Sancta **Lucia*** with the kind of excitement surrounding **Halloween** in North America.

Lucy and Light

In the Catholic and Anglican Churches, the feast of **Saint Lucy** used to be followed by one of the four **Ember Weeks** of prayer and fasting set aside for the ordination of the clergy. In current liturgical calendars, it has however been reduced to the Wednesday, Friday, and Saturday after the third of the four Sundays of **Advent** preceding **Christmas**.

The holy virgin Lucy was martyred in 303 during the Roman Emperor Diocletian's persecution of Christians, because she had broken off her engagement to a young patrician gentleman for the sake of Jesus. The December 13 anniversary of Lucy's death is marked in her native Sicily by bonfires and torchlight processions. In Syracuse where she was born, a heavy silver statue of Lucy is carried from the cathedral to the Church of Santa **Lucia**, to be taken back eight days later amidst much pomp and festivity. There is a similar procession in the Calabrian town of Amaroni, which also includes its patron Saint Barbara. In Tuscany too, ceremonies are held in Siena's church of Santa Lucia, while an outdoor pottery fair fills the adjacent streets with stands displaying ceramics and terracotta. West of Venice, the children of Verona receive gifts in remembrance of **Saint Lucy**'s role in protecting them from a plague in the fourteenth century.

The association of Lucy's name with light (since it is derived from the Latin *lux*) may be the source of the story on the basis of which the devout have turned to her to be cured of eye problems. They say that Lucy gouged out her own eyes to send them to her ex-fiancé, but that the Virgin Mary then gave her a new pair of even more beautiful ones. In many cases, her feast day took over from pagan winter solstice festivals of light. The shortest day of the year, after which light increases anew, actually tended to fall toward **Saint Lucy**'s on December 13, before the Gregorian calendar came into general use and brought the year in step with the actual length of days, from 1582 onward in Catholic countries. In France, there used to be a saying reflecting the pre-Gregorian situation: *À la Sainte-Luce, les jours croissent d'un saut de puce*; it could be rendered as: "On Saint Luce's, days grow by one leap of a louse's." (Some French Canadians still know its counterpart about **Epiphany**, at an equal distance from **Christmas** as **Saint Lucy**'s on the other side, and reflecting the steady waxing of daylight be-

tween the opening and the closing of the holiday season around the solstice: "*À la Fête des Rois, les jours allongent du pas d'une oie,*" which could be translated as: "On the **Twelfth Night** of **Christmas**, days lengthen by one step of a goose's.") In Burgundy, one of the box-tree branches blessed on **Palm Sunday** the previous spring would be lit at noon on this day—as though to greet the slightly increasing force of light as the distant promise of a new spring. Because of this old connection between **Saint Lucy**'s and the winter solstice, churches would begin to ring in **Christmas** on December 13 in some parts of southwestern France, and in parts of Hungary, people might plant some wheat or a peach-tree branch in a pot so it would produce shoots or blossoms on **Christmas**. As if the doors to the beyond swung open on this hinge between two cycles of time to allow communication with the mysteries of past and future, in Hungary on **Saint Lucy**'s Day, young women might try to tell how many years they still had to go before finding a husband by the number of grunts swines would make when they kicked their pigsty, and a chair would be left empty at the family table for a dead ancestor or for some passing stranger. This custom from pagan times is known in Poland too—but on **Christmas**, when Swedes also put some food for the dead on the dinner table.

Swedish Lucia: A Little Christmas

In Sweden, **Saint Lucy**'s Day or *Lucia* is even called *Lille Jul* or "Little Christmas." It marks the time of the official beginning of the month-long **Christmas** season extending in that country from December 13 to January 13, which is **Saint Knut**'s Day or *Knut*. On **Lucia**, Swedes are supposed to start preparing for **Christmas** proper, by cleaning the house from top to bottom and shining the copper and silverware, as well as by getting all of the food ready (which in olden times meant slaughtering the pigs). The legend of the Sicilian saint was only imported in the eighteenth century in this Nordic coun-

Eva Nycander, a nineteen-year-old Swede, is crowned by her maids of honor during the traditional festival of Saint Lucia at a Swedish church in Marylebone in London, England, in 1954. (Hulton-Detsch Collection/ Corbis)

try where, ironically, the Lutheran Church resorted to Catholic hagiography to provide a thin veneer of Christian piety for ancient pagan rites. Runic inscriptions from Viking times already mentioned this day as the darkest one of the year—after which light comes back. As if to embody the imminent return of light in the darkest of winter, in every Swedish household, the eldest girl, wearing a long white dress with a flowing red belt and a crown of lighted candles (electric ones are mostly used nowadays for safety reasons), appears at dawn to bring breakfast in bed to each family member. It consists of a tray of coffee, gingerbread cookies, and seasonal saffron cakes of various shapes and sizes, each with their special name. The largest bun, with raisins in it, is called "parson's hair." A family's Lucia is normally accompanied by

handmaidens: the younger girls of the house, dressed in white, but holding candles in their hands instead of wearing them in their crowns. They all sing, in a Swedish version of the well known Italian tune (also broadcast on the radio): "Now in our dark house/there arises with kindled light/Sancta **Lucia**,/Sancta **Lucia**!" (There is also a whole repertoire of Lucia songs that is performed along with **Christmas** tunes at church choral concerts during **Advent**.)

As the day progresses, the girls in white dresses continue their rounds at home and at the workplace, except that instead of coffee, they offer *glögga*—spiced red wine toddy. In every Swedish town, a chosen **Lucia** is taken on people's shoulders in a torchlight procession through the crowds lining the streets all the way to City Hall. In Stockholm, she receives a piece of jewelry once she gets there, often from the hands of the new Nobel Prize for literature. That girl is the winner of the national **Lucia** contest sponsored by the Social-Democratic newspaper *Stockholms Tidningen* since 1927. This parade has included the collection of money for the poor since 1945 and was imitated throughout the country in many advertising gimmicks, until they were all gradually eclipsed by the televised broadcast of the national parade introduced in the nineteen-seventies. Many Nobel laureates have been startled and sometimes frightened by the sudden appearance in their hotel rooms at five in the morning of eight white-clad figures holding candles. So the singing **Lucias** were eventually banned from the places where the distinguished foreign guests were staying, just after having received their prizes from the King of Sweden in the Golden Room of Stockholm's City Hall around December 10.

The Fearful Face of Lucy

The folklore surrounding **Saint Lucy** makes clear that this propensity to frighten as well as charm has long been familiar to Europeans. Throughout southern German lands, she was made an equivalent of Frau Holle and of Berchta—fairies who visited spinners, and had both a favorable and a menacing aspect. **Saint Lucy** replaced them in this capacity among the German populations of western Hungary and of Bohemia, where she would frighten children. She thus took on the role played in other parts of Northern Europe by the Black Petes or by Knecht Ruprecht, going around to do the dirty work of **Saint Nicholas** on December 6, by punishing children when they had not been obedient. But Lucy also punished sloppy housemaids and the like. The eve of her feast, like **Walpurgis Night** and **Halloween**, was a time when witches were very active and went about in the sky. In Sweden, trolls and other evil little people were out, and masked processions were organized to scare them away. The

same practice was also observed in Berchtesgaden—a town of Upper Bavaria named after Berchta, the local counterpart of Lucy; but it was held on slightly different dates, on the first and second Sundays of **Advent** instead of December 13. Across the German border in Lower Austria, people who (like Greeks on **Christmas** night and **Ascension**) dared to stay up until midnight to catch a glimpse of a mysterious light (called the *Luzieschein*) were then supposed to be able to foretell the future. On the other hand, those who tried to see it, but who instead dozed off before midnight, would be struck by misfortune or disease over the coming year. On December 13, all household tasks were taboo: the spinning wheel was left idle, and there would be no weaving or sewing or baking of bread. This is true in Hungarian folklore too, which is full of stories of people who try to learn the secrets of witches on **Saint Lucy**'s. The best way to do it was to start secretly building a chair that day, spreading the work over thirteen days, and sometimes using thirteen kinds of wood from thirteen different hamlets. The chair could then be used at the Midnight Mass on **Christmas** Eve to spot the village's witches, but one had to quickly go away and burn the chair before it was over so as to escape their wrath at being found out. (This explains why so few of these magic chairs have survived.) On **Saint Lucy**'s itself, young men would undergo a hazing ritual of initiation, where their faces were blackened and they were called devils, and they would also go trick-or-treating at all village farms, imitating chickens and singing lewd songs to stimulate fertility in nature and humans.

In Bavaria, **Saint Lucy**'s Day is known for a local festival reminiscent of Far Eastern customs involving the setting adrift of lights on **days of the dead**, and called the "Floating of Lights"—*Lichterschwemmen*, in Fürstenfeldbrück. There, "Lucy houses" (*Luzienhäuser*) are built by schoolchildren a month in advance in order to be blessed at the church on December

13, and then launched on the river Amper to float away into the darkness. These small-scale models of local houses have paper in the place of doors and windows to allow the light of the candles placed inside to shine through the openings. They are meant to be *ex-votos,* expressing gratitude for **Saint Lucy**'s intercession in preserving the town from a flood that threatened it in 1785, as well as offerings so that the river does not overflow its banks again.

Many traditions of **Saint Lucy**'s have been shifted to the next day on December 14, the feast of **Saint Odile** (660–720). She too is invoked against eye ailments, since she was born blind and was miraculously cured. This is especially the case in Alsace, a German province of France of which Odile is the patron saint. Her major pilgrimage site is the monastery she founded on Mont Sainte-Odile, which has been a sacred mountain from pagan times. It may have been initially associated with Odin—the god who gave up an eye to obtain knowledge; this made him supreme in the Germanic pantheon as the lord of runes, poetry, and war, with the power to fight demonic forces and uphold cosmic order. Something of this ambiguous power of pagan sky gods, beneficent and ferocious in turn, appears to have been inherited by Lucy as well as by Odile, as harbingers of light in the midst of winter. This was due in each case as much to the place of their feasts in the calendar as to the spiritual restoration of vision central to the stories of both saints.

See also Ascension; Christmas; Days of the Dead (West); Days of the Dead (China, Korea, Japan); Elevation of the Cross; Epiphany; Lent; May Day; Palm Sunday; Saint Nicholas; Samhain; Whitsuntide

References

Alain de Benoist. *Les Traditions d'Europe.* 2nd ed. Arpajon, France: Éditions du Labyrinthe, 1996.

H. Pomeroy Brewster. *Saints and Festivals of the Christian Church.* Detroit, MI: Omnigraphics, 1990.

Jules Ortutay. "La Sainte-Luce," in *Nouvelle Revue de Hongrie,* December 1939, pp. 414–417.

Mats Rehnberg. *Swedish Holidays and Annual Festivals.* Stockholm: Swedish Institute, 1970.

Jennifer M. Russ. *German Festivals and Customs.* London: O. Wolff, 1982.

SAINT MARK

See Rogations, Samhain

SAINT MARTIN

See Martinmas

SAINT MARY'S FEAST OF HARVEST

See Assumption

SAINT MAVRA

See May Day

SAINT MENAS

See Saint Nicholas

SAINT MICHAEL

See **Saint George**, Samhain

SAINT NICHOLAS (CHRISTIANITY)

The feast of **Saint Nicholas** is celebrated on December 6 and was for centuries in the West an important part of popular year-end celebrations. Except within Eastern Orthodoxy, where it remains a full-fledged church feast, since the Protestant Reformation and Catholic Counterreformation, there has been a pattern of official Church disengagement from this sometimes rowdy festival. Yet this was never enough to stop the proliferation in secular forms of the folk customs associated with it in Northern European countries, which were deliberately imitated in nineteenth-century America in an invented tradition of the **Christmas** season. This feast provided much of the imagery of Santa

Claus by way of the forms it took in the Low Countries, where on December 6 they live on side by side with the now universal American trappings of **Yuletide**.

Origins, Development, and Spread of the Nicholas Cult

The feast of **Saint Nicholas** has always marked the symbolic start of winter. Aside from its date (that of his death in 343), little is known with any certainty about Nicholas himself. It does seem that he was the first bishop of Myra in Anatolia (the Asian part of present-day Turkey) to hold this office after the end of Roman persecutions, when the Empire first recognized and soon embraced the Christian faith in the fourth century, as it shifted its center to its new Eastern capital Constantinople (now Istanbul). Not being primarily, if at all, a martyr, Nicholas was a new kind of saint: the type of the bishop in his public function as guide and protector of everyday secular pursuits, as opposed to the path of monastic or eremitic life that was simultaneously emerging in Egypt and Palestine as a model of Christian sanctification. His recognition was due to the maritime role of Myra on the coast of Asia Minor, as well as to the date of his feast, for it coincided with the **Poseidonia**, when protection on stormy winter seas was sought from the competent Greek gods. **Saint Nicholas** of Myra took over this function as the new patron of sailors, becoming known as the "Wonder-Worker" partly on account of miraculous rescues at sea. His cult thus spread along the coast and the sea routes to Constantinople and from there throughout the Empire, all the way to its main Italian outposts Rome and Ravenna.

Anxious for maritime success, imperial authorities naturally fostered the new cult, especially when it became clear that naval victories could no longer be taken for granted with the constant encroachments of Islam from the eighth century onward. Veneration for **Saint Nicholas** therefore took off spectacularly, once

that period's iconoclastic heresy against the cult of holy persons' images had been defeated. In Eastern Christendom, the cult of Nicholas became perhaps second only to the cult of Mary in newly converted Slavic lands like Russia just as in Greece. Greek sailors still take his icons to sea and cover those in his many coastal churches with silver and gold *ex-votos* representing the ships he has saved from danger. December 6 (or 19 if it is the Julian calendar that is used) thus marks the feast of Orthodoxy's most popular saint, with a liturgy in his honor.

After the Great Schism of 1054 divided the Eastern and Western Churches, the Eastern Roman Empire suffered two major setbacks in 1071: it lost Anatolia to the Seljuk Turks at Mantzikert, and the Normans captured its last remaining Italian outpost of Bari. Already a center of the Nicholas cult, the Adriatic port of Bari overtook its rival Venice in a bold seafaring raid to a now unsafe Myra in 1087, in order to secure the saint's relics for itself. After their translation to the West, the relics were housed in a new basilica in Bari. Their delivery is reenacted there on a special commemorative feast on the first weekend of May. They drew a great many pilgrims during the Middle Ages, largely because those proceeding to the Holy Land embarked for the perilous journey in this port. If they made it back, in their gratitude, they took the Nicholas cult home with them.

This diffusion was favored by a special property of the relics of **Saint Nicholas**: they ooze with a holy oil called myrrh. This miraculous power to generate renewable relics, which pilgrims could easily take away in little bottles, seems to have been derived from the circulation along the same maritime routes of flasks of the holy water of **Saint Menas**—taken from the Egyptian oasis where his cult was centered (in conjunction with a booming ceramics industry producing these earthen containers). In the East, the November 11 feast of **Saint Menas** still announces the coming of winter with **Saint Philip**'s **Lent** that lasts from his November 14 feast to **Christmas** Eve, and corresponds to the West's **Advent**. Oil from the candles burning at the shrine of **Saint Menas** was sometimes added to the holy water bottles, resulting in a holy oil. It did not take long before pilgrims came to expect, and obtain, similar "myrrh" from the shrine of **Saint Nicholas** of Myra by virtue of an association of sounds and ideas. Thus began a long-standing pattern for the veneration of the relics of saints in the East.

It began to be reproduced in the West, namely in Normandy, at the turn of the second millennium, in connection with an emerging cult of **Saint Catherine**, due to developing exchanges with the latter's Egyptian center in the Sinai on the eve of the Crusades. The liturgy for **Saint Catherine**'s November 25 feast day was composed in Normandy by German clerics from Franconia, who took over this miraculous theme of the holy oil from the service they used as a model: a popular **Saint Nicholas** liturgy composed by their countryman Reginold in the tenth century. While countless other saints would soon start exuding myrrh like Nicholas and Catherine by virtue of their life stories being cast in the same liturgical mold, the biographical elements contained in his liturgy made of Nicholas "the first subject of Western scholastic and secular drama; he was, as it were, drama's patron saint," according to the great historian of his cult Charles W. Jones (Jones 1978, p. 111). The little school plays put on during the occasion of his feast-day were known for their satirical rowdiness; official authorities often disapproved of them. Reflecting the resentment this caused among the lower clergy, the association of **Saint Nicholas** with schools may have developed in part from the following legend: some said the saint had appeared one night using a whip to drill his new liturgy into a prior who had turned down his monks' requests to adopt it. A common feature of German storytelling, this kind of pedagogical whipping into shape of naughty

Saint Nicholas, the original Dutch Santa Claus (Sinter Klaas), and his assistant Black Pete visit a Dutch town for his Feast of December 6. Black Pete carries a birch for bad children, an empty bag to put the bad children in, and a bag of gifts for the good children. (Hultan-Deutsch Collection/Corbis)

pupils stuck to the saint's popular image as one side of it: the punisher of bad children.

The Nicholas cult spread in Western Europe along sea routes and major rivers, especially in the Low Countries, the Rhineland, and Lotharingia—where Nicholas would become patron saint of the French province of Lorraine. This process was favored by the dedication to Nicholas of a number of churches sponsored by the Greek-born Western Empress Theophano, her entourage and descendants, starting with the birth of her son Otto III on the way to her favorite palace in Nijmegen—the Valkhof overlooking the Rhine. All that remains of it today on the river's Dutch banks is the **Saint Nicholas** chapel built around 980, no doubt in thanks for the safe delivery of the imperial heir, for whom she would soon act as regent. This constitutes an early instance of the association of **Saint Nicholas** with childbirth (and so with childhood) and also of his cult in the Low Countries.

From Northern European Folklore to American Popular Culture

By the thirteenth century, twenty-three churches had been built in honor of **Saint Nicholas** on the territory of what is now the Netherlands. In the fourteenth century, this favorite saint of sailors and merchants became associated, there as elsewhere, with children and gift giving. There was a basis for this in various elements of his legend, such as his bringing back to life three boys whom an innkeeper had butchered or the episode when he secretly threw bags of gold into the house of a bankrupt neighbor so he would not have to give his daughters over to prostitution as the only way left for them to survive without a dowry. In convent schools, the **Saint Nicholas** Day customs were adapted to pedagogical ends. A monk would put on a long white beard and a red cloak to act as Nicholas rewarding good students with gifts. Throughout Europe, the choirboys of **Saint Nicholas** churches—and eventually of all churches—took to marching through the streets on their patron's December 6 feast day, begging for "bishop money" in quests called "nixies." The custom survives in Mainz, capital of the Rhineland-Palatinate, as a major folk festival, where a parade of thousands of children follows a "Nicholas Bishop," like the one traditionally elected among children in all corners of late medieval Europe.

But official recognition was gradually withdrawn from the public celebration of **Saint Nicholas** Day in Protestant and Catholic countries alike in the sixteenth century, when it reached its apex; it was eventually downgraded from a feast of obligation to an optional one by the Vatican in 1969. As if to counter this banishment from church, a story soon arose in the Low Countries and the German-speaking world that the saint rode over the rooftops and dropped candy and gifts down the chimneys, into a newfound domestic setting. He was assisted in his rounds by *Zwarte Piet* ("Black Pete"), a devil he had chained to his service for the day, rather like the *Knecht Ruprecht* ("Servant Robert") of German folklore. Zwarte Piet and Knecht Ruprecht conveniently took over the functions of **Saint Nicholas** when it came to punishing children, leaving him the popular role of the "nice guy" who handed out gifts—except in regions where it was reserved for Kris Kringle (*Christkindl*, or "Christ Child" in German) or *Père Noël* ("Father Christmas" in French), and it was Nicholas who wielded a whip and took naughty children away in sacks!

The entrenched expectations created in children by seasonal gifts moved their parents to successfully resist attempts by Dutch civic authorities to suppress as idolatrous the public sale of dolls, gingerbread men, candies, and cookies, which often bore the effigy of *Sinter Klaas* (as **Saint Nicholas** was known), such as a 1663 proclamation by the magistrates of Amsterdam. With the outbreak of the Second Anglo-Dutch war the following year, Nieuw Amsterdam fell to England to become New York. There, these *Sinter Klaas koekjes* (hence the American word "cookie") continued to be imported from Dutch confectioneries by the colony's predominantly British merchant classes. They became part of their **New Year** celebrations due to the length of overseas delivery. The old Manhattan families' custom of visiting each other on **New Year**'s Day and being served brandy with **Saint Nicholas** cookies would be fondly remembered by the United States's first antiquarian, John Pintard. Aside from launching a number of new national holidays, he attempted to revive as a proper family affair a practice that had lost its respectability by the early nineteenth century, overshadowed and displaced by the riotous seasonal partying of the urban masses. Searching for an alternative celebration, Pintard traced the **New Year** visits to Dutch colonial observance of **Saint Nicholas** Day. But today, it is thought unlikely that it was ever commonplace among mostly Calvinist Dutch settlers who, like the Puritans, disapproved of saints' days as idolatrous. Pintard's unfounded reconstruction of the feast was embraced by the Knickerbockers, a circle of New York notables named after the title of a collection of stories by Washington Irving. This book, set in a bucolic colonial New Amsterdam, is the first publication to name and describe the figure of Santa Claus, albeit still in connection with **Saint Nicholas** Day.

There remained some hesitation on the proper date for observing this invented tradition: December 6, December 25, or January 1? **Christmas** was fixed upon in the 1820s with Clement Clarke Moore's popular poem *A Visit from Saint Nicholas*, shifting the bishop's appearance to children away from the saint's feast day.

The public observance of the feast of **Saint Nicholas** on December 6 in Dutch and Belgian towns is regarded by some more as a revival due to American interest in the "original" Santa Claus than as a genuine continuation of old local customs. It involves a parade where **Saint Nicholas**, with a bishop's miter and staff, rides to City Hall on a white horse or in a carriage with minstrel-faced adolescents playing his Black Petes, as Nicholas look-alikes, dressed in red, walk the streets handing out sweets. Oranges used to be singled out in Dutch folklore, as a reminder of the lesson given to Spain by the royal House of Orange when it led the Low Countries' revolt against foreign oppression. Indeed, Nicholas is supposed to come from Spain and take naughty children back with him. In Southern Italy, though, Nicholas is still revered as patron saint in Bari with folk celebrations on his feast day, while in Mezzojuso near Palermo in Sicily, there is the traditional blessing and distribution of *panuzze*, small loaves of bread stamped with the image of **Saint Nicholas**—like a distant cousin or prototype of colonial American cookies.

> **See also** Christmas; Epiphany; Feast of Fools; Lent; Martinmas; Matzu's Birthday; New Year (China, Korea), New Year (Japan); New Year (West); Saint Lucy

References

Fr. Thomas Hopko. *The Winter Pascha. Readings for the Christmas-Epiphany Season.* Crestwood, NJ: St. Vladimir's Seminary Press, 1984.

Charles W. Jones. *Saint Nicholas of Myra, Bari and Manhattan.* Chicago: University of Chicago Press, 1978.

Stephen Nissenbaum. *The Battle for Christmas.* New York: Knopf, 1997.

▌ SAINT ODILE
See Saint Lucy

▌ SAINT PATRICK
See Candlemas

▌ SAINT PETER
See Midsummer

▌ SAINT PETER IN FETTERS
See Lugnasad

▌ SAINT PHILIP
See Lent, Saint Nicholas

▌ SAINT POLYCARP
See Caristia

▌ SAINT ROMANOS THE MELODIST
See Protection of the Mother of God

▌ SAINT STEPHEN
See Christmas

▌ SAINT THOMAS (MONDAY, SUNDAY OF)
See Easter

▸ **SAINT VALENTINE**
See Lupercalia

▸ **SAINT VINCENT**
See Dionysia

▸ **SAINT WALBURGA**
See May Day

▸ **SAINTS CONSTANTINE AND HELENA**
See Dionysia

▸ **SAINTS' DAYS**
See Kermis, Lent, Pardon

▸ **SAINTS PETER AND PAUL**
See Assumption, Lent

▸ **SAINTS THEODORE (SUNDAY OF THE TWO)**
See Lent

SAMHAIN (CELTS)

The ancient Irish festival of **Samhain** (pronounced "Sah'win") is the only well-documented form of what used to be the high point of the Celtic calendar as its **New Year**'s Day in the British Isles and on the Continent alike before their Romanization and Christianization. It is attested in Roman Gaul as *Samonios,* while in modern Irish *Lá Samhna* ("the day of **Samhain**") has given its name to the month of November that starts with it. Much of the folklore of **All Souls** Day, **All Saints** Day and **All Hallows' Eve** (**Halloween** on October 31) can be traced back to **Samhain**, for in Celtic reckoning it began at sunset the day before.

A Fall Festival

Samhain seems to have also included the three or six days before and after November 1, depending on the source, which may well have to do with the scale of the territory where it was observed. For **Samhain** actually involved much more than the yearly return of the souls of the dead (the *anaon* of Breton folklore) to seek warmth and food at their living relatives' hearth at the onset of the cold and dark season. It has been suggested that this behavior closely parallels the return of the herds from their summer pastures to their stalls for the winter, which would have made this day the turning point of the year for the Celts' distant pastoral ancestors, as opposed to the winter solstice with its more agrarian daylight index. This explanation for their feast of **Samhain** finds indirect confirmation in the close parallel offered by the strikingly similar festival of **Käyri** or **Kekri**, long observed by the wholly unrelated Finnish and Estonian peoples. Originally falling on **Michaelmas** on September 29, it marked the end of the agricultural season, when the cattle were gathered from their pastures to spend the winter closer to home in the barn, so that in some places all the men of a village would sacrifice a sheep together. Until the twentieth century in Estonia, it was customary to prepare mutton dishes integrating fresh blood from this **Michaelmas** slaughter. It was likewise during this critical period between the old and new years that the ancestors' spirits came back to visit their former homes, where food and drink were left for these so-called holy men and the sauna was heated, while the living members of the family feasted together. It thus proved easy in Finland to shift these observances to the November 1 feast of **All Saints**, set aside to honor the dead in the rest of Western Christendom from the turn of the first millennium—as the Church's way of absorbing the many survivals of **Samhain**, the Celtic **New Year**.

Samhain even surpassed **Christmas** in festive importance in Ireland until relatively recently (though the nearest Monday is still a **bank holiday** in the Republic, like **Saint Stephen**'s Day after **Christmas**), with joyous celebrations and feasting reminiscent of **Yuletide**. Yet they are more directly related to an end-of-summer festival of slaughter and good cheer like **Martinmas** that comes on its heels on November 11, when there used to be a custom of offering an animal to **Saint Martin** (no doubt harking back to an old **Samhain** sacrifice). The continuity between **Halloween** and **Martinmas** as a holiday season was especially underlined in Scotland, where country people used to sing: "This is Hallaevan,/The Morn is Halladay,/Nine free nights till **Martinmas**,/An' sune they'll weare away!" But these are only the more popular, peripheral aspects of **Samhain**, which could best survive Christianization by confirming the spurious medieval etymology of the festival's name as "the summer's end."

A Celtic Potlatch

The correct Indo-European derivation of the word *samhain* actually makes it a close equivalent of Germanic words for "together," like the Dutch *samen*. The festival of **Samhain** meant just that: a gathering, at every conceivable level. It gathered the three functional groupings of Indo-European society in their different capacities as providers, warriors, and priests, around their ruler the king, under the aegis of the king of the gods Lug, in the dark aspect evident at this moment, when time gave way to eternity. For this was the gate of the year, when the old one dissolved and another cycle set in out of the timeless Other World, now brought within easy reach, as at the holy places called *síde*.

The gathering places for royal banquets replicating those of the gods at a local, provincial, or national level were also hallowed grounds of the *síd* or Other World (pronounced "shee" as in "banshee"—a "woman of the Other World," or Irish fairy). The election of a king at each level was held on the occasion of **Samhain** in the respective symbolic centers of these jurisdictions, during assemblies and fairs of proportional periodicity and length. As in other cultures, the year's end was a dangerous time for the old king; in a warlike, stormy climate, when both the world and society

seemed near a cataclysmic end, he stood out as an alternative sacrificial victim if he failed to perform his priestly-*cum*-sovereign role adequately. But other people could also be sacrificed on **Samhain** as scapegoats for the community's failings, to appease hostile powers like the Fomoire race of demons, and as an offering to the god Cromm Craich.

It is always at the **Samhain** banquet that Irish tales are set whenever they involve conflict with the denizens of the *síd*'s hollow hills due to intrusions by mortals, or the intervention of these otherworldly powers in human affairs, and the death of a king or a hero on account of taboo transgressions, or of their social counterpart in unjust war or misconduct at a formal gathering. There, one thing often led to the other, as such **Samhain** feasts were the focus of a warrior society's intense competition for prestige, which was only heightened by the fact that it could now paradoxically be regulated and stabilized by religious specialists: the druids. The druids were assisted by historians, assigning to each noble landholder or warrior a seat consistent with his rank, title, and genealogy, by ceremonially taking the shields representing them first to their proper places, so as to prevent fatal scuffles between their owners about seating arrangements. This was the origin of the symmetrical and egalitarian Round Table of Arthur's pacified kingdom, as the French sociologist Marcel Mauss could argue in concluding his famous 1924 *Essay on the Gift*. For **Samhain** can actually be seen as a close Celtic equivalent of the Amerindian **potlatch** on which Mauss based his paradigm of the gift, as a festival where debts and social obligations were periodically renegotiated by warriors vying for recognition of their valor. It was symbolized in this case by the coveted and hotly disputed "hero's share" of the sacred pork meat (usually the thigh). **Samhain** also took place in a festive atmosphere charged with volatile high spirits—in both senses—coinciding in this context where mead and beer too were sacred, as they opened up mental perceptions to the primal scene of an Other World that founded the very social order loosened by the feast. For legitimate order could now be reaffirmed afresh in otherworldly terms. Attendance was therefore mandatory under pain of madness (as possession by the Other World, or death) if society needed to enforce the sacred rules that were its binding agent. For beyond the pale of these rules lurked unrestrained rivalry, tantamount to crime, sacrilege, chaos, and ruin. As a sacred barrier against these perils, priestly authorities monitored an elaborate etiquette, relying on their ability to channel and transmute violent competitive impulses into the sacred sphere of peaceful coexistence within universally recognized social norms.

The Pagan Easter

But whenever druids were not there to play this pacifying priestly role, or warriors disregarded it as they got carried away by their quarrels, all hell broke loose—literally. Aside from epic battles, the land was then ravaged by magic swine from the Other World, as reflected in Welsh folklore about the monstrous Black Sow that used to be run away from or run after (depending on local variants) by country boys once **Halloween** fires had died out. Only this malevolent aspect of the now neglected sacred animal of war and knowledge could still haunt the popular imagination after Christianity had displaced the sacrifices the druids used to perform on **Samhain**, rightly seen by some chroniclers as the "pagan **Easter**." It was in view of it that in the seventh century, as Saint Adamnan reported, vast herds of swine were fattened over the fall in order to be slaughtered at **Samhain**. This also happened to mark the end of the campaign season; these swine sacrifices have thus been likened to that of the **October Horse** in ancient Rome as a typical rite of the second, military function of Indo-European society according to Georges Dumézil. But the druids of the first, priestly function have also been

known (from the scant sources that have come down to us) to sacrifice other animals when opening **Samhain**: a horse in Ulster, a bull elsewhere in Ireland, and two white bulls in Gaul, where the druids collected mistletoe that day, as Roman naturalist Pliny the Elder noted.

The Sacred Flame of a New Year

The most spectacular rite of the eve of **Samhain** endured beyond the demise of the druids. As they lit the sacred fires on the hill of Tlachtga that night to open the gate of the Other World to another year, heavy fines ensured that all other fires throughout Ireland had been put out, to be rekindled from their eternal source later. People would then jump through the new fires to take in their life-giving force. Until the beginning of the twentieth century, bonfires likewise dotted the countryside of Scotland on **Halloween**. They still do in the United Kingdom on **Guy Fawkes Day**, having merely been postponed a few days, in honor of the anniversary of the foiling, on November 5, 1605, of the Gunpowder Plot of Roman Catholic extremists to blow up Parliament along with King James I of the new Scottish Stuart dynasty (which makes this patriotic holiday a fitting vindication of Celtic Britain after all!). Other typical **Halloween** customs have been transferred to **Guy Fawkes Day** as a Protestant substitute for Catholic **All Saints**, and especially to its eve as **Mischief Night**. (On the other hand, the setting off of Roman candles and fireworks as an echo of the Gunpowder Plot would appear to have been transferred from **Guy Fawkes Day** to **Halloween** in Vancouver, British Columbia, where they feature prominently and still cause much property damage every year at this only time they can be sold legally.) Thus, aside from the topical persecution and burning of mock popes and of beggars' dummies known as "guys" after the leader of the popish plot, there are more traditional children's torchlight parades with jack-o'-lanterns (beets or pumpkins carved out to contain burning coals). These are meant to guide in the dark the old pagan spirits and ghosts, demoted first to evil beings, then to comical ones, that the fires are now supposed to drive back, no longer invite. "Ge's a peat t' burn the witches!" boys used to shout in Scotland, as they collected fuel from every homestead for the fire around which they would dance and play some seasonal competitive games.

In Wales, as in Scotland, it was common to mark a white stone and expose it to the fire before going to bed. To find it in bad shape, out of place, or not to find it at all among the ashes in the morning would be a bad omen for the coming year. This was also at stake in other conditional games like "lating the witches" in northern Lancashire—that is, climbing up a hill with a candle between eleven and midnight on **Halloween** and trying to keep it from being blown out (like one's own life, which otherwise might also be snuffed out over the next year).

Such folklore implies that the entire year is one beyond time with the eerie otherworldly day that was **Samhain** to the Celts. Most epic adventures of their mythology took place during the closed period of **Samhain**, or from one to the next yearly opening of the Other World within its brackets, or even a much later one. Thus, a hero who had wandered inside a *síd* might emerge from it years later without having aged (not unlike Washington Irving's Rip Van Winkle from his twenty-year sleep), or he might on the contrary spend weeks and months in the wondrous Other World and still return to the everyday world of humans only a few minutes after having left it.

All Hallows' Eve

Generally speaking, the living and the dead, mortals and immortals, gods and men, fairies and hobgoblins were all gathered at this point in time, especially in the fairy mounds or hollow hills known for being portals to the Other World. "For the *síde* of Ireland were always open on **Samhain** and people did not know how to keep them secret," as is reported among the *Boyhood Deeds* of the hero Cúchulainn (*Macgnímartha Find*, in Le Roux and Guyonvarc'h 1995, p. 75) in the epic tale of the *Cattle Raid of Cooley* (*Táin Bó Cuailnge*). Between these hills, there was a heavy traffic of fairies—and the dead souls indistinguishable from them—on **Samhain**, as there still is on **Halloween**. This used to make it possible to obtain prophecies from a fairy woman, especially about events due to occur in the temporal interval from the current to the next opening of the Other World beyond time at **Samhain**.

The same principle was preserved in a custom known in Wales and the north and west of England until the nineteenth century as the Church Porch Watch. From the vantage point of this threshold between the space consecrated to God and the burial ground surrounding it, a vision might be had at midnight on **Halloween** (and other turning points of the year like **New Year**'s Eve, **Saint John**'s Eve on June 23, and **Saint Mark**'s Eve on April 24) of the people of the parish who were to die over the coming year—albeit at the risk of joining them as the ghostly "churchyard walker" until another person was foolhardy enough to take it. From pagan times, precautions were in order to prevent recently departed souls (walking among the dead and the fairies but still reluctant to take the next step in the circuit of births, or *tuirgen*) from coming back to haunt the living in their former dwelling places. This is why there is still a custom throughout Britain and Ireland on **Halloween** of setting candles and lanterns in the windows, to guide them back where they belong: with the evil spirits that people dress up as to scare the real ones off, or just to mix with them on their night out—one long associated with shapeshifting by the Celts (as was **Beltane** as the source of **Walpurgis Night** on April 30). While there was a widespread prohibition on using brooms on **Halloween** to avoid sweeping away wandering souls, as soon as their time to mix with the living was up, in Cheshire and

Shropshire, "soulers" would roam the countryside to take them away on the back of their hobbyhorse on November 2—**All Souls** Day, the one set aside for prayers for the restless dead by the medieval Church, just after **All Saints,** or **All Hallows'** Day.

> **See also** Chiao; Christmas; Days of the Dead (West); Easter; Inti Raymi and Huarachicu; Martinmas; May Day; Midsummer; New Fire Ceremony; New Year (Japan); New Year (West); Potlatch; Saint George; Saint Lucy; Whitsuntide

References

Françoise Le Roux and Christian-J. Guyonvarc'h. *Les Fêtes celtiques.* Rennes: Ouest-France, 1995.

Proinsias Mac Cana. *Celtic Mythology.* New York: Peter Bedrick Books, 1983.

Caitlín and John Matthews. *The Encyclopedia of Celtic Wisdom: The Celtic Shaman's Sourcebook.* Shaftesbury, UK: Element Books, 1994.

Nicholas Rogers. *Halloween. From Pagan Ritual to Party Night.* Oxford: Oxford University Press, 2002.

Jack Santino. *The Hallowed Eve. Dimensions of a Culture in Northern Ireland.* Lexington: The University Press of Kentucky, 1998.

▷ SANFERMINES
See Games (Rome)

▷ SAN GIUSEPPE
See Lent

▷ SANJA MATSURI
See Matsuri

▷ SANKTHANS
See Midsummer

▷ SAN ROCCO
See Martinmas

▷ SANTA CROCE
See Elevation of the Cross

▷ SÃO JOÃO
See Midsummer

▷ SARASVATI PUJA, SARVAPITRI AMAVASHYA
See Navaratra and Dusshera

SATURNALIA (ROME)

The public festival of **Saturnalia** was celebrated in Rome starting on December 17. It lasted a week, during which all distinctions of rank or class were put aside. They were often reversed even, in honor of the god Saturn, who was thought to have ruled Italy during a Golden Age of plenty and carefree spontaneity, prior to civilization and its constraints. European folklore has preserved many traces of the **Saturnalia**'s rites of social inversion.

The Golden Age when Time Was King

The **Saturnalia** may have been partly modeled on the **Chronia** held in Athens on the twelfth of the month of Hekatombeion (around August), in which social order was likewise dissolved before being reaffirmed ten days later at the great festival marking the official start of the civic **New Year:** the **Panathenaea.** In the hellenizing interpretation of the Italo-Roman deity Saturn that prevailed from the late third century B.C.E. onward, he was actually identified with Chronos, the god of time who had been driven from Greece when his son Zeus (or Jupiter for Romans) replaced him as king of the gods on Mount Olympus. Before Time (Chronos) came to Italy by ship, Janus was already there to welcome him, as the god of beginnings—preceding time, yet setting it in motion, along with all institutions. This was true of the calendar too, starting with January as the month of Janus, the god or deified king (as sophisticated late Romans preferred to view many of their ancient deities) who was said to have established the **Saturnalia** near his fortress town of Janiculum after the sudden disappearance of Saturn, his co-ruler in this distant Golden Age. Writing at the decline of the Roman Empire in the West, the scholarly official Macrobius (*Saturnalia* I, ch. 7, par. 24, p. 59) maintained that "Janus then devised means to add to his honors. First he gave the name *Saturnia* to all the land which acknowledged his rule, and then he built an altar, instituting rites as to a god and calling these rites the **Saturnalia**—a fact which goes to show how very much older the festival is than the city of Rome."

This may help account for the fact that the liturgical year of the archaic Arval Brotherhood of priests of Mars had always been counted from **Saturnalia** to **Saturnalia**, and partly explain why the **calends of January**—the first day of the civic year—were observed in much the same way as the **Saturnalia**, with mutual gift-giving as well as the suspension and reversal of social roles. While the **calends of January** eventually overtook the **Saturnalia** in popularity after the latter's heyday in early imperial times, both Roman festivals were probably the ancestors not only of Christian Europe's winter solstice and **New Year** customs of social inversion like the December 28 **Feast of Fools**, but also of **Shrove Tuesday** and **Carnival**, closer to the end of winter. It has sometimes been suggested that the word "**carnival**" might be derived from *carrus navalis,* a boat-shaped carriage (also known in some local Greek and Near Eastern festivals of **Dionysus**) that was used during the **Saturnalia** to parade masked men and women who sang obscene songs on the streets.

Trading Places

The **Saturnalia** were reformed in 217 B.C.E. in the midst of the religious crisis caused by early defeats in the Second Punic War against Carthage, Rome's African rival. We know from Livy's *Roman History* (XXII, 1:19) that, in December of that year, a sacrifice was performed in the temple of Saturn (the founding of which in 497 B.C.E. the festival commemorated).

Among Greek religious customs adopted for the occasion, the senators gave a lectistern—that is, a banquet in honor of a deity who attends it in effigy, as an image set up on a ceremonial bed. A public banquet was also given, and for a day and a night the entire population was on the streets shouting "*Io Saturnalia!*" The decision was taken to do the same annually, so that the **Saturnalia** became an official year-end celebration.

According to Macrobius (*Saturnalia* I, ch. 10), it was initially set fourteen days before the **calends of January**, "but, after Gaius Caesar had added two days to December, the day on which the festival was held became the sixteenth before the **Kalends of January**, with the result that, since the exact day was not commonly known—some observing the addition which Caesar had made to the calendar and others following the old usage—the festival came to be regarded as lasting for more days than one" (par. 2, p. 70) from December 15 (the **Consualia** marking the onset of winter) to December 17. It comes "when men have gathered in the fruits of the earth" (par. 20, p. 72), and feel free to squander them in a wild winter holiday, as all caution and reserve are dropped to evoke the boundless abundance of the Golden Age, so as to invoke the future bounty (Latin *ops,* as in "opulence") of Mother Earth: Saturn's wife Ops (or the Greek Rhea). The climax of the **Saturnalia** was her December 19 feast of **Opalia**; "it was on this day alone that the shout of 'Io **Saturnalia**' would be raised, in the temple of Saturn, at a riotous feast" (par. 18, p. 72).

On the first day, as had been done in 217 B.C.E., no one was to put on a formal toga, not even the magistrates at the official banquet. Instead, while the statue of Saturn, whose feet were normally bound, was freed for a day, everyone wore a casual tunic instead of a toga, along with the *pileus libertatis,* an ancient Italian felt hat that had become the symbol of freed slaves. It was the masters who for once served the unusually impudent slaves at the banquet. Women were excluded, although slaves could have their way with their masters' concubines. After the meal and excessive drinking, all the men would play dice together—a game normally forbidden (to slaves especially), in which they used coins and nuts as stakes. Improvisational games and satire were the parlor games of educated circles, while less sophisticated ones exchanged riddles. No work at all was to be done on this civic holiday, when courts and government, as well as schools, were closed. It was thus under the name of *feriae servorum* that the **Saturnalia** were still observed as "the slaves' holidays" at the fall of the Christianized Roman Empire in the mid-fifth century, when they were also known as the **Brumalia**.

Ancient Trappings of the Holiday Season

Since the first century B.C.E. "however, the addition of the feast of the **Sigillaria** has extended the time of general excitement and religious rejoicing to seven days" (Macrobius 1969 ch. 10, par. 24, p. 73), during "which we amuse infants in arms with little masks of clay" (ch. 11, par. 1, p. 74), also giving a special allowance, the *sigillaricum,* to dependents like slaves and clients, so they could buy small gifts such as wax candles and pottery figurines called *sigilla* as inexpensive symbolic substitutes for the (often facetious) presents to be exchanged on that day. Thus, until what is now **Christmas** Eve, men and women would take part in candlelight parades, wearing garlands around their necks and leaves in their hair. Roman homes, especially doors, were also decorated with foliage and lights between **Saturnalia** and the **calends of January**, much as today during the holiday season; holly was already favored for this in Antiquity. But the early Church tended to disapprove of the custom. "You are the light of the world and the ever verdant tree. If you have renounced the temples, do not make a temple of your door,"

wrote Tertullian (155–222) in Roman Carthage, in one of the first Christian books in Latin (Tertullianus 1987, 15: 11, p. 55). As a way to compete with, and eventually absorb, the **Saturnalia**, the Roman Church instituted **Christmas** on December 25 as the feast of the birth of Jesus Christ, previously celebrated as part of **Epiphany** on January 6, along with other events of his life. But this only shifted vestiges of the **Saturnalia** to the latter date, when the King of the Bean would be randomly selected in medieval Europe, just as the Bishop of Fools was on **Innocents' Day**, December 28, to rule over a partying crowd for a limited time, like the **Carnival** king of many former provinces of the Roman Empire in Italy, France, and Spain. This king for a day is also mentioned by some Roman authors as a feature of the **Saturnalia** banquet: someone who would order people around, to do ludicrous things at his whim. This was done in good fun in ancient Rome as in medieval Europe.

Killing the Carnival King

Yet this rather marginal practice of the **Saturnalia** probably goes back to archaic customs that did not stop at choosing someone to impersonate a god and irresponsibly exert the divine right of kings for a while. Originally, this king was killed at the end of his term of office, as a way to exorcise his ambiguous powers, or to send him off to the safe distance of a divine realm. This is why the image of **Carnival** kings is often destroyed by fire or other means at the end of the pre-**Lent** festival. But in remote corners of the Roman Empire, where many soldiers were recruited, harsher, more primitive forms of the **Saturnalia** survived, or were revived or reinvented. They have been recorded in the story of the martyrdom of **Saint Dasius** on November 20, 303. This Christian soldier had been selected by lots to put on the royal dress of Saturn as king of the Golden Age. He was killed by the other soldiers for refusing to do what was expected of him as part of year-end celebrations: indulge all shameful passions until the festival of Saturn, when he was supposed to cut his own throat on the altar of the god he stood in for. Preferring to die the way of the God he actually stood for—Christ—Dasius gave up his life a month early.

> **See also** Carnival; Dionysia; Christmas; Epiphany; Feast of Fools; New Year (West); Panathenaea; Thesmophoria

References

Sir James George Frazer. *The Golden Bough. A Study in Magic and Religion.* One-Volume Abridged Edition. New York: Macmillan, 1985.

Macrobius. *The Saturnalia.* Tr. Percival Vaughan Davies. New York: Columbia University Press, "Records of Civilization" No. 79, 1969.

Tertullianus. *De idololatria.* Tr. J. H. Waszink and J. C. M. Van Winden. Leiden, The Netherlands: E. J. Brill, 1987.

H. S. Versnel. *Inconsistencies in Greek and Roman Religion.* Vol. 2: *Transition and Reversal in Myth and Ritual.* Leiden, The Netherlands: E. J. Brill, 1993.

SCHOLARS' FESTIVAL
See Lag ba-Omer

SECULAR GAMES
See Games (Rome)

SED
See Khoiak and Heb-Sed

SEE OF SAINT PETER (FEAST OF THE)
See Caristia

SEGAVECCHIA
See Lent

SEIJIN-NO-HI
See New Year (Japan)

SEKKU (JAPAN)

A *sekku* is any one of the five Japanese "sacred festivals" derived from Chinese festivals introduced into the imperial calendar of **annual events** (*nenchu gyoji*) over a thousand years ago and still observed today. The five sekkus are now known as: the **Day of Mankind** (*Nanakusa no Sekku*) on January 7, the **Doll Festival** (*Joshi no Sekku*) on March 3, **Children's Day** (*Tango no Sekku*) on May 5, the **Festival of the Weaver** (*Tanabata no Sekku*) on July 7, and the **Chrysanthemum Festival** (*Choyo no Sekku*) on September 9.

Children's Day

Tango no Sekku, the **First of the Five** sekkus, has undergone a complicated gradual transformation from its Chinese model, the **Dragon Boat Festival**, as preserved in the Peiron Boat Race in Nagasaki. It was already combined with martial exhibitions when it was first introduced in 611 under Empress Suiko. For archery contests and horse races were thought to have the same prophylactic effects of chasing away the evil spirits that often brought disease during the inauspicious fifth month (similar in this respect to the month of **May** in Western folklore). They were most active on the fifth day purposely chosen to hold the **Iris Festival**, as **Tango** was called during the Heian period (794–1185). This was because iris leaves as well as mugwort branches (both of them medicinal herbs helpful in controlling seasonal dysentery epidemics) would be hung on the roofs of every building and on the heads of every notable of the capital Kyoto, attached to swords and palanquins, made into pillows, and even drunk in *sake* rice wine, courtesy of the emperor, who wore an iris garland.

Officials of the Emperor's Bureau of Medicine were responsible for distributing supplies of medicinal herbs on his behalf, together with officers of the Guard, who would also bring the festival to a close by twanging their bowstrings to drive away the evil spirits. Archers would come to play a more active role with the ascendancy of the warrior class during the Muromachi Period from 1333 to 1568. For in addition to taking iris-steeped baths, these warriors put on *yabusame* contests of horseback shooting, of the kind still performed in period costume on September 16 at the Tsurugaoka Shrine to the popular war god Hachiman in Kamakura, the capital from 1185 to 1333.

By the Edo Period (1600–1868), paper warriors mounted on straw horses were often displayed at the gate of distinguished houses, while the populace staged mock pebble-throwing battles, called *injiuchi,* and flew kites—both ways to forecast the autumn harvest. Once Japan started to vie for the status of a modern power in the late nineteenth century, there arose the elaborate display of martial dolls and assorted battle gear that is now customary on **Children's Day** or **Kodomo no Hi**, which is a national holiday. Despite the reference to children in general (more aptly applicable to the **Seven-Five-Three** Festival), there is no mistaking the paraphernalia of a relatively recent **Boys' Festival** emphasizing military virtues in these impressive May 5 displays of miniature armor, weapons, battle streamers, and the like. Nonetheless, a small table at the bottom still holds two bottles of iris-steeped *sake*, as a reminder of the festival's much older, though not unrelated, hygienic purpose (which also comes through in the use of iris by women to wash their hair on the equivalent **Dano** Festival in Korea). Outside the house, families fly cloth or paper streamers shaped like carps (called *koi*)—as many as they have sons and reflecting their different ages in their respective sizes, because this fish is a symbol of virility on account of its strength and determination in swimming upstream. A favorite treat of the festival is *mochi*, which is glutinous rice wrapped in oak or bamboo leaves.

Chrysanthemum Festival

Perhaps as early as 686, Japan's **Chrysanthemum Festival** took over from Han China's **Chongjiu** or **Double Nine** Festival the custom of drinking chrysanthemum wine and composing poems. This is what would initially follow the Imperial Court's annual inspection of the chrysanthemums in the palace garden, at a banquet featuring dance performances by Palace Girls. They would offer the Emperor small white trout, which was also served to his guests later on. On the eve of the festival, chrysanthemums were covered with pieces of silk floss that people would later rub their faces with in order to prevent or erase signs of aging, since these flowers were thought to promote longevity. Now held in Nagasaki on October 7–9, the **Ninth Day** or *Okunchi* Festival features a parade of young men carrying umbrella-topped floats, with a Chinese dragon dance.

Day of Mankind

Along the same lines, the **Festival of Young Herbs**, or **Wakana no Sekku**, came to be one of the **Seven National Festivals** ordained in a 718 code, as well as part of **New Year** observances. On the seventh day of the first month, Imperial Storehouse officials went out to gather seven lucky herbs for a rice gruel that their colleagues of the Imperial Table Office would then present to the emperor. The Chinese custom of preparing this seven-herb gruel, called *nanakusagayu*, became widespread among townspeople of the Edo Period, and is still generally followed on January 7 as the **Day of Mankind**, or *Jinjutsu*, as a way of keeping evil spirits at bay and enjoying good health over the **new year**. The same health benefits were ascribed to the Ceremony of the Blue Horses (*Aouma no Sechie*) held on the same day since it was imported from China during the Nara Period (645–794). This was because horses are considered *yang* (of "male" polarity), even though those paraded before the Emperor and other nobles were white instead of steel gray as in China, due to both the rarity of such "lucky blue-green" (*aoi*) horses in Japan and the Shinto symbolism of the purity of white.

The movable **Feast of the Day of the Rat**, or *Nenohi no En*, started by 743 at Court. In the ninth century, it became a country outing to clear the mind of evil thoughts and pluck young herbs for longevity; it would therefore later be amalgamated with the **Festival of Young Herbs** as a popular form of picnic.

Festival of the Weaver

Known from 734 onwards, **Tanabata Matsuri** is a replica of China's **Chi Ch'iao T'ien** Festival about **Cowherd and Weaving Maid**'s yearly encounter over the Milky Way on a bridge of magpies. It became established as a weavers' festival during the Heian Period (794–1185), when young women would put a table in their garden and burn incense on it as they made offerings for skillfulness to the weaver star Vega and the shepherd star Altair. Among them were five needles holding silk threads of different bright colors, as well as long bamboo poles to which were attached decorations made from paper, either folded in the shape of cranes, as poem cards, or as multicolored streamers. Called *sasatake*, these poles remain a hallmark of this and other late summer and fall festivals in Japan, as ancient heralds of the coming rice harvest. As such, they were meant to be taken down and set afloat on a river with their decorations by the end of the festival. In the countryside, people believe rain is a sign of a good harvest since it brings purity by helping the poles flow downstream, while city folk hold to the Chinese version of this **Star Festival**'s story, in which clear skies on that night allow the celestial pair to meet.

In most towns where it is prominent, this festival is really just a tourist attraction by now, and the poles have grown to gigantic proportions while the decorations are made of plastic. Yet children still write poems on paper dragons, and small paper replicas of samurai clothes may also be seen on display on the street corners of the northern city of Sendai, in the most commercialized version of the festival, held

there from August 6 to 8. Another local variant is the **Lantern Festival**, or *Kanto,* in Akita, where it is celebrated on the fifth instead of the seventh day of the seventh month, with nighttime parades of young men balancing bamboo poles hung with tiers of lanterns.

Doll Festival

The **Doll Festival** developed during the late medieval Muromachi Period from elaborate doll displays at homes where there were little girls, which had long been part of the **Festival of the Snake (*Jomi*)** first recorded in 485. It was called that because of its original date on the First Day of the Snake, when dolls were thrown into the water as a purification rite, as mentioned in Court Lady Murasaki Shikibu's classic *Tale of Genji* at the turn of the last millennium. It had actually originated in China, where, as in the Roman festival of **Argei,** known and unknown evil spirits were transferred to the dolls and dispatched in this way.

But the focus eventually shifted to the dolls for their own sake, as they became so richly elaborate that they were put on display and kept from year to year and generation to generation, just to appear in a traditional arrangement that took shape during the Tokugawa Period (1603–1868). A set is made up of at least fifteen dolls, which are laid out on five to seven shelves covered with red cloth on March 3. On the top shelf are the *dairibina*, representing the Emperor and Empress holding court, with three ladies-in-waiting, five musicians, two retainers, and three guards, placed according to their rank. The lower shelves hold miniature weapons, armor, and musical instruments, as well as lacquered doll furniture (chests of drawers and toilet cases) and tableware, and tiny folding screens and lanterns, as well as a small palanquin and carriage. Food offerings are put at the bottom, and two flower arrangements and two lanterns are put to the sides. It would bring bad luck not to put away the dolls immediately after March 3, resulting in delayed mar-

Observance of Tanabata no Sekku, the Festival of the Weaver. This is the Japanese version of the Chinese celebration of Cowherd and Weaving Maid. Two lovely stars, known as Kenguy and Shokugo in Japan, are set apart on either side of the Milky Way, and they are suppposed to have their joyous reunion during one of the nights between July 6th and 8th. (Bettmann/corbis)

riage for the girl they belong to, who has received them from her parents or grandparents when she was born or on her first birthday as part of her dowry. That nearly every family therefore needs its own set of dolls helps explain that Japan is second only to the United States as a producer of dolls.

The traditional craft of making dolls is showcased at the Doll Fair (*Hina Ichi*) of Kurayoshi in Tottori Prefecture. There, the original link of the doll display with purification by water may still be seen. Children buy strings of paper dolls and untie them to form pairs, which they lay in small straw baskets, along with rice cakes and peach blossoms. After having first joined the standard **Doll Festival** display, these Floating Doll Boats fulfill the older ritual function by being set adrift on the nearby Mochigase River. By the eleventh century, the related seasonal custom of Winding Water banquets, also imported from China, had lost its religious significance but was observed at Court and in private houses alike for its sheer aesthetic appeal. Guests sat along a stream running around the house, or even through it. The stream was often punctuated by elegantly disposed rocks in order to provide inspiration for some verse to be composed by each guest every time a cup of *sake* rice wine floated by, or else he or she would have to drink it and set it back on the water to drift on. Nowadays on **Girls' Day** (as the **Doll Festival** is also known), sweet sake sprinkled with peach blossoms is served with seafood on sushi rice and with pink, green, or white diamond-shaped *mochi* rice cakes.

See also Argei; Cherry Blossom Festival; Cowherd and Weaving Maid; Double Nine; Dragon Boat Festival; Lantern Festival; Matsuri; May Day; New Year (Japan)

References

G. Caiger. *Dolls on Display; Japan in Miniature, Being an Illustrated Commentary on the Girls' Festival and the Boys' Festival.* Tokyo: The Hokuseido Press, 1933.

U. A. Casal. *The Five Sacred Festivals of Ancient Japan: Their Symbolism and Historical Development.* Rutland, VT: C. E. Tuttle Co. (for Tokyo's Sophia University), 1967.

Ivan Morris. *The World of the Shining Prince. Court Life in Ancient Japan.* New York: Knopf, 1964.

▌ SEOL

See New Year (China, Korea)

▌ SENSA (FESTA DELLA)

See Ascension

▌ SEPTUAGESIMA

See Lent

▌ SET-NIGHTS

See Candlemas

▌ SETSUBUN

See New Year (Japan)

▌ SEVEN-FIVE-THREE (JAPAN)

In Japan on November 15, boys aged three and five and girls aged three and seven are taken by their parents to the Shinto shrine of their patron deity to offer thanks for having reached

Two young Japanese girls dressed in kimonos for the Shichi Go San Festival, celebrating the birthdays of seven-, five-, and three-year-olds in Japan. (Michael S. Yamashita/Corbis)

their respective ages and to invoke the blessings of their continued safety and healthy growth. The day is therefore known as *Shichi Go San,* meaning "**Seven-five-three**" in Japanese. But since it is not an official holiday, many parents now combine it with **Culture Day** on November 3, which is a national holiday, or most often just visit the shrine on the weekend closest to the normal date.

Critical Early Years

The prototypes of the day's combined observances may be found in much older rites still present mainly in rural areas, where a child is taken to the shrine of his or her tutelary deity shortly after birth in order to be introduced, and later goes through ceremonies that are meant to allow his or her spirit from wandering away. For the latter's connection to the body is thought to remain tenuous during a child's early years, as the high infant mortality rates of former times seemed to demonstrate. If he or she survived a certain number of critical years, the youngster was again taken to the shrine to be introduced to the god under whose jurisdiction he or she lived—this time as a full-fledged person with his or her spirit firmly in place.

Three Samurai Rites of Passage

Although the **Seven-five-three** festival that preserves these rites in an urban guise retains this religious significance mostly for the poor, it actually goes back to the era of the samurais as a combination of three rites of passages practiced in this warrior class—hence the triple name. At age three, boys and girls stopped having their heads shaved and could grow hair to have it arranged on top of their heads for the first time. It was at five that boys first got to wear *hakama,* which are skirt-like trousers, in order to be introduced to their respective feudal lords. When they reached seven, girls began to wear an *obi* (the proper stiff sash on a kimono) instead of a cord belt. In the seventeenth century, the habit of visiting a shrine on each of these occasions to pray for the health of children aged three, five, and seven spread through the general population, but still within the framework of a specifically samurai celebration.

A Single Children's Day

It was only in the late nineteenth century that these traditions took on their current format, after the single, fixed date of November 15 was chosen for their joint observance, being a lucky day in the Japanese calendar. It remains one of a couple of special festival days each year when brightly colored traditional dress can be seen, such as *hakama* trousers and *haori* half-coats for the boys and kimonos for the girls, who also wear their elaborate hairdos. However, wearing Western formal suits and party dresses is also acceptable nowadays. This is an ideal photo opportunity, and professionals are often hired to record the occasion.

After a purification ceremony has been performed by the shrine's Shinto priest, the children are given *shitose ame,* or "thousand-year old candy," in colored bags. As its name indicates, this red and white rock candy, displaying the colors of luck and celebration, is meant to convey the parents' prayers for their child's longevity, also symbolized by the cranes and turtles on the bags. Once they are back home, families conclude the celebration with a party meal of *sekihan* (boiled rice with red beans) and *okashiratsuki no tai* (sea bream, complete with head and tail).

See also Apaturia; Liberalia; Lag ba-Omer; Sekku

References

Robert N. Bellah. *Tokugawa Religion: The Values of Pre-Industrial Japan.* Glencoe, IL: Free Press, 1957.

Tamotsu Iwado. *Children's Days in Japan.* Tokyo: Board of Tourist Industry, Japanese Government Railways, 1936.

Dianne M. MacMillan. *Japanese Children's Day and the Obon Festival.* Springfield, NJ: Enslow Publishers, 1997.

▶ SEVEN NATIONAL FESTIVALS
See Sekku

▶ SEVENTEENTH OF TAMMUZ
See Tisha be-Av

▶ SEXAGESIMA
See Lent

▶ SHABBAT
See Sabbath

▶ SHALAKO (ZUÑI)

Of all the festivals of the elaborate ceremonial calendar of the Zuñi tribe of Pueblo Indians in

New Mexico, the most spectacular is without a doubt the fall ritual drama commonly referred to as the **Shalako**. Its true name is actually *Kokowawia*—the feast of the **Coming of the masked gods**, that is of the *katchinas*, who come on other occasions too. But at this festival, the six **Shalakos** stand out like ten-foot tall horned penguins with their eagle-feather crests and long articulate beaks, as impersonated on this occasion.

Year-Long Preparations

The **Shalako** is the most important and prestigious ceremony of the Zuñi tribe. For the first couple of days it is celebrated in late November or early December, it draws numerous onlookers from all the other Indian tribes of New Mexico and Arizona, not to mention non-Indian tourists from nearby Gallup and elsewhere. This hunting and war ceremony functions as a generic memorial for all the dead, but is mainly aimed at bringing on rain and making the fields fertile, in addition to blessing new houses and granting longevity and happiness to the people. As these depend largely on rainfall, the deities controlling it are most visible in the ritual drama through which they are made present by ascetically prepared impersonators, while the general population looks on. In a wider sense, the **Shalako** also includes a series of rituals that go on after the day the six **Shalakos** spend at the village of Zuñi and conclude with the Corn Maiden ceremony after almost a week. But the **Coming of the Gods** (which includes their departure) is really the culmination of a whole year of preparatory ritual acts.

It is on the ninth day of the ceremonies of the winter solstice (starting on a date set as the start of the year by a shifting compromise between the solar and lunar calendars) that feathered prayer sticks are given to the actors officially designated to represent the principal gods: Pautiwa, Kyaklo, Shulawitsi, Sayatasha, the two Yamuhaktos, Hututu and the two Salimopias, as well as the six **Shalakos** and the ten Koyemshis. Such *telikinawe* are also given the next day to the men whose houses are to be built or rebuilt during the summer, which will therefore be known as **Shalako** houses. A prayer stick is kept for each of them. Up to eight in number, these are to be planted in the fields over eleven months later at the end of the **Shalako** ceremony by the Koyemshis. Also known as "mudheads" in English, these ten are among the most important and peculiar-looking of the masked gods or *Kokos* (otherwise known as *Katchinas* among Pueblo Indians in general, such as the Hopis, who also have their own **Katchina Festivals**). The nine hideously deformed children of the incestuous union of "their father" *Awantachu* with his sister take after this parent who joins them, in that they inherited the muddy complexion he acquired when he rolled on the ground because his face had started to swell and bubble as a result of his unnatural act. With their relatively realistic masks (in contrast to the elaborate abstract symbolic patterns on all the others) and transgressive behavior as sacred clowns, these particular impersonators are likely to be a survival of the religion of the Salado element absorbed by Pueblo refugees from drought-stricken cliff-dwellings to form the Zuñi people close to eight centuries ago.

The people chosen to impersonate the gods visit various sacred spots each month until the **Shalako** to deposit prayer sticks in their holy springs or bury them in the ground. If they were to neglect any of their complicated ritual duties, the tribe would be exposed to serious misfortune (above all drought, since it is mostly rain gods they represent). Their daily meetings get to last until later at night, and the stick plantings take place every ten days with the start of a countdown of the forty-nine days before the **Shalako**. Each day is matched by a knot on the two cotton ropes given to Awantachu and Sayatasha, who untie one every morning. Forty days later, coming from Hepatina, the shrine that marks the center of the world (or

Itiwana, which is a term also applied to the middle of the year that is the winter solstice), the Koyemshis begin to play their part as salacious sacred clowns, once they cross a small sacred bridge into the village to announce the coming of the council of the gods in four days, and that of the **Shalako**s after four more days. Until then, they do a retreat in the house of the fraternity of the man chosen as their leader Awantachu. They may eat what they want, but touching a woman is strictly taboo. So is even seeing one for the people standing for the Council of the gods, after it arrives at midnight four days later and starts its own retreat in the house of the impersonator of Sayatasha, as do the **Shalako**s in the houses of their assistants, albeit still out of costume.

On that day, Zuñis have thrown food in the fire as offerings to the dead in general. (Since a man's ancestors do not belong to his clan in this matrilineal society, they are not personally remembered, and the departed remain as abstract a presence as the patterns on the masks that make them present.) From then on, the men frantically finish up the new or renovated houses by cleaning and bleaching them, as the women prepare the great banquets to be hosted in them; not to mention celebrations going on in all other houses. Sometimes, delays in wrapping up all the necessary preparations cause the Koyemshis to come out of their retreat one at a time to announce the postponement of the festival by a day or two. No further delay is possible, since the Gallup local newspapers have to publish the exact date a few days ahead, with a proclamation from the Zuñi governor reminding non-Indians that it is forbidden to take notes, shoot photographs, or make sketches in the *pueblo* (Indian village). If anyone should happen to catch a glimpse of the masks and the secret preparations of those who are to wear them before they appear in costume, that person would need to be severely flogged in order to dissipate the bad luck that would surely cause a **Shalako** to trip and fall, with dire con-

sequences for the whole people. The Spanish language is also taboo around the masks, being that used in the past by Catholic missionaries from Mexico, who have tried in vain to stamp them out or even burn them all.

The Coming of the Gods

On the eve of the day on which the new houses are to be consecrated, the principal gods assemble at Hepatina. They cross the river on the sacred bridge to enter the village, and, after depositing prayer sticks in various places, they use ladders to go into the house they are to dedicate via the formal entrance through the terrace on the roof. The householder throws corn meal on the gods as they come, and a line of it also connects the foot of the ladder to his fraternity's altar, at which a priest offers basketsful of grain after holding them to the six directions (including above and below). The gods impersonated then perform similar blessings as one of the most important acts of the **Shalako** ritual, before sitting on benches in front of their respective priests to share with them a sacred cigarette and launching upon a repetitive litany that lasts several hours. In it, each god in turn explains the route he took from their underwater village of Kothluwalawa to visit humans at the midpoint of the six directions, in order to bring them long life and prosperity with the sacred grain.

Meanwhile, night is falling, and the crowd amassed outside the house moves south to welcome the **Shalako**s at the bridge by throwing flour on their passage. Their impressive, eerie procession breaks up into six as each of the **Shalako**s then makes his way to the house he is to bless on the same pattern as the Council of the gods (except that a **Shalako** has to remove his oversized attire to climb on the rooftop and down into the house). By then, it is around half past eight, and it is the turn of the Koyemshis to make their entrance in the village and go inside a new house to bless it, although they first stop to sing and fool around in front of the other houses where ceremonies are underway. In a departure from the norm among masked gods, theirs are not leather masks but are made of cotton covered with the pink clay of a sacred lake, with thick stuffing around their round eyes, gaping mouths, and variously placed bumps, which recall their father's hitting his head on trees in horror at his melting face. These bumps are filled with seeds and earth from the footsteps of the villagers, which makes them into powerful love charms. Touching the Koyemshis while they wear their masks can therefore make one sex-crazed or hysterical, and refusing them anything can bring on severe hardship. Not unlike similar secret societies of masked men in Rumania's **Whitsuntide** folklore, they are known for their obscene language and behavior—such as exhibiting their genitals from below their black kilts, though the penis is often tied up so as not to become erect. Paradoxically, this would be out of character, for the Koyemshis are supposed to be sexually immature retarded children. Zuñis invoke this as an excuse for such explicit antics, but remain so sensitive to non-Indians' frowning at this kind of behavior that it has tended to subside over the years. For the **Shalako** is now largely driven by the need to proudly display and openly validate Zuñi cultural identity over against the pressures of the outside world, which makes the opinion of outsiders critical—even as they are purposely left out of the inner meaning and workings of the ritual. This ambiguity is reflected in the Koyemshis' self-censorship of obscene gestures as they go on telling dirty jokes under cover of the Zuñi language. As it is, they represent a strictly delimited manifestation of a layer of out-of-control transgressive revelry amid the otherwise highly formal proceedings and self-controlled behavior of other actors.

Inside each of the **Shalako** houses, once the particular gods who have come to bless it are finished with their litany (the Council of the gods earlier and the Koyemshis later than the six **Shalako**s), someone dips a feather in holy water and blesses them before the crowded home is rearranged—first for the banquet in their honor and then to give them space to dance. Over the years, Zuñis have tended to lose patience with visiting Navajos (a neighboring Athapaskan tribe they disliked in the first place), who would try to take advantage of this occasion for hospitality to gatecrash parties to which they were not invited. Both Navajos and Zuñis used to drink a lot that night, but for many decades now, authorities on the reserve have made sure it remained alcohol-free for the duration of the **Shalako** festival, which has always been relatively immune to festive excess anyway. For this is really just the beginning: it is only when the morning star appears that Sayatasha and Awantachu untie the last knot on their countdown strings as part of a **thanksgiving** ceremony they perform at the house where they have been celebrating all night. As the party dissolves and most outside visitors get in their cars and trucks to leave town, women ritually wash the heads of the men who have personified the gods. The village then gives in to slumber until the noontime ceremony called *Koane*. This ceremony, which is forbidden to non-Indians, is one in which, until the next year, most of the gods take leave of Itiwana, the middle of the earth and home to the Zuñis.

The Shalako Race

On the ceremonial plot across the river where the gods previously gathered before entering the village, fourteen holes about thirty centimeters square are dug in two parallel rows of seven holes, some distance apart. The fire god Shulawitsi leads his six colleagues in the council in depositing a prayer stick in a hole before they all do a kind of square dance around it, much as they did at each spot in the village where they deposited a *telikinawe* the previous day. They deposit some more after parading in front of the singers. They then follow Sayatasha when he goes to bury the string he has untied that morning, before most of them go take off their sacred masks and their costumes in the nearby shack they have been using as a dressing room. Only the two Salimopias remain behind to run on the same spot with long yucca stems for the duration of the **Shalako** race that follows, in the unlikely event a **Shalako** should fall under the weight of his heavy attire. The ill omen this brings to the community could then be immediately dissipated by indiscriminately whipping the audience. At intervals, each of the **Shalako**s runs from the singers' line to deposit a prayer stick in the corresponding hole of the north and south rows of the field before returning to his point of departure, where the impersonator's alternate will take his place inside the dummy to repeat the operation. The same process is followed to then throw some sacred flour onto the sticks in the holes, before the **Shalako**s can go remove their sacred costumes, which are brought into village houses wrapped in blankets, to be stored until the next year's **Shalako**. This relay race of giant birds is meant to facilitate the arrival of rain, being a symbolic representation of the function of the **Shalako** gods as messengers between the rain gods (*unwanami*) of the six directions. For the feathered prayer sticks are the messages they exchange when they need to cooperate to send rain to a given point of the land on the order of the Council of the gods, presided by Sayatasha.

Five Nights of Dances

Both kinds of gods have now gone back to their own realms, leaving the Zuñis in a sad mood. This is partly a throwback to the mythical times when these gods or ancestors used to take some of them along to the realm they shared with the dead, which may point to human sacrifice as an element in these rituals a long time ago. The last outside visitors have now gone too, and the village seems to go back to the quiet of its everyday routines. However, as the gods promised, they left "their children"—the secondary Katchinas—to perform in the evening over the next five days, along with unmasked dancers, in the plazas and at the **Shalako** houses. In addition to these teams, appointed by the various houses of the village (but which have sometimes proven more difficult to recruit in recent years), the Koyemshis also appear at various points and times until the last day of **Shalako**. From its eve, they stop their clowning, refrain from eating and sleeping, and suddenly become solemn on their last tour of the **Shalako** houses, being blessed along the way with the throwing of flour. In the morning and early afternoon of the sixth day of **Shalako**, as part of elaborate farewell ceremonies, each of them is washed by women of their clan and given some gifts of food, clothing, and money, before bringing these to the main plaza. Each of the ten piles of gifts is then increased by truckloads of further gifts, brought by the rest of the people of their respective clans. All the dancers gather there and perform their dances one last time simultaneously, before leaving for the village of the masked gods at the bottom of the Lake of Sighs.

The Corn Maidens

This is also where the Corn Maidens are said to have found refuge from the advances of the musicians of the god Payatamu, who was therefore entrusted with persuading them to come back to Itiwana to bring corn cobs for the priests of the six directions, so as to allow corn to grow again. Their procession from *Kushilowa* ("Red Sands," a sacred spot one kilometer southeast of the pueblo) is reenacted in the late afternoon by the young men who have been delegated by young women (so as to spare them this journey in the autumn cold) to play the Corn Maidens. They come back to the village square and the adobe house (*kiwissiné* or *kiva* for other Pueblo Indians) to the north preceded by the Pekwin or high priest of the sun, by Bitsitsi (as Payatamu is mostly known after the whistling sounds he makes), by Awantachu, and by Pautiwa, high priest of the masked gods of Kothluwalawa and fairest of the **Katchinas**. Many people leave after the rare appearance of this supreme sun god as

Native American (Pueblo, Zuñi) men participate in a Shalako race near Zuñi Pueblo, New Mexico, in 1896. They wear tall kachina costumes while spectators look on. (Western History/Geneology Department of The Denver Public Library)

he emerges from the kiwissiné, his beautiful mask whitened by the flour used to bless him inside.

The Corn Maidens are led around the plaza by Awantachu and taken one by one on the rooftop of the kiwissiné, where Bitsitsi leads them in blessings in all directions. Once they are all inside, the Pekwin empties their scarves of the grain offerings they held. After their silent ceremony, the Corn Maidens follow Bitsitsi to Kushilowa to bring offerings and prayer sticks to this starting point of the **Katchina**s' visit to Itiwana, as all other Zuñi initiates have already done during the day. As soon as the Corn Maidens have left the plaza, which is now lit by a bonfire, a bustling crowd rushes in to bring gifts to the Koyemshis to the respective houses of their impersonators. Ayantachu then assigns to each of his nine sons a section of the village to bring thanks and blessings to before they all convene at his house to remove their masks. The Koyemshis' priestly function comes to the fore as they then declare: "My father, we have ended our task, which was to see to the happiness of our people." Ayantachu collects in a blanket the masks that had made them divine beings for eight days and goes to put them in storage before he formally dismisses them with a speech and blessing, relieving them of their twenty-four hour fast and vigil, as well as a year of strenuous duties as stand-ins for the masked gods.

See also Carneia; Whitsuntide

References

Ruth L. Bunzel. *Zuñi Ceremonialism.* Albuquerque: University of New Mexico Press, 1992.

Edward S. Curtis. *The North American Indian,* Vol. 17: *The Tewa—The Zuñi Mythology.* New York: Johnson Reprint Corp., 1970.

Paul Radin. *Primitive Religion: Its Nature and Origin.* New York: Dover Publications, 1957.

Matilda Coxe Stevenson. *The Zuñi Indians: Their Mythology, Esoteric Fraternities, And Ceremonies.* Glorieta, NM: Rio Grande Press, 1985.

> ## SHANG YUAN
See Lantern Festival

> ## SHAO YI JIE
See Days of the Dead (China, Korea, Japan)

SHAVUOT (JUDAISM)

This second of the three Jewish **pilgrim festivals** is mentioned in the Biblical Book of Pentateuch as coming fifty days after **Passover**—hence its Greek name of **Pentecost**, meaning "fiftieth." The idea of the time between the two feasts is also expressed in the Hebrew name *shavuot,* or "weeks," and is complemented by other Biblical references to the **Harvest Feast** or *Hag ha-Qatzir* and the **Day of the First-Fruits** (*Yom ha-Bikkurim*). Celebrated on the sixth of the month of Sivan, as well as on the seventh in the Diaspora outside Israel, it used to mark the end of the barley harvest and the beginning of the wheat harvest, but now it mostly celebrates the giving of the Torah to Moses by God on Mount Sinai.

An Agricultural Festival

Some have suggested that **Shavuot** may have been derived from a Canaanite **Midsummer** festival. On this occasion, two loaves of bread made from the finest wheat grown in Israel would be offered in the Temple of Jerusalem. This confirmed that harvest time, which had been ushered in by the eating of unleavened bread at **Passover**, was now at an end, so that the more normal course of daily life could resume. Some time between **Shavuot** and the third **pilgrim festival** of **Sukkot,** the villagers of every district were to bring the first ripe fruits of their crops to the Temple, where the priests welcomed them with singing. By extension, in the Hellenistic period after Alexander the Great's conquests, the feast was also understood to renew the Covenant made by God with Noah after the Flood to provide for the continued existence of all creatures. Thus, in the Mishnah law code of that period, **Shavuot** is said to be the time when God judges trees and determines how much fruit they are going to give that year.

The Giving of the Law

But after the Romans destroyed the Temple in 70, rabbis replaced its priests as the chief religious authorities; since they turned to the Law instead of sacrificial ritual as the sole focus of the Jewish faith, the character of the festival of **Shavuot** changed altogether. As the other **pilgrim festivals** of **Sukkot** and **Passover** already had in biblical times, **Shavuot** had first tended to lose its early agricultural significance to the benefit of a historical commemoration linked to the Exodus. It did retain an emphasis on nature's bounty in the final goal of this forty-year journey: the Promised Land of milk and honey (Deuteronomy 26:1–11). Now its focus was shifted to a crucial event on the way there in the wasteland, as **Shavuot** came to celebrate "the time of the giving of our Torah" on Mount Sinai, when God made his Covenant with the people of Israel. This change was done on the basis of a verse placing the Hebrews' arrival in its vicinity in the third month after they left Egypt (Exodus 19:1), just as **Passover** and **Shavuot** were spread over three months of the Jewish calendar.

The Essene sect associated with the Dead Sea Scrolls found at Qumran soon started to celebrate **Shavuot** as a yearly renewal of the Covenant. The new rabbinical interpretation of **Shavuot** also dates back to the second century. It motivated the inclusion in the first day's synagogue readings of the biblical episodes of the manifestation of God on Mount Sinai, when Moses was given the Ten Commandments. It is also described in the morning service's *piyyut,* a poem interpolated after the Shema (the first cycle of *berakhot* in praise of the Creator). But the rabbis had long been uneasy about reciting these passages outside the Temple where they had used to be read out loud every day, because this could appear to confer on the Ten Commandments a special status over against the rest of the Torah, and they claimed this oral law had been given as a whole to Moses on Mount Sinai. Since this was the source of their authority, some of them, feeling it threatened, were led to protest against the practice of standing for the reading of the Ten Commandments at **Shavuot** that had become established by the Middle Ages. It has remained until now, along with the commemoration of dead relatives in *yizkor* prayers on the festival's second day.

Secondary Customs

Another medieval custom made of **Shavuot** the time to introduce children to the Torah at the Hebrew school in some communities, and the idea survives in the practice of many modern synagogues of holding Bar Mitzvahs on this festival of the giving of the Torah. However, under Kabbalistic influence, traditionalists have made a point of spending the previous night in a study vigil, devoted to selections from all of Jewish religious literature, and called *Tikkun lel Shavuot*. Sometimes, the entire Book of Psalms is read on the second night, because its author King David is said to have been born and to have died on a sixth of Sivan. This is also one of the reasons given for the standard practice of reading the Book of Ruth on **Shavuot**, as Ruth was the Psalmist's ancestor. Others include the time of year of the events it relates, Ruth's conscious conversion to Judaism, and her loyalty to the Torah as symbolic of Israel's. The latter is the theme of the eleventh-century Aramaic hymn *Akdamut* by Meir ben Isaac Nehorai of Orléans, chanted by Ashkenazis before the Torah reading.

All that remains of **Shavuot**'s original agricultural content is the symbolism of the greenery that is used to decorate the synagogue—over the objections of certain authorities—to its striking resemblance with Church practices like those of the Christian version of **Pentecost**.

Dairy products are consumed at home on **Shavuot**, because the laws concerning milk and **first-fruits** appear next to each other in the Bible. In some communities, triangular stuffed pancakes are made for this festival on account of the third month since the Exodus, when the Torah in three parts was given to Moses, a third child, for a threefold people made up of the Levite priestly tribe, of an élite of priests descended from Moses' brother Aaron, and of all the rest of the Israelites.

See also Conception and Birth of the Virgin Mary; Midsummer; Passover; Sukkot; Whitsuntide

References

Philip Goodman, ed. *The Shavuot Anthology.* Philadelphia, PA: Jewish Publication Society, 1992.

Ronald H. Isaacs. *Every Person's Guide to Shavuot.* Northvale, NJ: Jason Aronson, 1999.

Dianne M. MacMillan. *Jewish Holidays in the Spring.* Hillside, NJ: Enslow Publishers, 1993.

▌ **SHEMINI ATZERET**
See Sukkot

▌ **SHICHI GO SAN**
See Seven-Five-Three

▌ **SHIVARATRI**
See Mahashivaratri

▌ **SHO PUJA**
See Divali

▌ **SHOGATSU**
See New Year (Japan)

▌ **SHROVE TUESDAY**
See Carnival

▌ **SIGILLARIA**
See Saturnalia

▶ SIMHAT TORAH

See Sukkot

▶ SITUA (INCAS)

One of several Andean festivals incorporated by the Incas into their imperial calendar, **Situa** was celebrated toward September, in the month of Coya Raymi. This sidereal month's symbolic breastplate character points to the lunar origins and nocturnal setting of **Situa**. Coinciding with the first rains, when the Andes are most susceptible to disease and food shortages, this festival was meant, on the one hand, to keep such calamities at bay through rites of purification by water and fire, and on the other hand, to bring together the *huaca*s or relics from the four quarters of the Empire for their annual visit to its capital Cuzco, where their oracles would be assessed.

Domestic Rites

The precise details of **Situa** observances (in particular the questions to be put to divinatory huacas) were planned and decided each year by the Inca's entourage on the day of the moon's conjunction with the sun. In preparation for the expulsion of evils at **Situa**, foreigners and the physically handicapped would leave Cuzco, while a fast was held on the first day of the moon following the spring equinox. Once night had fallen, a coarse paste of maize called *sanco* was baked. A separate batch was kneaded with blood drawn between the eyebrows of children aged five to ten. Then each family gathered at the house of the eldest brother in the absence of one, the eldest relative next in line would do. After all family members had washed themselves and rubbed some of the blood-kneaded paste over their head, face, breast, shoulders, arms, and legs, so that it would imbibe their infirmities, the head of the family applied it to the threshold, leaving it there to attest that the prescribed ablutions had been performed in the house. Sanco was also offered

to the deities and to the clan's ancestral mummies. The same steps were followed by the high priest at the Temple of the Sun in Cuzco. When the Sun appeared in the morning, the people prayed that he should drive out all evils. At a set time, so that all would worship the Sun simultaneously throughout the Empire, they broke the fast by eating sanco, which made their communion effective.

Expelling Evils from the Land

But it is actually upon first sighting the new moon that the high priest would have first proclaimed the feast to 400 representatives of the highest clans, assembled fully armed in front of the Temple of the Sun; they shouted in response: "Diseases, disasters, misfortunes, leave this land!" (MacCormack 1991, p. 196). An Inca of royal blood then stood forth as a messenger of the Sun in full regalia, holding a lance to which feathers of many colors were fastened by golden rings. He brandished it as he ran down from the fortress to the middle of the open space in front of the Temple of the Sun, where stood the golden urn used for the sacrifice of *chicha*, as the Spaniards would call the Incas' maize liquor. There, the messenger touched the lances of four other Incas of royal blood who headed four companies of a hundred men each, facing the four quarters of the world (in other words, of the Empire). Every quarter or *suyo* corresponded to the quarter of the twenty lineages of Cuzco represented by each company. The herald told them that the Sun was requesting them, as his messengers, to drive all evils out of the world's center—Cuzco. They then separated, to start a kind of relay race of a few leagues with the four lances as they brandished firebrands and shouted "Evils go forth!"(MacCormack 1991, p. 197), down the four royal roads leading out of the city, along which squadrons of local state settlers would relieve them. The company facing south ran as far as present-day Angostura, to bathe in the river at Quiquisana, while that facing west ran to the river Apurimac, that facing east went over the plateau of Chita and down into the Vilcamayu valley, and those who went north also bathed in a stream that was supposed to wash out all evils, carrying them downstream and out to sea (not unlike the scapegoat dummies thrown into the river Tiber in the Roman festival of **Argei**). Having bathed and washed their weapons, the final runners set up the lances to mark a boundary within which the banished evils might not return (as is done by other means at West African **New Yam Festival**s).

Along the runners' path and on every street in the realm, people of all walks of life stood on their doorsteps and shook their clothes as if to make dust fall off, while they gladly shouted: "Let the evils be gone. How greatly desired has this festival been by us. O Creator of all things, permit us to reach another year, that we may see another feast like this" (Frazer 1985, p. 642). They would then pass their hands over their heads, faces, arms, and legs, to wash away evils. For the next twenty-four hours, they would also wash for real in rivers and fountains, dance through the night, and play with great straw torches called *pancurcu,* passing them on and striking each other with them as they made this wish: "Let all harm go away" (Frazer 1985, p. 642). The firebrands were finally taken out of city limits to be discarded in streams. Although people were less careful in early colonial times, throwing them in the water within the city itself, they still avoided them as charged with evil if they failed to be washed away by the current. Originally, cloth, llamas, coca, and flowers were also thrown into the water (as positive offerings this time) at the confluence of the rivers Huatanay and Tullumayu. All were to enjoy themselves; there was to be no scolding or any exchange of angry words on that day.

Gathering Local Relics at the Imperial Center

The following days saw grand ceremonies accompanied by sacrifices of cloth and llamas.

Their blood was sprinkled on platters of sanco given as communion to all present once they had vowed to serve the gods and the monarch with a pure heart, while their lungs were examined for signs of the future, before their meat was distributed among the people. The main event was a ceremony of tribute that would bring to the capital all the provincial huacas, such as relics and other sacred objects, although mummies were foremost. Accompanied by their priests and followed by colorful delegations of subject populations, they were solemnly received at the Imperial Court and displayed on the main square. The huacas were then expected to give oracles on the events of the coming year, after being asked specific questions about war and peace, the harvest, and the Inca's well being. Their respective priests would respond on their behalf, once the huacas had been given time to ponder the future and had received the proper sacrifices. If it turned out by the following year that their prophecies had been correct, they would then be rewarded by a solemn procession bearing gifts of gold and silver, textiles and llamas to their local shrines; this was the imperial obligation or *capacocha* in the Quechua language (in which the same word was used for human sacrifice). The huacas that had failed to deliver accurate prophecies would have to forego the official sanction of such offerings from on high and suffer a corresponding decline in reputation. As the city's handicapped were allowed to come back, provincial subjects were given permission to return home with gifts of gold and silver, cloth, women, and retainers (though not with the huacas they had just brought, but only with those they had left behind in Cuzco the previous year). On the occasion of **Situa**, the integrity of the Inca Empire was thus reaffirmed at every level simultaneously: spiritual and physical, cosmic and sociopolitical, securing the ties of the Andean provinces to Cuzco as the center of authority.

See also Argei; Busk; Inti Raymi; Naked Festivals; New Yam Festival; Thargelia; Yom Kippur

References

Sir James George Frazer. *The Golden Bough. A Study in Magic and Religion.* One-Volume Abridged Edition. New York: Macmillan, 1985.

Sabine MacCormack. *Religion in the Andes. Vision and Imagination in Early Colonial Peru.* Princeton, NJ: Princeton University Press, 1991.

Sir Clements Markham. *The Incas of Peru.* London: Smith, Elder and Co., 1910.

▶ SKIROPHORIA

See Thesmophoria

▶ SNAKE (FESTIVAL OF THE)

See Sekku

▶ SNOW FESTIVAL

See Bear Festival

▶ SOMBA DAMBA

See Mawlid

▶ SOTIRIA

See Games (Greece)

▶ SOUL SATURDAYS

See Days of the Dead (West)

▶ SPECIAL SABBATHS

See Sabbath

▶ SPRING BREAK

See Lent

▶ SPRING DRAGON (CHINA)

"On the second day of the second moon, the Dragon rears its head," goes the Chinese saying about the festival of the **Spring Dragon**. This fantastical being (whose hybrid forms and cosmic expanse straddle and connect all realms of Nature) is thought to stir from its yearly hibernation with the Awakening of Insects, or *Jing Zhe,* the third of the twenty-four periods into which the Chinese year was divided over 2,000 years ago to reflect the agricultural cycles of the middle and lower Yellow River. In central China, they still say that "once Jing Zhe day is over, there is no end to Spring plowing."

As the very voice of the Dragon, thunder then gives the signal for unrelenting activity to insects and men alike. To protect their cattle and themselves against the swarms that the awakening Dragon's tail lifts from the ground and spreads through the air, in some places the peasants stir-fry soybeans with sugar as "scorpions' legs." In others, they make lantern-shaped dishes out of the leftover dough from the **Lantern Festival** of a couple of weeks before. In Jiangsu province, they eat "cakes for supporting the loins," kept from the previous year as a protection against backaches, to ensure the ability to work hard so as to be able to feed the family over the coming year. There as in Shantung, they draw concentric "barn circles" with straw ashes to read the fortune of the new harvest, and sometimes add a ladder design to symbolize the plenty they hope for. In Shensi, they use sugar or lime to literally draw in the Serpent from its dwelling in the well in the courtyard through the door to a water jug inside the house—inviting in the good fortune in its power. For fear of antagonizing the Dragon and facing retribution in misfortune, women do not even dare to do needlework on this day, as they might unwittingly prick its eyes.

Such regional folkloric practices aside, the day of the **Spring Dragon** is generally one for outings, long walks, dragon-lantern processions, and launching **dragon boat**s.

See also Lantern Festival; Dragon Boat Festival

References

Juliet Bredon and Igor Mitrophanow. *The Moon Year: A Record of Chinese Customs and Festivals.* Hong Kong: Oxford University Press, 1982 (reprint of the 1927 Shanghai edition).

Qi Xing. *Folk Customs at Traditional Chinese Festivities.* Tr. Ren Jiazhen. Beijing: Foreign Language Press, 1988.

C. K. Yang. *Religion in Chinese Society.* Berkeley: University of California Press, 1962.

▶ SPRING FESTIVAL

See New Year (China, Korea), Passover

▶ SPRING FESTIVAL OF CYBELE AND ATTIS (ROME)

Imported to Rome from Asia Minor at the end of the third century B.C.E., the cult of Cybele was at first officially restricted to April **games** and a procession led by foreign clergy. But it gained state recognition in early Imperial times, when its focus shifted more to March rituals re-enacting the death of her lover Attis and his resurrection as a herald of spring. These rites were known for sexual self-mutilation performed in trance states, as well as for **carnival** inversion practices. Later, the **Spring Festival** of **Cybele and Attis** developed into a mystery cult calling for the initiation of devotees through a baptism in bull's blood.

How Cybele Came to Rome

The cult of the Near Eastern Great Mother of the Gods, the *Mater Deum Magna Idaea* or *Magna Mater,* had its major seat in Phrygia (an ancient land in the Asian part of present-day Turkey), at the foot of Mounts Ida and Cybele—the two names by which she was known. She was worshipped there in the shrine of Pessinus in the form of a black stone called a betylus. But this sacred stone was eventually taken all the way to Rome by a delegation sent from there for this purpose after solemnly consulting the Sibylline Books of prophecies for a way to obtain divine help against the armies of Hannibal from Rome's rival Carthage. They had seemed about to overcome all of Italy; yet within a year, they had gone back to Africa.

Even before this providential retreat, bumper crops had made it clear that the foreign fertility goddess had gone to work from the moment she was installed in the Temple of Victory on Palatine Hill by Rome's aristocracy on April 4, 204 B.C.E. It was on this day that the first scenic **games** were organized by the nobles in her honor. These **Ludi** *Megalenses* would become annual and last until April 10 from that date in 191 B.C.E., when the *Magna Mater*'s very own temple was dedicated on the Palatine. The Great Mother's strange "Phrygian rites" were long confined to her temple and left to foreign clergy. Yet Rome's patricians made of her **games**, for a long time the first **games** of the year, their answer to those of the wheat goddess Ceres, the **Cerialia**, which immediately followed from April 12 to 19, put on by the plebeians. The nobles seized this opportunity to emulate the common people's seasonal practice of *mutitationes,* that is of inviting each other in turn to extravagant sacred banquets. On these occasions, an old peasant dish of white cheese and ground herbs, called *moretus,* was set aside for Cybele.

After over a century of restricting the actual cult of Cybele to a colorful annual procession, the Senate finally had to bow to popular pressure caused by the fascination it exerted and allow her clergy to recruit devotees among Roman citizens. They had previously been barred from full participation, because it involved castration, which was illegal in Rome. Officially protected by Emperor Augustus (63–14 B.C.E.), the public cult of the goddess Cybele was incorporated and regulated by Emperor Claudius (10–54 B.C.E.), likely under the influence of his powerful entourage of former slaves. It thus came to feature a full-fledged liturgy meant to reenact the associated myth of Attis, down to sexual self-mutilation as its centerpiece. This was the price to be paid for the renewed fertility of spring, as part of rites extending from March 15 to 27. They began with a procession of reed-bearers (*cannophori*), introducing eight days of

The introduction of the Cult of Cybele at Rome, a painting by Andrea Mantegna from 1505–1506. The imported Oriental cult of Cybele gained state recognition in early Imperial times, when its focus shifted more to March rituals reenacting the death of her lover Attis and his resurrection as a herald of spring. (National Gallery collection, London/Corbis)

fasting that particularly concerned bread and other flour-based products. This was both a sign of mourning for the death of the wheat god Attis and a way to achieve purification before partaking of the sacramental mysteries of his annual resurrection.

Mourning for Attis

The Great Mother had by then been assimilated to the Mother of the Gods of classical mythology: Rhea. She had caused her husband Saturn's emasculation by saving one of their offspring, which until then he had been swallowing as soon as they were born. Jupiter, having escaped this fate, would unseat his father as king of the gods, slashing his father's male organs in the process. But as Cybele, remembering how her fertility had long been thwarted by the divine patriarch, the Mother of the Gods would not allow her young lover Attis (whom she had actually *fathered* from the nymph Nana in her guise as the hermaphrodite Agdistis—named after Mount Agdis or Cybele) to ever grow to manhood and into a husband—to her or to anyone. She had him swear to always remain just a boy and never to love anybody else. As a result, when Attis came of age and fell in love with a fair wood nymph, Cybele killed her. Attis then went mad with regret, cutting off with a sharp stone the male organs that had caused the anger of the

jealous Great Mother. The blood from his wound, splattered at the foot of a pine tree, turned into violets. Pines are evergreens bearing cones that are full of seed and have the shape of testicles, which makes them an obvious symbol of fertility. At the time of year when violets actually do blossom in the shade of pines, one of these trees used to be cut in the forest on March 22, to be brought to the temple of Cybele by ceremonial tree-bearers. The trunk was wrapped around with woollen bands and wreathed with violets, to further underline that it stood for the dead Attis, and an effigy of the poor boy was tied to it. It would be buried until the next year, when it would be burned and replaced with a new tree.

Cybele's Day of Blood

On March 23, trumpets were blown, as if to call the spring. But the love sacrifice of Attis to the Great Mother had yet to be performed on March 24, Cybele's **Day of Blood**. The *Archigallus* was head of her priests, the *Galles*. They were named after the river Gallus that flowed from Mount Cybele, and whose waters were said to make whoever drank from them go mad. This was a condition that the mythical, half-demonic attendants of Cybele, the Corybantes, were thought able to cure with the wild dances of their orgiastic cult. (Likewise in the

Whitsuntide folklore of Rumania and Bulgaria, only initiated *Calūşari* mummers embodying the **Rusalii** water spirits had the power to cure the madness they caused with their dances.) It was among the reeds on the banks of the Gallus that Cybele was reputed to have found the body of her son and lover Attis. This event is commemorated on March 15.

On the **Day of Blood**, the high priest of the Galles set an example worthy of the Corybantes by drawing blood from his arms and offering it to Cybele. Entranced by the rhythm of cymbals and drums and the grating sound of horns and flutes, the rest of the clergy used shards, knives, and whips to gash their skin so as to splash blood on the altar and the tree, ecstatically whirling their long hair. In their frenzy, some would go so far as to cut off their genitals and dash them against the image of the Great Mother. It might even have been expected of the novices as an initiation into a new estate of exclusive devotion to the jealous goddess. It is known to have been done on the spur of the moment by ordinary devotees from the general public at Asian cultic centers of a similar Great Goddess, be it Diana of Ephesus or Astarte of Hierapolis. It may have happened in Rome too, since Catullus (87–54 B.C.E.), in his poem on "Attis," movingly captured the devotee's appalling realization, upon coming back to his senses, of an irreparable act performed while possessed by a divine spirit.

Hilaria

After these wild expressions of mourning for the god, mad rejoicing followed his nightlong funeral wake as dawn broke on March 25, which was the spring equinox in the Ancients' reckoning. For spring was experienced as the rebirth of the young god Attis. It was celebrated in the streets of Rome and elsewhere as the **Festival of Joy** or **Hilaria**. Known also on November 3 for the resurrection of Osiris in the similar foreign cult of Isis, this was a **thanksgiving carnival** of laughter, where people dressed up to assume and parody other social stations. None was too high or too sacred to escape such derision amidst the universal license that prevailed for a day when nothing was forbidden. This suspension and confusion of social roles was even once used (however unsuccessfully) by conspirators to get within stabbing distance of Emperor Commodus (161–192); they dressed as his Imperial Guard and mingled with the partying crowd that surrounded him. The following day of rest allowed people to recuperate before the closing procession of March 27. To the accompaniment of tambourines and pipes, it took the silver image of the Great Mother, with the black betylus set on her forehead, through a gate called the Porta Capena to the brook Almo that flowed into the Tiber just outside city walls. The high priest, wearing purple vestments, and usually named Attis, would now wash the image of Cybele and other sacred objects, as well as the wagon itself, in a rite known as *lavatio.* This wagon, along with the oxen drawing it, would be decorated with fresh spring flowers for the merry ride back to town.

Baptism of Blood

The **Spring Festival of Cybele and Attis** came to be very popular throughout the Roman Empire, from Africa to Bulgaria. But from the end of the third century onward, it was experienced more and more as a mystery religion of personal salvation. On March 28, the candidate for higher initiation would partake in a sacramental meal, eating out of a tambourine and drinking out of a cymbal, which were the ceremonial instruments of the festival. First he would have to go through what was known as a taurobolic baptism of blood. Initially performed on behalf of the Emperor and his realm and soon very widespread throughout its Western half, it was derived from the bull sacrifice introduced into the cult of Cybele in 160 in imitation of other foreign cults like that of Mithra, and possibly influenced by the Christian baptism of water as well. Wearing headbands and a golden crown, the candidate had to go down into a pit. The hole was then closed behind him with a wooden grating, and a bull was pressed onto it, garlanded with flowers, with gold leaf stamped on its forehead. The bull would then be stabbed to death with a consecrated spear, bleeding profusely on the initiate underneath it. Leaving behind as in a grave the old man and his sins, he would eventually emerge from the pit drenched with the reeking blood of the bull sacrificed to Cybele. It was supposed to purify and revitalize him for ten or twenty years, as a foretaste of a blissful life everlasting beyond death, it was later assumed (though the sacrifice was generally done for its own sake). His fellows would worshipfully welcome him to this new life by nursing him on milk like a newborn child for a while.

The devotee's regeneration was thus carried out at the same time as that of his god Attis on the spring equinox. These rites were observed in Rome and were most popular among urban women for a long time after the Empire's formal adoption of Christianity as its only official religion. They were practiced chiefly on the very spot of Vatican Hill where the Roman Church's symbolic center, St. Peter's Basilica, would later stand. Likewise, before the date of **Easter** was universally set as a movable feast in 325, March 25 was taken to be the date of Christ's Resurrection in the very places where the rebirth of Attis (like him a "solar" god in later times) had long been celebrated on that day as part of the **Spring Festival of Cybele**: namely Phrygia, Cappadocia, Gaul, and perhaps Rome as well. And of course, March 25 was eventually retained by the Church as the date for the celebration of the **Annunciation** to Mary that she would be Mother of God, on a day when the Great Mother of the Gods Cybele (also from the Near East) already used to be honored. These coincidences in time and place seem to suggest a hidden continuity in Western man's quest for regeneration, whether seasonal or personal; for whether it ensured natural renewal or granted supernatural realization, its high-point was always set in the spring.

See also Annunciation; Dionysia; Easter; Games (Rome); Khoiak and Heb-Sed; May Day; Palm Sunday; Venus Verticordia and Virile Fortune; Whitsuntide

References

Robert Duthoy. *The Taurobolium. Its Evolution and Terminology.* Leiden, The Netherlands: E. J. Brill, "Etudes préliminaires aux religions orientales dans l'Empire romain" series, Vol. 10, 1969.

Eugene N. Lane. *Cybele, Attis, and Related Cults. Essays in Memory of M. J. Vermaseren.* New York: E. J. Brill, 1996.

Giulia Sfameni Gasparro. *Soteriology and Mystic Aspects in the Cult of Cybele and Attis.* Leiden, The Netherlands: E. J. Brill, 1985.

Maarten J. Vermaseren. *Cybele and Attis, the Myth and the Cult.* Tr. H. Lemmers. London: Thames and Hudson, 1977.

▶ **SRÉTENYE**
See Candlemas

▶ **STANDARD MONTH**
See New Year (Japan)

▶ **STAR FESTIVAL**
See Sekku

▶ **STUDENTS' DAY**
See Lag ba-Omer

▶ **SUGÔ FESTIVAL**
See Gion Festival

▶ **SUKKOT (JUDAISM)**

Sukkot is the principal of the three **pilgrim festivals** of Judaism (alongside **Passover** and **Shavuot**), and its oldest festival altogether. It started out as a one-day harvest festival. Later on, the Hebrew word *sukkot* was attached to it

Sukkot. Goldsmidt House, Jerusalem, 1930. (Library of Congress)

and has been taken to refer to the **booths** (sometimes called "tabernacles") in which the Jews camped in the wilderness after their flight from Egypt. To celebrate this time of trial and triumph joyfully, Jews still build huts, eating their meals in them over a weeklong festival, followed by a day for honoring the Torah.

The Festival of Ingathering

Sukkot was long known simply as *Hag* or "the Festival." It was derived from a Canaanite autumn feast of ingathering from the threshing floor and the winepress. Unlike most other Jewish festivals, which start on the **New Moon**, this one, like **Passover**, begins on the full moon, namely in the middle of the month of Tishri, in late September or early October. The autumn pilgrimage initially lasted one day; it was then known as the **Festival of Ingathering** (*hag*

ha'asip) in the Book of Exodus (23:16). But by the time it was mentioned again in Leviticus (23:33–43) and Deuteronomy (16:13–15), it had become the **Festival of Booths** (*hag hassukkot*) and lasted seven days, followed by an eighth day for a sacred assembly. It then started a little later than the **Ingathering**, when the harvest had already been processed. This delaying and extension of the original festival was probably due to the increasing centralization of all pilgrimage at the Temple of Jerusalem, to the exclusion of any local shrines, which compelled Jews to be on the move for a longer period. The **booths** may well have arisen as temporary shelters for the countless pilgrims who came to the capital especially for this festival (even from abroad) after the Jewish people spread out in the Diaspora. The greenery still used to adorn the **sukkot** attests to their original connection with a fertility ritual.

Sukkot grew into the major yearly gathering of the Jews at the Temple in Jerusalem, after King Solomon first dedicated it on the occasion of this festival around 966 B.C.E. By the same token, he turned it into an enthronement feast of his dynasty and a consecration of its royal capital. So much so that after Solomon's death, when the Northern Kingdom of Israel split away, its king Jeroboam made sacrifices at his own shrine in Bethel on **Sukkot**, as King Solomon had done at the Temple of Jerusalem—only a month later than remained the use in Jerusalem, capital of the Southern Kingdom of Juda. There, the seventh month of Tishri, when **Sukkot** was held, eventually became the first month (as was the case in neighboring Assyria) so that its **new moon** signaled the Jewish **New Year**: **Rosh Hashanah**. It was itself derived from the Mesopotamian **New Year** festival **Akitu** as the proper time for the solemn enthronement of kings—an idea Solomon seems to have been emulating.

Coming straight on the heels of the ascetic period of fasting between **Rosh Hashanah** and **Yom Kippur**, the feast of **Sukkot** has always been characterized by joy, even before these other festivals existed. According to a vision of the prophet Zechariah from the year 520 B.C.E., joy will also overflow at the end of time when all the nations of the world come to Jerusalem to celebrate **Sukkot** along with the Jews. Three huge golden candlesticks used to be lit in the Temple courtyard during the festival's **intermediate days**, for water-libation rites that were meant to bring rain. They called for priests to carry in procession water from the pool of Siloam in a golden jar to pour it on the southwestern side of the altar of burnt offerings—the one facing the direction rain clouds came from. A flute-playing procession also circled the altar with willow branches for a ceremony called *Simhat Bet ha-Sho'evah,* as the epitome of joy. Some of these customs have been translated to the context of the local synagogue after the destruction of the Second Temple of Jerusalem in

70. Every day of **Sukkot**, the congregation circles the pulpit and waves branches of the "four species"—citron, myrtle, palm, and willow—from which the **sukkot** used to be made in Jerusalem's squares and courtyards and on the city's rooftops. On the seventh day, known as *Hoshana Rabba* (**"Great Hosanna"**), the faithful sing *hoshana* prayers for a good harvest in the coming year as they circle the Scrolls of the Law seven times inside the synagogue. This day is now regarded as a supplement to **Yom Kippur**, when God can still finalize his judgment for the year. **Sukkot** itself may be seen as a kind of popular counterpart of the priestly **New Year**'s Day of **Rosh Hashanah** leading up to **Yom Kippur**; all three festivals come within a couple of weeks of each other in the same month of Tishri.

Shemini Atzeret and Simhat Torah

The twenty-second of Tishri marks the eighth day of **Sukkot**, but is treated by the rabbis as a separate festival called **Shemini Atzeret**. It features a great prayer for rain, as well as the *yizkor* memorial prayer for the dead after the Book of Ecclesiastes has been read out. This was on account of its seasonal melancholy mood and of the justification for this extra day drawn from the following verse (11:2): "Divide a portion into seven, yea, even into eight" ("Sukkot," in *Encyclopedia Judaica* 1971, p. 502).

On this eighth day in Israel (but on the next day in the Diaspora), the festival has been closing for over a thousand years with *Simhat Torah,* or "Rejoicing in the Torah," because the annual reading of the Torah from the scroll at the synagogue is then completed, and the new cycle of readings is immediately started. One member of the congregation, "the bridegroom of the Torah," reads the last portion, and another picks up from the very beginning as "the bridegroom of Genesis," after which the two of them will invite the other members to a party. Both on the eve and on the day of **Simhat Torah**, the scrolls are taken in a singing (and often dancing) procession around the synagogue by a few of the faithful, while the others wave small, colorful handmade flags. Little boys race around the synagogue with them in Hasidic communities, while girls may only look on from another room. Later that evening, babies are cuddled as they are passed from lap to lap, and well-to-do businessmen outbid each other at a ritual auction of opportunities for their less fortunate or elderly brethren to have the honor of reading aloud from the Torah. If the first and the eighth day of the festival are days of rest, certain sacrifices are prescribed for all eight days by the Bible's Book of Leviticus and Book of Numbers: seventy on the first seven days for the seventy nations of which mankind is symbolically made up, and one ram and one bullock on the eighth day, to denote Israel's special relationship to God as His chosen people. Yet they can no longer be done without priests or Temples.

Symbolism of the Sukkah

In principle, unless it is facing severe hardships, a Jewish household (limited to its male members in Hasidic communities) is still supposed to eat and sleep (as well as celebrate with rhythmic singing and clapping of hands) within the frail temporary shelter of a *sukkah* for the duration of the festival. According to the Book of Leviticus (23:43), this was ordained by God to Moses as a reenactment of the living conditions of the tribes of Israel during the forty years of their wanderings in search of the promised land. In the words of the festival's *kiddush* or blessing over wine: "Blessed are You, *YHVH* our God, King of the Universe, who has sanctified us by His commandments and commanded us to dwell in the sukkah"(Fine 1984, p. 335). The roof of the cabin should be made of foliage under open sky, so that rain can come through. This probably represents not so much a hazard of life in the Sinai desert as a seasonal invitation for rain to come down and to water the plants. But there remains the idea of being in touch with nature, and with the clouds in particular, as a reminder of God's providence, which protected the Jews in a hostile environment during the Exodus, under the guise of clouds of glory. In the Talmudic commentary of Rabbi Eliezer (*Sukkah* 11b), the **sukkot** themselves are the clouds of glory, of which there are seven according to a *midrash* by Rabbi Hoshaya (Numbers Rabbah 1:2). Kabbalists have thus been able to identify them with the seven lower *sefirot* or power points on the cosmic Tree of Life of their esoteric teachings. In its branches or *sefirot*, the Community of Israel (*Knesset Yisrael* in its heavenly aspect as opposed to the earthly people of Israel) is sheltered and lodged by the Divine Presence (the female *Shekhinah*), both of them corresponding to the lowest *sefira: Malkhut,* or the Kingdom, as the basis for the manifestation of all the others, leading back to God.

For all its associations with the austerity of exile, the seasonal sukkah has always been richly decorated (according to the respective standards of every walk of life of course) with constructions ranging from a ramshackle outhouse to a luxurious pavilion. A variety of fruits will often be hung from the ceiling. Although the walls can be made of any material, they will usually be wood, and they will often be covered with tapestries and pictures. Some of these are termed *ushpizim* or guests, since they depict Biblical heroes who are thus invited to join the celebration, following a Kabbalistic custom that matches each of them with a sefira: Abraham with *Hesed* or Mercy, Isaac with *Din,* meaning Justice, Jacob with *Tiferet,* or Beauty, Moses with *Nezah,* Victory, Aaron with *Hod,* Majesty, Joseph with *Yesod,* Foundation, and David with *Malkhut* or Kingship. A different patriarch is invited on each night of the festival, using formulas such as this one for the first: "O Abraham, my exalted guest, may it please you to have all the exalted guests dwell with us—Isaac, Jacob, Joseph, Moses, Aaron and David" (Fine 1984, p. 334). In their guise, the different divine attributes dwell in turn in the sukkah—or rather, their presence is contemplatively dwelt upon by every celebrant in this Kabbalistic ritual. It has found its way into many prayer books, including most Sephardic ones. At its source in the *Zohar* (III:104a), the ethical remains inseparable from the mystical, as it clearly states:

> Nevertheless, he must make the poor happy.
> Why?
> Because the portion of those guests whom he has invited belongs to the poor.
> One who sits in this shade of faith
> And invites these sublime guests, guests of faith,
> And does not give them their portion—
> All of them rise to leave, saying:
> 'DO NOT EAT THE FOOD OF A STINGY PERSON . . .' (Proverbs 23:6)
> It turns out that the table he set is his own, not divine . . .
>
> (Fine 1984, pp. 335–336)

Though rarely observed in such elaborate forms, the practice of building **sukkot** has recently been enjoying a comeback after years of neglect in North America, as shown by the sudden mushrooming of wooden back-patios in Jewish neighborhoods at this time of year. Often, it is the children who love the fun idea of moving for a while to a small makeshift house in the backyard of their everyday homes and press for its realization. The trend is seen by some as evidence of a spiritual reawakening among Jewish communities. To feed its flames, **Sukkot** will often be the occasion of a "gathering of souls" around a religious elder in a home setting, where young and old may raise questions about proper living as a Jew.

See also Akitu; Passover; Rosh Hashanah; Shavuot; Yom Kippur

References

Lawrence Fine. "Kabbalistic Texts," in Barry W. Holtz, ed. *Back to the Sources—Reading the Classic Jewish Texts.* New York: Summit Books, 1984, pp. 305–359.

Philip Goodman, ed. *The Sukkot and Simhat Torah Anthology.* Philadelphia, PA: Jewish Publication Society of America, 1973.

The Living Festivals (video series), *Part 2 (Sukkot, Divali, Guru Nanak's Birthday).* Exeter, UK: Pergamon Educational Productions in association with RMEP, 1987.

Dianne M. MacMillan. *Jewish Holidays in the Fall.* Hillside, NJ: Enslow Publishers, 1993.

"Sukkot," in *Encyclopedia Judaica.* New York: Macmillan, 1971.

▶ SUMMER FESTIVAL

See Dragon Boat Festival

▶ SUN DANCE (PLAINS INDIANS)

The most dramatic and public religious ceremony of the Plains Indians is the **Sun Dance**. Known in about twenty different cultures (both Siouan and Algonquian) across North America, it had its heyday in the nineteenth century. All the bands of a tribe would then converge in large encampments every summer (while the bison gathered and food was abundant) for an intense festive period during which its belief systems and social bonds were reaffirmed.

A Name's Origin

The term "**Sun Dance**" was first applied to this ceremony by the fur trader Jean-Baptiste Truteau in recollections of the late eighteenth century, when he had observed it among its classic exponents and likely originators along with the Sioux: the Algonquian-speaking Arapaho and Cheyenne. The expression was popularized by Mary Eastman's description of the Santee version in the mid-nineteenth century, since the ceremony had meanwhile spread to tribes from the Kiowa in Texas to the Plains Ojibwa in Saskatchewan. The name stuck in English, even among Indians, though some anthropologists regard it as no more than "a convenience that historians, travelers, and ethnologists have fallen back upon to refer to a range of **midsummer** tribal ceremonies" (Hall 1997, p. 20). They all have names of their own, reflecting both their diversity of purposes and local variations in the rites involved. Most of them have to do with a temporary lodge built to hold sacred dances, so the Arikara call it **House of Whistling** (since dancers pray by blowing through eagle bone whistles), while the Ute, Shoshone, Plains Cree, and Plains Ojibwa know it as the **Thirsting Dance** (since dancers could not eat or drink). In certain versions, the sun hardly figured at all in the ceremony, which was only named after it by the Ponca and Sioux, as the **Sun-Gazing Dance** (*Wi wan' yank Waci'pi,* for the latter's Dakota tribe).

Personal Sacrifice and Cosmic Renewal

The **Sun Dance** is a typical instance of individual quests for spiritual power, mystical knowledge, and supernatural assistance, that grew into elaborate collective ceremonies with a body of songs, ritual, and sacred lore specific to each tribe, reinforcing communal ties by involving everyone in their preparation over many months and their performance over several days. For one thing, like other festivals of the Plains Indians, the **Sun Dance** was normally carried out every year or so in fulfillment of a particular individual's vow in a time of crisis—be it a woman who wanted to keep illness away from her family, as for the Blackfoot and Sarcee, or a man who had pledged to sponsor this event if he returned safely from a war party, as among the Plains Cree and Ojibwa, or either a man or a woman looking for spiritual protection and was instructed by a vision, as with the Cheyenne. Yet it was usually men who did the actual dancing, while women might fast and perform other rites.

For the **Sun Dance** owed its specific features to the warrior culture of Plains nomads, though their more sedentary neighbors took over and adapted some of them. The full ritual entailed the discovery of a special tree that was treated as a captured enemy, being carried in triumph to the center of a specially built circular arbor, often the same structure as the lodge. This pole could start out being the focus of abuse, since the Sioux hung it with buffalo hide images of the infectious spirit of licentiousness. But it was mostly the focus of prayerful offerings, which were hung on it (as on the "thunderbird nest" set at the top by the Plains Cree and Ojibwa) by spectators who wanted to have a share in the sacrifice effected through the ascetic exertions of the fasting dancers.

These were derived from tests of manhood common in such warrior cultures, and also part of other Native American festivals like the Southeastern **Busk**. The best known example of this kind of ordeal is the very similar four-day **Okeepa** ceremony practiced by the Mandan in North Dakota until the late nineteenth century and documented in paintings by George Catlin, who first witnessed it in 1832. At the **Sun Dance** of the Sioux, Cheyenne, Arapaho, and Blackfoot, spectators might join the dancers in cutting tiny pieces of flesh from their arms. But only the dancers had the privilege of being themselves hung on or tied to the central pole by pegs inserted below the muscles of their chest or back. They would dance, gazing at the sun and imbibing its energy through the cables, for as many hours as it took for the flesh to tear away and free them from its bonds. This gave them access to the spirit realm where visions came from, either on the spot or later on during the year. Alternatively, the thongs hooked in their flesh might drag the heavy buffalo skulls they gazed at, like the ones hung on the central pole, as the world axis connecting the earth with the Cosmic Buffalo.

Called Wakan Tanka in Sioux mythology, this Great Spirit is identifiable with the sun as the head of all the spirits who manifest him in the special visions he grants, while he remains unseen as their common source and that of the

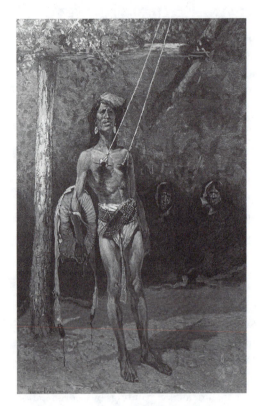

Reproduction of a lithograph by Frederick Remington showing a Blackfoot (Siksika) Native American man enduring a portion of the Sun Dance that includes a piercing of both nipples with thongs that are attached to ropes drawn tight. (Western History/Genealogy Deparment of the Denver Public Library)

world they structure. Among the Cheyenne, as stated by a religious leader a century ago, "the object of the ceremony is to make the whole world over again" (Dorsey 1971, p. 186). The Sioux attribute its origin to the White Buffalo Woman who, perhaps a thousand years back, taught them how to find buffalo and other necessities of life in their new Plains habitat by using the sacred pipe of peace she brought as a gift from the Buffalo people to revere the sky, the earth, and the four winds. Representing the breath of life, it presumably empowered the bison skull next to which it was set on the altar drawn on the ground at the base of the pole. Most Plains tribes who practiced the **Sun Dance** were likewise "buffalo cultures" for which the increase of herd and tribe were one and the same thing, in a celebration of the sun's fertile power that usually involved sacrifice, if not always bloodletting. This feature was thus altogether absent from the distinctive springtime version of the **Sun Dance** found among the Kutenai people of obscure origin, living in southern British Columbia and the north of the states of Idaho and Montana.

From Apparent Suppression to Ambiguous Revival

Regardless of such differences, it was partly on account of some tribes' inclusion of self-torture and mutilation in its rites that the **Sun Dance** as a whole was banned in Canada by an amendment to the Indian Act that was only repealed in 1951. American efforts at suppressing such outwardly militaristic, potentially seditious displays of tribal identity and pride culminated in April 1921, when Commissioner of Indian Affairs Charles Burke called for the abolition of "the **sundance** and all other similar dances and so-called ceremonies" (Archambault 2001, p. 988). They had first been outlawed in 1904, though for the most part they just went underground, even as part of **Fourth of July** celebrations, like the **powwow**. Many federal agents turned a blind eye to them, but others, along with Christian missionaries, went on discouraging the **Sun Dance** and other Native American practices even after Commissioner of Indian Affairs John Collier reversed repressive official policy in his historic 1934 circular on "Indian Religious Freedom and Indian Culture."

By the 1960s, only seven groups from among the nineteen reported at the beginning of the twentieth century still held a **Sun Dance**. But by its end, all but two of these (namely the Ponca and the Sarcee) performed one—either as a traditional tribal ritual, or as an adaptation of that of another tribe if the original version had died out in the interval. "Of all the twentieth-century tribal **Sun Dance**s that either survived or were renewed, the Sioux traditions, particularly those originating on the Pine Ridge and Rosebud reservations, played the most significant role in the diffusion of an intertribal, interracial **Sun Dance** that became international in scope" (Archambault 2001, p. 992). This was largely due to the development of the American Indian Movement, whose leadership was largely Sioux. It was thus at the **Sun Dance**s held on these Sioux reservations that, by the 1970s, many uprooted urban Indian young people got their first taste of Native American spirituality, regardless of their tribal background. Aside from traditional revivals that often allowed piercing to reemerge openly, more or less politicized versions of the **Sun Dance** appeared among the Sioux. They spread to communities beyond the Plains as part of an intertribal movement of Indian pride, reaching northward as far east as Micmac territory on Cape Breton Island in Atlantic Canada in 1988, and as far west as the Rocky Mountains, for supporters in a land dispute with the Canadian government at Gustafsen Lake, British Columbia, in 1994 and 1995.

Non-Indian sympathizers were also welcome to participate as helpers and workers, if not as dancers, increasingly for spiritual as well as political reasons. For since the 1970s too, there has been a renewed emphasis on the universal scope of this ritual for the benefit of all beings, with many Native American religious leaders coming back from vision quests with specific instructions to help people of all backgrounds through the **Sun Dance**, in a spirit of reconciliation between races and with the earth. This new openness has often been taken advantage of by non-Indian spiritual seekers, leaving these mostly Sioux ecumenicists open to charges of being seduced by their fawning attentions to the point of selling out sacred lore to outsiders, and even of lending a spurious air of traditional legitimacy to New Age versions of the **Sun Dance**, such as have been held for this new con-

stituency as far away as Britain, France, and Germany.

See also Busk; Midsummer; Powwow

References

Hartley Burr Alexander. *The World's Rim. Great Mysteries of the North American Indians.* Foreword by Clyde Kluckhohn. Lincoln: University of Nebraska, 1953.

JoAllyn Archambault. "Sun Dance," in Raymond J. DeMallie, *Handbook of North American Indians,* Vol. 13: *Plains* (Part 2). Washington, DC: Smithsonian Institution, 2001, pp. 983–995.

G. A. Dorsey. *The Cheyenne II: The Sun Dance.* Field Columbian Museum Publication 101, Anthropological Series 9(2), Chicago, 1905, reprinted with *The Cheyenne I: Ceremonial Organization.* New York: Kraus Reprints, 1971.

R. L. Hall. *An Archeology of the Soul: North American Indian Belief and Ritual.* Urbana: University of Illinois Press, 1997.

V. M. Roediger. *Ceremonial Customs of the Plains Indians.* Berkeley: University of California Press, 1961.

SUNDAY (CHRISTIANITY)

Among Christians, **Sunday** has always been set aside for weekly worship in common to commemorate the Resurrection of Christ following the Jewish **Sabbath**, which it initially displaced as a festive holy day, and gradually replaced as a solemn day of rest. It was enforced with varying strictness in different periods, places, and church denominations.

Primitive Sunday Worship

New Testament writings do not explain how **Sunday** worship began in the time of the Apostles. While they were still mostly of Jewish background, many early Christians probably kept the **Sabbath** at the synagogue before gathering as a distinct group the following day, which was the first of the week, for the celebration of the Eucharistic sacrifice, as indicated in

Acts, 20:7 and I Corinthians 16:2. In Revelation 1:10, it is called "the **Lord's Day**," marking the triumph of Christ in his Resurrection, and the beginning of a timeless new Creation beyond the completion of the old one on the **Sabbath** as a time of rest on its seventh day. The next day was thus known as "the eighth day," because of the "other day" fixed by God for his people to reach the "place of rest" after the work of Creation in Hebrews 4:4–11.

Around 150, Saint Justin Martyr's *First Apology* to Emperor Antoninus Pius on behalf of Christians, to refute charges of atheism and subversion, is the first text that equates (in chapter sixty-seven) the eighth day (as that of Christ's Resurrection) with the first one (as that of God's Creation of the world) in the still unofficial Roman planetary week—starting with the sun's day to end on Saturn's day. His description of **Sunday** worship remains largely valid in basic outline for all apostolic Churches and some mainline Protestant ones.

On the day known as that of the sun, Justin relates, "all who live in cities or in the country gather together to one place, and the memoirs of the apostles or the writings of the prophets are read, as long as time permits; then, when the reader has ceased, the president verbally instructs, and exhorts to the imitation of these good things. Then we all rise together and pray, and . . . when our prayer is ended, the bread and wine and water are brought." Known as the two species of the Eucharist, bread and wine mixed with warm water were originally available to all the faithful, but laypeople have until recently (for example, the Second Vatican Council for Catholics) had to be content with the bread alone in the Western Church, since about the same time as its separation from the Eastern Church was triggered a thousand years ago by the Roman papacy's claim to unilaterally and universally impose such innovations as the use of unleavened bread for this sacrament, on the model of Jewish **Passover**. This schism between the two halves of the Christian Church still prevents their respective members from communing in each other's sacraments, starting with the Eucharist.

The latter's name is the Greek word for the "**thanksgiving**" as which the priest offers the consecrated bread and wine to God with devotion. The congregation then answers with one voice: "*Amen*"—a Hebrew word meaning "so be it." According to Justin already, to partake in the Eucharist, one has to believe in the truth of Christian doctrines and live by them in practice, having been born again through baptism as the washing away of sins and the putting on of Christ. For "in like manner as Jesus Christ our Saviour, having been made flesh by the word of God, had both flesh and blood for our salvation, so likewise have we been taught that the food which is blessed by the prayer of His word, and from which our blood and flesh by transmutation are nourished, is the flesh and blood of that Jesus who was made flesh. For the apostles, in the memoirs composed by them, which are called Gospels, have thus delivered unto us what was enjoined upon them; that Jesus took bread, and when He had given thanks, said, 'This do ye in remembrance of me, this is my body;' and that, after the same manner, having taken the cup and given thanks, he said, 'This is my blood;' and gave it to them alone." In Justin's time however, "when the president has given thanks, and all the people have expressed their assent, those who are called by us deacons give to each of those present to partake of the bread and wine mixed with water over which the **thanksgiving** was pronounced, and to those who are absent they carry away a portion." Deacons are also responsible for a collection from all those in the congregation who have the means and the desire to give—at their own discretion. They then hand it over to the presiding priest or bishop, who "takes care of all who are in need:" orphans and widows, the sick and the poor, prisoners and strangers, and the like (Roberts and Donaldson 1867, pp. 64–66).

A Day of Rest Begins the Week

Born around the same time as Saint Justin's text was written, the Latin Christian author Tertullian added in chapter twenty-three of his treatise *Concerning Prayer* (1919, pp. 40–41) that "we, according to the tradition we have received, on the day of the Lord's Resurrection, and on it alone, ought to refrain carefully not only from this [kneeling], but from every attitude and duty that cause perplexity putting off even our daily business, 'lest we give any place to the devil' [Ephesians 4:27]. The same thing, too, at **Whitsuntide**, which is distinguished by the same solemnity of its rejoicing," except that the solemn reintroduction of the kneeling banned since **Easter** (as though to draw out the joy of this original **Sunday** over fifty days) in Orthodox Churches now takes center stage at vespers. This is an evening service marking the feast's end, but in practice, on **Pentecost**, it is usually held right after the morning liturgy. Otherwise, to this day, there is no kneeling on **Sunday** (except for **Cross Veneration Sunday**, the third one in **Lent**) in Eastern rite Churches, because of such a concern to uphold a dignified demeanor befitting the glorification of liberated mankind in its worship of God, reflected in the need to avoid servile labor and make time for this higher purpose.

In the Latin West, Tertullian's North African countryman Saint Augustine of Hippo (354–430) took the **Sabbath** rest from servile work on **Sunday** to mean abstention from sin. But more literal approaches were steadily gaining ground. In 300, the Council of Elvira decreed: "If anyone in the city neglects to come to church for three **Sunday**s, let him be excommunicated for a short time so that he may be corrected" (Slater 1999). In 321, the Roman Emperor Constantine issued an edict calling on townspeople and craftsmen to refrain from work, and for magistrates not to sit "on the venerable day of the Sun," a day sacred to both Mithraism and Christianity, for different reasons. It is not clear which of the two increasingly popular Oriental religions the Roman Emperor was tacitly acknowledging (if not both) by making **Sunday** into a civic holiday, thus for the first time giving official standing to the seven-day planetary week that had become generally accepted throughout the Greco-Roman world over the previous couple of centuries (Rybczynski 1991, p. 70).

If Constantine had still followed Roman tradition by allowing agricultural work on **Sunday** as on all other feasts (*feriae*), two centuries later, the Third Council of Orléans (538) deemed it "better to abstain" from it too, "so that people may the more readily come to the churches and have leisure for prayers" (Rybczynski 1991, p. 71). But it also denounced as a Judaizing practice the application to **Sunday** of **Sabbath** rules that had gone on being followed on Saturday by the Ethiopian and other Eastern Churches until they were officially forbidden in the twenty-ninth canon of the Synod of Laodicea (360s). For even in the Roman Church there were still those who claimed, like Saint Cæsarius of Arles (470–543), that the whole glory of the Jewish **Sabbath** had been transferred onto **Sunday**, so that Christians had to keep it holy in the same way as the Jews had their own day of rest. Other Church councils and imperial edicts though sought to restrict various activities on this day, especially public amusements in the theater and circus.

Christian Sabbath and Weekly Fair

In the wake of the collapse of the Roman Empire in the West, the Roman Church insisted more and more on the obligation of **Sunday** rest, preceded by Saturday fasting. The latter practice was the earliest bone of contention with Eastern Churches, since they forbade such austerity on a day commemorating both the completion of Creation and Christ's victorious Harrowing of Hell while he walked among the dead between his Crucifixion and Resurrection. As for the prohibition on work, it was meant to humanize the lot of a new underclass of rural serfs and laborers and to give them the opportunity to attend mass and absorb Christian teachings. From the eighth century onward, local councils forbade servile labor, public buying and selling, pleading in law courts, and the public taking of oaths. The breaking of the law of **Sunday** rest was punished like other crimes and misdemeanors in Saxon England. But it was not until the twelfth century that **Sunday** came to be referred to and earnestly thought of as the "Christian **Sabbath**," with unnecessary work accounted a mortal sin and the clergy relying on civil laws to enforce an increasing number of sabbatarian regulations on **Sunday** and other holidays.

Laypeople had long been taught that they had to hear mass and the preaching of the Word of God on **Sunday**s in their parish church. But by the end of the thirteenth century, certain monastic orders began to teach that they might also do it in their own churches and private chapels, and this controversial new practice was eventually allowed by the papacy. Still, in the Middle Ages, as a regular time for people to meet for worship, **Sunday** was also the usual market day (the meaning of its Hungarian name *vasárnap*), taking over this function from the last day of an earlier eight-day Roman week. This was an occasion for both business and entertainment—be it as sports, jousts, plays, pageants, parish ales, or other public amusements. Open-air markets are still held on **Sunday** in many Catholic countries in Europe and elsewhere.

The Strictures of the Protestant Sabbath

Much of the bustling, boisterous spontaneity of medieval **Sunday**s, which the clergy had vainly tried to control, was lost with the advent of the Protestant Reformation. Its denial of sacred time as expressed in a regular cycle of festivals took different forms. For Calvin, no particular day was fitter than others for religious worship, but for practical reasons he maintained the ob-

servance of **Sunday**, and liked to go bowling after the service. But for Luther (Rybczynski 1991, p. 72), "everything is governed and ordained by the Gospel, baptism, and **Sunday** prayer"—which now carried the full weight of religious observance with the canceling or downplaying of a multitude of medieval feasts at the Church and parish level. There was now a renewed insistence on doctrine, which would be imparted to Lutheran adults in catechism classes after the **Sunday** service, as the first model of the **Sunday** schools later aimed at children in many denominations. On its part, the Catholic Counterreformation stressed attendance at **Sunday** morning mass, and even at **Sunday** evening vespers for a while in the eighteenth and nineteenth centuries.

Protestant states where the monarch was given tight control over the national Church, such as Sweden and England, had civil laws making attendance at **Sunday** services compulsory, and absence a punishable offence. In England, the **Sunday** Observance Act of 1677 was applied to the widest variety of trades and occupations. In 1781, any public entertainment charging an entrance fee was banned by a law that remained in force until the 1930s. It was after the blue paper on which an edict of this kind was issued that same year in New Haven, Connecticut that such "Blue Laws" came to be known in all of Britain's former American colonies—even as the strict interpretation given to them by their Puritan founders began to lapse with the War of Independence. For Puritans referred to **Sunday** as "the **Sabbath**" and meant it to be as strict as the Old Testament suggested. The same Calvinist strain of sabbatarian intransigence also prevailed in Scotland until about fifty years ago, when people still spent their **Sunday** afternoons doing nothing but making sure nobody else did anything of any kind.

But nowhere were the civil laws governing **Sunday** observance so severe as in Puritan colonies. In Virginia, failure to attend **Sunday** morning services and afternoon catechism was punishable with flogging and even death for repeat offenders. More common were the laws passed to enforce church attendance and prohibit work, travel, sports, and other frivolous pastimes in colonies such as Maryland and Massachusetts, where sabbatarian restrictions on various activities remain strongest, though they are also still found in some form in a majority of American states as well as countless municipalities. They may aim at a disconcerting variety of specific activities, such as bowling and bingo, pool and polo, boxing and wrestling, gambling and hunting, going to the movies or a dance, digging oysters, selling fresh meat, and especially drinking liquor.

The Pressures on the Catholic Sunday

By contrast, few Catholic countries have ever instituted **Sunday** laws. In Spain for instance, it is on **Sunday** afternoon that bullfights are traditionally held. In Canada, a large Catholic population came under the jurisdiction of British **Sunday** laws with the conquest of this French colony in 1759. Their application was rather lenient until 1906, when a lobbying campaign by the Protestant **Lord's Day** Alliance, aimed against streetcars, rail travel, public spectacles as well as commerce on **Sunday**s, resulted in the full adoption of the proposed **Lord's Day** Act. However, an amendment was made that left its enforcement to the discretion of the provinces, so that it remained a dead letter in mostly French Quebec. A Catholic **Sunday** League was formed in 1923 to combat this laxity and promote sabbatarian restrictions in that province—especially against movie theaters. But it remained the only one in Canada where they remained open on **Sunday**s, as local politicians were well aware that the laity did not share the clergy's censorious attitude in these matters. The only success of this *Ligue du Dimanche* was the abrogation of a provision of the law allowing Jews to do business on **Sunday**—since they already kept the original **Sabbath** as their day of rest. Quite aside from such petty bigotry, a main objective of many Catholic social reformers since the nineteenth century had been the restoration of **Sunday** rest for industrial workers, because employers paid it little heed and long insisted on making them work practically all week long. However, in the latter half of the twentieth century, the popularization of the weekend away from home and parish, or wholly given over to leisure in an increasingly secular consumer society, would prove even more disruptive of religious **Sunday** observance. Its collapse was nowhere as dramatic as in Quebec in the 1960s, where it signaled that of the Catholic Church's long pervasive influence, along with the demise of the *Ligue du Dimanche*.

The Long Decline of the Lord's Day

From then on, the commercial pressures that have gradually imposed **Sunday** shopping in most of North America over the second half of the last century could meet with little resistance. In 1950 already, the **Lord's Day** Alliance had lost a key plebiscite in Toronto, long the center of Canadian sabbatarianism, as baseball games were allowed on **Sunday**. In response to the enshrinement in the new Canadian Constitution in 1982 of American principles of separation of Church and State, the organization tried to shed its religious cast and to rely more on labor support in a short-lived new incarnation as "People for **Sunday**." Its rearguard actions against **Sunday** shopping and related causes did not prevent its prompt demise after the **Lord's Day** Act was struck down by the Supreme Court of Canada in 1985 as an unconstitutional abridgement of religious freedom. Interestingly enough, the last Canadian bastion of the traditional ban on **Sunday** shopping, reaffirmed by popular demand in a province-wide referendum in October 2004, is Nova Scotia, the Scotland of the New World. Otherwise,

Canada tends to closely follow American patterns of **Sunday** behavior, only with a delay of a decade or so.

See also Day of Assembly; Easter; Games (Rome); Kunapipi; Lent; Nineteen-Day Feast; Passover; Sabbath; Whitsuntide

References

Paul Laverdure. *Sunday in Canada. The Rise and Fall of the Lord's Day.* Yorkton, Canada: Gravelbooks, 2004.

Rev. Alexander Roberts and James Donaldson, eds. *Ante-Nicene Christian Library: Translations of the Writings of the Fathers Down to A.D. 325,* Vol. II: *The Writings of Justin Martyr and Athenagoras.* Tr. Rev. Marcus Dods, Rev. George Reith, and Rev. B. P. Pratten. Edinburgh: T. and T. Clark, 1867.

Witold Rybczynski. *Waiting for the Weekend.* New York: Viking Penguin, 1991.

Thomas Slater. "Sunday," in *The Catholic Encyclopedia,* Vol. XIV. New York: Robert Appleton Company, 1912 (Online Edition: Kevin Knight, 1999).

Winton U. Solberg. *Redeem the Time: The Puritan Sabbath in Early America.* Cambridge, MA: Harvard University Press, 1977.

Tertullian. *Concerning Prayer,* with *Concerning Baptism.* Tr. Alexander Souter. New York: Macmillan, 1919.

SUNDAY OF ORTHODOXY, SUNDAY OF SAINT THOMAS

See Easter

SUNDAY OF THE LAST JUDGMENT, SUNDAY OF THE PRODIGAL SON, SUNDAY OF THE PUBLICAN AND THE PHARISEE, SUNDAY OF THE TWO SAINTS THEODORE

See Lent

SUN-GAZING DANCE

See Sun Dance

SVIATKI

See Christmas

SWAN

See Divali

SWING (FESTIVAL OF THE), SWING FULL MOON

See Holi

SWITCHING DAY

See Easter

T

TANABATA NO SEKKU
See Sekku

TANGO NO SEKKU
See Sekku

TA'SUA
See Ashura

TEDUDU
See New Yam Festival

TENNÔ FESTIVAL
See Gion Festival

TEPEILHUITL
See Rain Festivals

TERMINALIA (ROME)

On February 23, the festival of **Terminalia** marked both the temporal delimitation of the Roman religious year—from the early days when it started on March 1—the spatial delimitation of Roman territory politically as well as in terms of property.

Private Property's Common Deity

Upon the close of the **Parentalia** novena devoted to making peace with dead relatives, Roman families turned to the living at the **Caristia** festival, putting aside their quarrels amidst good cheer to bring concord to the home. Then, the next morning, to preserve harmony between neighbors, a festival was devoted to Terminus. This minor god of boundaries (*termini*) personified the divine force they held and which made them sacred—literally intangible, from both sides of the fence.

A law ascribed to King Numa Pompilius, who was also believed responsible for making January 1 the beginning of the **New Year**, declared *sacer* or cursed by a taboo whomever disturbed a *terminus* while plowing his fields, along with the oxen in question. The installation of such a marker required a ceremony in which the blood of a sacrifice was spilt in the hole dug out for it, along with other offerings. The collaboration of both owners of the lands it delimited required the ongoing cult of the common divinity dwelling in this stone or stump, in joint recognition of this boundary's immutable and sacrosanct character. On **Terminalia**, they would each crown the god with a garland and give him a sacrificial cake. A woman would bring embers from the home fire to a makeshift outdoor altar, while a man would build a pyre. Beside him, a young boy would take some grain from a big basket to throw it into the flames three times, while a lit-

Terminalia festival, February 23, painting by Vittorio Benisson, early 19th century. Owners of adjacent land gathered at a common boundary stone, and each garlanded his own side of the stone. Offerings were made, and a lamb or pig was sacrificed to the god Terminus. (The Art Archive/Galleria d'Arte Moderna, Turin, Italy/ Dagli Orti)

tle girl gave him honeycombs, and others brought wine. A sample of each offering was cast into the fire, as the white-clad neighbors looked on in religious silence, so as not to utter inauspicious words that might disturb the supernatural power thus invoked. The immolation of a lamb or a suckling sow would be followed by a sacred meal where the praises of Terminus would be sung; they went like this in Ovid's rendition: "You confine peoples and cities and great kingdoms;/All land would be disputed without you" (*Fasti* 2:659–660, p. 47).

This very basic civilizing function of Terminus was acknowledged not only in private agrarian rites, but also in public observances that betrayed the archaic roots of **Terminalia**, such as a sheep sacrifice on the sixth milestone on the Via Laurentina. It was located about nine kilometers from the central Terminus of Rome (to which all roads led): the god's ancient shrine on the Capitol. The temple of Jupiter, king of the gods, had to be built around it (with a hole in the ceiling as Terminus demanded open-air sacrifices) by the city's last king, Tarquinius Superbus, who had closed down other shrines on the site to make room for this prestigious project. But the augurs had read into the flight patterns of birds that the god Terminus refused to be moved, which was taken as a sign of stability for the city (Livy, *Ab urbe condita* I,

55). For Ovid (*Fasti* 2:673–676, p. 47), it was a pledge of the internal boundaries of private property: "Terminus, after this you lost the freedom to move./Remain on guard where you have been posted,/And surrender nothing to a neighbor's demands/Lest you appear to prefer mankind to Jove" (another name for Jupiter). Was such stability truly compatible with Rome's imperial destiny, then becoming manifest at the same time as the first Emperor Augustus Caesar (63–14 B.C.E.) combined the cult of his own *genius* or personal protecting spirit as new founder with that of the *lares* or ancestral spirits on **Caristia**, on the eve of **Terminalia**? Despite the massive expropriations of farmers also occurring in his lifetime, the great poet of the dawning era liked to think so: "For other nations the earth has fixed boundaries; Rome's city and the world are the same space" (*Fasti* 2:683–684, p. 47).

A Square City Founded on a Round Pit by a Priest-King

The jurist Carl Schmitt (1888–1985) was fond of relating the words "Rome" and *Raum*, German for "space," since he defined political institutions as being meant to take hold of space, to portion it out, and to cultivate it. Schmitt had in mind *Roma quadrata,* the territory around Palatine Hill delimited by the city walls. According to legend, their outline had been plowed by Romulus after he became king, whereupon he hallowed this furrow with the blood of his twin brother and rival Remus by killing him when he dared to cross it in jest. Under the late Republic, shortly before the Common Era, this event came to be commemorated as the actual foundation or birthday (*dies natalis*) of Rome on the April 21 festival of **Parilia,** just when shepherds, facing the horizon before dawn, prayed their patron goddess Pales to be forgiven such transgressions—that is, those of which they or their sheep might be guilty for having trespassed in bushes or in brooks where gods and nymphs were thought

to dwell. On **Terminalia** itself, in parallel to the rededication of private property markers, a public sacrifice was performed on the sixth milestone of the Via Laurentina to reaffirm the symbolic limit of Rome's earliest territory, thus securing civic space.

A round sacrificial pit was also associated with the city's foundation, as well as with **Terminalia**, and was said (according to one tradition) to have been the original location of the altar of the hearth goddess Vesta, later moved to her round temple housing Rome's *palladium* or civic totem. Similarly, Vesta's Greek counterpart Hestia was thought to have had her seat on the *omphalos* of Delphi—the round navel of the world. Much like the hole for a new country *terminus,* this civic hole contained samples of all good and licit things, except that it was closed with earth brought by the first settlers of Rome from their respective homelands. It was at this *mundus rotundus* or "round world" on the Comitium that, down to Imperial times, a sacrifice used to be offered on the public holiday following **Terminalia** by the King of the Sacred Rites, Rome's high priest. His job done, this residual Roman king would flee from the Forum; hence the ancient ceremony's name of *regifugium.*

Sir James George Frazer has conjectured that an actual sacred king may have originally been running for office (and probably for his life) in an annual race where the incumbent was deposed whenever he proved to be past the peak of his vigor by failing to win it. He had to match the growing strength of vegetation in the budding spring as its king for the coming year, or else be done away with as the king of the dying year, just as in the execution of a winter **carnival** king in a lot of European folklore. Roman space thus appears to have squared with the close of a cycle of Roman time in the round sacrificial pit that the god Terminus filled with his mediating presence at the point when the killing of an ailing king would previously have cleared the air through his purifying absence.

This would recall, channel, and defuse Rome's foundational violence—still inscribed in the boundary-markers of private and public land, where it was most prone to erupt again between neighboring citizens, as between the rival kings of archaic folklore.

See also Carnival; Days of the Dead (West); Eleusinian Mysteries; Games (Greece); New Year (West); Rogations; Saint George; Vestalia

References

Georges Dumézil. *Archaic Roman Religion, with an Appendix on the Religion of the Etruscans.* Tr. Philip Krapp. Baltimore, MD: Johns Hopkins University Press, 1996.

Livy. *The Rise of Rome: Books One to Five.* Tr. T. J. Luce. Oxford: Oxford University Press, 1998.

Ovid. *Fasti.* Tr. A. J. Boyle and R. D. Woodard. London: Penguin Books, 2000.

Giulia Piccaluga. *Terminus: I segni di confine nella religione romana.* Rome: Edizioni dell'Ateneo, 1974.

▶ TÊT

See New Year (China, Korea)

▶ THAIPUSAM (HINDUISM)

Tamils in Malaysia and other countries of South Indian emigration celebrate a festival of the god Murukan, featuring body-piercing vows long outlawed in peninsular India itself.

The Murukan Cult in India and Overseas

When the full moon is in conjunction with the star Pusam in the month of Tai that straddles January and February, devotees of Shiva honor their god in the **Thaipusam** festival. But it has a more specific, even paramount significance when celebrated in temples of Murukan, a fertility god of the Tamils of South India, who have identified him with Shiva's first-born son Skanda—another cannibalistic warrior-god from North India—and even with the Greek god **Dionysus** in ancient times. The constellation segment of Pusam is also known by the name of Dandapani, alluding both to an ascetic's staff and to a warrior's army, which is used for Murukan as a subduer of spiritual passions as well as temporal enemies. Murukan is like Skanda in this and also as the lord of time who initiated its measurement, presiding over both the solar year and the lunar cycle, and even the current dark age or Kali Yuga, aside from the yearly coming of the rains and the blossoming of certain trees. Celebrated shortly after the Tamils' winter solstice and harvest festival of **Pongal, Thaipusam** is a timely expression of the youthful virility and creativity of Murukan. But if his worship used to include orgiastic dancing in the distant past, it has more recently become notorious for the ecstatic states his devotees get into in order to commune with him as conqueror of base desires and malevolence, allowing them to fulfill a vow to pierce their bodies. In Tamil Nadu on **Thaipusam**, devotees of Karttikeya (as Skanda is also known) display their faith in his grace by walking unscathed on a path of burning coals instead. Otherwise, since Indian law forbids public self-mutilation, it is only in the Tamil diaspora—from Fiji to the West Indies—that **Thaipusam** rites may still be observed in their complete form. They are performed on the largest scale at the Sri Suhramaniaswamy temple (dedicated to Subrahmanya, another name for Skanda) outside Kuala Lumpur, capital of Islamic Malaysia, in the Batu Caves (from the word for "rock" in Bahasa Malaysia). Each year, a million pilgrims and tourists gather to witness the penitents' spectacular austerities.

Ascetic Preparations and Worldly Distractions

These slowly begin three weeks in advance as the penitents pray for spiritual progress and worldly help while they observe sexual abstinence and a fast that allows them only one meal a day, cooked to strict specifications. Their diet

Malaysian Hindu devotees with pierced bodies walk to the Batu Caves Temple during the Thaipusam festival in Kuala Lumpur on February 5, 2004. Thousands of Hindus participate in the annual Hindu festival and subject themselves to painful rituals in a demonstration of faith and penance. (Zainal Abd Halim/Reuters/Corbis)

includes milk as the purifying substance also used to wash idols. It actually takes a month in time and (average) wages to build a *kavadi,* the 30-kilo portable shrine the penitent will carry at the festival. He is not to wear it until then, so a friend has to model it for him while it is being built. With the endless variations of their rich symbolism, no two kavadis are alike, aside from the picture of the god mounted on top. Meanwhile, during the three days prior to **Thaipusam**, the sleepy suburban road leading to the Batu Caves is transformed into a fairground, with all the loud, garish, at times unedifying at-

tractions this entails, for the benefit of the many visitors. The pilgrims among them have come assuming that what they ask of God will be granted, even if their offerings are not on the scale of the penitents' vow to be pierced by representations and equivalents of *vel*—the spear that is Murukan's most powerful weapon, which he uses to drive evil out of the world.

By four in the morning of the first day, the faithful gather to wait for the god's statue and escort its silver chariot more than eight kilometers to the incense-shrouded Batu Caves, which they will reach by midmorning. This human stream will go on for twenty-four hours, including both the fit and infirm from every walk of life and at all levels of seriousness, be it the curious bystander, the pious bearing small pots of milk as symbols of purity, or the devout—who may already be seen doing stunts like pushing ahead while weighted hooks pull them back. This is but a foretaste of the second day.

Divine Bliss through Bodily Ordeals

Before dawn, devotees purify themselves by bathing in a sacred river. Though they often need little coaxing by now, this is when those who have made vows—wearing red bandanas—are placed in a trance-state by their respective gurus, who will only join them in it and skewer themselves after they have done this for all of their disciples. When the sun is up, frantic drumbeats accompany the screams of the possessed who dance wildly. Their weeks of concentration and purification have brought them to a point where they can utterly forget themselves and have no idea of what they are doing once they have let the spirit take over. God then helps the body become more ready, for if the dung ash that is regularly dusted on the skin helps stem the flow of blood, pain is only overcome by devotion, and any serious bleeding is seen as a result of faulty spiritual preparation. Conversely, the level of union with Murukan is felt to be proportionate to the extremity of the mutilations endured.

Penitents often start by inserting a miniature vel through their tongue vertically and another one through their cheeks horizontally (thereby puffing up the latter in a way that makes them look like the monkey-god Hanuman who possesses some of them). Mutilations escalate as the day progresses, and the temperature sometimes rises to 40° C. The music pulsates hypnotically and votaries reel rapturously as more and more hooks are skewered into their bodies. Each hook may be weighted with a food offer-

ing, such as apples and oranges by the dozens. Some tow heavy chariots with chains tethered to the skin of their back. The standard practice is to have a kavadi, adorned with peacock feathers, fastened to one's shoulders and back to walk the last couple of kilometers to the Batu Caves, with a relative such as a child carrying the symbolic milk pot. Supporters shout "*Vel! Vel!*" as the votaries ascend the 272 steps to the cave's entrance, making their way in bliss rather than pain into the divine embrace of Murukan. The god receives them in the 122-meter high natural cathedral of limestone standing for the place where he first received the vel himself. It can hold crowds of up to a thousand, who come in wave after wave. Having reached the goal of their mystical journey, those who have vowed to come there as penitents are each relieved of their kavadi, given water, and gently slapped out of their trance. What remains is indescribable happiness, with no memory of pain. On the contrary: participants look forward to going through it all again every year as long as they still can, gaining more intimate union with God each time.

See also Ashura; Dionysia; Matzu's Birthday

References

P. V. Jagadisa Ayyar. *South Indian Festivities.* Madras, India: Higginbothams Ltd., 1921.

Fred W. Clothey. "Chronometry, Cosmology, and the Festival Calendar in the Murukan Cult," in Guy R. Welbon and Glenn E. Yocum. *Religious Festivals in South India and Sri Lanka.* New Delhi: Manohar, 1982, pp. 157–188.

Bruce David Klein and Anja Baron (producers). *Rituals of the World.* (Television documentary for The Learning Channel.) Atlas Media Corporation in association with All American Fremantle, 1997.

▶ **THANKSGIVING**

See Christmas, Martinmas, Mid-Autumn, New Year (China, Korea)

▌ THARGELIA (GREECE)

Peculiar to Ionia, a major festival of the Greek god Apollo was held on the sixth and seventh days of the month of Thargelion named after it in the calendar of Athens. This city was the home of the best-known version of **Thargelia** (aside from those of some Ionian cities and their colonies). Much older than the cult of the sun god, it is at base a vegetation ritual unto which has been grafted a ceremony of collective purification through the scapegoating of a couple of unpopular individuals.

First-Fruits

In Athens, the entire month of Thargelion, devoted to purification, was sacred to Apollo because the seventh was his birthday, around the twenty-second of May. Its name comes from the word *thargelos,* which may refer to the fair season's **first-fruits**. These would have been the boiled vegetables- and fresh bread from the new wheat, or the grain porridge or cake, that were offered in thanksgiving for the new harvest on that day. That same word may also have referred to the vessel in which these **first-fruits** were taken in a procession in honor of Helios and the Horai—the Sun and the Hours (or Seasons). This procession seems to have included *eiresionai,* which are known from the songs accompanying it to be olive or laurel branches bound with wool on which were suspended fruits of the season (including wine and oil flasks) and pastries, as on other festivals like the **Panathenaea** or especially the Ionian **Pyanopsia** on the seventh of Pyanopsion—the parallel October festival of Apollo that closed the season. But it is on **Thargelia** that some of these cakes are known to have been lyre-shaped—in honor of this god as patron of the arts and on account of the musical competitions at which the tripods given as prizes were first dedicated in one of his temples. The magical boughs themselves were hung over the door of every citizen's house as boys sang a spell over it so as to turn away famine; they were left there until they were replaced by new ones at the next year's **Thargelia.** The official registration of adopted persons would follow this private agrarian rite going back to prehistory, long before the worship of the sun god Apollo. There were also offerings in honor of Demeter Chloe ("Greening Demeter") that day.

Human Scapegoats

In spite of the historic origin alleged by the third-century writer Helladios (Farnell 1907, pp. 270–271), the same may be said of the previous day's "custom at Athens of leading two *pharmakoi,* one for the men and one for the women, to be a purification for the city. The one intended for the men had black figs hung around his neck, the other had white: and they were called *Sivakkhoi.* This purification was to avoid the troubles of plague, and arose from Androgeos the Cretan, for in consequence of his lawless death the Athenians were smitten with the plague, and so the custom prevailed always to purify the city with *pharmakoi*" on the eve of the ceremonies of the early harvest—also in order to remove any hindrance to it. A ram was sacrificed to the goddess Demeter on the sixth of Thargelion for similar purposes.

The term *pharmakos* refers to one or two men (or a man and a woman), chosen among the ugliest. They were first led through the city and hit with squill stems and fig branches along the way to transfer unto them the miasma of defilements as well as to egg them on. They were thus finally driven out as scapegoats for the community's guilt, thus diverting divine retribution for all its sins and impurities toward expendable, removable substitutes in which evil was first concentrated.

This is a classic instance of the ritual transference of everything undesirable in a society on designated public enemies, as represented in many festivals of other cultures, from the ancient Hebrews' **Yom Kippur** to the **Naked Festi-**

val of Inazawa in Japan. No less typical is the ambiguity of this role as scapegoat, for the one who takes out evil also brings in the good and can thus also represent the deity. In this case, this would be the god of vegetation, as suggested by the figs. Occasionally, the *pharmakoi* were nonetheless even sacrificed on pyres of wild fruit trees or thrown into the sea in times of peril or calamity, but this is unlikely to have occurred on a regular basis on **Thargelia** in historical times. For one thing, we know that the execution of Socrates was postponed for several weeks after sentencing, because the sacred ship taking the *theoria* or delegation of Athens' pilgrims who brought the **first-fruits** of the year's new wheat to the pan-Hellenic shrine of Apollo at Delos had just set sail for the great festival of the god. (The **Delia** likely started on his birthday on the seventh of Thargelion, which was the second day of **Thargelia**, when, aside from being a condition set by Apollo to appease his wrath so he would relieve a famine plaguing the city, the *eiresionai* custom was related to the hero Theseus' stop at Delos on his way back from killing the Minotaur in Crete.) As Lewis Richard Farnell (1907, pp. 278–279) has argued:

> This respite was given, not for the sake of mercy, but in order that the city might contract no stain, since as long as the ship was absent in the service of the 'pure' god, to whom contact with death was unclean, the city must remain 'pure' and no one could be put to death. Now it is difficult to dissociate this period of purity from that which was consummated by the *pharmakoi* on the sixth of Thargelion . . . Therefore those victims—in the time of Socrates at least—by public ordinance could not be slain.

See also Anna Perenna; Busk; Dionysia; Naked Festivals; Panathenaea; Presentation of the Virgin Mary; Yom Kippur

References

Thomas C. Brickhouse and Nicholas D. Smith. *The Trial and Execution of Socrates: Sources and Controversies*. New York: Oxford University Press, 2002.

Lewis Richard Farnell. *The Cults of the Greek States*. Vol. IV. Oxford: Clarendon Press, 1907.

Robert Parker. *Miasma. Pollution and Purification in Early Greek Religion*. Oxford: Clarendon Press, 1996.

▶ THEOINIA

See Dionysia

▶ THEOPHANY

See Epiphany

▶ THESMOPHORIA (GREECE)

In ancient Greece, the agrarian festival of **Thesmophoria** was noted for its archaic rites, making it a pure example of the type (unlike the **Eleusinian Mysteries** of related origin): a fertility cult reserved to women because of their magical kinship with that side of life which is manifested in nature by the yearly cycle of death and renewal in vegetation. Its twin goddesses, Demeter Thesmophoros (an epithet possibly meaning "bringer of wealth") and her daughter Persephone or Korê, were honored on this occasion by free married women of good repute in Athens and many other Greek cities, such as Thebes in southeast Boeotia or Syracuse near Argos in Laconia (there were also temples of Demeter Thesmophoros in Megara, Egina and Paros), though the Dorians of the Peloponnese did not have **Thesmophoria**, according to the ancient historian Herodotus (2:171). The festival originally lasted from the twelfth to the fifteenth days of the month of Pyanopsion (in late October), but in Attica it was eventually extended to five days, from the ninth to the thirteenth. In spite of its importance, these were still officially business days, as only women were directly involved in the celebration. Men could therefore still hold their political assemblies, though not necessarily in their usual venue, sometimes left to women for their exclusive ceremonies that day.

Preparations: Abstinence and Obscenity

In preparation for the **Thesmophoria**, Athenian women observed some rules of ritual purity such as abstinence from sexual intercourse for three days beforehand, and would not eat the seeds of pomegranates during it. For these fruits, associated with the promise of sex, were supposed to have sprung from the blood of **Dionysus**, another underworld divinity honored at the **Thesmophoria**, with characteristic revelry (including the foul language and obscenities common in fertility rituals as a way to purify oneself and ward off evils). They were indulged in with special glee if a man fell into the hands of Athens' women as they went after dark in small groups to Cape Kolias in the Halimos deme or country borough for the first nocturnal mysteries, playfully demanding identification from each other as they met on the way. For men were only allowed to sponsor their wives' participation in the festival as a public service known as a liturgy, while women chose two officials called *archousai* among themselves to run it, in the seclusion of a tent city they erected on the Pnyx sacred grounds for the duration, and called the Thesmophorion, where they slept on beds made of withy. This is a kind of willow that was said to dispel sexual impulses. The closed women's assemblies, unique in the context of the exclusively male public life of Athens, provided Aristophanes with the topic of his seasonal comedy *Thesmophoriazusae* of 411 B.C.E., in which a spy in drag, sent by the tragic playwright Euripides (the object of the satire), is exposed as an old man, and nearly comes to grief for violating the secrecy of the women's mysteries, including bloody sacrifices of which we know next to nothing. This was one of many

activities and attitudes normally forbidden to them that they could temporarily assume as part of this role reversal, as a rare reversion to a fantasized "prehistoric" wild stage prior to the establishment of patriarchal Greek civilization, which put the **Thesmophoria** in the same class of festivals of social inversion as the **Chronia** and their Roman counterpart the **Saturnalia**.

First Day: The Snake-Pit of Rotten Pigs

The following day at the beach in Halimos was spent in purifying baths, with plenty of fun and games until another day came, and the laws of Demeter, the *Thesmoi,* were carried to Athens on the heads of sacred women. The festival was probably named on account of these "carriers of the things laid down," and was held at the city's Thesmophorion and another temple of the same name at its port, the Piraeus. This first day was known both as *Kathodos* ("going down") and *Anodos* ("rising up" or "road up"), in reference to the sacred task of going down into the snake-infested caves of Demeter and Persephone to recover and bring up to the meeting grounds the decayed remains of the sacrificed pigs that had been thrown there either the previous year or possibly at another, early summer secretive women's festival sometimes attributed to Demeter, called the **Skirophoria.** The "drawers" or "bailers" (*antletriai*) designated to fetch the pigs from the underworld (along with the dough figures of snakes, pigs, and human beings, and the pinecones also thrown in as fertility agents) clapped as they went down, to scare away the sacred snakes. This descent was their way of reenacting Demeter's rescue of the spring goddess Persephone from the cold realm of Hades to which she had been carried off through this suddenly gaping chasm, along with the pigs of the swineherd Ebuleus, who happened to be there at the time. He was thus able to reveal Persephone's fate to a grateful Demeter, from whom he would receive (along with his brother the wheat god Triptolemus) the gift of growing corn. This story may have been a rationalization of the central place of pigs at this corn festival, witness to an earlier stage of ritual and myth where the pig itself was the corn-spirit; was not its flesh partaken of at the **Thesmophoria** as if to commune with a divinity? It also happens that the pig is often likened to female genitals in classical Greco-Roman culture, as an ambivalent being that has power for both harm and good, and can stand for the lack of patriarchal control it most feared, yet allowed within the strictly delimited boundaries of festivals of social inversion like this one.

Second Day: Mourning for Persephone

Whatever was left of the pigs from the cave (*megaron*) was mixed with seed, ceremoniously placed on an altar and kept there for the next day, when council meetings and law courts were suspended and prisoners were freed from their chains. On this twelfth day of the month (in the five-day version of the festival), devoted to fasting—*Nesteia,* the women took the part of Demeter in sitting on the ground to bewail the loss of Persephone to Hades. The Greek historian Plutarch (who lived from about 46 until some time after 119) already saw such mournful rites as a common heritage of the ancient Mediterranean world:

> The Greeks also enact, round about the same time, many ceremonies that are similar to those performed by the Egyptians in their sacred rites [of Osiris during **Khoiak**]. For the women at Athens fast in the **Thesmophoria**, sitting on the ground, and the Boeotians move the halls of Achaea, calling that festival one of grief because Demeter bewails the descent of Korê to the underworld. This month is indeed, at the time of the (setting of the) Pleiades, the season for sowing; the Egyptians call it Athyr, the Athenians Pyanepsion, and the Boeotians Damatrius [named after Demeter] . . .

> . . . At this time men saw the fruits entirely disappearing from the trees and failing, while others they planted themselves, though scantily and unskillfully, scraping the earth away with their hands and throwing it on again. They put the seed away with no certainty that it would be brought to fruition and reach full growth, and thus they did much that resembled burial and mourning ceremonies. (*Plutarch's De Iside et Osiride*, pp. 227–229: 378D9-E16, 379A1–5 in par. 69–70)

Third Day: The Rebirth of Nature

But then came the third day of **Thesmophoria**, that of "beautiful offspring" (*Kalligeneia*), whose name signals women's hope of bringing into the world new generations of Athenian citizens and their mates. It was a day of joy at the resurrection of nature from winter—at the rescue of sweet Persephone from cold Hades by bountiful Demeter—pledged on the remains of her sacred pigs and cakes as they were taken from the altar to be scattered in the fields with the seed corn, in order to secure a good crop with the return of fair weather. A banquet was then offered, with light entertainment such as games and lascivious dances. No doubt women's fecundity was also thought to be favored by the oblations and merriment evoked by the leader of the circle dance of the chorus in Aristophanes' play (Aristophanes 2001, v. 947–948, p. 109) *Thesmophoriazusae*:

> Come now, let us disport ourselves as is the custom for women in this place,
> when we faithfully celebrate the holy secret rites of the Two
> Goddesses at the sacred seasons

Parallels in European Folklore

Sir James George Frazer (1854–1941) saw many analogies with classical Greece's great autumn festival in the folk customs of preindustrial Western and Central Europe, from France to Hungary through Germany, wherever the corn-spirit was killed in animal form, to be partly consumed as a sacrament by the community and partly kept until the next harvest or sowing time as a token of renewal of the vegetative energies it stood for:

> So in the neighbourhood of Grenoble the goat killed on the harvest-field is partly eaten at the harvest-supper, partly pickled and kept till the next harvest; so at Pouilly the ox killed on the harvest-field is partly eaten by the harvesters, partly pickled and kept till the first day of sowing in spring, probably to be then mixed with the seed, or eaten by the ploughmen, or both; so at Udvarhely the feathers of the cock which is killed in the last sheaf at harvest are kept till spring, and then sown with the seed on the field; so in Hesse and Meiningen the flesh of pigs is eaten on **Ash Wednesday** or **Candlemas**, and the bones are kept till sowing-time, when they are put into the field sown or mixed with the seed in the bag; so, lastly, the corn from the last sheaf is kept till **Christmas**, made into the **Yule** Boar, and afterwards broken and mixed with the seed-corn at sowing in spring. (1985, p. 545)

See also Candlemas; Carnival; Christmas; Dionysia; Eleusinian Mysteries; Khoiak and Heb-Sed; Lent; Saturnalia

References

Aristophanes. *The Comedies of Aristophanes*, Vol. 8: *Thesmophoriazusae*. Tr. and ed. Alan H. Sommerstein. Warminster, Wiltshire, UK: Aris and Phillips, 2001.

Hugo Blümner. *The Home Life of the Ancient Greeks*. Tr. Alice Zimmern. London: Cassell, 1893; reprint New York: Cooper Square Publishers, 1966.

A. M. Bowie. *Aristophanes: Myth, Ritual and Comedy*. Cambridge, UK and New York: Cambridge University Press, 1993.

Sir James George Frazer. *The Golden Bough: A Study in Magic and Religion*. One-Volume Abridged Edition. New York: Macmillan, 1985.

Plutarch. *Plutarch's De Iside et Osiride*. Tr. J. Gwyn Griffiths. Cardiff: University of Wales Press, 1970.

Sarah B. Pomeroy. *Goddesses, Wives, Whores, and Slaves. Women in Classical Antiquity*. New York: Schocken Books, 1975.

H. S. Versnel. *Inconsistencies in Greek and Roman Religion*. Vol. 2: *Transition and Reversal in Myth and Ritual*. Leiden, Holland: E. J. Brill, 1993.

▶ THINGYAN
See Water-Splashing-Festival

▶ THIRSTING DANCE
See Sun Dance

▶ THREE FOR THE DEAD
See Days of the Dead (China, Korea, Japan)

▶ THREE FOR THE LIVING
See Days of the Dead (China, Korea, Japan), Dragon Boat Festival

▶ THREE MIRACLES (FESTIVAL OF THE)
See Epiphany

▶ THREE WEEKS
See Tisha be-Av

▶ THREE YUAN
See Days of the Dead (China, Korea, Japan)

▶ THYIA
See Dionysia

▶ TIHAR
See Divali

▶ TIJ
See Ganesha Chaturthi

▶ TIKA PUJA
See Navaratra and Dusshera

▶ TIMQAT

See Epiphany

▶ TISHA BE-AV (JUDAISM)

The ninth day of the fifth month of Av (which can fall any time between June and August), known in Hebrew as *Tisha be-Av,* is classified as a minor festival. Though Jewish tradition holds that it will be the greatest festival of the time to come, in the meantime, it is actually a mourning fast. For it is supposed to be on a **Ninth of Av** that both the First and the Second Temples of Jerusalem were destroyed, and that several other historical disasters struck the Jewish people.

Three Weeks Between Two Ordeals

Three weeks earlier, the fast of the **seventeenth of Tammuz** commemorates the day in 586 B.C.E. when the troops of Babylonian King Nebuchadnezzar made a breach in the walls of Jerusalem and took the city. The intervening period of mourning between this fast and Tisha be-Av as the commemoration of the subsequent destruction of the Temple is therefore called *yeme ben hametzarim,* which is Hebrew for "between two ordeals." No weddings are to be performed while it lasts, and the **New Moon** blessing is omitted. In some communities, the devout will not shave or wear new clothes, nor eat meat or drink wine except on the **Sabbath**, when prophecies of doom from Isaiah and Jeremiah are read in the synagogue. The first nine days of Av are observed most strictly.

Mourning the Lost Temple and Recurrent Exile

At the culmination of these **Three Weeks** on the **Ninth of Av**, it has become customary to sit on the ground in the synagogue and not to put on prayer shawls and phylacteries for the morning service as would be done any other day (though they are exceptionally worn at the afternoon service). These are signs of mourning for the loss of the religious and national center of the Jews, the "eternal house" that used to be their one fixed place of worship. The sacrifices that could only be performed in the Temple have thus been replaced in Judaism by liturgical prayer and the study of the law. This profound transformation first began during the Babylonian exile of the Jews after the destruction of the First Temple in 586 B.C.E. The event is recalled in the scroll of Jeremiah's Book of Lamentations which is read at the synagogue on this day at candlelight, along with elegies (*qinot*) about the destruction of the Second Temple by the Romans in 70, that allowed this process to be completed in the Diaspora of the Jews. For they were sent away from the Holy Land and had to resettle in distant places after the fall of Bethar and the collapse of the second Jewish revolt against Rome in 135. The next year, a pagan temple was established in Jerusalem, and Jews were banned from their own city. Both events are said in the Talmud to have taken place on a **Ninth of Av**, as is God's decree centuries earlier that the Jews would wander forty years in the wilderness after Moses led them out of Egypt. There is also a tradition that the expulsion of the Jews from Spain in 1492 took place on that date as well. All these historical calamities are therefore jointly commemorated on the **Ninth of Av**.

It is not surprising then that on this day, the thoughts of many Jews turn to their dead, and they go visit them in cemeteries. As a day of mourning, **Tisha be-Av** is second only to **Yom Kippur**, coming two months earlier with a fast that is just as rigorous (except for Reform Jews): it lasts from one sunset to the next, beginning on the eve of the ninth—unless it falls on a Saturday. In this case, the fast is postponed until the end of a **Black Sabbath** of mostly nominal mourning.

Ever since the surviving portion of the Temple's ruins, the Western Wall in Jerusalem's Arab quarter has been captured by the Israeli

A Jewish man, lying on a mattress, reads from a prayer book late August 9, 2000, on the plaza before the Western Wall, Judiasm's holiest site, as he and thousands of Jews mark the solemn fasting day of Tisha be-Av. (Reuters/Corbis)

army during the Six-Day War of June 1967, thousands of Jews every year have made a point of going on its esplanade to recite elegies on **Tisha be-Av**—each community according to its own rite, the way so many generations had done for centuries prior to Jordan's conquest of the Old City in 1948. For the Wailing Wall has kept on functioning as a holy place of Judaism; according to a *midrash* or Bible commentary, through all the vicissitudes of Jewish history, "the divine presence has never left it" (Malka 1989, p. 97).

A False Messiah's Birthday

As for **Tisha be-Av**, it used to be a very festive occasion rather than one of mourning for the Dönmeh—a crypto-Jewish sect of staunchly loyal followers of the false messiah Shabbetai Tsevi, who was born on this day in 1626. Seven years after his death in 1676, 300 Sephardic families of Salonica in the Ottoman Empire (present-day Thessaloníki in Greece), led by his successor Jacob Querido, converted to Islam in imitation of his shocking gesture of 1666, which had thrown into sudden disarray his numerous followers in the Jewish world, the Sabbatians. Like him, having seemingly renounced their ancestral faith, they became known as "apostates," or *dönme* in Turkish, outwardly leading impeccable Muslim lives while remaining clandestinely faithful to their Jewish heritage, assumptions, and practices. Among their descendants, many played an important part in the emergence of the Turkish nationalist movement that would lead to the establishment of a secular republic after the fall of the sultanate in the aftermath of the First World War. They assimilated so well into the new Turkey that, a century later, Dönmeh customs and identity have all but disappeared.

See also Rosh Hodesh, Sabbath, Yom Kippur

References

Encyclopedia Judaica. New York: Macmillan, 1971.

Gates of Prayer. New York: Central Conference of American Rabbis, 1975.

Victor and Salomon Malka. *La Petit Retz* du judaïsme. Paris-Retz, 1989.

Bezalel Naor. *Post-Sabbatian Sabbatianism: Study of an Underground Messianic Movement.* Spring Valley, NY: Orot, 1999.

Prayers for the Festivals. New York: Union of Sephardic Congregations, 1963.

▶ TITITL

See Rain Festivals

▶ TOURNAMENT OF ROSES

See Carnival

▶ TOXIUHMOLPILIA

See New Fire Ceremony

▶ TOZOZTONTLI

See Rain Festivals

▶ TRANSFIGURATION (CHRISTIANITY)

The August 6 feast of the **Transfiguration** celebrates the luminous manifestation of Christ to three apostles on Mount Tabor as a foretaste of his eternal glory as God, which his Passion and Resurrection were meant to allow human beings to share with him fully upon his Second Coming. One of the **Twelve** Great **Feasts** of the Eastern Church, it was belatedly adopted in the West, but as a minor feast.

History

The feast of the **Transfiguration** seems to have developed in the Eastern Churches by the seventh century, soon settling on an August 6 date. The **Transfiguration** of Christ was held to have taken place forty days prior to his Rising from the dead at **Easter**, and its feast was appropriately set forty days before the Raising or **Elevation of the Cross** on September 14. The emphasis in the latter was on the Cross as a symbol of Christ's triumph within history through the conversion of human society, just as the **Transfiguration** stands for the visible manifestation within earthly life of Christ's invisible glory. Since this divine light is none other than the risen life of his Resurrection at **Easter**, which is followed by his **Ascension** to heaven in glory after forty days, the **Transfiguration** is likewise followed after the same interval by the **Elevation of the Cross**—yet another crowning vertical translation to a victorious position. However, the **Transfiguration** was also commemorated on the second Sunday of **Lent** early on in the West.

Like Syrian Christians, Armenians, who may have invented this feast and observe it most solemnly over three days, still keep it as a movable feast on the seventh Sunday after **Pentecost**. The feast was already well established throughout the Eastern Roman Empire by the middle of the ninth century, when it appeared in Spain on August 6. Yet in spite of the efforts of the great French Benedictine abbey of Cluny to propagate it in the twelfth century, this feast long remained almost unknown in the Western Church at large. Then a Spanish Pope, Calixtus III, in thanksgiving for a victory over the invading Ottoman Turks before Belgrade on that date in 1456 (a high point of his otherwise unsuccessful campaign to retake Constantinople after the Eastern imperial capital fell to them in 1453), gave it official recognition in 1457, and in 1458 he even died on the very day of the new feast he had just instituted. Still, in the Roman Catholic Church, it is just a double of the second class, without an octave of special prayers for the following week. There were neither prayers nor readings for the **Transfiguration** in the Anglican communion for several centuries, until well into the last one. Some Lutheran bodies mark the **Transfiguration** on a Sunday after **Epiphany**.

Mystical Theology

By contrast, the **Transfiguration** of Christ on Mount Tabor provides the key to the mystical theology of the Orthodox Church, being the feast of divine glory as such. This uncreated light without beginning nor end, beyond time, space, and the natural senses, shone through Christ's humble human form to show his closest disciples Peter, James, and John that in him, in spite of appearances, it was God Himself who would voluntarily suffer death on the Cross. If, prior to the Resurrection, this light could only be seen by a chosen few of Christ's apostles, through a miraculous transmutation of their physical senses, as an outer brilliance shining through his body, the sacrament of the Eucharist instituted by Christ at the Last Supper allows the faithful to be part of his risen body and discover (in whatever degree) the same light within themselves, in their heart. The goal of Orthodox contemplative life is to be able to actually see this inner, uncreated light, called precisely the Taboric light by those (chiefly monks and nuns) who strive for the grace to see it and be in turn "transfigured" by it through the ascetic discipline of the prayer of the heart. Monastics are therefore seen as the prophets of the New Covenant established by Christ, since they may already experience in their own beings the exchange mortal humans will make with God's immortal glory at Christ's Second Coming, first shown when he was transfigured on Mount Tabor, according to the Orthodox matins of the feast.

A Summer Epiphany

The apostle Peter already seemed to suggest that the **Transfiguration** of his master on the Tabor was a glimpse of the Kingdom of God, recalling in his Second Letter (1:17) that "we had seen his majesty by ourselves. He was honored and glorified by God the Father, when the Sublime Glory

Transfiguration by Fra Angelico, 1438–1445. (Arte and Immagini srl/Corbis)

itself spoke to him and said, 'This is my Son, the Beloved; he enjoys my favor.' We heard this ourselves, spoken from heaven, when we were with him on the holy mountain" (*Jerusalem Bible* 1968). This witness of the Father on behalf of the Son has a precedent in Christ's baptism in the Jordan, when the Holy Spirit descended upon him in the shape of a dove as the same words were heard coming from heaven. Orthodoxy celebrates this event on the January 6 feast of **Epiphany**, calling it instead the **Theophany**, as a feast of the Trinity, since it marks the first time God became manifest as the unity of Three Persons. The August 6 feast of the **Transfiguration** echoes it in this respect, provided that the light shining out of the Son's body and the bright cloud from which the voice of the Father came are both taken to be the Holy Spirit itself as God's "Sublime Glory." In this sense, the **Transfiguration** is a lot like **Epiphany**: a feast of Light as revealed in the Holy Trinity, for according to its exapostilarion in the Greek rite, in the manifestation of the Light of the Son as divine

Word on Mount Tabor, the Father and the Spirit were also seen as Light, guiding as such all of Creation.

Greek Folklore

Though the custom is also part of **Christmas** and **Ascension** folklore, it is appropriate then that many Greeks sit up all night on the eve of the feast of the **Transfiguration** in hopes of catching a glimpse of the divine light of the heavens as they burst open. They think any wish they make at this very moment is sure to be granted. Most of them take August 6 to be the date that puts an end to the *dhrimes,* which are a sequence of inauspicious days when evil spirits of the same name are active at the beginning of that month (as of that of March), so that certain activities are taboo. People prefer to refrain from cutting wood, washing their hair, bathing in the sea, and so on, and they make sure their children are not outdoors at noon, just to be on the safe side.

Fishermen are the only people allowed to work on this day, because it is at sea that they will find omens about their success over the rest of the year. Cod or some other fish is the centerpiece of the day's special meal, as a small festive departure from the two-week vegetarian fast that precedes the August 15 feast of the **Dormition** of the Mother of God. The first baskets of grapes are also brought to church to be blessed after the service, and are then shared out among the congregation. Other fruits may be included in this **thanksgiving** ritual (probably taken over from an unknown pagan harvest festival) that is observed not just in Greece, but in Orthodox Christian communities throughout the world.

> **See also** Ascension; Assumption; Easter; Elevation of the Cross; Epiphany; Holy Week; Lent; Whitsuntide

References

Jerusalem Bible. New York: Doubleday, 1968.

John Anthony McGuckin. *The Transfiguration of Christ in Scripture and Tradition.* Lewiston, NY: Edwin Mellen Press, 1986.

A. D. A. Moses. *Matthew's Transfiguration Story and Jewish-Christian Controversy.* Sheffield, UK: Sheffield Academic Press, 1996.

Michael Ramsey. Archbishop of Canterbury, *The Glory of God and the Transfiguration of Christ.* London: Darton, Longman and Todd, 1967.

▶ TRIETERIDES

See Dionysia

▶ FEAST OF THE TRINITY, TRINITY SUNDAY

See Whitsuntide

▶ TRO-BREIZ

See Pardon

▶ TRUT

See Water-Splashing Festival

▶ TSUKIMI

See Mid-Autumn

▶ TU BI-SHEVAT (JUDAISM)

The fifteenth of the month of Shevat, or *Tu bi-Shevat* in Hebrew, is a minor Jewish festival that falls in January or early February. It is based on the fiscal year deadline for tithes (sacrifices of a tenth) on fruits that went to the priesthood or to the poor, depending on the year. According to the Talmud, this is the time when winter rains come to an end in Israel. The ancient Hebrews would take this opportunity to plant trees, and this tradition has been kept up in the Diaspora.

New Year for Trees

Tu bi-Shevat is considered to be **New Year for Trees.** There also used to be a **New Year for Animals** on the day they were likewise tithed on the first day of the month of Ellul. On the pattern of an analogy between man and a tree that is found in the Torah, the fate of trees depends on an auspicious beginning on this **Day of**

A young boy pats down the soil around a sapling he has just planted for the Tu bi-Shevat holiday in Herzlia, Israel. (Hanan Isachar/Corbis)

Judgment comparable to **Rosh Hashanah**— the **New Year for Years** from which they are counted in the system of four functional **New Year**'s days laid down by early rabbis in the Mishnah by the second century. By then, however, the **New Year for Kings** had lost its relevance as a way to date legal documents from their official accession on the first day of Nisan, since the Romans had already abolished the Jewish monarchy. But as for **Tu bi-Shevat**, coming at a point of the year when there is no water left in the ground and trees only live on their own sap, this **New Year for Trees** might still decide the amount they could expect to receive from the sky as rainfall, just as any **New Year** observance is seen to reflect upon the entire coming year in practically all of world folklore.

It would therefore be inappropriate to fast on this day. Instead, the **New Year** wish for fruitfulness has been expressed since medieval times in the Ashkenazi custom of partaking of fifteen varieties of the first fruits of the season on the fifteenth of Shevat. This was the date arrived at by Hillel the Elder at the turn of the Common Era, and handed down in the canonical law code, the Mishnah, for this critical point in the life of trees in the interior of Israel, where this doctor of the law was living.

While this celebration has little impact on the synagogue's liturgy (only the omission of some penitential prayers), the influence of the Kabbalistic school of Isaac Luria (1534–1572) has encouraged more elaborate home observances among Sephardi Jews than among Ashkenazis. They center on a special meal on the pattern of the **Passover** seder, where they ponder the inner meaning of the different fruits of the land and sing seasonal hymns called *complas* in the Ladino language of Spanish Jewry—scattered since the fifteenth century.

Reclaiming the Promised Land

Tu bi-Shevat acquired a new layer of meaning with the spread of Zionist agricultural colonies in Palestine at the end of the nineteenth century. In this context, planting trees became a symbol of national rebirth and continuity, since they could stand for the Jewish people laying new roots in the land of Israel, to reclaim from the desert its promise of plenty. This frontier spirit has spread to the Diaspora; on this Jewish **Arbor Day**, families will make financial contributions to reforestation projects in Israel, while there, school-children go out in groups to plant trees and sing songs. This festival of earth and nature was thus bound to become a day of environmental awareness for Jews by the late twentieth century.

> **See also** New Year (China, Korea); New Year (Japan); New Year (West); Passover; Rosh Hashanah

References

Ari Elon, Naomi Mara Hyman and Arthur Waskow, eds. *Trees, Earth, and Torah: A Tu b'Shvat Anthology.* Philadelphia, PA: Jewish Publication Society, 1999.

Lillian Ross, ed. *The Judaic Roots of Ecology.* Miami, FL: Central Agency for Jewish Education, 1983.

Hayyim Schauss. *Jewish Festivals. A Guide to their History and Observance.* Tr. Samuel Jaffe. New York: Schocken Books, 1996.

▌ TWELFTH DAY, TWELFTH NIGHT
See Epiphany

▌ TWELVE DAYS
See Christmas, Epiphany

▌ TWELVE FEASTS
See Easter

▶ VAISHAKHA AND VAISAKHI (HINDUISM, BUDDHISM, SIKHISM)

In much of the Indian subcontinent, the solar year begins in mid-April with the month known as **Vaishakha** in Sanskrit. But the latter has acquired a universal significance for two world religions having their roots there. The first day of this month in Punjab and North India, called **Vaisakhi**, marks the anniversary of the institution of the Khalsa as the community of Sikhs. The full moon of the lunar month of **Vaishakha** is regarded as the traditional date not only for the birth of the Buddha in the south of Nepal, where it is celebrated soon after the **New Year**, but for his enlightenment and death as well. All three events tend to be observed on an equivalent date by the followers of different Buddhist traditions, and since half a century as an ecumenical **Buddha Day** on the original date to manifest the universality of their founder's teachings, called the *Dharma*, and their worldwide unity as a community, called the *sangha*. The custom of illuminating temples as centers of religious community is found in the Sikhs' **Vaisakhi** as in the Buddhists' **Vesakha**.

A Hindu New Year (Among Many)

In April, the first day of the month of **Vaishakha** ushers in the solar **New Year** for a sizable por-tion of Hindus, though it is observed under a variety of names as the time when the spring harvest is ready to be either stored or sold. **Vaisakhi** is celebrated not only with partying and worshipping, but also with holy bathing. This is when the goddess Ganga is thought to have descended to earth in the mythical past, and many Hindus gather in her honor for ritual baths in the sacred river Ganges in North India, in the Tawi River at Jammu or in the Jhelum River at Srinagar (the winter and summer capitals of Jammu and Kashmir State in the country's northwest frontier) or anywhere in the southern state of Tamil Nadu, where great processions featuring caparisoned elephants are organized.

In the southwest of the subcontinent, the festival is called **Vishu** in Kerala, and includes fireworks (like a Western **New Year**'s Eve), alms-giving and cash gifts from elders to dependents and younger relatives (also a custom of the Parsis' **Naw Ruz** and the Chinese **New Year**), shopping for new clothes at the **New Year** fair or *Vishuwela*, as well as *Vishukkani*—Malayalam for the "lucky sight" of arrangements of auspicious items like flowers, grains, fruits, cloth, gold, and money that are ceremoniously placed before a lamp and should be viewed early in the morning to ensure prosperity over the coming year (rather like the *Sofrah*

Navrozi table of Parsis on their own March 21 New Year, or **Naw Ruz**).

In the northeast, **Poila Baishakh** is observed with rites and customs for invoking wealth, as an official **New Year** holiday in both West Bengal and Bangladesh. In the east, in Assam, the festival is called **Bohag Bihu** or **Rangoli Bihu** and features massive feasts, music, and dancing, in addition to the associated **Goru Bihu** cattle festival, in which the beasts are bathed, decorated, and fed delicacies. Many Hindus hang brass, copper, or silver pots on top of poles wrapped in flags of gold-embroidered silk that they raise like maypoles in front of their homes. Children wear flower garlands and run through the streets singing wishes for many returns of the New Year.

Sikh Vaisakhi: Anniversary of the Pure

In India's northern states, the first of **Vaishakha** is celebrated with fairs, dances, and folksongs as a public holiday on April 13 (or 14 every thirty-six years), on account of their sizeable Sikh communities. Elsewhere in the country and overseas, each Sikh temple or *gurdwara* can choose to observe it on the following or preceding weekend. **Vaisakhi** (often spelled **Baisakhi**) is especially important in Panjab State as the homeland of the Sikhs. Their third Guru Amar Das first enjoined them to assemble in the presence of their spiritual leader on this day of the **New Year** over 450 years ago. The tenth Guru Gobind Singh, having abolished the *masand* order of deputies of the Guru in local congregations, asked Sikhs to contribute directly to his treasury on **Vaisakhi**. It was on this occasion in 1699 that he established the *Khalsa* as the new structure of the Sikh community, centered on individual initiation and adherence to a strict code of conduct symbolized by the five "k"s, since "k" is the first letter of the Punjabi names of five items (long hair, a comb, a steel bracelet, a sword, and a pair of shorts) to be worn by every male member, since Gobind maintained

that "where there are five, there am I." The "Land of the Five Rivers" that Punjab's name refers to is thus seen by Sikhs as a gift from their last human Guru, so that Sikh rule in Punjab is entailed as a political aim in the institution of the Khalsa—the "Pure" in Punjabi.

This idea of forming a chosen people of warrior-saints has been the most powerful force in shaping Sikh identity ever since. The importance of the celebration of the Khalsa's birth on **Vaisakhi** has only been underscored by a number of tragic events that have marred this festive occasion in the holy city of Sikhism. The 1919 Amritsar Massacre also helped convince many Indians of the need to end British rule of the subcontinent. On the same day in 1762, the Afghan invader Ahmed Shah Abdali even destroyed the main Sikh temple, the Harimandir, but the Sikh king of Punjab Maharaja Rajit Singh rebuilt it in the early nineteenth century as Amritsar's famous Golden Temple. It is now illuminated on **Vaisakhi**, like many such gurdwaras wherever there are Sikhs. In most of them, the sacred "First Book" appointed by Guru Gobind Singh as his successor for all time: the *Adi Granth,* is read from cover to cover by a relay of readers (*akhand paath*) over two days. More *kirtan* hymns of praise are sung over this time than as part of regular worship, and as always, all are welcomed to eat together after services and during breaks at the "kitchen of the Guru" (*Guru ka langar*), as a demonstration of Sikh egalitarianism against Hindu caste segregation. This is also the time to clean the flagpole and raise a new flag. Elections are held for temple presidents and management committees, and new initiates young and old are inducted into the Khalsa brotherhood by the same five men who may walk in front of the holy book with swords drawn in parades to be seen in larger centers. They are spiritual elders chosen to represent the "Beloved Five" (*Panj Piarey*)—volunteers who formed the nucleus of the Khalsa by first answering their Guru's call to sacrifice their lives and so went into a tent where he pretended to slay them, substituting a goat for each one out of the view of the others. These ceremonies are followed by feasting, music, and dance. In Punjabi villages, men perform the strenuous *bhangra* dance, depicting every stage of the agricultural process, from tilling the soil to celebrating the harvest.

Nepal's New Year and the Buddha's Birthday

The first day of **Vaishakha** is also **New Year**'s Day for the Hindus of the Indian state of Himachal Pradesh, as well as in the neighboring Himalayan kingdom of Nepal, where Hindus and Buddhists coexist and largely participate in each other's festivals. Like the Sikhs' **Vaisakhi**, the Nepalese **New Year** is the only religious festival determined by a solar calendar system rather than a lunar-based one like all other feasts. It is celebrated in a host of different ways following local usage. The best known version is that of the Newars of Bhadgaon, called **Bisket** after the slaying of two snakes that used to come out of the nostrils of a princess to devour all her suitors until the coming of the victorious founder of a local dynasty. It is celebrated with the raising of a 27-meter-tall phallic maypole from which banners representing the two slain serpents are unfurled, as well as with the processions of idols of many gods. As the terrifying, destructive aspects of Shiva, Bhairava and his consort Bhadra are each carried in a huge temple-shaped chariot called a *ratha*, pulled by ropes through the streets of Bhadgaon (or Bhaktapur as the city is also known). At a certain square, crews from the rival upper and lower parts of town vie in a tug-of-war for the good omen of inflecting its course toward their own quarter.

Nepal's **New Year**, or **Nava Varsha**, is soon followed by *Buddha-Jayanti Purnima,* that is the "Full Moon of the **Buddha's Birth**" in Lumbini, a village now called Rummindei near the southern border with India that was then the capital of the Shakya kingdom. This feast is also widely known as the "Triple Blessing," since it is on the same date that, thirty-five years later, the Shakya Prince Gautama Siddhartha is said to have become the *Buddha*—the Enlightened One in Sanskrit—by meditating under the *bodhi* tree of "awakening" in Bodh Gaya, and to have passed away into nirvana, or liberation from death and rebirth, in Kushinagar around 483 B.C.E., at the age of eighty.

As Nepalese Buddhists go on pilgrimage to the latter two Indian sites on this occasion, so Buddhists come from all over the world not so much to Lumbini as to Kathmandu. Some relics of the historical Buddha are said to be preserved there within the massive, lotus-bud-shaped, white-domed Swayambunath stupa, which is illuminated at night during this festival. It was actually built 2,000 years ago to cover the divine flame of light of the pre-eternal, "Self-Existent" (*Swayambu*) and "Primordial," that is, *Adi Buddha,* of which the historical Shakyamuni Buddha was but one among an infinity of cyclical manifestations, according to some schools of Mahayana Buddhism. But this "Great Vehicle" represents a more recent strand of Buddhism than its original Theravada form, the "Way of the Elders" that experienced a revival in Sri Lanka from the tenth century. This was just when Buddhism ceased to be a significant presence in India with the onslaught of Islam. In the land of its first blossoming, Buddhists are now a small minority found in scattered pockets, as in the northeastern Tripura State enclaved by Bangladesh, where the **Buddha's birthday** is celebrated on *Vaisakhi Purnima*.

From Theravadin Vesak to World Buddha Day

Every full moon is considered holy by Buddhists, since it symbolizes the unobstructed fullness of enlightenment. But two of them have come to stand out as special occasions: that of the month of Asalha ushering in the rainy season's monastic retreat on the anniversary of the Buddha's first sermon in a Benares park, and that of **Vaishakha**. The latter is called *Vesakha* in the Pali language of the ancient Theravada canon, in which the "Great Chronicle" (*Mahavamsa*) of Sri Lanka's history was written by the Buddhist monk Mahanama in the middle of the first millennium. It records the number of times **Vesakha** Puja was celebrated under the reigns of various kings from the time of Dutthagamani (101–77 B.C.E.), champion of the Sinhalese Buddhists against the Hindu Tamils from India who had taken over the country after the death of the early Buddhist convert King Tissa in 207 B.C.E. But this festival was probably observed on the island from the earliest years of the introduction of Buddhism and had become an established tradition by the fourth century, as an occasion for kings to make offerings of robes to the monks and of food and clothing to the poor.

Nowadays, food and drink are brought to temporary alms halls by the devotees and sightseers who flock to temple rituals in greater numbers than on any other holiday to observe the "Eight Precepts" (*asta-sila*) out of the ten observed by monks. This is in contrast to the basic five normally followed by laypeople. Those who are taking on extra silas (with some combined to give eight) wear white attire for the day of the full moon and the next one, which is set aside for commemorative activities, while others attend to their many needs around the temples. Processions circle these three times (for the Buddha, the Dharma, and the Sangha). For up to four days in bigger towns, there is extra traffic as large, happy crowds circulate to view the sights of **Vesak**. These include rows of coconut oil lamps of various sizes and shapes (some intricate and traditional, others fanciful and contemporary, for example, planes and spaceships) on temples and houses, street plays based on the life stories of Gautama Buddha and his previous incarnations or the history of Buddhism in Sri Lanka, impressive archways with panels illustrating these same stories and flashing lightbulb patterns, *tableaux-vivants* on

the same themes (plus the cautionary tales of Buddhist hells), and children's devotional choirs. Sending colorful **Vesak** cards has recently become a widespread custom.

Aside from the purchase of fish and birds to permit their release in memory of the Buddha's compassion for all sentient beings, this festival is observed in similar ways as a public holiday in Southeast Asian countries whose national Buddhist traditions are offshoots of the Theravada form they adopted from Sri Lanka. In Thailand and Burma, Laos and Cambodia, it is thus known as **Vesakha** Puja. But in Sri Lanka itself, **Vesak** was cancelled as a public holiday in 1815 by British colonial authorities as part of a policy of undermining native culture, which was only reversed in 1885 with the reestablishment of its official status. It was in this context that the American Colonel Henry Steele Olcott, a co-founder of the Theosophical Society (with Madame Blavatsky) who became a Buddhist there in 1880, devised a Buddhist flag based on the five colors of the Buddha's aura. They reflect the five energies of the awakened state as ultimate reality, with blue, yellow, red, white, and orange vertical bands, along with a sixth one repeating the same sequence horizontally, being their harmonious synthesis.

This flag was adopted by Sinhalese Buddhist organizations for their flag-raising ceremonies, and especially for **Vesak,** when it also adorns temples, houses, and streets and features in solemn processions. On May 25, 1950, it was also unanimously adopted by the delegates of twenty-six nations at the annual congress of the World Fellowship of Buddhists in Colombo, capital of Sri Lanka, as the official flag of Buddhism. It was to be proudly displayed by Buddhists everywhere (especially on **Vesak** as **Buddha Day**) as the banner or right belief and a beacon of peace and harmony for all beings, beyond race and class distinctions and national and ideological allegiances. Thus, ever since the monk To Lien brought it back with him from Colombo to Vietnam in 1951, it has been raised in front of Buddhist temples over the objections of Communist authorities there. Nowadays, these colors are flown at **Buddha Day** ceremonies in over fifty nations, as well as at UNESCO headquarters in Paris, where, since 1976, **Vesak** is observed every year in the presence of many diplomats, academics, Buddhist monks of both the Theravada and Mahayana traditions, and the representatives of other world religions. In countries where most of them are either immigrants or converts, Buddhists gather in their temples or meditation centers to listen to lectures about the Buddha's universal message and perform pious acts and express their devotion, be it with offerings of oil lamps, flowers, and incense before an image of the Buddha, or by lighting paper lanterns as in Sri Lanka.

Mahayana Variations from Tibet to Japan

However, the many strands of the Mahayana tradition of Buddhism observe this festival over a range of slightly different dates according to its many national calendars. Their adherents in non-Buddhist countries may then invite their fellow Buddhists of other traditions to their own celebrations and vice versa, since there is no conflict between them. Thus, in the Tibetan calendar, the **Buddha's birthday** is commemorated around May on the eighth day of the fourth lunar month, while his death and passing into nirvana are celebrated on the fifteenth (but sometimes on the same day in certain meditation centers). On this occasion in Tibet, pilgrims visit the monasteries to bring offerings and view religious paintings, while lamas perform symbolic dances in special costumes. The eighth day of the Fourth Moon is **Buddha's birthday** in Korea, where it also used to be called "Buddha's Bathing Day" (in reference to the local version of a custom known from Hong Kong to Japan, described next). People would visit temples and pray for the happiness of the dead while lighting lanterns. Some Buddhist temples are still spectacularly illuminated with lanterns on this festival, though the influence of Buddhism has lessened under the staunchly Confucian Choson Dynasty that ruled the country from 1392 to 1910, when it was annexed by Japan. In that country, the Buddhist religion has always remained at the center of national life, and its founder's birth in a flower bush according to a local account is celebrated on April 8 with *Hana Matsuri*, the **Flower Festival**. In front of every Buddhist temple, monks set up a temporary wooden shrine to hold a small black bronze statue of the young Buddha pointing to the sky with one hand and to the earth with the other, in the middle of a water basin. Both the basin and the shrine are covered with flowers, and beside them is a bucket full of a sweet green tea in which visitors can dip with a bamboo ladle to pour some on the Buddha's head in a "baptism" ceremony called *kambutsue*. He is also offered flowers, and children dance before his image. Rice flour cakes are a festive treat.

See also Gurpurb; Kathina; Matsuri; May Day; Naw Ruz; New Year (China, Korea); New Year (West)

References

Pategama Gnanarama. "Full Moon," pp. 283–286, and Vinnie Vitharana. "Festivals," pp. 228–234, in W. G. Weevarathi, ed. *The Encyclopedia of Buddhism*. Vol. V, Fascicle 2. Colombo, Sri Lanka: Government of Sri Lanka, State Printing Corporation, 1991.

Harbans Singh. *Encyclopaedia of Sikhism*. Patiala, India: Panjabi University, 1992.

▶ VALENTINE'S DAY

See Lupercalia

▶ VAPPU

See May Day

▶ VASANTA-MAHOTSAVA

See Holi

▶ VASANTA NAVARATRI

See Navaratra and Dusshera

▶ VEIL (FEAST OF THE)

See Protection of the Mother of God

▶ VENUS VERTICORDIA AND VIRILE FORTUNE (ROME)

On the first day of April, which was the month of Venus, the women of Rome, whether they were respectable or not, "turned to" the goddess, and asked her to "turn their hearts" (*verso corde*) to virtue, at a festival accordingly called that of **Venus Verticordia**. It is Venus, too, they were invoking that same day at the misleadingly named festival of **Virile Fortune**, with the idea of preserving their beauty, along with their reputation and moral virtue.

Festivals of Feminine Force

The two linguistic origins suggested by Ovid's account of the festival of **Venus Verticordia** ("turning to Venus," "turning to virtue") reinforce one another. But since the Latin word *virtus* for "virtue" comes from *vis* for "force," and is related as such to *vir* for "man," Verticordia's orientation toward virtue may link it to the festival of **Virile Fortune**. Its name refers to men, as opposed to Fortuna Muliebris as a force protecting women. Yet **Virile Fortune** too concerned women directly. Women of the people could use the men's public baths for the day. There, they burned incense as they prayed Venus to give them the good fortune of keeping their physical imperfections a secret to men (*viros*).

Setting an Example of Virtue

Following the poet Ovid and the historian Valerius Maximus, Venus came to get the surname Verticordia because of the change of heart she had caused in the women of Rome after a temple was built for her for this very purpose. Its construction was decided as a result of a scandal that revealed how little virtue the city's women had. In 114 B.C.E., three Vestal virgins were buried alive, as prescribed if they ever broke their vow of perpetual chastity. (This way, the stain of their presence was removed from the city, without violating the sacredness of their persons.) It appears that they were guilty of having committed sexual indiscretions with knights. At least, this is what the Cuman sibyl or prophetess maintained when she was consulted about a disturbing omen. A knight's daughter had been struck by lightning on horseback; oddly enough, not only did she lose her life, but she was also stripped of her clothes on the spot. Matrons and prostitutes alike were urged from then on to look up to Venus for modesty.

This was symbolized on April 1 by the myrtle crowns they wore as they bathed in her honor. The goddess Venus was said to have once reached for myrtle leaves to cover her hair while she was letting it dry on the shore of a river after bathing: she had just realized that satyrs (lewd goat-footed beings) were watching her. The marble image of Venus was also carefully washed (like the silver one of **Cybele** at the closing of her **Spring Festival** a few days before or in Greece the statue of Athena some six weeks later at Athens' **Plynteria**) by Roman women on that day. Having first removed its rich ornaments and golden necklace, they would put them back on once the sculpture had been thoroughly dried. The women would then offer fresh roses to the sparkling effigy of **Venus Verticordia**.

See also Spring Festival of Cybele and Attis; Vestalia

References

William Warde Fowler. *Roman Festivals of the Period of the Republic. An Introduction to the Study of the Romans*. Port Washington, NY: Kennikat Press, 1969.

Ovid. *Fasti*. Tr. A. J. Boyle and R. D. Woodard. London: Penguin Books, 2000.

▶ VESAK, VESAKHA

See **Vaishakha** and **Vaisakhi**

▶ VESTALIA (ROME)

On June 9, after the famous angling competition of June 8: the *ludi Pescatorii,* the ritual focus of the ancient Roman calendar shifted from water to fire at the high point of the **Vestalia**, a festival extending over nine unlucky days from June 7 to 15. Weddings were proscribed for two weeks prior to the purification of the temple of Vesta, with its eternal flame tended by the Vestal virgins. Bakers had a holiday in honor of their patron, the goddess of the hearth—at once fire and earth.

A Round Temple for Vesta, a Royal Palace for the Vestals

Since time immemorial, the goddess Vesta had been worshipped in certain cities of Latium, such as Lavinium and Alba. Some Romans thought her cult had been brought from Alba to their city by the mother of its founder Romulus, the Vestal virgin Silvia. Others believed it was King Numa Pompilius who, forty years after Rome was founded in 753 B.C.E., had introduced Vesta's cult there, housing her virgins of royal blood on the premises of his palace on the Forum. Representing Rome's permanence, it survived the monarchy as the Atrium of Vesta, the convent of her six priestesses (standing for the original six princesses) beside the temple proper. The ruins of the temple of Vesta are among the most remarkable in Rome, because of its unusual round shape, echoing that of early Italian huts, and suggesting the private origins of the public hearth within.

The Invisible Goddess of Intangible Fire

According to the poet Ovid (*Fasti* 6, p. 146), the reason for this shape was that the earth is round, and "Vesta equals Earth. Sleepless fire underlies both;/Earth and hearth denote their own fixity" (267–268). For Vesta is "nothing but living flame" (291), kept in her temple by virgins (since this proud daughter of Saturn and Ops had remained unwed, unlike her two older sisters Juno and Ceres who had children). But "you see no substances born from flame" (292), giving or receiving seed. Nor could she be seen in a body as a statue like other gods, since "that temple encloses an undying fire/but no image of Vesta or of fire" (297–298, p. 147), even though Ovid himself had long assumed there was a statue hidden inside the round temple. This was because access to its inner sanctum, open to matrons who came barefoot during the festival between June 7 and 15, remained denied to males at all times. The only exception was the Great Pontiff, who was thus able to rescue from the flames that consumed the temple in 241 B.C.E. one of the sacred talismans on which Rome's fate depended: the Palladium, a statue of Athena brought from Troy after its fall to the Greeks by the city's mythical founding ancestors, led by Aeneas.

The Public Cult of Jupiter as Baker

According to Ovid, Vesta had also played a crucial part in the rescue of Rome from the besieging Gauls after the disastrous defeat of the Allia in 390 B.C.E., when they finally became convinced the Romans would not give in for lack of food after being pelted by them with loaves of bread from Capitol Hill. This had been done on Jupiter's counsel to his starving people, once he had addressed his half-sister thus: "Now make their dwindling corn appear plentiful,/Vesta, and do not desert your site./Have the hollow mill grind all their uncrushed grain,/hands soften it and hearth fires bake it" (*Fasti* 6:379–382, p. 149). Having leaned on the functions of Vesta, the king of the gods was henceforth annually honored by Romans at a shrine that was dedicated on her great festival day of June 9 to Jupiter Pistor or "Jupiter the Baker." Vesta's public cult was thus of vital importance to the city, even if the all-male citizenry was not a party to its essential acts and can tell us only so much about it. But we do know that the festival's nine days of ill omen only came to an end once the sweepings from the ceremonial cleaning of the temple of Vesta on June 15 had been either put away at a special spot next to Capitol Hill or thrown into the Tiber.

The Private Worship of Vesta by Bakers

The **Vestalia** had their roots in ancient private rites of which we know little more than the traces they left in such relatively late (second century B.C.E.) celebrations as those of the bakers' corporation in honor of their patron goddess. They would not work on that day but would garland their idle grindstones with flowers and put collars of bread loaves around the necks of the donkeys that turned them the rest of the time. Though the bakers were by then using ovens to provide the population with bread, it is to the hearth goddess Vesta that they turned for protection. This was a holdover from the time when all households baked their own bread under the ashes of the home fire. It was so vital to placate this most familiar yet most impalpable of divinities that in Ovid's day, at the turn of the Common Era, a small purified plate still used to be set aside by the hearth with food for Vesta. The name of this protector of all altar fires comes from an Indo-European root for "burning," like that of her Greek counterpart Hestia; but whereas Hestia's name was the first one to be invoked in Greek prayers, Vesta's was the last to be mentioned when Romans turned to their gods. There was among them a special patron for ovens too: the goddess Fornax, whose festival of **Fornacalia** was on February 17.

> ***See also*** Fordicidia and Parilia; Fornacalia and Quirinalia; Games (Rome); Hollyhock Festival; Terminalia

References

Georges Dumézil. *Archaic Roman Religion, with an Appendix on the Religion of the Etruscans.* Tr. Philip Krapp. Baltimore, MD: Johns Hopkins University Press, 1996.

Ovid. *Fasti.* Tr. A. J. Boyle and R. D. Woodard. Harmondsworth, Middlesex, UK: Penguin Books, 2000.

Sir Thomas Cato Worsfold. *The History of the Vestal Virgins of Rome.* London: Rider and Co., 1932.

▶ VETERANS DAY

See Martinmas

▶ VIJAY DASHAMI

See Navaratra and Dusshera

▶ VIRGIN MARY DAY

See Conception and Birth of the Virgin Mary

▶ VISAKHA, VISHU

See Vaishakha and Vaisakhi

▶ VISITATION OF HOLY MARY

See Sacred Heart

WAKANA NO SEKKU

See Sekku

WALPURGIS NIGHT

See May Day

WATER-SPLASHING FESTIVAL (CHINA, THAILAND)

The Tai Lue people, native to the southernmost part of China's Yunnan Province as well as areas of northern Thailand, celebrates the Theravada Buddhist **New Year** from the twenty-fourth to the twenty-sixth day of the sixth month of its traditional calendar. It falls in April, about ten days after the **Qing Ming** festival of China's majority Han population. The People's Republic of China has been promoting this event to tourists as the **Water-Splashing Festival**, after a practice central to its celebrations. This is only one of a number of typical seasonal games, aside from the **dragon boat** races known to all Chinese people. The legends relating to this festival deal with the fight against tyrants and with the purification needed to preserve peace in the community after their violence has had to be met with more violence.

First Day

After the washing of Buddhist images to favor good crops, the festival begins with a **dragon boat** race between teams of young men wearing red turbans. The first team to reach the goal waves a flag as it disembarks. It is then rewarded with wine, fruits, and candy, as boys and girls dance on the shore to the sound of drums and gongs. This victory is meant to recall a kind of local equivalent of the Biblical story of David and Goliath. Once upon a time, a young man was challenged to a **dragon boat** race by the king of Sipsongpanna (or Xishuangbanna in the official Pinyin transliteration of Chinese, where Tai is written "Dai"). The tyrant said he would have the boy's head cut off and thrown in the river to the fishes if he lost. This seemed a foregone conclusion, since the king's boat was much bigger than the boy's. But the Dragon King and the Heavenly King, moved by the latter's courage, decided to help him out: the Dragon turned into a splendid boat, and the King into a strong, steady gust of wind. It propelled the young man's boat to the finish line and threw the evil ruler overboard so that he drowned.

Second Day

The demise of another legendary tyrant of Sipsongpanna is invoked as an explanation for the

People of Tai ethnicity celebrate during the Water-Splashing Festival, 2002. (Liu Liqun/Corbis)

playful aspersion rites typical of the second day of the Tai Lue Water Festival (although similar ones are part of **Pi Mai**, the Laotian **New Year**, **Trut**, the Thai **New Year**, and **Thingyan**, Burma's **New Year**, rooted in ancient rituals marking the onset of the monsoon season when all these festivals take place). A powerful demon wizard who oppressed the Tai Lue people was not afraid of anything—be it weapons, fire, or water. He was thus able to abduct seven women to keep them as his wives. They still hated him just as much as anybody else and wondered how to overcome him. The beautiful and clever seventh concubine managed to manipulate him into revealing his weak spot. That same night, she proceeded to take advantage of his sleep to get him in this way: by ripping off his head with one of his hairs tied around his neck. However, the head provoked a fire when it fell onto the ground. It

then rolled into the river, which started to boil, killing all the fish. They tried to bury the head, but from underground it spread a nauseating stink. So the seventh wife had to hold it, and the others took turns to relieve her when she was tired. Each wife threw water on the one she was replacing, because of the need to wash off the blood still streaming without cease from the fiend's gaping neck. They have been at it ever since, in a god realm where a day lasts a full human year. In honor of the seven wives who are condemned to forever do the dirty job that somebody had to do, the Tai Lue soak each other with water. Just as their heroines keep on cleansing the stains of their act, they wash off the stains of the year gone by and try to bring better luck for a new one. Buckets and basins will generally do for these water fights, but a more delicate method is used with due respect for old people. As they sit motionless, the Tai

Lue sing their elders' praises, while pouring a few drops of clear water on their head or down their necks, with either a spoon or an olive branch. One way or another, everyone is soaked (not to mention a little tipsy) at the end of the day.

This is when performances begin. To the sound of elephant-foot drums, gongs, and bamboo flutes, young and old can join in the *xu-la-he* dance. Some hearty villagers dress up for the famous Peacock Dance, impersonating the Tai country's lucky symbolic bird. *Zan ha* singers relate seasonal tales as the song and dance go on into the night.

Third Day

Then comes the Tai Lue **New Year**'s Day and its typical games. *Gao sheng* means "rocket-launching" and refers to a powder-filled bamboo rocket containing five objects. These objects bring luck to everyone (especially children) who rushes to pick them up from the ground after the primitive missile explodes. *Diu bao* means "throwing ball," namely a special diamond-shaped, cotton-filled ball with colored fringes, between two rows of players: one for boys and one for girls. The one who drops the ball must offer a fresh flower to the last thrower of the other gender, by way of an apology. Players take this opportunity to edge nearer every time. When a girl has the boy she likes within her reach, she grabs his knife and scarf without warning. Once she gets home that night, she prepares a nice meal, in expectation of the moment he comes to get his belongings back. Many marriages are decided this way on **New Year**'s Day among the Tai Lue of the upper basin of the Mekong River.

See also Days of the Dead (China, Korea, Japan); Dragon Boat Festival; Easter; New Year (China, Korea)

References

Marie-Luise Latsch. *Traditional Chinese Festivals.* Singapore: Graham Brash, 1988.

Michael Moerman. "Ethnic Identity in a Complex Civilization: Who Are the Lue?" in *American Anthropologist,* Vol. LXVII (1965), pp. 1215–1230.

Qi Xing. *Folk Customs at Traditional Chinese Festivities.* Tr. Ren Jiazhen. Beijing: Foreign Language Press, 1988.

▸ WEAVER (FESTIVAL OF THE)
See Sekku

▸ WHEAT FESTIVAL
See Assumption

▸ WHITE SUNDAY, WHITE WEEK
See Easter

▸ WHITSUNTIDE (CHRISTIANITY)

Whitsuntide is the name of the festive season surrounding **Whitsunday**, as **Pentecost** is also known in the British Isles. Its original Greek name identifies it as the "fiftieth day" after **Easter**, commemorating the descent of the Holy Spirit on Jesus Christ's disciples during the Jewish **Pentecost** or **Shavuot**, fifty days after his Resurrection during **Passover**. Beyond this celebration of the Church's birthday, **Whitsuntide** is also the focus of a wide range of remarkably similar folkloric practices of pagan origin from one end of Europe to the other. They revolve around the ambiguous power of rain charms and vegetation spirits when summer is around the corner, much as on **May Day** a little earlier.

Pentecost: The Descent of the Holy Spirit

Early Christians referred to the entire fifty-day period following **Easter** as **Pentecost**. The last day was merely the formal closing of the "seven weeks" of Paschal joy when kneeling and fasting were therefore not allowed, according to Saint Irenaeus of Lyon. There would then be a continuous reading of the Acts of the Apostles to remind the faithful of what God had accomplished through his Church. The latter's founding (as described in chapter two) when the Holy Spirit descended on Christ's disciples fifty days after his Resurrection and ten days after his **Ascension**, only became the focus of a distinct feast on the fiftieth day in the last third of the fourth century in Constantinople. In Rome, the descent of the Spirit that bestows grace in Christ was likened to the giving of the Law to Moses on Mount Sinai. Rabbis had recently made this the main focus of the original Jewish **Pentecost** or **Shavuot**, coming fifty days after **Passover**. This is the Jewish feast during which Christians believe Jesus died and rose again, and the basis for their own **Easter** celebration.

If baptism used to be administered both at the beginning (**Easter**) and end (the day of **Pentecost**) of the Paschal season, **Pentecost** eventually came to be favored for this over **Easter** in Northern Europe. While the Roman Catholic Church dissociated the feast's vigil from baptism in 1955, the feast itself is still commonly called **Whitsunday** in English, after the special white garments worn by the newly baptized. Attested (as *hwitan sunnan daeg*) in the *Anglo-Saxon Chronicle* in 1067, the term was soon borrowed in Norway and Iceland, then in the process of full conversion to Christianity by largely English clergy. With the separation in the Western Church around the same time of the gift of the Spirit from baptism—as the new independent sacrament of confirmation, it became customary for Catholic children to receive it (as a kind of rite of passage) toward the age of puberty on a **Pentecost** Sunday. This was after all the anniversary of the original descent of the Holy Spirit and hence that of the Church of which they now became active members. Thus, a century ago, children could still be seen all dressed up riding with their godparents through Vienna's thoroughfares in carriages decorated with white lilacs and roses, down to their two horses. In France for most of

the second millennium, **Whitsunday** or **Whitmonday** were also days for electing the captains of youth, where it was organized into a hierarchical society.

A million pilgrims from all over the world (including close to a hundred specialized lay brotherhoods) still trek through the coastal marshlands east of the Andalusian port of Huelva on jeeps, horses, and carriages decorated with flowers of many colors to the shrine of the *Virgen del Rocío* (the "Virgin of the Dew"—an ancient symbol of the descending, vivifying Spirit in liturgical language), for the statue's hectic annual **Whitsunday** night rosary procession in the petal-strewn streets of the village of Almonte, starting with a mad crush of young men to touch her when she is first taken out. To the east in the village of Peñas de San Pedro in La Mancha on **Whitmonday**, the bearers of an articulated statue of Christ in a cross-shaped coffin run with it to a shrine located fifteen kilometers away.

From Italy to Rumania, Whitsunday is often popularly known by names derived from the ancient Roman festival of **Rosaria** or **Rosalia**, which may help explain the role that roses and other flowers frequently play in its customs. In the Catholic Church, roses are sometimes thrown to symbolize the descent of the Holy Spirit on the apostles in the guise of tongues of fire. This symbolism may also account for the red color of liturgical vestments for **Whitsunday** in the Anglican communion, where it is followed in the church calendar by two **Red-letter Days** (indicating important feast-days), not to mention Wednesday, Friday, and Saturday as **Ember Days** of fasting and prayer. In England, the **Pentecost** procession was long the occasion for parishioners to make yearly payments to their local church or diocesan cathedral on the basis of the number of chimneys on their houses— hence the term "Smoke Money" often used for these "**Whitsun** Farthings" or "**Pentecost**als."

It is to the Sunday following **Pentecost**, as the full revelation of the Holy Spirit, that the recitation of the Office of the Holy Trinity composed in the early tenth century by Bishop Stephen of Liège was initially assigned in some places. This date was retained by Pope John XXII when he instituted a mandatory Catholic feast called **Trinity Sunday** in 1334, only with a new office composed in the previous century by the Franciscan John Peckham, Archbishop of Canterbury. **Trinity Sunday** started out as a double of the second class, but was upgraded to a primary of the first class by Pope Pius XI on July 24, 1911. Its mass features the ancient preface by the late fifth-century Pope Saint Gelasius distinguishing canonical scriptures from apocryphal writings and three series of three readings taken from the Books of Exodus, Deuteronomy, and Proverbs. In certain Spanish villages just north of Portugal, people (mostly children) who have survived some mortal peril over the past year get to be carried inside caskets in a **Trinity Sunday** procession to thank Saint Martha for their new lease of life.

If Anglican and Lutheran churches count the following Sundays as "Sundays after **Trinity**," up to 1969, the Roman Catholic Church reckoned them until the start of **Advent** in their order as "Sundays after **Pentecost**," as is still done in the Eastern Church until the start of **Lent**. There, however, **Whitsunday** itself is often referred to as the **Feast of the Trinity** (which it specially manifests alongside **Epiphany** and the **Transfiguration**), unless the term is reserved by local use for **Whitmonday**, otherwise dedicated to the Holy Spirit. Though the one Orthodox prayer to the Holy Spirit, with which every other prayer and service begins, is taken from the **Pentecost** vespers that immediately follow **Whitsunday**'s Divine Liturgy, this divine Person is otherwise only alluded to in the seven lengthy prayers said by the priest at intervals during this service as the people kneel with him. These prayers are addressed either to the Father, to the Son, or to God in general (understood as the Trinity of Father, Son, and Spirit), to ask for the gift of the Holy Spirit as on the original **Pentecost**, kneeling in penitence to set the tone for the rest of the Church year, until the next fifty-day season of joyful **Easter** celebrations, when it is forbidden.

In Greece, wherever churches are named after the Holy Trinity, lambs are sacrificed for a large communal meal on this **Kneeling Sunday**, which may also be the final opportunity for graveside meals and offerings to the dead, such as rice pudding and sour milk. For not only is this the one time of the year when the Orthodox liturgy includes prayers for all the dead since the beginning of the world (even including suicides and other lost souls in hell), but there is also a belief that the souls of the dead are released from Hades following Christ's Resurrection on **Easter** Sunday and roam the earth freely for fifty days afterwards (or alternatively forty days to **Ascension**, up until the moment Resurrection hymns are sung for the last time). While they are thus "on parole," the deceased enjoy the sweets that the living set aside for them. To make sure the dead do not meet their relatives' gaze and risk becoming unable to bear parting from them again, some Greek villagers cover their eyes with leaves or rose petals and bow their heads very low during the particular kneeling invocations for the repose of the departed, while others light candles in front of them as they kneel to light the latter's way back to the beyond. During these kneeling prayers, Serbian women weave wreaths of tall grasses; they will decorate the home with foliage, in addition to the church as is the practice in many Eastern European cultures—down to covering the floor with grass among some like the Carpatho-Rusyn, in which women also used to throw roses into rivers that evening. Whitsunday is thus often actually known as **Green Sunday** in Slavic Churches.

Whitsuntide: Rain-Charms and Tree-Spirits

This is usually explained in terms of the role of plants in the celebration of Jewish **Pentecost** as a feast of **first-fruits**, which after all the Apostles were probably observing like the rest of the Jews gathered in Jerusalem for the occasion, when they received the Holy Spirit that now set them apart, with a **Pentecost** of their own as the fruition of the new Christian dispensation. And indeed, from East to West, the gathering of produce and other food to be blessed in a church full of greenery confirms that **Pentecost** very much remains a harvest festival along Jewish lines. Yet abundant folklore betrays another source for the **Whitsuntide** greening of churches, in the seasonal pagan worship of vegetation spirits. In Saxony and Thuringia, this was the time for "fetching the Wild Man out of the wood," into which a leaf-clad lad would hide and let other boys seek and capture him for a mock execution and resurrection, before they would parade him through the village, expecting gifts at every house—usually eggs as an obvious fertility symbol, in endless variations of this ceremony throughout Central Europe on **Whitsunday** or **Whitmonday**. These often involved the cutting, parading, decoration, and erection of a May-tree as another object of contest, sometimes directly connected to the slain leaf-clad man as its counterpart: the personified tree-spirit, like Attis in the **Spring Festival of Cybele** in ancient Rome. Another common practice, "the drenching of the *Pfingstl* [from German *Pfingst* for **Whitsunday**] with water and his wading up to the middle into the brook are, therefore, no doubt rain-charms," as Sir James George Frazer has argued in the chapter on "The **Whitsuntide** Mummers" that opens his discussion of "The Killing of the Tree-Spirit" in *The Golden Bough,* his classic "Study in Magic and Religion" (Vol. 4, 1935, p. 211). The Leaf King or Grass King was selected by (often equestrian) contests, only to be symbolically killed and replaced by a fresh representative of vegetation. But in Bohemia for instance, he was sometimes accompanied by a Hangman or Frog-Flayer who actually hanged or beheaded frogs. This was a rain charm that finds

parallels throughout Europe as well as in South and Central America, where, on the Aztec rain festival of **Etzalqualitzli**, priests used to swim around in a lake imitating frogs in honor of the rain goddess Chalchihuitlicue, the "Emerald Lady."

Hungary is one country where there is still a custom of electing a **Whitsun** Queen, whose attendants carry her from door to door throwing petals (as is done for a **May** Queen), and lifting her up before each house as they wish the owners that their hemp grow just as high (a kind of analogy that governs many **Midsummer** customs). In Silesia, the **Whitsuntide** Bride was the sweetheart of the lad who had reached the top of a smooth maypole to bring down the prize that made him **Whitsuntide** King, much as a **May** King was elsewhere matched by contest to a **May** Queen on **May Day**. In parts of Denmark, a little girl and boy were dressed up as a **Whitsun** Bride and Groom and escorted by the other children, also adorned with flowers and ribbons of many colors, as they collected from all the farmhouses the food (starting with eggs) needed for the wedding feast, at which they would all dance in their clogs until the dawn of **Whitmonday**. In Russia, it was on the previous Thursday that villagers fetched a birch tree in the wood, dressing it up in women's clothes and colorful ribbons for a feast, at the end of which they took it to one of their houses as an honored guest. All would visit "her" there until **Whitsunday**, when "she" was thrown into a stream along with the season's garlands, like Morena (as a dummy often carried by girls on a pole) or Green George (usually in the guise of a tree) at other times in other Slavic lands, and countless other embodiments of tree-spirits across Europe around **Whitsun**. It may not be too far-fetched to count among them the magic flagpole, or *steag,* used for their secret oath by the *Căluşari*, a men's society of **Whitsuntide** dancers found in the rural areas of southern Rumania (and in the past well into Bulgaria); for in parts of Oltenia, they too would throw it in the water at the end of their annual rites. They used to be active for a full week after **Whitsunday**, until the pressures of modern life gradually reduced this period to a couple of days. In Rumanian, the word *Rusalii* is synonymous with both the feast of **Pentecost** and all of **Whitsuntide** as a period when beautiful white-clad fairies also known as *Rusalii* (or just *iele*, which is the feminine form of "they") are most dangerous. Aside from Călușari who disobey some of their own rules, "they" will possess fertile women who transgress certain taboos peculiar to this period, like that on cleaning house or oneself (in time for spring cleaning), that on work in the fields and with animals (just when it starts in earnest), or on climbing trees (as they begin to be fruitful). At this delicate time of transition between winter and summer (rather like **May Day**), nature spirits can still turn either way, and they demand to be treated with fear and trembling, or else people fall ill with a kind of epilepsy, "possessed by the Căluș."

In contrast to the rest of the year when people can come to sorceresses for their ailments, this one can only be cured by the dancers embodying the Căluș as male counterparts of the **Rusalii**. Their name is also that of a similar winter ritual exclusive to Macedonian men, but related to Bulgaria's **Carnival** *Kukeri* processions and those of Rumanian mummers during **Yuletide**, while only women fall into trance at the **Whitsun** *Rusalje* processions of northeastern Serbia. Eastern Slavs think the *rusalki* live in streams, ponds, and lakes, and have the power to cause storms. Likewise, many Rumanian Călușari receive their power from these water fairies, and indeed, some of their societies take their ritual oath by immersing their hands in a body of water on **Whitsunday** Eve. Reminiscent of the flower-bedecked flagpole Greeks carry from door to door the weekend after **Easter**, singing folksongs called *Roussalia*, the flag the Călușari then raise is magically empowered by placing within a red

cloth bundle at the top wormwood and garlic as protection against evil (which they also wear in their belts) and sometimes also a bottle of dew (which in many places is endowed with the power to beautify the face on **May Day**). In this case, the dew is collected at the beginning of preparations for **Rusalii**, often as far back as **Mid-Pentecost**.

Among Albanian Christians, this minor Orthodox feast (known to them as **Rusicat**), based on the Jewish **Sukkot** but placed at the midpoint of the Paschal time between **Easter** and **Pentecost** (**Rushajet**, in their language), is actually reserved for women, who may then sleep over on monastery porches in the old country or visit each other between parishes all through **Eastertide** in the New World. In Rumania, women speak with deceased relatives in long tearful laments during meals at their graves that begin before dawn on **Rusalii** as a major collective day of mourning (as the pagan **Rosalia** likely was), though it is still only one of several private and public **days of the dead** when such a *pomana* or food offering is held. This one takes place so early because, in Rumanian folklore, all spirits can only be fully active and on the move from sunset to sunrise, as we all know from the vampire film genre drawn from the Dracula story about *Nosferatu*, meaning "undead" in Rumanian parlance for such restless dead people. The same rule applies to the dead these black widows seek out to bring them comfort and keep them quiet, and to the Căluș embodied by the white-shirted male dancers who eventually join them in village cemeteries early that morning. The latter are otherwise not allowed to have any intimate contact with women during **Whitsuntide** and may even stay together in one house just to be on the safe side.

Protracted preparations, secrecy, seclusion, and sexual abstinence also characterize the all-male **katchina** dancers' societies of the Pueblo village of Zuñi in New Mexico at the annual November celebration known as **Shalako**, after the ten-foot tall embodiments of rain spirits, whose accidental fall would spell disaster for the community. The same is true of the Căluşari's flag, and its raising and other preparations are as taboo to outsiders as those surrounding the **katchina**, with comparably dire consequences for any transgression. Just as among the latter in their tours of the village, there are oddly masked, kilt-wearing fools notorious for their obscenity and exhibitionism, the Căluşari are often led by an androgynous mute character—the only dancer wearing a mask (usually wooden and bearded, but sometimes a gas mask, or even a kind of Indian feather headdress!), who likes to flash from under his skirt a red wooden phallus as he chases women and children. Ritual silence is observed by the other Căluşari at various points of their ceremonies, as it often was in European folklore involving the early morning collection of magical "speechless water" on **Easter** or **New Year**'s Day.

Sometimes, the mute's phallus is diplomatically replaced by a stick sculpted with a horse's head, which makes it even more reminiscent of the hobbyhorses that would playfully chase people and invade houses on **May Day** or **Saint George**'s Day in Britain. Alternatively, the more serious *vătaf*, master of the order and holder of its secrets, would figure prominently and instead carry a stick called a *cioc*, or "beak," also known as *iepure* ("rabbit") after the animal whose pelt is pulled over it. This too is an obvious phallic symbol, since the rabbit represents fertility throughout Eurasia. It is usually connected as such with a moon goddess like the Greek Artemis or the Roman Diana, models of Irodeasa, the so-called "patron saint" Căluşari pray to for protection from her attendants or *iele* (or "they") who must not be named: the **Rusalii**. Rabbits were seen as a form witches took on **May Day** in Irish and Manx folklore. Similarly, the rabbit stick is kept at a secret burial site (somewhat like feathered prayer sticks in the course of **Shalako**) at the crossroads "they" are said to inhabit, because of its potential to harm mortals by causing them to be possessed,

as well as to cure them from this trance state. The latter is what the Căluşari use the stick for on people who fall possessed during **Rusalii.** They otherwise perform their suggestive comic plays and elaborate spirit dances (some of which others may join in) in all courtyards, and engage in a ritual fight or contest wherever two groups happen to cross paths in a village, as when they later on go from one village to the next in a competitive spirit.

Decline and Fall of English Whitsun

Actual brawls long went had in hand with the rough traditional games (including blood sports such as dog or cock fights and badger or bull baiting) that used to be played at **Whitsuntide** feasts in English villages. This is where they would hold competitions between each other's Morris "sides"—troupes of Morris dancers also seen on **May Day** and other festive occasions (depending on local custom) since the Middle Ages, but mostly associated with **Whitsuntide** by the nineteenth century. Like Romania's Căluşari (or other Balkan sword and stick dancers such as Bulgaria's Kukeri), they wore hats and a white shirt crossed with bands. At the Kirtlington Lamb Ale for instance, these bands were the same pink and blue ribbons that adorned (along with flowers and other plants) the "forest feathers" (wooden clubs carried by the two men who closed their procession), as well as the season's finest, first-born lamb carried by the man who opened it and the selected **Whitsun** Lord and Lady, whose badges of office were called "maces." The latter were followed by a Squire—a fool who prodded the crowd and cleared space for the dancers with a long staff (strung with a cow's tail at one end and a bladder at the other), much like the mute with his phallic rod in Rumania. There, a similar role was played by his colleague the *vătaf*, who in turn had an equivalent in the foreman of Morris sides. In the latter's Lancashire version, the Leader clearly stands aside to call the

Whitsun celebrations at London's Hamstead Heath, 1921. (Hulton-Deutsch Collection/Corbis)

figures with the help of a whistle, while the men carry ropes or short sticks bound with colored ribbons, though they never strike the sticks together as in the more widespread Cotswold Morris.

Pink and blue ribbons also adorned the maypole that was raised before **Whitsuntide** (sometimes on the previous "Holy Thursday"—a term used in England for **Ascension** a week earlier—as well as during **Holy Week**), as was the Căluşari's ribboned flagpole before **Rusalii.** In this case, the pole was provided by the Duke of Marlborough, along with the Bowery, "a shed made of green boughs set up on the village green, where the ale previously brewed was sold during the nine days of the feast without a license, the proceeds going towards the expenses incurred" (P. Manning, in Howkins 1973). Such events were therefore called "Whit

Ales," except in other parts of Oxfordshire where instead a "Youth Ale" followed the "Whit Hunt," which originated in a common right of local villagers to go within the bounds of the old Royal Forest around Wychwood to get a deer for the occasion.

Yet there as elsewhere in England, the old Whit Ales had disappeared by the second half of the nineteenth century. Tamer versions of some customs lived on in their wake. Children might still go from door to door with maces or garlands to collect pennies or dance around a maypole. A dwindling number of local Morris sides were sometimes replaced by more regional Morris troupes in the twentieth century. Over that time, as in Rumania later on, **Whitsuntide** celebrations were gradually reduced to three or four days, and then to a single holiday, as recommended by the **Bank Holidays** Act of

1871, which included among these **Whitmonday**. This was replaced by the last Monday in May in the 1980s (although shops still close on **Whitmonday** in France and Denmark). But in addition, these festivities also changed in character and became sober, orderly, respectable affairs, as the Anglican Church tightened its control over rural parish life, and the puritanical influence of dissenting groups like the Baptists and Methodists also spread. The latter had long made a point of holding "camp meetings" (open-air evangelical gatherings) in direct competition to wakes, fairs, and feasts such as **Whitsun**.

Representing an early cooperative form of social welfare on a local and increasingly national scale, "the growth of friendly societies in the countryside was another major influence, and so far as **Whitsun** was concerned the most directly important, since they 'expropriated' **Whitsun** and turned it into their 'Club' day. There can be little doubt that the gentry and clergy, who played a large part in promoting them, saw the Friendly Societies as active agencies of social control," slowly but surely spreading "the change in manners which swept through the upper classes in the last half of the eighteenth century . . . over the whole society. The change in **Whitsun** took place unevenly and in stages, first by the rise of Club Day and the Clubs, then by the change in their character, as temperance and 'rational recreation' gradually encroached. The rise of the [national] affiliated orders shifted the focus of **Whitsun** from the village to the district fete or rally. **Whitsun** as a village festival was on its way out when the clubs began to disappear, when the survivors stopped marching through their own villages behind their own village bands, to sing and dance till the early hours of the morning, and when the Foresters and Oddfellows [national "friendly" orders], banners triumphant, marched into Headington Hill Hall for their annual fete and sports day, to run, jump and parade with nary a drop to drink or a bit of fatty bacon to eat" after the formal procession to the **Whitsunday** or **Whitmonday** "club" service at the parish church (Howkins 1973, p. 62). For even this formal procession was abandoned by clubs and churches alike in favor of the fundraising afternoon fete, "offering a more controlled and elevating alternative to the general village feast," according to rural historian Alun Howkins, who recalled from his own mid-twentieth-century Oxfordshire childhood that "**Whitsun** was indistinguishable from two things: the Buff[aloes]s outing, and the **Sunday** School treat. The club outing replaced club day in the course of the 1920s, by which time too the **Sunday** School treat often took the form of an outing," the prospect of which was dangled in advance as a carrot to bribe children into behaving, or a stick if they failed to behave, as they risked being left behind. (Howkins 1973, pp. 58–59). Throughout Europe, **Whitsuntide** has always been, and largely continues to be, a favorite time for country outings for the entire family.

> ***See also*** Ascension; Carnival; Christmas; Days of the Dead (West); Dionysia; Easter; Elevation of the Cross; Epiphany; Holy Week; Lent; May Day; Midsummer; New Year (West); Rain Festivals; Sacred Heart; Saint George; Saint Lucy; Samhain; Shalako; Shavuot; Spring Festival of Cybele and Attis; Sukkot; Sunday; Transfiguration

References

Sir James George Frazer. *The Golden Bough,* Vol. 4: *The Dying God.* New York: Macmillan 1935.

John Gunstone. *The Feast of Pentecost: The Great Fifty Days in the Liturgy.* London: Faith Press, 1967.

Alun Howkins. *Whitsun in Nineteenth Century Oxfordshire.* Oxford [Ruskin College]: History Workshop Pamphlets No. 8, [1973].

Gail Kligman. *Căluş Symbolic Transformation in Romanian Ritual.* Foreword by Mircea Eliade. Chicago: University of Chicago Press, 1981.

Arthur Peck. *The Morris and Sword Dances of England.* Letchworth Garden City, Hertfordshire, UK: The Morris Ring, 1978.

A. R. Wright. *British Calendar Customs. England.* Vol. I: *Movable Festivals.* London: The Folk-Lore Society, 1936.

▌ **WOMEN'S FESTIVAL**

See Cowherd and Weaving Maid

▌ **WOMEN'S NEW YEAR**

See New Year (Japan)

▌ **WORLD DAY OF ORTHODOX YOUTH**

See Candlemas

▌ **WREN (DAY OF THE)**

See Christmas

XIA YUAN

See Days of the Dead (China, Korea, Japan)

XOCOTL HUETZI

See Days of the Dead (West)

Y

YAM CUSTOM, YAM FESTIVAL
See Adae

YAMA DWITITYA
See Divali

YANAYER
See New Year (Islam)

YANDATSA
See Days of the Dead (West)

YAWM AL-JUM'A
See Day of Assembly

YEME BEN HAMETZARIM
See Tisha be-Av

YOM HA-BIKKURIM
See Shavuot

YOM HA-DIN, YOM HA-ZIKKARON, YOM TERU'AH
See Rosh Hashanah

YOM KIPPUR (JUDAISM)
Yom Kippur, the "**Day of Atonement**" (meaning literally "covering over" in Hebrew), is the most solemn High Holy Day of the calendar for all Jewish people, regardless of religious and political differences. It comes on the tenth day of the month of Tishri (straddling September and October), at the culmination of several weeks of penitential preparation. The faithful spend most of this day at the synagogue saying confessional prayers, singing thanksgiving hymns, and asking for God's favor over the coming year.

Sacrifice and Scapegoat
The **Yom Kippur** service describes the feast's origin (known from Chapter 16 of Leviticus) in a purification ceremony for the First Temple of Jerusalem and its priesthood in view of the fall festival of booths or *Sukkot*. A Talmudic treatise entitled *Yoma* (Aramaic for "Day") is devoted to the rules that used to govern this "sacred service" of the High Priest. This was the only day of the year where he could publicly say aloud God's Unutterable Name, encrypted in the Tetragram as *YHWH*, and enter the Holy of Holies—the most sacred part of the Temple, where the Ark of the Covenant was kept. The incense he took to burn inside the shrine symbolized by its fragrance God's forgiveness of the sins of Israel. Most important though was the blood of a goat he sprinkled on and before the Ark's mercy seat and then on the altar just outside the Holy of Holies. For this life substance is

Jews on synagogue steps on Yom Kippur, New York City, ca. 1910. (Library of Congress)

what restored the bonds of community between Yahweh and His people of Israel, obtaining His forgiveness for its sins and those of the priests.

Yet this first sin offering was apparently not enough to ritually take the community out of harm's way. Popular pressure seems to have imposed the practice of drawing lots between two goats: one to be sacrificed to God, and the other to be sent to the devil called Azazel, meaning "to carry away a goat." The people's sins were laid on the head of the second goat with the hands of the priest as he confessed them again, so that they could physically be expelled by sending the beast away to die in the wilderness, and so join the demon Azazel. If this was the literal scapegoat, singled out to receive and take away the evils threatening the community, it was far from being original, as such "scapegoating" rituals, though named after this Biblical example, are well known in all cultures. They may have provided the ambiguous sacrificial foundation for human society, as French literary critic René Girard argued in his widely influential 1972 book *Violence and the Sacred.*

Personal Penitence

Yet the God of the Bible came to privilege a more original sense that ritual observances alone cannot secure atonement, since He ordained "as a perpetual law" that His people "fast and refrain from work" on this day in order to be "clean of all [their] sins" (Leviticus 16:29–31). This is why, even though it may fall on a weekday, **Yom Kippur** is always treated as the "**Sabbath** of **Sabbaths**," as the Bible calls it. According to a second century B.C.E. Bible commentary on **Yom Kippur**, "the Day of Atonement, on which there is no food or drink, the Torah states that one must honor it with clean clothes." These are often white, as they stand for both purity from sin and the white linen robes worn by the High Priest as he entered the Holy of Holies, like the *kippelot* also worn by Orthodox Jews.

Tradition has extended prohibitions to sexual intercourse, to all washing except for ritual ablutions, to the use of cosmetics and oils to anoint oneself, and to the wearing of shoes with leather soles or heels (since it would not do to ask forgiveness for oneself while standing on another creature's skin). In this spirit, it used to be on the **Yom Kippur** of a jubilee year, which occured every fifty years (Leviticus 25:9–10), that all debts were canceled just as sins were forgiven, so that tenant-farmers became owners of their land, and even slaves were given back their freedom. A trace of this practice survives in the special **Yom Kippur** synagogue collection, when people pledge to make a given material contribution for the needy. The strict twenty-four-hour fast (from sunset to sunset) is the only one still observed in some form by a majority of Jews throughout the world. But in consideration of its hardships, **Yom Kippur** is not celebrated over two days in the Diaspora like the other biblical Jewish festivals.

It is largely after the destruction of the Temple of Jerusalem in 586 B.C.E. that what had begun as a cosmic ritual of expiation came to be internalized as a day of personal repentance. In this ethical format, it marks the end of the ten-day penitential season, which was ushered in by the blowing of the *shofar* at **Rosh Hashanah** (the **New Year**) and that is brought to a close by the sound of this horn during the *neila* service peculiar to **Yom Kippur**. The latter goes back to the ancient evening prayers said by the laity throughout Israel while sacrifices were being made at the Second Temple or on public fasts. The *neila* is above all the most solemn service of the yearly liturgical cycle, as it marks the symbolic closing of heaven's gates, when the judgment of God on sinners is ratified. The whole process of critically looking inward and turning to God in repentance was actually initiated even before the **New Year**, with the *selihot* prayers of the preceding month of Ellul, the last one of the year gone by. By the time of **Yom Kippur**, Jews are supposed to take care of forgiving others' transgressions and being forgiven their own by them, so they can now focus on their remaining sins against God on this day for facing Him. Though the liturgy proper is hardly any longer than that of the **Sabbath**, the five **Yom Kippur** services go on from the morning to the evening of the tenth of Tishri. This is due to the many additional materials that are interpolated to sustain the moment, be it Torah readings, *selihot*, *yizkor* memorial prayers for the recently deceased, or optional *piyyutim*, poems for the festivals, collected in *mahzorim*. The largest *mahzor* is for the Ten Days of Penitence (*Aseret Yeme Teshuva*) between **Rosh Hashanah** and **Yom Kippur**.

Proclamation of a People

The opening of the **Day of Atonement** is proclaimed by the whole congregation at the evening service on the ninth of Tishri. All are standing in front of the Ark of the Law, from which the scrolls have been taken out. Two respected "pillars" of the community hold them up on either side of the rabbi. An eighth-century Aramaic text is then sung, starting with the words *Kol nidre* ("All vows") to express repentance for all unfulfilled vows, oaths, and promises made to God over the past year. It is read out three times over, so latecomers can hear it too. It is important that no Jews be left out—so much so that, in the Middle Ages, the Roman community added a sentence aimed at the victims of forced conversions to Christianity or to Islam. Many of them would pray in hiding on **Yom Kippur**, but those who dared to come to the synagogue could thus hear these comforting words of solidarity and trust in divine mercy: "We proclaim that it is permitted to pray together with those who have transgressed."

The plaintive medieval melody used for the *Kol nidre* proclamation in the Ashkenazi rite has such wide appeal that it has been taken as the basis for classical compositions by Max Bruch and Arnold Schoenberg. The power of its meaning in the face of the many trials of Jewish people's loyalty to their heritage finds a compelling witness in the German religious thinker and Bible translator Franz Rosenzweig (1886–1929). After an intense discussion with his philosopher colleague Eugen Rosenstock (also born a Jew) through the night of July 7, 1913 in Leipzig, he decided to take the same step his friend already had and convert to Protestantism. However, he insisted on going through it not as a pagan, but as a Jew, coming to the consummation of his faith, which he barely knew at this point. On October 11 of that year, to test out his idea, he decided to attend the High Holy Day services at a small Orthodox synagogue in Berlin before undergoing baptism. But the *Kol nidre* got through to him. He came out realizing that, as a Jew, he was already with God and did not need to seek Him elsewhere than within his own heritage, with its keen awareness of human sinfulness and responsibility, of divine love and forgiveness—

central themes of the **Yom Kippur** service. Rosenzweig decided to recover this Jewish tradition for himself and for others like him who had lost touch with it in a Gentile and secular environment. His theology would revolve around the Jewish liturgical cycle and its calendar of festivals as the record of God's revelatory intrusions into human history.

It is true that the **Day of Atonement** is the only one of the Jewish festivals that is not based on a historical event. Yet it does supremely reveal and highlight their common premise: the healing efficacy of the acknowledgment of misdeeds in turning toward God for justice and mercy, both personally and as a community.

See also Akitu; Rosh Hashanah; Sabbath; Sukkot

References
René Girard. *Violence and the Sacred.* Baltimore, MD: Johns Hopkins University Press, 1977.

Mitch and Zhava Glaser. *The Fall Feasts of Israel.* Chicago: Moody Press, 1987.

Philip Goodman. *The Yom Kippur Anthology.* Philadelphia, PA: Jewish Publication Society, 1992.

Jules Harlow, ed. *Mahzor for Rosh Hashanah and Yom Kippur.* New York: Rabbinical Assembly of America, 1972.

Jerusalem Bible. Garden City, NY: Doubleday & Co., 1968.

❯ YOM KIPPUR KATAN
See Rosh Hodesh

❯ YOUNG HERBS (FESTIVAL OF)
See Sekku

❯ YU LAN PEN
See Days of the Dead (China, Korea, Japan)

❯ YUAN SHUO
See New Year (China, Korea)

❯ YUAN XIAO
See Lantern Festival

❯ YUAN ZHENG
See New Year (China, Korea)

❯ YULETIDE
See Christmas

▶ **ZAGMUK**
See Akitu

▶ **ZHONG YUAN JIE**
See Days of the Dead (China, Korea, Japan)

▶ **ZWÖLFER**
See Epiphany

APPENDIXES

APPENDIX I: Main Hindu Festivals and Buddha Day in North India 2001–2031

N.B.: Vikram years are grouped according to the sequence of months dictated by the irregular presence and varying location of an intercalary lunar month (Adhik Maas) in this lunisolar calendar.

HINDU FESTIVALS	Vikram Year: 2057 Gregorian Year: 2001		Vikram Year: 2076 Gregorian Year: 2020	
Vasant Panchami	Monday	29-01-2001	Thursday	30-01-2020
Mahashivaratri	Wednesday	21-02-2001	Saturday	22-02-2020
Holi	Friday	09-03-2001	Tuesday	10-03-2020
Hindu New Year	Monday	26-03-2001	Wednesday	25-03-2020
Ramayana Week	Monday	26-03-2001	Wednesday	25-03-2020
To	Monday	02-04-2001	Thursday	02-04-2020
Ramanavami	Monday	02-04-2001	Thursday	02-04-2020
Raksha Bandhan	Saturday	04-08-2001	Monday	03-08-2020
Krishna Janmashtami	Sunday	12-08-2001	Wednesday	12-08-2020
Ganesha Chaturthi	Wednesday	22-08-2001	Saturday	22-08-2020
Pitripaksha	Sunday	02-09-2001	Thursday	03-09-2020
To	Monday	17-09-2001	Thursday	17-09-2020
ADHIK MAAS EXTRA MONTH	*Lunar*	*Calendar*	*Lunar*	*Calendar*
From	*Tuesday*	*18-09-2001*	*Friday*	*18-09-2020*
To	*Tuesday*	*16-10-2001*	*Friday*	*16-10-2020*
Navaratra	Wednesday	17-10-2001	Saturday	17-10-2020
To	Thursday	25-10-2001	Saturday	24-10-2020
Sarasvati Puja	Thursday	25-10-2001	Thursday	22-10-2020
(forms part of Navaratra)				
Vijay Dashami (Dusshera)	Friday	26-10-2001	Sunday	25-10-2020
Divali	Wednesday	14-11-2001	Saturday	14-11-2020
Vikram New Year	2058 Thursday	15-11-2001	2077 Sunday	15-11-2020
Buddha Day (Vaishakha)	Monday	07-05-2001	Thursday	07-05-2020

(Continued on next page)

(Appendix I Cont.)

HINDU FESTIVALS	Vikram Year: / Gregorian Year:	2058 / 2002	Vikram Year: / Gregorian Year:	2059 / 2003	Vikram Year: / Gregorian Year:	2061 / 2005	Vikram Year: / Gregorian Year:	2062 / 2006
Vasant Panchami	Sunday	17-02-2002	Thursday	06-02-2003	Sunday	13-02-2005	Thursday	02-02-2006
Mahashivaratri	Wednesday	13-03-2002	Saturday	01-03-2003	Tuesday	08-03-2005	Sunday	26-02-2006
Holi	Thursday	28-03-2002	Monday	17-03-2003	Friday	25-03-2005	begins on Tuesday as the Full Moon, celebrations on **Wednesday**	14-03-2006 **15-03-2006**
Hindu New Year	Saturday	13-04-2002	Wednesday	02-04-2003	Saturday	09-04-2005	Thursday	30-03-2006
Ramayana Week	Saturday	13-04-2002	Wednesday	02-04-2003	Saturday	09-04-2005	Thursday	30-03-2006
To	Sunday	21-04-2002	Friday	11-04-2003	Monday	18-04-2005	Thursday	06-04-2006
Ramanavami	Sunday	21-04-2002	Friday	11-04-2003	Monday	18-04-2005	Thursday	06-04-2006
Raksha Bandhan	Thursday	22-08-2002	Tuesday	12-08-2003	Friday	19-08-2005	Wednesday	04-08-2006
Krishna Janmashtami	Friday (Smarta sect)	30-08-2002	Wednesday	20-08-2003	Saturday	27-08-2005	Wednesday	16-08-2006
Krishna Janmashtami	Saturday (Vaishnava)	31-08-2002						
Ganesha Chaturthi	Tuesday	10-09-2002	Sunday	31-08-2003	Wednesday	07-09-2005	Sunday	27-08-2006
Pitripaksha	Saturday	21-09-2002	Wednesday	10-09-2003	Sunday	18-09-2005	Friday	08-09-2006
To	Sunday	06-10-2002	Friday	26-09-2003	Monday	03-10-2005	Friday	22-09-2006
Navaratra	Monday	07-10-2002	Saturday	27-09-2003	Tuesday	04-10-2005	Saturday	23-09-2006
To	Tuesday	15-10-2002	Saturday	04-10-2003	Wednesday	12-10-2005	Sunday	01-10-2006
Sarasvati Puja (forms part of Navaratra)	Sunday	13-10-2002	Thursday	02-10-2003	Tuesday	11-10-2005	**Friday**	**29-09-2006**
Vijay Dashami (Dusshera)	Tuesday	15-10-2002	Sunday	05-10-2003	Wednesday	12-10-2005	Monday	02-10-2006
Divali	Monday	04-11-2002	Saturday	25-10-2003	Tuesday	01-11-2005	Saturday	21-10-2006
Vikram New Year	2059 Tuesday	05-11-2002	2060 Sunday	26-10-2003	2062 Wednesday	02-11-2005	2063 Sunday	22-10-2006
Buddha Day (Vaishakha)	Sunday	26-05-2002	Friday	16-05-2003	Monday	23-05-2005	Saturday	13-05-2006

HINDU FESTIVALS	Vikram Year: 2060 / Gregorian Year: 2004		Vikram Year: 2063 / Gregorian Year: 2007		Vikram Year: 2066 / Gregorian Year: 2010		Vikram Year: 2074 / Gregorian Year: 2018		Vikram Year: 2079 / Gregorian Year: 2023		Vikram Year: 2082 / Gregorian Year: 2026	
Vasant Panchami	Monday	26-01-2004	Tuesday	23-01-2007	Wednesday	20-01-2010	Monday	22-01-2018	Thursday	26-01-2023	Friday	23-01-2026
Mahashivaratri	Wednesday	18-02-2004	Friday	16-02-2007	Friday	12-02-2010	Wednesday	14-02-2018	Sunday	19-02-2023	Monday	16-02-2026
Holi	Saturday	06-03-2004	begins on Saturday as the Full Moon, celebrations on **Sunday**	03-03-2007 **04-03-2007**	begins on Sunday, celebrations on **Monday**	28-02-2010 **01-03-2010**	Friday	02-03-2018	Wednesday	08-03-2023	Tuesday	03-03-2026
Hindu New Year	Sunday	21-03-2004	Monday	19-03-2007	Tuesday	16-03-2010	Sunday	18-03-2018	Wednesday	22-03-2023	Thursday	19-03-2026
Ramayana Week	Sunday	21-03-2004	Monday	19-03-2007	Tuesday	16-03-2010	SundayTo	18-03-2018	Wednesday	22-03-2023	Thursday	19-03-2026
To	Tuesday	30-03-2004	Tuesday	27-03-2007	Wednesday	24-03-2010	Monday	26-03-2018	Thursday	30-03-2023	Friday	27-03-2026
Ramanavami	Tuesday	30-03-2004	Tuesday	27-03-2007	Wednesday	24-03-2010	Monday	26-03-2018	Thursday	30-03-2023	Friday	27-03-2026
ADHIK MAAS EXTRA MONTH	*Lunar*	*Calendar*	*Lunar*	*Calendar*	*Lunar*	*Calendar*	*Lunar*	*Calendar*	*Lunar*	*Calendar*	*Lunar*	*Calendar*
From	*Sunday*	*18-07-2004*	*Thursday*	*17-05-2007*	*Thursday*	*15-04-2010*	*Wednesday*	*16-05-2018*	*Tuesday*	*18-07-2023*	*Sunday*	*17-05-2026*
To	*Monday*	*16-08-2004*	*Friday*	*15-06-2007*	*Friday*	*14-05-2010*	*Wednesday*	*13-06-2018*	*Wednesday*	*16-08-2023*	*Monday*	*15-06-2026*
Raksha Bandhan	Monday	30-08-2004	Tuesday	28-08-2007	Tuesday	24-08-2010	Sunday	26-08-2018	Wednesday	30-08-2023	Thursday	27-08-2026
Krishna Janmashtami	Monday	06-09-2004	Tuesday	04-09-2007	Thursday	02-09-2010	Monday	03-09-2018	Thursday	07-09-2023	Friday	04-09-2026
Ganesha Chaturthl	Saturday	18-09-2004	Saturday	15-09-2007	Saturday	11-09-2010	Thursday	13-09-2018	Tuesday	19-09-2023	Monday	14-09-2026
Pitripaksha	Tuesday	28-09-2004	Thursday	27-09-2007	Friday	24-09-2010	Tuesday	25-09-2018	Saturday	30-09-2023	Sunday	27-09-2026
To	Wednesday	13-10-2004	Thursday	11-10-2007	Thursday	07-10-2010	Monday	08-10-2018	Saturday	14-10-2023	Saturday	10-10-2026
Navaratra	Thursday	14-10-2004	Friday	12-10-2007	Friday	08-10-2010	Tuesday	09-10-2018	Sunday	15-10-2023	Sunday	11-10-2026
To	Friday	22-10-2004	Saturday	20-10-2007	Saturday	16-10-2010	Thursday	18-10-2018	Monday	23-10-2023	Tuesday	20-10-2026
Sarasvati Puja (forms part of Navaratra)	Thursday / Friday	21-10-2004 22-10-2004	**Thursday** / Friday	**18-10-2007** 19-10-2007	**Thursday** / Friday	**14-10-2010** 15-10-2010	Tuesday	16-10-2018	Saturday	21-10-2023	Sunday	18-10-2026
Vijay Dashami Dusshera	Friday	22-10-2004	Sunday	21-10-2007	Sunday	17-10-2010	Friday	19-10-2018	Tuesday	24-10-2023	Wednesday	21-10-2026
Divali	Friday	12-11-2004	Friday	09-11-2007	Friday	05-11-2010	Wednesday	07-11-2018	Sunday	12-11-2023	Sunday	08-11-2026
Vikram New Year	2061 Saturday	13-11-2004	2064 Saturday	10-11-2007	2067 Saturday	06-11-2010	2075 Thursday	08-11-2018	2080 Monday	13-11-2023	2083 Monday	09-11-2026
Buddha Day (Vaishakha)	Tuesday	04-05-2004	Wednesday	02-05-2007	Thursday	27-05-2010	Sunday	29-04-2018	Friday	05-05-2023	Friday	01-05-2026

(Continued on next page)

(Appendix I Cont.)

HINDU FESTIVALS	Vikram Year: 2064 Gregorian Year: 2008		Vikram Year: 2065 Gregorian Year: 2009		Vikram Year: 2067 Gregorian Year: 2011	
Vasant Panchami	11-02-2008	Monday	31-01-2009	Saturday	08-02-2011	Tuesday
Mahashivaratri	06-03-2008	Thursday	23-02-2009	Monday	03-03-2011	Thursday
Holi	21-03-2008 **22-03-2008**	begins on Friday as the Full Moon, celebrations on **Saturday**	11-03-2009	Wednesday	19-03-2011 **20-03-2011**	begins on Saturday, celebrations on **Sunday**
Hindu New Year	06-04-2008	Sunday	27-03-2009	Friday	04-04-2011	Monday
Ramayana Week	06-04-2008	Sunday	27-03-2009	Friday	04-04-2011	Monday
To	14-04-2008	Monday	03-04-2009	Friday	12-04-2011	Tuesday
Ramanavami	14-04-2008	Monday	03-04-2009	Friday	12-04-2011	Tuesday
Raksha Bandhan	16-08-2008	Saturday	05-08-2009	Wednesday	13-08-2011	Saturday
Krishna Janmashtami	24-08-2008	Sunday	14-08-2009	Friday	22-08-2011	Monday
Ganesha Chaturthi	03-09-2008	Wednesday	23-08-2009	Sunday	01-09-2011	Thursday
Pitripaksha	16-09-2008	Tuesday	05-09-2009	Saturday	13-09-2011	Tuesday
To	29-09-2008	Monday	18-09-2009	Friday	27-09-2011	Tuesday
Navaratra	30-09-2008	Tuesday	19-09-2009	Saturday	28-09-2011	Wednesday
To	08-10-2008	Wednesday	27-09-2009	Sunday	05-10-2011	Wednesday
Sarasvati Puja	**06-10-2008**	**Monday**	**25-09-2009**	**Friday**	**03-10-2011**	**Monday**
(forms part of Navaratra)	07-10-2008	Tuesday	26-09-2009	Saturday	04-10-2011	Tuesday
Vijay Dashami (Dusshera)	09-10-2008	Thursday	28-09-2009	Monday	06-10-2011	Thursday
Divali	28-10-2008	Tuesday	17-10-2009	Saturday	26-10-2011	Wednesday
Vikram New Year	29-10-2008	2065 Wednesday	18-10-2009	2066 Sunday	27-10-2011	2068 Thursday
Buddha Day (Vaishakha)	19-05-2008	Monday	08-05-2009	Friday	17-05-2011	Tuesday

HINDU FESTIVALS	Vikram Year: Gregorian Year:	2068 2012	Vikram Year: Gregorian Year:	2087 2031
Vasant Panchami	Saturday	28-01-2012	Monday	27-01-2031
Mahashivaratri	Monday	20-02-2012	Thursday	20-02-2031
Holi	Thursday	08-03-2012	begins on Saturday, celebrations on Sunday	09-03-2031
Hindu New Year	Friday	23-03-2012	Sunday	23-03-2031
Ramayana Week	Friday	23-03-2012	Sunday	23-03-2031
To	Sunday	01-04-2012	Monday	01-04-2031
Ramanavami	Sunday	01-04-2012	Monday	01-04-2031
Raksha Bandhan	Thursday	02-08-2012	Saturday	02-08-2031
Krishna Janmashtami	Friday	10-08-2012	Sunday	10-08-2031
ADHIK MAAS EXTRA MONTH	*Lunar*	*Calendar*	*Lunar*	*Calendar*
From	*Saturday*	*18-08-2012*	*Tuesday*	*19-08-2031*
To	*Sunday*	*16-09-2012*	*Tuesday*	*16-09-2031*
Ganesha Chaturthi	Wednesday	19-09-2012	Saturday	20-09-2031
Pitripaksha	Sunday	30-09-2012	Wednesday	01-10-2031
To	Monday	15-10-2012	Thursday	16-10-2031
Navaratra	Tuesday	16-10-2012	Friday	17-10-2031
To	Tuesday	23-10-2012	Friday	24-10-2031
Sarasvati Puja (forms part of Navaratra)	Sunday	21-10-2012	Wednesday	22-10-2031
Vijay Dashami (Dusshera)	Wednesday	24-10-2012	Saturday	25-10-2031
Divali	Tuesday	13-11-2012	Friday	14-11-2031
Vikram New Year	**2069** Wednesday	14-11-2012	**2088** Saturday	15-11-2031
Buddha Day (Vaishakha)	Sunday 06-05-2012 or Saturday 05-05-2012		Tuesday	06-05-2031

(*Continued on next page*)

HINDU FESTIVALS	Vikram Year: 2069 / Gregorian Year: 2013		Vikram Year: 2070 / Gregorian Year: 2014		Vikram Year: 2071 / Gregorian Year: 2015		Vikram Year: 2072 / Gregorian Year: 2016		Vikram Year: 2073 / Gregorian Year: 2017	
Vasant Panchami	Friday	15-02-2013	Tuesday	04-02-2014	Saturday	24-01-2015	Friday	12-02-2016	Wednesday	01-02-2017
Mahashivaratri	Sunday	10-03-2013	Friday	28-02-2014	Tuesday	17-02-2015	Tuesday	08-03-2016	Saturday	25-02-2017
Holi	Wednesday	27-03-2013	Monday	17-03-2014	Friday	06-03-2015	Wednesday	23-03-2016	Monday	13-03-2017
Hindu New Year	Thursday	11-04-2013	Monday	31-03-2014	Saturday	21-03-2015	Friday	08-04-2016	Tuesday	28-03-2017
Ramayana Week	Thursday	11-04-2013	Monday	31-03-2014	Saturday	21-03-2015	Friday	08-04-2016	Tuesday	28-03-2017
To	Saturday	20-04-2013	Tuesday	08-04-2014	Saturday	28-03-2015	Friday	15-04-2016	Wednesday	05-04-2017
Ramanavami	Saturday	20-04-2013	Tuesday	08-04-2014	Saturday	28-03-2015	Friday	15-04-2016	Wednesday	05-04-2017
Raksha Bandhan	Wednesday / Tuesday	21-08-2013 / 20-08-2013	Sunday	10-08-2014	Sunday	29-08-2015	Thursday	18-08-2016	Monday	07-08-2017
Krishna Janmashtami	Wednesday	28-08-2013	Sunday	17-08-2014	Saturday	05-09-2015	Thursday	25-08-2016	Tuesday	15-08-2017
Ganesha Chaturthi	Monday	09-09-2013	Friday	29-08-2014	Thursday	17-09-2015	Monday	05-09-2016	Friday	25-08-2017
Pitripaksha	Friday	20-09-2013	Tuesday	09-09-2014	Monday	28-09-2015	Saturday	17-09-2016	Thursday	07-09-2017
To	Friday	04-10-2013	Wednesday	24-09-2014	Monday	12-10-2015	Friday	30-09-2016	Wednesday	20-09-2017
Navaratra	Saturday	05-10-2013	Thursday	25-09-2014	Tuesday	13-10-2015	Saturday	01-10-2016	Thursday	21-09-2017
To	Sunday	13-10-2013	Friday	03-10-2014	Wednesday	21-10-2015	Monday	10-10-2016	Friday	29-09-2017
Sarasvati Puja (forms part of Navaratra)	Friday	11-10-2013	Wednesday	01-10-2014	Tuesday	20-10-2015	Saturday	08-10-2016	Wednesday	27-09-2017
Vijay Dashami (Dusshera)	Monday	14-10-2013	Saturday	04-10-2014	Thursday	22-10-2015	Tuesday	11-10-2016	Saturday	30-09-2017
Divali	Sunday	03-11-2013	Thursday	23-10-2014	Wednesday	11-11-2015	Sunday	30-10-2016	Thursday	19-10-2017
Vikram New Year	2070 Monday	04-11-2013	2071 Friday	24-10-2014	2072 Thursday	12-11-2015	2073 Monday	31-10-2016	2074 Friday	20-10-2017
Buddha Day (Vaishakha)	Saturday	25-05-2013	Wednesday	14-05-2014	Sunday	03-05-2015	Saturday	21-05-2016	Wednesday	10-05-2017

HINDU FESTIVALS	Vikram Year: 2075 Gregorian Year: 2019		Vikram Year: 2077 Gregorian Year: 2021		Vikram Year: 2078 Gregorian Year: 2022		Vikram Year: 2080 Gregorian Year: 2024		Vikram Year 2081 Gregorian Year: 2025	
Vasant Panchami	10-02-2019	Sunday	16-02-2021	Tuesday	05-02-2022	Saturday	14-02-2024	Wednesday	02-02-2025	Sunday
Mahashivaratri	05-03-2019	Tuesday	12-03-2021	Friday	01-03-2022	Tuesday	09-03-2024	Saturday	26-02-2025	Wednesday
Holi	21-03-2019	Thursday	29-03-2021	Monday	18-03-2022	Friday	25-03-2024	Monday	14-03-2025	Friday
Hindu New Year	06-04-2019	Saturday	13-04-2021	Tuesday	02-04-2022	Saturday	09-04-2024	Tuesday	30-03-2025	Sunday
Ramayana Week	06-04-2019	Saturday	13-04-2021	Tuesday	02-04-2022	Saturday	09-04-2024	TuesdayTo	30-03-2025	Sunday
To	14-04-2019	Sunday	21-04-2021	Wednesday	10-04-2022	Sunday	17-04-2024	Wednesday	06-04-2025	Sunday
Ramanavami	14-04-2019	Sunday	21-04-2021	Wednesday	10-04-2022	Sunday	17-04-2024	Wednesday	06-04-2025	Sunday
Raksha Bandhan	15-08-2019	Thursday	22-08-2021	Sunday	11-08-2022	Thursday	19-08-2024	Monday	09-08-2025	Saturday
Krishna Janmashtami	23-08-2019 24-08-2019	Friday (Smarta) Saturday	30-08-2021	Monday	19-08-2022	Friday	26-08-2024	Monday	16-08-2025	Saturday
Ganesha Chaturthi	02-09-2019	Monday	10-09-2021	Friday	31-08-2022	Wednesday	07-09-2024	Saturday	27-08-2025	Wednesday
Pitripaksha	14-09-2019	Saturday	21-09-2021	Tuesday	11-09-2022	Sunday	18-09-2024	Wednesday	08-09-2025	Monday
To	28-09-2019	Saturday	06-10-2021	Wednesday	25-09-2022	Sunday	02-10-2024	Wednesday	21-09-2025	Sunday
Navaratra	29-09-2019	Sunday	07-10-2021	Thursday	26-09-2022	Monday	03-10-2024	Thursday	22-09-2025	Monday
To	07-10-2019	Monday	14-10-2021	Thursday	04-10-2022	Tuesday	12-10-2024	Saturday	01-10-2025	Wednesday
Sarasvati Puja (part of Navaratra)	05-10-2019	Saturday	12-10-2021	Tuesday	02-10-2022	Sunday	10-10-2024	Thursday	29-09-2025	Monday
Vijay Dashami (Dusshera)	08-10-2019	Tuesday	15-10-2021	Friday	05-10-2022	Wednesday	13-10-2024	Sunday	02-10-2025	Thursday
Divali	27-10-2019	Sunday	04-11-2021	Thursday	24-10-2022	Monday	01-11-2024	Friday	21-10-2025	Tuesday
Vikram New Year	28-10-2019	2076 Monday	05-11-2021	2078 Friday	25-10-2022	2079 Tuesday	02-11-2024	2081 Saturday	22-10-2025	2082 Wednesday
Buddha Day (Vaishakha)	18-05-2019	Saturday	26-05-2021	Wednesday	16-05-2022	Monday	23-05-2024	Thursday	12-05-2025	Monday

(Continued on next page)

HINDU FESTIVALS	Vikram Year:	2085	
	Gregorian Year:	2029	
Vasant Panchami	Friday	19-01-2029	
Mahashivaratri	Sunday	11-02-2029	
Holi	Thursday	01-03-2029	
ADHIK MAAS EXTRA MONTH	*Lunar*	*Calendar*	
From	Friday	16-03-2029	
To	Friday	13-04-2029	
Hindu New Year	Saturday	14-04-2029	
Ramayana Week	Saturday	14-04-2029	
To	Monday	23-04-2029	
Ramanavami	Monday	23-04-2029	
Raksha Bandhan	Thursday	23-08-2029	
Krishna Janmashtami	Saturday	01-09-2029	
Ganesha Chaturthi	Tuesday	11-09-2029	
Pitripaksha	Sunday	23-09-2029	
To	Sunday	07-10-2029	
Navaratra	Monday	08-10-2029	
To	Monday	15-10-2029	
Sarasvati Puja (forms part of Navaratra)	Saturday	13-10-2029	
Vijay Dashami (Dusshera)	Tuesday	16-10-2029	
Divali	Monday	05-11-2029	
Vikram New Year	**2086** Tuesday	06-11-2029	
Buddha Day (Vaishakha)	Sunday	27-05-2029	

HINDU FESTIVALS	Vikram Year: Gregorian Year:	2083 2027	Vikram Year: Gregorian Year:	2084 2028	Vikram Year: Gregorian Year:	2086 2030
Vasant Panchami	Thursday	11-02-2027	Monday	31-01-2028	Thursday	07-02-2030
Mahashivaratri	Saturday	06-03-2027	Wednesday	23-02-2028	Saturday	02-03-2030
Holi	Monday	22-03-2027	Saturday	11-03-2028	Wednesday	20-03-2030
Hindu New Year	Wednesday	07-04-2027	Monday	27-03-2028	Wednesday	03-04-2030
Ramayana Week	Wednesday	07-04-2027	Monday	27-03-2028	Wednesday	03-04-2030
To	Thursday	15-04-2027	Monday	03-04-2028	Friday	12-04-2030
Ramanavami	Thursday	15-04-2027	Monday	03-04-2028	Friday	12-04-2030
Raksha Bandhan	Tuesday	17-08-2027	Saturday	05-08-2028	Tuesday	13-08-2030
Krishna Janmashtami	Wednesday	25-08-2027	Sunday	13-08-2028	Wednesday	21-08-2030
Ganesha Chaturthi	Saturday	04-09-2027	Wednesday	23-08-2028	Sunday	01-09-2030
Pitripaksha	Thursday	16-09-2027	Monday	04-09-2028	Thursday	12-09-2030
To	Wednesday	29-09-2027	Monday	18-09-2028	Friday	27-09-2030
Navaratra	Thursday	30-09-2027	Tuesday	19-09-2028	Saturday	28-09-2030
To	Friday	08-10-2027	Tuesday	26-09-2028	Saturday	05-10-2030
Sarasvati Puja (forms part of Navaratra)	Wednesday	06-10-2027	Sunday	24-09-2028	Thursday	03-10-2030
Vijay Dashami (Dusshera)	Saturday	09-10-2027	Wednesday	27-09-2028	Sunday	06-10-2030
Divali	Friday	29-10-2027	Tuesday	17-10-2028	Saturday	26-10-2030
Vikram New Year	2084 Saturday	30-10-2027	2085 Wednesday	18-10-2028	2087 Sunday	27-10-2030
Buddha Day (Vaishakha)	Thursday	20-05-2027	Monday	08-05-2028	Friday	17-05-2030

These tables are based on those appearing on the award-winning website hinduism.co.za (http://www.hinduism.co.za/newpage3.htm), first published on the Internet on June 24, 1998.

APPENDIX II: Main Muslim Festivals 2001–2050

A.H.	Day of the Hegira	Ashura	Mawlid	Ramadan	Eid-al-Fitr	Eid-al-Adha
1422	26-03-2001	05-04-2001	05-06-2001	17-11-2001	17-12-2001	25-02-2002
1423	15-03-2002	25-03-2002	25-05-2002	06-11-2002	06-12-2002	13-02-2003
1424	05-03-2003	15-03-2003	15-05-2003	27-10-2003	26-11-2003	03-02-2004
1425	22-02-2004	03-03-2004	03-05-2004	15-10-2004	14-11-2004	22-01-2005
1426	10-02-2005	20-02-2005	22-04-2005	04-10-2005	03-11-2005	11-01-2006
1427	31-01-2006	10-02-2006	12-04-2006	24-09-2006	24-10-2006	01-01-2007
1428	20-01-2007	30-01-2007	01-04-2007	13-09-2007	13-10-2007	21-12-2007
1429	10-01-2008	20-01-2008	21-03-2008	02-09-2008	02-10-2008	10-12-2008
1430	29-12-2008	08-01-2009	10-03-2009	22-08-2009	21-09-2009	29-11-2009
1431	18-12-2009	28-12-2009	27-02-2010	11-08-2010	10-09-2010	18-11-2010
1432	07-12-2010	17-12-2010	17-02-2011	01-08-2011	31-08-2011	08-11-2011
1433	26-11-2011	06-12-2011	06-02-2012	20-07-2012	19-08-2012	27-10-2012
1434	15-11-2012	25-11-2012	25-01-2013	09-07-2013	08-08-2013	16-10-2013
1435	04-11-2013	14-11-2013	15-01-2014	29-06-2014	29-07-2014	06-10-2014
1436	25-10-2014	04-11-2014	04-01-2015	18-06-2015	18-07-2015	25-09-2015
1437	15-10-2015	25-10-2015	25-12-2015	07-06-2016	07-07-2016	14-09-2016
1438	03-10-2016	13-10-2016	13-12-2016	27-05-2017	26-06-2017	03-09-2017
1439	22-09-2017	02-10-2017	02-12-2017	16-05-2018	15-06-2018	23-08-2018
1440	12-09-2018	22-09-2018	22-11-2018	06-05-2019	05-06-2019	13-08-2019
1441	01-09-2019	11-09-2019	11-11-2019	24-04-2020	24-05-2020	01-08-2020
1442	20-08-2020	30-08-2020	30-10-2020	13-04-2021	13-05-2021	21-07-2021
1443	10-08-2021	20-08-2021	20-10-2021	03-04-2022	03-05-2022	11-07-2022
1444	30-07-2022	09-08-2022	09-10-2022	23-03-2023	22-04-2023	30-06-2023
1445	19-07-2023	29-07-2023	28-09-2023	11-03-2024	10-04-2024	18-06-2024
1446	08-07-2024	18-07-2024	17-09-2024	01-03-2025	31-03-2025	08-06-2025
1447	27-06-2025	07-07-2025	06-09-2025	18-02-2026	20-03-2026	28-05-2026
1448	17-06-2026	27-06-2026	27-08-2026	08-02-2027	10-03-2027	18-05-2027
1449	07-06-2027	17-06-2027	16-08-2027	28-01-2028	27-02-2028	07-05-2028
1450	25-05-2028	04-06-2028	04-08-2028	16-01-2029	15-02-2029	25-04-2029
1451	15-05-2029	25-05-2029	25-07-2029	06-01-2030	05-02-2030	15-04-2030
1452	04-05-2030	14-05-2030	14-07-2030	26-12-2030	25-01-2031	04-04-2031
1453	23-04-2031	03-05-2031	03-07-2031	15-12-2031	14-01-2032	23-03-2032
1454	12-04-2032	22-04-2032	22-06-2032	04-12-2032	03-01-2033	13-03-2033
1455	01-04-2033	11-04-2033	11-06-2033	23-11-2033	23-12-2033	02-03-2034
1456	21-03-2034	31-03-2034	31-05-2034	12-11-2034	12-12-2034	19-02-2035
1457	11-03-2035	21-03-2035	21-05-2035	02-11-2035	02-12-2035	09-02-2036
1458	28-02-2036	09-03-2036	09-05-2036	21-10-2036	20-11-2036	28-01-2037
1459	17-02-2037	27-02-2037	29-04-2037	11-10-2037	10-11-2037	18-01-2038
1460	06-02-2038	16-02-2038	18-04-2038	30-09-2038	30-10-2038	07-01-2039
1461	26-01-2039	05-02-2039	07-04-2039	19-09-2039	19-10-2039	27-12-2039
1462	16-01-2040	26-01-2040	27-03-2040	08-09-2040	08-10-2040	16-12-2040
1463	04-01-2041	14-01-2041	16-03-2041	28-08-2041	27-09-2041	05-12-2041
1464	24-12-2041	03-01-2042	05-03-2042	17-08-2042	16-09-2042	24-11-2042
1465	14-12-2042	24-12-2042	23-02-2043	07-08-2043	06-09-2043	14-11-2043
1466	03-12-2043	13-12-2043	12-02-2044	26-07-2044	25-08-2044	02-11-2044
1467	22-11-2044	02-12-2044	01-02-2045	16-07-2045	15-08-2045	23-10-2045
1468	11-11-2045	21-11-2045	21-01-2046	05-07-2046	04-08-2046	12-10-2046
1469	31-10-2046	10-11-2046	10-01-2047	24-06-2047	24-07-2047	01-10-2047
1470	21-10-2047	31-10-2047	31-12-2047	13-06-2048	13-07-2048	20-09-2048
1471	09-10-2048	19-10-2048	19-12-2048	02-06-2049	02-07-2049	09-09-2049
1472	28-09-2049	08-10-2049	07-12-2049	22-05-2050	21-06-2050	28-08-2050
1473	17-09-2050	27-09-2050	27-11-2050	12-05-2051	10-06-2051	08-08-2051

Dates of Mi'raj 1997–2020: 28 Nov 1997; 17 Nov 1998; 06 Nov 1999; 26 Oct 2000; 15 Oct 2001; 04 Oct 2002; 24 Sep 2003; 12 Sep 2004; 01 Sep 2005; 22 Aug 2006; 11 Aug 2007; 31 Jul 2008; 20 Jul 2009; 09 Jul 2010; 28 Jun 2011; 17 Jun 2012; 06 Jun 2013; 27 May 2014; 16 May 2015; 05 May 2016; 24 Apr 2017; 13 Apr 2018; 03 Apr 2019; 22 Mar 2020. The dates of Mi'raj are taken from the web page http://www.holidayfestival.com/Islam.html (© Brian Prescott-Decie, 1998, 1999), last modified on Sunday, 28 April, 2002. Other dates, except for corrections, are taken from the table provided in Michel Coireault, *Les Fêtes. Judaïsme, Christianisme, Islam*. Paris: Éditions du Cerf, 1994, pp. 192–195.

APPENDIX III: Main Jewish Holidays in Israel 2001–2050

JEWISH HOLIDAYS	5762/2001–02	5763/2002–03	5764/2003–04	5765/2004–05	5766/2005–06	5767/2006–07	5768/2007–08	5769/2008–09	5770/2009–10	5771/2010–11
Rosh Hashanah	18-09-2001	07-09-2002	27-09-2003	16-09-2004	04-10-2005	23-09-2006	13-09-2007	30-09-2008	19-09-2009	09-09-2010
Yom Kippur	27-09-2001	16-09-2002	06-10-2003	25-09-2004	13-10-2005	02-10-2006	22-09-2007	09-10-2008	28-09-2009	18-09-2010
Sukkot	02-10-2001	21-09-2002	11-10-2003	30-09-2004	18-10-2005	07-10-2006	27-09-2007	14-10-2008	03-10-2009	23-09-2010
To	07-10-2001	26-09-2002	16-10-2003	05-10-2004	23-10-2005	12-10-2006	02-10-2007	19-10-2008	08-10-2009	28-09-2010
Hoshana Rabba	08-10-2001	27-09-2002	17-10-2003	06-10-2004	24-10-2005	13-10-2006	03-10-2007	20-10-2008	09-10-2009	29-09-2010
Simhat Torah	09-10-2001	28-09-2002	18-10-2003	07-10-2004	25-10-2005	14-10-2006	04-10-2007	21-10-2008	10-10-2009	30-09-2010
Hanukkah	10-12-2001	30-11-2002	20-12-2003	08-12-2004	26-12-2005	16-12-2006	05-12-2007	22-12-2008	12-12-2009	02-12-2010
To	17-12-2001	07-12-2002	27-12-2003	15-12-2004	02-01-2006	23-12-2006	12-12-2007	29-12-2008	19-12-2009	09-12-2010
Purim	26-02-2002	18-03-2003	07-03-2004	25-03-2005	14-03-2006	04-03-2007	21-03-2008	10-03-2009	28-02-2010	20-03-2011
To	27-02-2002	19-03-2003	08-03-2004	26-03-2005	15-03-2006	05-03-2007	22-03-2008	11-03-2009	01-03-2010	21-03-2011
Passover	28-03-2002	17-04-2003	06-04-2004	24-04-2005	13-04-2006	03-04-2007	20-04-2008	09-04-2009	30-03-2010	19-04-2011
Shavuot	17-05-2002	06-06-2003	26-05-2004	13-06-2005	02-06-2006	23-05-2007	09-06-2008	29-05-2009	19-05-2010	08-06-2011

JEWISH HOLIDAYS	5772/2011–12	5773/2012–13	5774/2013–14	5775/2014–15	5776/2015–16	5777/2016–17	5778/2017–18	5779/2018–19	5780/2019–20	5781/2020–21
Rosh Hashanah	29-09-2011	17-09-2012	05-09-2013	25-09-2014	14-09-2015	03-10-2016	21-09-2017	10-09-2018	30-09-2019	19-09-2020
Yom Kippur	08-10-2011	26-09-2012	14-09-2013	04-10-2014	23-09-2015	12-10-2016	30-09-2017	19-09-2018	09-10-2019	28-09-2020
Sukkot	13-10-2011	01-10-2012	19-09-2013	09-10-2014	28-09-2015	17-10-2016	05-10-2017	24-09-2018	14-10-2019	03-10-2020
To	18-10-2011	06-10-2012	24-09-2013	14-10-2014	03-10-2015	22-10-2016	10-10-2017	29-09-2018	19-10-2019	08-10-2020
Hoshana Rabba	19-10-2011	07-10-2012	25-09-2013	15-10-2014	04-10-2015	23-10-2016	11-10-2017	30-09-2018	20-10-2019	09-10-2020
Simhat Torah	20-10-2011	08-10-2012	26-09-2013	16-10-2014	05-10-2015	24-10-2016	12-10-2017	01-10-2018	21-10-2019	10-10-2020
Hanukkah	21-12-2011	09-12-2012	28-11-2013	17-12-2014	07-12-2015	25-12-2016	13-12-2017	03-12-2018	23-12-2019	11-12-2020
To	28-12-2011	16-12-2012	05-12-2013	24-12-2014	14-12-2015	01-01-2017	20-12-2017	10-12-2018	30-12-2019	18-12-2020
Purim	08-03-2012	24-02-2013	16-03-2014	05-03-2015	24-03-2016	12-03-2017	01-03-2018	21-03-2019	10-03-2020	26-02-2021
To	09-03-2012	25-02-2013	17-03-2014	06-03-2015	25-03-2016	13-03-2017	02-03-2018	22-03-2019	11-03-2020	27-02-2021
Passover	07-04-2012	26-03-2013	15-04-2014	04-04-2015	23-04-2016	11-04-2017	31-03-2018	20-04-2019	09-04-2020	28-03-2021
Shavuot	27-05-2012	15-05-2013	04-06-2014	24-05-2015	12-06-2016	31-05-2017	20-05-2018	09-06-2019	29-05-2020	17-05-2021

(Continued on next page)

(Appendix III Cont.)

JEWISH HOLIDAYS	5782/2021-22	5783/2022-23	5784/2023-24	5785/2024-25	5786/2025-26	5787/2026-27	5788/2027-28	5789/2028-29	5790/2029-30	5791/2030-31
Rosh Hashanah	07-09-2021	26-09-2022	16-09-2023	03-10-2024	23-09-2025	12-09-2026	02-10-2027	21-09-2028	10-09-2029	28-09-2030
Yom Kippur	16-09-2021	05-10-2022	25-09-2023	12-10-2024	02-10-2025	21-09-2026	11-10-2027	30-09-2028	19-09-2029	07-10-2030
Sukkot	21-09-2021	10-10-2022	30-09-2023	17-10-2024	07-10-2025	26-09-2026	16-10-2027	05-10-2028	24-09-2029	12-10-2030
To	26-09-2021	15-10-2022	05-10-2023	22-10-2024	12-10-2025	01-10-2026	21-10-2027	10-10-2028	29-09-2029	17-10-2030
Hoshana Rabba	27-09-2021	16-10-2022	06-10-2023	23-10-2024	13-10-2025	02-10-2026	22-10-2027	11-10-2028	30-09-2029	18-10-2030
Simhat Torah	29-09-2021	18-10-2022	08-10-2023	25-10-2024	15-10-2025	04-10-2026	24-10-2027	13-10-2028	02-10-2029	20-10-2030
Hanukkah	29-11-2021	19-12-2022	08-12-2023	26-12-2024	15-12-2025	05-12-2026	25-12-2027	13-12-2028	02-12-2029	21-12-2030
To	06-12-2021	26-12-2022	15-12-2023	02-01-2025	22-12-2025	12-12-2026	01-01-2028	20-12-2028	09-12-2029	28-12-2030
Purim	17-03-2022	07-03-2023	24-03-2024	14-03-2025	03-03-2026	23-03-2027	12-03-2028	01-03-2029	19-03-2030	09-03-2031
To	18-03-2022	08-03-2023	25-03-2024	15-03-2025	04-03-2026	24-03-2027	13-03-2028	02-03-2029	20-03-2030	10-03-2031
Passover	16-04-2022	06-04-2023	23-04-2024	13-04-2025	02-04-2026	22-04-2027	11-04-2028	31-03-2029	18-04-2030	08-04-2031
Shavuot	05-06-2022	26-05-2023	12-06-2024	02-06-2025	22-05-2026	11-06-2027	31-05-2028	20-05-2029	07-06-2030	28-05-2031

JEWISH HOLIDAYS	5792/2031-32	5793/2032-33	5794/2033-34	5795/2034-35	5796/2035-36	5797/2036-37	5798/2037-38	5799/2038-39	5800/2039-40	5801/2040-41
Rosh Hashanah	18-09-2031	06-09-2032	24-09-2033	14-09-2034	04-10-2035	22-09-2036	10-09-2037	30-09-2038	19-09-2039	08-09-2040
Yom Kippur	27-09-2031	15-09-2032	03-10-2033	23-09-2034	13-10-2035	01-10-2036	19-09-2037	09-10-2038	28-09-2039	17-09-2040
Sukkot	02-10-2031	20-09-2032	08-10-2033	28-09-2034	18-10-2035	06-10-2036	24-09-2037	14-10-2038	03-10-2039	22-09-2040
To	07-10-2031	25-09-2032	13-10-2033	03-10-2034	23-10-2035	11-10-2036	29-09-2037	19-10-2038	08-10-2039	27-09-2040
Hoshana Rabba	08-10-2031	26-09-2032	14-10-2033	04-10-2034	24-10-2035	12-10-2036	30-09-2037	20-10-2038	09-10-2039	28-09-2040
Simhat Torah	10-10-2031	28-09-2032	16-10-2033	06-10-2034	26-10-2035	14-10-2036	02-10-2037	22-10-2038	11-10-2039	30-09-2040
Hanukkah	10-12-2031	28-11-2032	17-12-2033	07-12-2034	26-12-2035	14-12-2036	03-12-2037	22-12-2038	12-12-2039	30-11-2040
To	17-12-2031	05-12-2032	24-12-2033	14-12-2034	02-01-2036	21-12-2036	10-12-2037	29-12-2038	19-12-2039	07-12-2040
Purim	26-02-2032	15-03-2033	05-03-2034	25-03-2035	13-03-2036	01-03-2037	21-03-2038	10-03-2039	28-02-2040	18-03-2041
To	27-02-2032	16-03-2033	06-03-2034	26-03-2035	14-03-2036	02-03-2037	22-03-2038	11-03-2039	29-02-2040	19-03-2041
Passover	27-03-2032	14-04-2033	04-04-2034	24-04-2035	12-04-2036	31-03-2037	20-04-2038	09-04-2039	29-03-2040	17-04-2041
Shavuot	16-05-2032	03-06-2033	24-05-2034	13-06-2035	01-06-2036	20-05-2037	09-06-2038	29-05-2039	18-05-2040	06-06-2041

JEWISH HOLIDAYS	5802/2041–42	5803/2042–43	5804/2043–44	5805/2044–45	5806/2045–46	5807/2046–47	5808/2047–48	5809/2048–49	5810/2049–50	5811/2050–51
Rosh Hashanah	26-09-2041	15-09-2042	05-10-2043	22-09-2044	12-09-2045	01-10-2046	21-09-2047	08-09-2048	27-09-2049	17-09-2050
Yom Kippur	05-10-2041	24-09-2042	14-10-2043	01-10-2044	21-09-2045	10-10-2046	30-09-2047	17-09-2048	06-10-2049	26-09-2050
Sukkot	10-10-2041	29-09-2042	19-10-2043	06-10-2044	26-09-2045	15-10-2046	05-10-2047	22-09-2048	11-10-2049	01-10-2050
To	15-10-2041	04-10-2042	24-10-2043	11-10-2044	01-10-2045	20-10-2046	10-10-2047	27-09-2048	16-10-2049	06-10-2050
Hoshana Rabba	16-10-2041	05-10-2042	25-10-2043	12-10-2044	24-10-2045	21-10-2046	11-11-2047	28-09-2048	17-10-2049	07-10-2050
Simhat Torah	18-10-2041	07-10-2042	27-10-2043	14-10-2044	04-10-2045	23-10-2046	13-10-2047	30-09-2048	19-10-2049	09-10-2050
Hanukkah	18-12-2041	08-12-2042	27-12-2043	15-12-2044	04-12-2045	24-12-2046	14-12-2047	30-11-2048	20-12-2049	10-12-2050
To	25-12-2041	15-12-2042	03-01-2044	22-12-2044	11-12-2045	31-12-2046	20-12-2047	07-12-2048	27-12-2049	17-12-2050
Purim	17-03-2042	06-03-2043	26-03-2044	13-03-2045	03-03-2046	22-03-2047	12-03-2048	28-02-2049	18-03-2050	08-02-2051
To	18-03-2042	07-03-2043	27-03-2044	14-03-2045	04-03-2046	23-03-2047	13-03-2048	29-02-2049	19-03-2050	09-02-2051
Passover	16-04-2042	05-04-2043	25-04-2044	12-04-2045	02-04-2046	21-04-2047	11-04-2048	29-03-2049	17-04-2050	07-04-2051
Shavuot	05-06-2042	25-05-2043	14-06-2044	01-06-2045	22-05-2046	10-06-2047	31-05-2048	18-05-2049	06-06-2050	27-05-2051

Dates are taken from the table provided in Michel Coireault, *Les Fêtes. Judaïsme, Christianisme, Islam*. Paris: Éditions du Cerf, 1994, pp. 184–187.

Some Minor Jewish Holidays 2000–2015:

Tu bi-Shevat: 5760: Sat. 22 January 2000 5761: Thu. 8 February 2001 5762: Mon. 28 January 2002 5763: Sat. 18 January 2003 5764: Sat. 7 February 2004 5765: Tue. 25 January 2005 5766 : Mon. 13 February 2006 5767: Sat. 3 February 2007 5768: Tue. 22 January 2008 5769: Mon. 9 February 2009 5770: Sat. 30 January 2010 5771: Thu. 20 January 2011 5772: Wed. 8 February 2012 5773: Sat. 26 January 2013 5774: Thu. 16 January 2014 5775: Wed. 4 February 2015.

Lag ba-Omer: 5760: Tue. 23 May 2000 5761: Fri. 11 May 2001 5762: Tue. 30 April 2002 5763: Tue. 20 May 2003 5764: Sun. 9 May 2004 5765: Fri. 27 May 2005 5766 Tue. 16 May 2006 5767: Sun. 6 May 2007 5768: Fri. 23 May 2008 5769: Tue. 12 May 2009 5770: Sun. 2 May 2010 5771 Sun. 22 May 2011 5772 Thu. 10 May 2012 5773 Sun. 28 April 2013 5774: Sun. 18 May 2014 5775: Thu. 7 May 2015

Tishah be-Av: 5760: Thu. 10 August 2000 5761: Sun. 29 July 2001 5762: Thu. 18 July 2002 5763: Thu. 7 August 2003 5764: Tue. 27 July 2004 5765: Sun. 14 August 2005 5766: Thu. 3 August 2006 5767: Tue. 24 July 2007 5768: Sun. 10 August 2008 5769: Thu. 30 July 2009 5770: Tue. 20 July 2010 5771: Tue. 9 August 2011 5772: Sun. 29 July 2012 5773 Tue. 16 July 2013 5774: Tue. 5 August 2014 5775: Sun. 26 July 201

Dates generated with the HaYom© On-Line Hebrew Calendar program (http://www.hayom.com).

APPENDIX IV: Main Moveable Feasts of the Western Church 2001–2050

Year	Ash Wednesday	Palm Sunday	Easter	Ascension	Pentecost	Year	Ash Wednesday	Palm Sunday	Easter	Ascension	Pentecost
2001	28-02-2001	08-04-2001	15-04-2001	24-05-2001	03-06-2001	2026	18-02-2026	29-03-2026	05-04-2026	14-05-2026	24-05-2026
2002	13-02-2002	24-03-2002	31-03-2002	09-05-2002	19-05-2002	2027	10-02-2027	21-03-2027	28-03-2027	06-05-2027	16-05-2027
2003	05-03-2003	13-04-2003	20-04-2003	29-05-2003	08-06-2003	2028	01-03-2028	09-04-2028	16-04-2028	25-05-2028	04-06-2028
2004	24-02-2004	04-04-2004	11-04-2004	20-05-2004	30-05-2004	2029	14-02-2029	25-03-2029	01-04-2029	10-05-2029	20-05-2029
2005	09-02-2005	20-03-2005	27-03-2005	05-05-2005	15-05-2005	2030	06-03-2030	14-04-2030	21-04-2030	30-05-2030	09-06-2030
2006	01-03-2006	09-04-2006	16-04-2006	25-05-2006	04-06-2006	2031	26-02-2031	06-04-2031	13-04-2031	22-05-2031	01-06-2031
2007	21-02-2007	01-04-2007	08-04-2007	17-05-2007	27-05-2007	2032	10-02-2032	21-03-2032	28-03-2032	06-05-2032	16-05-2032
2008	05-02-2008	16-03-2008	23-03-2008	01-05-2008	11-05-2008	2033	02-03-2033	10-04-2033	17-04-2033	26-05-2033	05-06-2033
2009	25-02-2009	05-04-2009	12-04-2009	21-05-2009	31-05-2009	2034	22-02-2034	02-04-2034	09-04-2034	18-05-2034	28-05-2034
2010	17-02-2010	28-03-2010	04-04-2010	13-05-2010	23-05-2010	2035	07-02-2035	18-03-2035	25-03-2035	03-05-2035	13-05-2035
2011	09-03-2011	17-04-2011	24-04-2011	02-06-2011	12-06-2011	2036	26-02-2036	06-04-2036	13-04-2036	22-05-2036	01-06-2036
2012	21-02-2012	01-04-2012	08-04-2012	17-05-2012	27-05-2012	2037	18-02-2037	29-03-2037	05-04-2037	14-05-2037	24-05-2037
2013	13-02-2013	24-03-2013	31-03-2013	09-05-2013	19-05-2013	2038	10-03-2038	18-04-2038	25-04-2038	03-06-2038	13-06-2038
2014	05-03-2014	13-04-2014	20-04-2014	29-05-2014	08-06-2014	2039	23-02-2039	03-04-2039	10-04-2039	19-05-2039	29-05-2039
2015	18-02-2015	29-03-2015	05-04-2015	14-05-2015	24-05-2015	2040	14-02-2040	25-03-2040	01-04-2040	10-05-2040	20-05-2040
2016	09-02-2016	20-03-2016	27-03-2016	05-05-2016	15-05-2016	2041	06-03-2041	14-04-2041	21-04-2041	30-05-2041	09-06-2041
2017	01-03-2017	09-04-2017	16-04-2017	25-05-2017	04-06-2017	2042	19-02-2042	30-03-2042	06-04-2042	15-05-2042	25-05-2042
2018	14-02-2018	25-03-2018	01-04-2018	10-05-2018	20-05-2018	2043	11-02-2043	22-03-2043	29-03-2043	07-05-2043	17-05-2043
2019	06-03-2019	14-04-2019	21-04-2019	30-05-2019	09-06-2019	2044	02-03-2044	10-04-2044	17-04-2044	26-05-2044	05-06-2044
2020	25-02-2020	05-04-2020	12-04-2020	21-05-2020	31-05-2020	2045	22-02-2045	02-04-2045	09-04-2045	18-05-2045	28-05-2045
2021	17-02-2021	28-03-2021	04-04-2021	13-05-2021	23-05-2021	2046	07-02-2046	18-03-2046	25-03-2046	03-05-2046	13-05-2046
2022	02-03-2022	10-04-2022	17-04-2022	26-05-2022	05-06-2022	2047	27-02-2047	07-04-2047	14-04-2047	23-05-2047	02-06-2047
2023	22-02-2023	02-04-2023	09-04-2023	18-05-2023	28-05-2023	2048	18-02-2048	29-03-2048	05-04-2048	14-05-2048	24-05-2048
2024	13-02-2024	24-03-2024	31-03-2024	09-05-2024	19-05-2024	2049	03-03-2049	11-04-2049	18-04-2049	27-05-2049	06-06-2049
2025	05-03-2025	13-04-2025	20-04-2025	29-05-2025	08-06-2025	2050	23-02-2050	03-04-2050	10-04-2050	19-05-2050	29-05-2050

Dates are taken from the table provided in Michel Coireault, *Les Fêtes. Judaïsme, Christianisme, Islam.* Paris: Éditions du Cerf, 1994, pp. 188–189.

APPENDIX V: Gregorian Dates of Orthodox Easter 1875–2124

A) By Year

Year	Date	Year	Date	Year	Date	Year	Date	Year	Date	Year	Date	Year	Date	Year	Date	Year	Date
1875	4/25	1876	4/16	1877	4/8	1962	4/29	1963	4/14	1964	5/3	2049	4/25	2050	4/17	2051	5/7
1878	4/28	1879	4/13	1880	5/2	1965	4/25	1966	4/10	1967	4/30	2052	4/21	2053	4/13	2054	5/3
1881	4/24	1882	4/9	1883	4/29	1968	4/21	1969	4/13	1970	4/26	2055	4/18	2056	4/9	2057	4/29
1884	4/20	1885	4/5	1886	4/25	1971	4/18	1972	4/9	1973	4/29	2058	4/14	2059	5/4	2060	4/25
1887	4/17	1888	5/6	1889	4/21	1974	4/14	1975	5/4	1976	4/25	2061	4/10	2062	4/30	2063	4/22
1890	4/13	1891	5/3	1892	4/17	1977	4/10	1978	4/30	1979	4/22	2064	4/13	2065	4/26	2066	4/18
1893	4/9	1894	4/29	1895	4/14	1980	4/6	1981	4/26	1982	4/18	2067	4/10	2068	4/29	2069	4/14
1896	4/5	1897	4/25	1898	4/17	1983	5/8	1984	4/22	1985	4/14	2070	5/4	2071	4/19	2072	4/10
1899	4/30	1900	4/22	1901	4/14	1986	5/4	1987	4/19	1988	4/10	2073	4/30	2074	4/22	2075	4/7
1902	4/27	1903	4/19	1904	4/10	1989	4/30	1990	4/15	1991	4/7	2076	4/26	2077	4/18	2078	5/8
1905	4/30	1906	4/15	1907	5/5	1992	4/26	1993	4/18	1994	5/1	2079	4/23	2080	4/14	2081	5/4
1908	4/26	1909	4/11	1910	5/1	1995	4/23	1996	4/14	1997	4/27	2082	4/19	2083	4/11	2084	4/30
1911	4/23	1912	4/7	1913	4/27	1998	4/19	1999	4/11	2000	4/30	2085	4/15	2086	4/7	2087	4/27
1914	4/19	1915	4/4	1916	4/23	2001	4/15	2002	5/5	2003	4/27	2088	4/18	2089	5/1	2090	4/23
1917	4/15	1918	5/5	1919	4/20	2004	4/11	2005	5/1	2006	4/23	2091	4/8	2092	4/27	2093	4/19
1920	4/11	1921	5/1	1922	4/16	2007	4/8	2008	4/27	2009	4/19	2094	4/11	2095	4/24	2096	4/15
1923	4/8	1924	4/27	1925	4/19	2010	4/4	2011	4/24	2012	4/15	2097	5/5	2098	4/27	2099	4/12
1926	5/2	1927	4/24	1928	4/15	2013	5/5	2014	4/20	2015	4/12	2100	5/2	2101	4/24	2102	4/9
1929	5/5	1930	4/20	1931	4/12	2016	5/1	2017	4/16	2018	4/8	2103	4/29	2104	4/20	2105	4/5
1932	5/1	1933	4/16	1934	4/8	2019	4/28	2020	4/19	2021	5/2	2106	4/25	2107	4/17	2108	5/6
1935	4/28	1936	4/12	1937	5/2	2022	4/24	2023	4/16	2024	5/5	2109	4/21	2110	4/13	2111	5/3
1938	4/24	1939	4/9	1940	4/28	2025	4/20	2026	4/12	2027	5/2	2112	4/17	2113	4/9	2114	4/29
1941	4/20	1942	4/5	1943	4/25	2028	4/16	2029	4/8	2030	4/28	2115	4/14	2116	5/3	2117	4/25
1944	4/16	1945	5/6	1946	4/21	2031	4/13	2032	5/2	2033	4/24	2118	4/17	2119	4/30	2120	4/21
1947	4/13	1948	5/2	1949	4/24	2034	4/9	2035	4/29	2036	4/20	2121	4/13	2122	5/3	2123	4/18
1950	4/9	1951	4/29	1952	4/20	2037	4/5	2038	4/25	2039	4/17	2124	4/9				
1953	4/5	1954	4/25	1955	4/17	2040	5/6	2041	4/21	2042	4/13						
1956	5/6	1957	4/21	1958	4/13	2043	5/3	2044	4/24	2045	4/9						
1959	5/3	1960	4/17	1961	4/9	2046	4/29	2047	4/21	2048	4/5						

(Continued on next page)

(Appendix V Cont.)

B) By Date

Date												
4/3	none											
4/4	1915	2010										
4/5	1885	1896	1942	1953	2037	2048	2105					
4/6	1980											
4/7	1912	1991	2075	2086								
4/8	1877	1923	1934	2007	2018	2029	2091					
4/9	1882	1893	1939	1950	1961	1972	2034	2045	2056	2102	2113	2124
4/10	1904	1966	1977	1988	2061	2067	2072					
4/11	1909	1920	1999	2004	2083	2094						
4/12	1931	1936	2015	2026	2099							
4/13	1879	1890	1947	1958	1969	2031	2042	2053	2064	2110	2121	
4/14	1895	1901	1963	1974	1985	1996	2058	2069	2080	2115		
4/15	1906	1917	1928	1990	2001	2012	2023	2085	2096			
4/16	1876	1922	1933	1944	2017	2028						
4/17	1887	1892	1898	1955	1960	2039	2050	2107	2112	2118		
4/18	1971	1982	1993	2055	2066	2077	2088	2123				
4/19	1903	1914	1925	1987	1998	2009	2020	2071	2082	2093		
4/20	1884	1919	1930	1941	1952	2014	2025	2036	2104			
4/21	1889	1946	1957	1968	2041	2047	2052	2109	2120			
4/22	1900	1979	1984	2063	2074							
4/23	1911	1916	1995	2006	2079	2090						
4/24	1881	1927	1938	1949	2011	2022	2033	2044	2095	2101		
4/25	1875	1886	1897	1943	1954	1965	1976	2038	2049	2060	2106	2117
4/26	1908	1970	1981	1992	2065	2076						
4/27	1902	1913	1924	1997	2003	2008	2087	2092	2098			

Date											
4/28	1878	1935	1940	2019	2030						
4/29	1883	1894	1951	1962	1973	2035	2046	2057	2068	2103	2114
4/30	1899	1905	1967	1978	1989	2000	2062	2073	2084	2119	
5/1	1910	1921	1932	1994	2005	2016	2089				
5/2	1880	1926	1937	1948	2021	2032	2100				
5/3	1891	1959	1964	2043	2054	2111	2116	2122			
5/4	1975	1986	2059	2070	2081						
5/5	1907	1918	1929	2002	2013	2024	2097				
5/6	1888	1945	1956	2040	2108						
5/7	2051										
5/8	1983	2078									
5/9	none										

From the web page http://www.smart.net/~mmontes/OrthEasttbl.html by Marcos Montes, April 12, 1997.

APPENDIX VI: Dates of Chinese Lunar New Year's Day 1995–2020

Chinese Year	Zodiac Animal	Gregorian Calendar
4693	Boar	January 31, 1995
4694	Rat	February 19, 1996
4695	Ox	February 7, 1997
4696	Tiger	January 28, 1998
4697	Hare/Rabbit	February 16, 1999
4698	Dragon	February 5, 2000
4699	Snake	January 24, 2001
4700	Horse	February 12, 2002
4701	Ram/Sheep	February 1, 2003
4702	Monkey	January 22, 2004
4703	Rooster	February 9, 2005
4704	Dog	January 29, 2006
4705	Boar	February 18, 2007
4706	Rat	February 7, 2008
4707	Ox	January 26, 2009
4708	Tiger	February 10, 2010
4709	Hare/Rabbit	February 3, 2011
4710	Dragon	January 23, 2012
4711	Snake	February 10, 2013
4712	Horse	January 31, 2014
4713	Ram/Sheep	February 19, 2015
4714	Monkey	February 9, 2016
4715	Rooster	January 28, 2017
4716	Dog	February 16, 2018
4717	Boar	February 5, 2019
4718	Rat	January 25, 2020

Adapted from L. E. Dogget. *Explanatory Supplement to the Astronomical Almanac*, P. Kenneth Seidelmann, editor, with permission from University Science Books, Sausalito, CA 94965, for an online exhibit on calendars by the Institute for Dynamic Educational Advancement (IDEA). ©2003 Michael Douma Productions, LLC, at http://webexhibits.org/calendars/calendar-chinese.html.

APPENDIX VII: Comparative Table of Main Festival Entries for Each Cultural Area by Time of Year

N.B.: Festivals unrelated to the seasonal cycle, like those of Islam, do not appear in this table, while Naw Ruz appears under "Miscellaneous."

	ANCIENT GREECE & ROME	ANCIENT NEAR EAST	JUDAISM	CHRISTIANITY	HINDUISM, BUDDHISM, JAINISM & SIKHISM	FAR EAST	AMERICAS	AFRICA	MISCELLANEOUS
WINTER		Heb-Sed	Hanukkah	Christmas, Feast of Fools		Bear Festival, New Year (Japan)	Capac Inti Raymi & Huarachicu, Tititl		New Year (West)
	Carmentalia, Lenaea			Epiphany		Day of Mankind, Laba	Potlatch, Izcalli		
			Tu bi-Shevat	Candlemas	Thaipusam, Vasant Panchami	Naked Festival of Inazawa, New Year (China, Korea)	Midwinter		
	Fornacalia & Quirinalia, Lupercalia, Caristia				Mahashivaratri	Naked Festival of Okayama, Lantern Festival			
	Anthesteria, Terminalia, Matronalia		Purim	Carnival	Holi	Doll Festival	Atlcaulo		
	Lesser Eleusinian Mysteries, Liberalia, Anna Perenna, Quinquatrus			Lent		Spring Dragon, Kasuga Festival			

	ANCIENT GREECE & ROME	ANCIENT NEAR EAST	JUDAISM	CHRISTIANITY	HINDUISM, BUDDHISM, JAINISM & SIKHISM	FAR EAST	AMERICAS	AFRICA	MISCELLANEOUS
SPRING	Spring Festival of Cybele and Attis, City Dionysia, Venus Verticordia & Virile Fortune	Akitu		Annunciation	Nyepi		Totoztontli		Naw Ruz
	Fordicidia & Parilia				Vaisakhi	Qing Ming, Matzu's Birthday			Ridvan, Kunapipi
	Isthmian Games, Floralia			Saint George, Palm Sunday, Holy Week	Vaishakha	Water-Splashing Festival, Cherry Blossom Festival, Children's Day			May Day
	Argei		Passover	Easter		Asakusa Shrine Festival, Hollyhock Festival		Kokuzahn	
	Thargelia	Beautiful Festival of the Valley	Lag ba-Omer	Rogations, Ascension		Rice-Transplanting Festival	Etzalqualitzli		
	Vestalia, Matralia, Small Quinquatrus		Shavuot	Whitsuntide		Dragon Boat Festival			

(Continued on next page)

(Appendix VII Cont.)

	ANCIENT GREECE & ROME	ANCIENT NEAR EAST	JUDAISM	CHRISTIANITY	HINDUISM, BUDDHISM, JAINISM & SIKHISM	FAR EAST	AMERICAS	AFRICA	MISCELLANEOUS
SUMMER				Corpus Christi		Festival of the Weaver	Inti Raymi, Sun Dance, Powwow		Midsummer
			Tisha be-Av	Sacred Heart		Gion, Bon, Naadam			
	Carneia			Transfiguration		Cowherd and Weaving Maid	Busk		Lugnasad
	Panathenaea			Assumption	Janmashtami	Chung Yuan			
	Olympic Games, Pythian Games		Rosh Hashanah	Birth of the Virgin Mary	Ganesha Chaturthi, Paryushana	Chrysanthemum Festival		Ôsun Festival, Reed Dance	
	Greater Eleusinian Mysteries, Roman Games		Yom Kippur	Elevation of the Cross	Dashalakshana	Mid-Autumn	Tepeilhuitl	Geerewol, New Yam Festival	
FALL			Sukkot	Protection of the Mother of God	Navaratra & Dusshera	Double Nine	Situa		
	Oschophoria				Kathina	Jidai Matsuri		Adae Kese	
	Thesmophoria				Divali, Guru Nanak's Birthday				Samhain, Days of the Dead (West)
	Apaturia, Nemean Games, Plebeian Games			Martinmas, Presentation of the Virgin Mary		Seven-Five-Three			
				Saint Nicholas, Saint Lucy			Shalako		
	Country Dionysia, Saturnalia	Khoiak		Conception of the Virgin Mary		Kasuga Wakamiya Grand Festival, Dong Zhi	Atemoztli, Kukulcan Festival		

APPENDIX VIII: List of Full Festival Entries by Cultural Area

ANCIENT GREECE & ROME: Anna Perenna, Apaturia, Argei, Caristia, Carmentalia, Carneia, Dionysia, Eleusinian Mysteries, Floralia, Fordicidia & Parilia, Fornacalia, Games (Greece), Games (Rome), Liberalia, Lupercalia, Matralia, Matronalia, Noumenia, Panathenaea, Quinquatrus, Saturnalia, Spring Festival of Cybele and Attis, Terminalia, Thesmophoria, Thargelia, Venus Verticordia & Virile Fortune, Vestalia

ANCIENT NEAR EAST: Akitu, Beautiful Festival of the Valley, Khoiak & Heb-Sed, KI.LAM

JUDAISM: Hanukkah, Lag ba-Omer, Passover, Purim, Rosh Hashanah, Rosh Hodesh, Sabbath, Shavuot, Sukkot, Tishah be-Av, Tu bi-Shevat, Yom Kippur

CHRISTIANITY: Annunciation, Ascension, Assumption, Candlemas, Carnival, Christmas, Conception and Birth of the Virgin Mary, Corpus Christi, Easter, Elevation of the Cross, Epiphany, Feast of Fools, Holy Week, Kermis, Lent, Martinmas, Palm Sunday, Pardon, Presentation of the Virgin Mary, Protection of the Mother of God, Rogations, Sacred Heart, Saint George, Saint Lucy, Saint Nicholas, Sunday, Transfiguration, Whitsuntide

ISLAM, ZOROASTRIANISM & BAHA'ISM: Ashura, Day of Assembly, Eid, Mawlid, Mi'raj, Naw Ruz, New Year (Islam), Nineteen-Day Feast, Ridván, Ramadan

HINDUISM, BUDDHISM, JAINISM & SIKHISM: Divali, Ganesha Chaturthi, Gurpurb, Holi & Vasant Panchami, Janmashtami, Kathina, Mahashivaratri, Navaratra & Dusshera, Nyepi, Paryushana & Dashalaksana, Thaipusam, Vaishakha & Vaisakhi

FAR EAST: Bear Festival, Cherry Blossom Festival, Chiao, Cowherd and Weaving Maid, Days of the Dead, Dong Zhi, Double Nine, Dragon Boat Festival, Gion Festivals, Hollyhock Festival, Kasuga Festivals, Laba, Lantern Festival, Matsuri, Matzu's Birthday, Mid-Autumn, Naadam, Naked Festivals, New Year (China, Korea), New Year (Japan), Sekku, Seven-Five-Three, Spring Dragon, Water-Splashing Festival

AMERICAS: Busk, 8 Monkey, Inti Raymi & Huarachicu, Izcalli, Kukulcan, Midwinter, New Fire Ceremony, Potlatch, Powwow, Rain Festivals, Shalako, Situa, Sun Dance

AFRICA: Adae, Geerewol, Kokuzahn, Osun Festival, New Yam Festival, Reed Dance

MISCELLANEOUS: Days of the Dead (West), Kunapipi, Lugnasad, May Day, Midsummer, New Year (West), Samhain

INDEX

N

X

Xia Yuan, 90
Xocotl Huetzi, 97

Y

Yakke charm dance, 181
Yam Custom, 2
Yam Festival, 3
Yama Dwititya. *See* Divali
Yandatsa. *See* Days of the Dead
Yawm al-Jum'a, 85
Yeme ben hametzarim, 470
Yom ha-Bikkurim, 438
Yom ha-din, 397
Yom ha-Zikkaron, 397
Yom Kippur (Judaism)
    Annunciation and, 10
    Hegira and, 19
    Judgment Day and, 7, 395
    New Year and, 8
    overview, 501–504
    Rosh Hodesh and, 398
    Sukkot and, 448
    Temple and, 373
    Thargelia and, 465
    Tisha be-Av and, 470
Yom Kippur Katan, 399
Yom Teru'ah, 396
Yoruba people, 346–348
Young Herbs, Festival of, 428
Yu Lan Pen, 88, 91
Yuan Shuo, 319
Yuan Xiao, 90, 240, 242
Yuan Zheng, 319
Yule log, 193, 286, 321, 329, 337
Yuletide, 54, 66, 69, 244, 420, 493

Z

Zagmuk, 6
Zhong Yuan Jie, 88
Zoroastrianism, 311–315, 529
Zuñi, 432–437
Zwölfer, 143

ABOUT THE AUTHOR

CHRISTIAN ROY was born in Quebec City in 1963. He studied German and History at McGill University in Montreal and obtained his Ph.D. in History there in 1993, specializing in contemporary European intellectual history. He soon gained international recognition for his research on the French personalist tradition and related "third way" political movements in the twentieth century. In 1996–1997, he was Hoover Fellow in Applied Ethics at the Centrum voor Economie en Ethiek of the Katholieke Universiteit Leuven in Belgium. His dissertation, an intellectual biography of Alexandre Marc (1904–2000), a French personalist pioneer of European federalism, was published in 1999 in Nice, France, where he has lived several years. He has published numerous papers and articles, mostly on French intellectual life and its international connections (for example, in Germany and the Low Countries), on Scandinavian literature, and on Canadian political thought. Roy has also contributed entries to several reference works: the *Historical Dictionary of World War II France: The Occupation, Vichy, and the Resistance (1938–1946)* (1998) and the *Historical Encyclopedia of Christian Politics, 1789–Present* (2005), both published by Greenwood Press (Westport, CT), and *Personalisti nel XXᵐᵒ secolo* (2005) published by Edizioni Scientifiche Italiane (Naples). Among the not-yet-published topics covered are Roy's contribution to Ian Angus, ed., *Athens and Jerusalem: George Grant's Theology, Philosophy and Politics* (University of Toronto Press, 2006) and his general editorship of the complete works of Belgo-Canadian Thomist philosopher Charles De Koninck (1906–1965) for Quebec City's Université Laval. He is also a member of the latter's international Projet Tillich as one of the translators of the early German works of Paul Tillich (1886–1965) for a French edition (Paris: Cerf and Geneva: Labor et Fides) of the main works of this American Protestant thinker. Roy earns his living as a freelance translator from most Western European languages (especially German and Dutch) to either English or his native French. He is now pursuing a Master's degree in Orthodox theology at the Université de Sherbrooke's campus in Longueuil, the Montreal suburb where he is currently based.